Canadian Third Edition

INFORMATION AND IMAGE MANAGEMENT

A Records Systems Approach

BETTY R. RICKS, CRM
Associate Professor of Management
Old Dominion University
Norfolk, Virginia

ANN J. SWAFFORD
Office Administration Department
College of Applied Professional Sciences
University of South Carolina
Columbia, South Carolina

KAY F. GOW
Consultant
Records Management and Automated Office Systems
Norfolk, Virginia

GLEN M. FLEMMING
Associate Professor
Information Management Department
Mount Saint Vincent University
Halifax, Nova Scotia

I(T)P Nelson

an International Thomson Publishing company

Toronto • Albany • Bonn • Boston • Cincinnati • Detroit • London • Madrid • Melbourne •
Mexico City • New York • Pacific Grove • Paris • San Francisco • Singapore • Tokyo • Washington

I(T)P®
International Thomson Publishing
The ITP logo is a trademark under licence

© I(T)P Nelson
A division of Thomson Canada Limited, 1997

Published in 1997 by
I(T)P Nelson
A division of Thomson Canada Limited
1120 Birchmount Road
Scarborough, Ontario M1K 5G4

Visit our Web site at **http://www.nelson.com/nelson.html**

Canadian Cataloguing in Publication Data
Main entry under title:
Information and image management : a records
    systems approach

Canadian 3rd ed.
Includes index.
ISBN 0-17-604252-0

1. Business records - Management. 2. Business records - Management - Data processing. 3. Information resources management. I. Ricks, Betty R.

HF5736.163 1996   651.5   C96-930846-9

Publisher	Jacqueline Wood
Acquisitions Editor	Jennifer Dewey
Production Editor	Jill Young
Project Editor	Anita Miecnikowski
Senior Production Coordinator	Carol Tong
Assistant Art Director	Sylvia Vander Schee
Interior Design/Cover Design	Brian Lehen • Graphic Design Ltd.
Input Operator	Elaine Andrews

Printed and bound in Canada

2 3 4 (BBM) 99 98 97

Contents

Preface

During the process of adapting *Information and Image Management: A Records Systems Approach,* Canadian Third Edition, it has become clear that rapid changes are occurring in information management and that Canadians are actively involved with these changes. One trend concerns the disappearance of distinctions that formerly separated the professions of records manager, archivist, and librarian. By engaging in scholarly research, providing a variety of courses, and sharing expertise world-wide, information management professionals are developing a broad choice of careers. The Internet plays an increasingly important role in the world-wide exchange of information.

Another trend, influenced by advances in computer technology, is the current shift in focus from traditional management of paper records to electronic records management. To assist organizations of all sizes with their information management needs, professionals must therefore become knowledgeable about all aspects of the systems.

Features

To reflect these current trends, career opportunities in the information management profession are described from a Canadian perspective in Chapter 2, "The Records Manager and the Records Management Staff." Two new chapters have been developed for *Information and Image Management: A Records Systems Approach,* Canadian Third Edition: Chapter 9, "Electronic Records Management" and Chapter 10, "Integrated Information Systems." The topics of vital records and disaster prevention and recovery have been combined in Chapter 11, "Vital Records and Disaster Prevention." A growing concern about information privacy has resulted in the expansion of this topic in Chapter 12, "Records Security and Information Privacy."

Canadian terminology and illustrations are used throughout the book as much as possible. As one example, the legal aspects of Chapter 4, "Records Retention and Legal Considerations," are dealt with from a Canadian perspective. Recognizing the widespread use of the metric system in Canada, a table of metric equivalents is provided after Chapter 18.

Profiles of records management positions have been retained as a popular tool for allowing students, instructors, and professionals to have some quick looks at real-life opportunities for entry and progression in the records management profession.

Structure

The reorganized 18-chapter Canadian edition is divided into seven parts. Part 1, "Introduction to Records Management," gives an overview of records management as a system and the role of the records manager and the records management staff within the system. This part emphasizes preparation for and career opportunities within the field of information management.

Part 2, "Records Evaluation," contains information about records inventory, analysis and appraisal, and records retention and legal considerations from a Canadian perspective. Records retention and disposition schedules are the foundation upon which all records management programs are based.

"Active Records in Manual Systems" is the title of Part 3, in which the principles of managing paper records are described and applied in three chapters. Chapter 5, "Manual Systems of Active Records Management, Equipment and Supplies," describes the types of facilities for active records as well as the equipment and supplies to house the records. Chapter 6 examines indexing rules and classification systems selection, and Chapter 7 covers the manual storage and retrieval of records.

Part 4, "Imaging and Electronic Records Management Systems," concerns microfilm technology, electronic records management, and integrated information systems in three extensively revised chapters.

"Records Protection" is the title of Part 5, which includes two chapters. Chapter 11, "Vital Records and Disaster Prevention," combines two previous chapters into one. Chapter 12 addresses records security and information privacy. Protection of information and the right to privacy are important topics for today's records managers.

"Records Creation and Control" is the title of Part 6, which includes four chapters. Chapter 13 is about the communication of information through correspondence and directives. Chapter 14, "Forms and Reports Management," addresses the creation, distribution, and storage of forms and reports. Responsibilities of managers to control the records program through audits and reports are described in Chapter 15. The last chapter in Part 6 covers records management manuals.

Part 7, "Inactive Records," contains two chapters—one about inactive records facilities and the other about archives management. With the blurring of distinctions between records managers and archivists and the need to manage information from its creation to its disposition, these two topics have become important elements of all records management programs.

A Glossary containing all terms printed in bold provides easy reference for study and review of the important concepts introduced in the text material.

Learning Aids in the Text

Learning aids are distributed within and at the end of each chapter. For example, each chapter opens with learning goals. To enhance readability and highlight important points, key terms are printed in bold, and margin notes are used throughout. In Learning Checks, the reader is asked to verify that information discussed up to that point in the chapter can be recalled and understood. At the end of each chapter are a Terminology Review, Review and Discussion, two Applications, two Concluding Cases, and a list of suggested readings and resources. Answering the questions for review and discussion allows readers to verify that they have accomplished the chapter's learning goals. The Applications and Concluding Cases are designed to provide opportunities to apply the chapter's ideas to the solution of various records management problems. Suggested readings furnish sources of up-to-date information about topics in the chapter.

Comprehensive Cases appear in the Appendix. Solving each Comprehensive Case requires the application of concepts, techniques, or approaches examined in a particular group of chapters.

Illustrations that aid in understanding the material presented are used liberally throughout this textbook. Extensive use of records management forms and photographs of equipment enhance the value of the written materials appearing in the text.

Student Supplementary Items

Information and Image Management Applications, a manual and text-workbook, has been adapted to accompany *Information and Image Management: A Records Systems Approach,* Canadian Third Edition. Each application includes learning goals and step-by-step procedures for successfully completing the application. Students apply alphabetic indexing rules in manual applications of alphabetic, subject, numeric, and geographic filing.

Instructor Supplementary Items

The Instructor's Manual for *Information and Image Management: A Records Systems Approach,* Canadian Third Edition, contains an extensive Introduction. The main portions of the Manual are divided into four sections. Section One contains general teaching suggestions for using the cases, profiles, the term project, pre-test and post-test, test bank, teaching masters, records management videotape, and the supplementary text-workbook. Sources of additional information and teaching schedules are also included. Section Two contains the following important features in each chapter: (1) Learning Goals, (2) Chapter Outline, (3) Teaching Suggestions, (4) presentation of the Review and Discussion questions and their answers, (5) restatements of the Applications with suggested solutions, (6) presentation of the questions appearing at the end of the Concluding Cases along with suggested solutions. Suggested solutions to the Comprehensive Cases are presented.

Section Three consists of a test bank containing more than 1,000 objective questions that are evenly divided between true/false and multiple choice questions. Three essay/discussion questions are provided with each test. A pre-test and a post-test of alphabetic filing rules conclude Section Three.

Section Four contains teaching masters including key illustrations from the text.

A videotape entitled Records Management is available for use with the text. Active filing and special records equipment, image technology, and inactive records centre equipment are shown in colour. Equipment, supplies, and working situations are described in detail.

Acknowledgments

Betty Ricks and Ann Swafford, the authors of *Information and Image Management: A Records Systems Approach,* 3d Edition, provided the strong foundation on which to base this Canadian edition. Thanks are expressed to the following reviewers of portions of the Canadian edition expressed to the following reviewers of the Canadian edition:

    Dr. Dale H. Bent—Graduate School of Library and Information Science, The University of Western Ontario

    Marian Curtis—Confederation College

    Dorothy Haines—Northern Alberta Institute of Technology

    Anita Maria Henderson—Vancouver Community College

    Nina Nicholson—Camosun College

    Jennifer Prest—Southern Alberta Institute of Technology

    Margaret Russell—Seneca College

    Dr. Virginia Sullivan, CND—University of New Brunswick

In addition, the following also provided much appreciated assistance:

    Christine Ardern and Jill ten Cate—CIBC, Toronto

    Carman Carroll—Provincial Archivist, Province of Nova Scotia, Halifax

    Allan J. Fletcher—Command Services Atlantic, Halifax

    Dan Pittman—Workers' Compensation Board, Halifax

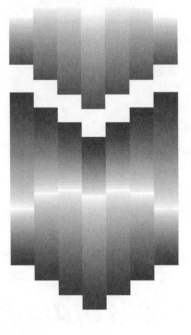

Part 1
Introduction to Records Management

The Records Management System

Learning Goals

After completing this chapter, you should be able to:

1. Define record and records management.
2. Describe legislative actions and other events that have had a major impact on the evolution of records management.
3. Specify major reasons for establishing a records management system.
4. Identify the components of a records management system and describe the relationships among the components.
5. Describe the life cycle of a record and state the methods for reaching each stage.
6. Distinguish between and classify examples of records as active, inactive; long-term, temporary; record, nonrecord; and provide a rationale for your decision.
7. Distinguish between records management and filing activities.

Information is one of an organization's most vital resources. Companies require information to grow or even to survive. Without knowledge based on current and accurate information, managers cannot make good, informed decisions. Where is the information kept? It is kept on records. Records contain information about and evidence of organizational functions, policies, decisions, procedures, operations, and other activities.

Records management requires systematic control of records.

To be useful, records must be managed. They must be available when they are needed. This function is called records management. **Records management** provides for the systematic control of records from creation, or receipt, through their processing, distribution, organization, storage and retrieval to their ultimate disposition.

The terms *records manager* and *records management* are used throughout this text; however, other terms such as *information manager* and *information resource management* are also used in the industry for the same position and function. These terms are often used interchangeably and should be regarded in that manner.

Records are required in the conduct of business.

The information to be managed takes the form of a record. A **record** is recorded information, regardless of medium or characteristics, made or received by an organization that is useful in the operation of the organization. Records include all books, papers, photographs, maps, or other documentary materials, regardless of physical form or characteristics, made or received for legal and operational purposes in connection with the transaction of business.

Records may be in different forms.

A record may take various forms—some traditional, some unique. A record may be in the form of paper, microfilm, computer tape, magnetic disk, microfiche, videotape, optical disk, or such unique forms as the original manuscript of *E.T.* or sacks of seed corn. Northrup King Grain Company in Minneapolis, Minnesota, stores grain seeds so that if a blight destroys one particular strain of corn, there will be a "record" (seed stock) to use to start over again. Regardless of the form, any recorded information constitutes a record. Figure 1-1 shows some of the many records forms.

 Learning Check: Can you define records management? What is a record? Can you give examples of different forms of records?

EVOLUTION OF RECORDS MANAGEMENT

The sophisticated records management technology that is in common use today has not always been available. But the need for evidence of previous transactions has been present from early recorded history.

Figure 1-1
Forms of Records

The earliest need recorded was the need for records of taxes collected—what was collected, from whom, by whom, and when. Even thousands of years ago, governments were collecting and recording taxes!

Early Recordkeeping Practices

Early records were in primitive forms.

The earliest record keepers obviously had none of today's technology to assist them in their task. Early records were carved into stone or clay tablets or recorded in wax, on wood, or on animal skins. This was quite time consuming and prohibited keeping any but the most important records. Papyrus was developed by the Egyptians and was in widespread use from about 400 B.C. to A.D. 400.

Places for storing government records were initially called *archives*. Archives are now defined as facilities where records of an organization are preserved because of their continuing value. There were some rather interesting methods of protecting records stored in the archives. Clay tablets were tagged and racked. Rolls of papyrus were often stored in hollow crocodile skins.

The first known retention schedule came into being about A.D. 1200. A **retention schedule** identifies the time records must be kept according to legal and/or organizational requirements. In A.D. 1200 the city states of northern Italy enacted statutes regulating the retention and disposal of files. Prior to that time, retention and disposition decisions had been made on an individual basis by the person currently in charge of the records. When records were no longer deemed to be of value, they were often dumped in an area that resembled a modern landfill.

Introduction of Paper Records

The fifteenth century brought the development of paper. Paper allowed a new ease of recording information, and the number of records made and preserved rapidly multiplied.

The typewriter had a major effect on the paperwork explosion.

By the early 1900s, the typewriter was coming into prominent use in business and government offices, and businesses and governments were generating even greater numbers of records. The paperwork explosion had begun; numerous steps were to be taken by all levels of government to control their records.

Major Actions Affecting Records Management

Many organizations as well as legislative and regulatory bodies have had an impact on the way records are created, maintained, stored, and discarded. The following is a summary of some of the major actions affecting records management from Confederation to the present.

1800s

1867   Canada became a country with a large volume of records already accumulated.

1868   The federal government passed an act creating the Department of the Secretary of State, which was made responsible for public records.

1897   The top floor of the West Block of the Parliament Buildings in Ottawa burned on February 11, 1897, destroying many valuable documents. This tragic event emphasized the need for protecting irreplaceable historical records.

Early 1900s

During this period, the Dominion Archivist was placed in charge of the government's records, and the Public Archives Act was passed. A royal commission in 1912 recommended that the permission of the federal government's Treasury Board should be sought before any "useless" documents were destroyed. By 1936 Treasury Board had become the final authority regarding disposal of records in case of any disagreement between a department and the Dominion Archivist.

1940s

1939–1945

World War II created many more government records than in any previous period. Microfilm became much more common after its use in wartime espionage activities.

1949–1951

The Massey Commission on National Development in the Arts, Letters, and Sciences recommended creating a records management program in Canada under the jurisdiction of the Dominion Archivist.

1950s

Early 1950s

In government the focus moved to developing a uniform filing system for active records. The Department of National Defence published a guide to its own subject classification system. Developed by Alfred James Brown, this block numeric system was later known internationally as the Canadian system.

1953   Treasury Board placed records management under the control of the Dominion Archivist.

1955   The first Public Archives records centre was built in Ottawa and immediately filled to capacity.

1959–1962

The Glassco Commission focused on the organization and methods of operation of the Government of Canada. Report Number 4 of the Commission's findings dealt with paperwork and systems management. Among other findings, the commission reported that more than 2.5 million records were stored on government premises, and in each successive year 250,000 cubic feet of records were being added.

1960s

1961   Responsibilities were defined for the management of public records in Canada under an order-in-council, which recommended that a statement of executive policy be developed for controlling the creation, use, retention, and disposition of public records.

1965–1977

The federal government built regional centres in Toronto (1965), Vancouver (1972), Winnipeg (1973), Halifax (1974), and Edmonton (1977).

1966   Treasury Board set policies regarding the protection of archival records and records scheduling (planning retention periods of records) and disposal. Roles of Treasury Board, the Public Archives of Canada, and government departments were clearly defined.

1968   Adopting the recommendations of the Ottawa Records Management Forum, which was chaired by Alfred James Brown, Treasury Board accepted its subject classification guide for housekeeping records. Published in 1968 under the title *Subject Classification Guide for Housekeeping Records,* this guide has served as the basis for most classification plans developed in Canada.[1]

1970s

1978   The Canadian Human Rights Act of March 1, 1978, states, "Every individual should have an equal opportunity with other individuals to make for himself or herself the life that he or she is able and wishes to have, consistent with his or her duties and obligations as a member of society." Part IV of the act provides limited protection of privacy and limited access to personal information.[2]

1980s

Early 1980s

In 1980 the Association of Records Managers and Administrators, Inc. (ARMA), an international organization, undertook a campaign to eliminate use of legal-size files called Project ELF (Eliminate Legal-size Files). During this period the concept of a paperless office became popular. Canadian educational institutions developed specific programs such as archival management, library science, and information studies. Provinces also influenced the development of archives and records management, for example, the Quebec Archives Act of 1983 concerning records retention periods and British Columbia's initiatives in retention scheduling.

1982   The Access to Information Act gave every Canadian citizen or permanent resident of Canada the right to examine or obtain copies of records of a federal government institution with limited exemptions and exclusions. To assist in identifying records, an Access Register was developed containing descriptions of government records and their likely location.[3] Expanding on Part IV of the Canadian Human Rights Act, the Privacy Act gave Canadians access to information about themselves held by the federal government, while protecting people's privacy by preventing others from having access to the information. Individuals can request that their files be corrected and appeal to the Privacy Commissioner if they are denied access.[4]

---

[1]Canadian Council of Archives, "Records Management in Canada," *Canadian Archives in 1992,* pp. 73-91.

[2]*The Canadian Human Rights Act: A Guide,* HRC 91/030, Cat. No. HR21-18-1991.

[3]*Access to Information Act Brochure,* Communications Division, Treasury Board of Canada.

[4]*Privacy Act Brochure,* Communications Division, Treasury Board of Canada.

Mid-1980s

The Association of Records Managers and Administrators, Region VIII (Canada), prepared an inventory of Canadian laws affecting records retention.

1987   The National Archives of Canada Act provided that the records of government institutions were to be destroyed or disposed of only with the consent of the National Archivist and that records of archival or historical value were to be transferred to the National Archives.

1989   The Canada Evidence Act defined a record to include "the whole or any part of any book, document, paper, card, tape or other thing on which information is written, recorded, stored, or reproduced."

1990s

1990   Treasury Board introduced a policy covering technological information to give government departments guidelines for handling information in forms other than paper, such as microfilm, microfiche, and optical disk.

1993   Representatives of various groups involved in libraries, archives, and records management throughout Canada formed an Industrial Adjustment Service Committee. The committee's work was to be jointly funded by Human Resources Development Canada and by participating groups that included the Canadian Library Association, the Canadian Council of Archives, and ARMA. They formed the Alliance of Libraries, Archives and Records Management (ALARM), which was charged with developing a national human resource strategy for those working in the information resources sector. ALARM's Phase I report appeared in early 1995.[5]

1995   With input from the Canadian Library Association, the first Information Rights Week was held in April 1995. A joint project of ARMA International established the First National Records Management Day (NMRD) on April 5, 1995, promoting records and information management in both the United States and Canada.[6]

 Learning Check: Can you identify major actions in Canada affecting records management?

---

[5]*Towards a Strategy for Human Resource Development in Libraries, Archives, and Records Management,* Report of the Alliance of Libraries, Archives and Records Management, December, 1994, and Communique dated February, 1995.

[6]*News, Notes, and Quotes,* Vol. 19, No. 4 (December, 1994), ARMA International.

NEED FOR RECORDS MANAGEMENT

Both government and business have recognized the need to manage records, as is evidenced by their actions. This management of all phases of records life is essential to the life of an organization. Major reasons for establishing a records management program are that records serve as the corporate memory, aid in management decision making, provide litigation support, reduce paperwork volume and produce cost reduction, aid organizational efficiency, meet legislative and regulatory requirements, and preserve organizational history.

Corporate Memory

Records are the corporate memory of the organization. Consider the inaccuracy of individual recollections of events. Ask any number of persons to observe a scene and report their individual observations. The results of this experiment are consistent—each person's memory of the event is different. An organization must not depend on elusive memory and conflicting recollections. Further, organizations depend on recorded past accomplishments to provide a foundation for future development. Accurate records are necessary to provide this background information when planning for the future while taking advantage of the past.

Records meet various business needs.

Records are, therefore, both an organizational resource and an organizational asset. As a resource, records provide information; as an asset, they provide documentation.

Management Decision Making

To make appropriate decisions, managers must have appropriate information. Decisions are only as good as the information on which they are based. Most of the information necessary for decision making is found in records.

Good decisions require good information.

The decision-making process includes defining the problem, developing alternatives, evaluating the alternatives, choosing and implementing the best solution, and evaluating that decision. To make professional decisions, managers should have background information (documentation provided by records), bases for evaluating the alternatives (forecasting, past experiences, consequences experienced by other organizations—provided by records), and means for evaluating the decisions (feedback and control mechanisms provided by records).

Records also provide the information required for routine or programmed decisions. These types of decisions are made based on established organizational policies, procedures, and rules, all of which are a part of organizational records.

Litigation Support

Records provide
documentation of
an organization's
actions.

The importance of documentation to the continuing life and success of organizations has become critical as more and more consumers, individuals, and organizations turn to the court systems as a forum for their concerns and as an avenue of recourse. In a 1984 landmark decision in the United States (*Carlucci v. Piper Aircraft Corporation*), a judge ruled that Piper Aircraft Corporation had to pay $10 million basically because its records management system did not provide necessary information.[7]

Virtually all organizations are vulnerable to discrimination and privacy violation suits, as well as suits such as the one above. Organizations rely on records for documentation that these practices do not occur and, further, that the organization has established policies and procedures to prevent their occurrence.

When an organization initiates legal action against another, records must provide the necessary documentation to prevail in court. Clear documentation of an organization's intent and subsequent actions is a safeguard for protection from litigation consequences and an imperative for their records system. Legal considerations are discussed further in Chapter 4.

Paperwork Volume and Cost Reduction

Many executives in North America are concerned with the increasing volume of records and the increasing costs associated with creating, using, maintaining, and disposing of these records. Illustrations of the massive volume of records that have accumulated and will continue to accumulate are common. It has been estimated that in the United States

Unnecessary
records represent
an unnecessary
cost.

- American businesses produce 370 million new documents daily, totalling 190 billion pages.[8]
- 18,000 pages of paper per white-collar employee are being created each year—almost 30 billion documents.[9]
- Photocopiers produce 100 billion pages per year.[10]
- Computer output equals approximately 350 billion pages per year.[11]

---

[7]Robert B. Austin, "10,000 Reasons for Records Management," *Records Management Quarterly,* Vol. 19, No. 3 (July, 1985), p. 3.

[8]Tom Jenkins, "Good Records Management," *Office Systems '89,* Vol. 6, No. 5 (May, 1989), p. 55.

[9]"Records and Information Management: Industry Profile," Brochure (Pasadena, California: Infologics, Inc., n.d.).

[10]Ibid.

[11]Ibid.

- While the projected volume increase is 62 million file drawers each year, 85 to 90 percent of the stored records are never referenced (used), and 95 percent of the references made are to records created within the past three years.[12]
- Eighty percent of references occur within 18 months.[13]

Concern over increasing paperwork is understandable when one considers that 130 billion of the 350 billion copies made in American offices each year are not needed: they are wasted, unnecessary, or for personal use.[14] The cost of processing these copies is more than $2.6 billion, not counting the time spent standing by the copier.[15] Although recognition is given to the problem of records proliferation, the recognition is primarily due to inconvenience created by the mass of records and to the spiralling costs of maintaining the records. It is only when space becomes a premium, records become difficult to locate, misfiles are prevalent, and the cost exceeds the benefits that organizations seriously consider implementing a records management system. The problems indicated by these figures apply to Canadian organizations as well.

In the 1990s a number of developments have appeared that are reducing paperwork volume. The use of **electronic data interchange (EDI)**, the technology that enables organizations to completely automate the ordering, inventory updating, shipping and payment cycle, eliminates the need for millions of paper documents. Electronic mail—including reports, spreadsheets, charts, and other attachments—can be sent, received, and stored without having to create paper copies. With CD-ROM technology becoming much less expensive, many offices and libraries have placed their reference information on CD-ROMs. Computers' increasing portability allows electronic document viewing away from the desktop. These and other innovations have led Leo Gotlieb to suggest that it is not far-fetched of vendors to predict over half the information in an organization will be in digital form within several years.[16]

---

[12]Ibid.

[13]Ibid.

[14]William Benedon, "Computer Records Management" (Presentation of a study sponsored by Accountemps at the 30th Annual Conference of the Association of Records Managers and Administrators, Inc., New York, September 9–12, 1985).

[15]Ibid.

[16]Leo Gotlieb, "Our Journey with Information Management," *CMA Magazine,* Vol. 68, No. 9 (November, 1994), p. 18.

Organizational Efficiency

Frustration and reduced efficiency occur when the individual responsible for making a decision is unable to locate the information necessary to efficiently develop and evaluate alternatives. Statistics show that employees spend an average of 50 minutes per day looking for misplaced files. Not only is this searching costly in terms of the records clerk's time, but it is also a loss of productive time to the person requiring the information.

Unavailable records and lost time are costly to an organization.

Organizational efficiency can be seriously impaired if needed information is not readily available. A systematic approach to records management provides the vehicle for information availability to enhance the efficiency of the employees and, ultimately, the organization.

Legislative and Regulatory Requirements

Many organizations are involved with provincial and federal government programs and must operate using established policies and procedures. The records of such organizations are subject to provincial and/or federal records retention and disposition criteria as well as the established corporate criteria. Organizations engaged in pharmaceutical, health records, insurance, banking, public utilities, investment activities, or in some interprovincial activities such as transportation and communication are subject to stringent regulatory constraints and are accountable to regulatory agencies. All of these organizations must be able to document their compliance and provide that documentation upon request.

Organizations must meet all legislative and regulatory requirements.

Each year, changes in departmental responsibilities and new statutes and regulations require companies to keep records longer, or keep different records, or reduce recordkeeping requirements. For example, changes in unemployment insurance legislation require employers to keep additional records about their employees' length and terms of employment.

Historical Reference

Records document the past and provide information for future events. Records preserve history for future generations. When recorded information is lost or destroyed, much of it is never regained. Those portions of the information regained are often a result of recollection and may contain considerable distortion from the original record.

Records provide a reference base for company history.

Records provide a reference base not only in a historical sense but also in a current sense. Technical reference files consist of specialized information for use as a technical reference library. Materials housed in a technical reference library include copies of books, periodicals, special reports and studies, catalogues, and data sheets. Project histories may be maintained as a historical reference base for researchers. Therefore, organizations must maintain this historical base both as evidence of their past achievements and as an introduction to the future.

 Learning Check: Can you describe reasons for implementing a records management system?

THE SYSTEM CONCEPT

A **system** is a group of interrelated parts acting together to accomplish a goal. To properly manage records, a system must be developed to control records throughout their life. This, in turn, enables the records management system to reach its goal, which is to provide the right information to the right person at the right time at the lowest possible cost. Reaching this goal is more easily accomplished by applying the system approach to records management.

All systems have inputs, processes, and outputs.

All systems are composed of three basic elements—input into the system, processing of the input, and generation of the output of the system. The input, processing, and output components of the records management system contribute to the achievement of the established goal of the system (see Figure 1-2).

Figure 1-2
Records
Management
System

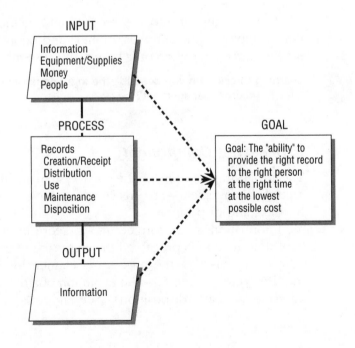

Input Component

The input of a records management system includes those factors that provide the necessary ingredients for the system to process in order to reach its goal. The input factors include information, equipment and supplies, money, and people. Each factor is essential to the system, and the factors are interdependent.

Information as an input may take any of the forms of recorded material. As discussed earlier, recorded material takes many forms and is generated by many sources.

Inputs are information, equipment and supplies, money, and people.

Equipment and supplies as an input to the system include all of the hardware, software, and supplies used in processing records. Organizations may choose traditional equipment such as four- or five-drawer cabinets or shelf units, or they may select automated equipment with computer-assisted retrieval, as discussed in Chapters 5, 8, 9, and 10.

The money input into the system provides the resources for expenditures necessary in planning, implementing, operating, and controlling the total system of records administration.

People as an input into the system include the administrative support personnel necessary to provide the "right record to the right person at the right time at the lowest possible cost." The "people input" also includes administrative and managerial personnel who generate records, which serve as an input in the form of information into the system.

The four inputs into the records management system—information, equipment and supplies, money, and people—provide the bases for the processing of records within the system.

 Learning Check: Can you describe the input component of a system as it relates to records management?

Processing Component

The processing portion of the total system includes the functions of records management—records creation/receipt, distribution, use, maintenance, and disposition.

Life cycle includes every phase of a record from its beginning to its end.

Information is transformed into a record in the processing component. Information is processed through each of the functions. The five functional phases of the processing element of the system represent the **life cycle** of a record—the evolution of a record from its birth (creation) to its death (disposition). (See Figure 1-3.)

Figure 1-3
Life Cycle of a
Record

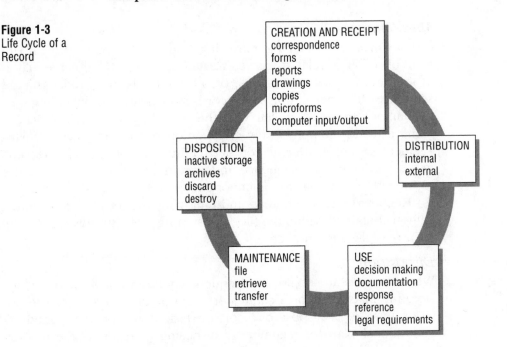

CREATION AND RECEIPT
correspondence
forms
reports
drawings
copies
microforms
computer input/output

DISTRIBUTION
internal
external

DISPOSITION
inactive storage
archives
discard
destroy

MAINTENANCE
file
retrieve
transfer

USE
decision making
documentation
response
reference
legal requirements

Creation and Receipt

Records originate internally from dictation, handwritten drafts, or word or data processors and externally from mail, computer output, telecommunication systems, or word and data processors. When a letter is written, an invoice typed, a report prepared, an engineering drawing made, or a new formula recorded, a record has been created; and information has been processed. Records are created by people at all levels of the organization—from clerk to chief executive officer.

Distribution

If the process stopped at the creation phase, information would not be available to persons requiring the data in the performance of their jobs. Following the creation phase, therefore, is the distribution phase, during which the information can be distributed to the appropriate persons. Distribution may be internal or external to the organization. Information may be distributed by electronic mail, Canada Post, special courier, interoffice mail systems, or direct access to computer databases.

Use

Records have many uses. They provide information for decision making, for documentation, for response to inquiries, for reference, or for supporting legal requirements. In this phase of the life cycle, information is put to its intended use.

Maintenance

Maintenance refers to filing, retrieving, and transferring records. A **file** is a collection of related records treated as a unit; filing is the action of arranging books, documents, or other records into predetermined sequences. The perception that records management is only filing persists among those unfamiliar with the records management function. Filing activities comprise only one portion of the total records management system. Differentiation between the act of arranging records into a predetermined sequence and creating a system to manage the records of an organization is important.

Retrieval refers to finding and removing a requested file or information contained within the file. Transferring refers to moving records from one place to another.

Disposition

Records may be disposed of in several ways.

When records are no longer frequently referenced, they are either stored in inactive records centres or archives, or disposed of. The decision to store or dispose of records is based on a predetermined organizational plan for retaining or disposing of records—the records retention schedule. This schedule takes into consideration the legal and business needs of the organization and is discussed in detail in Chapter 4.

Inactive Records and Archives Storage. Records may be stored in government, company-owned, or commercial records centres or in archives. Archives house public or private records that have been selected for long-term storage and preservation. Where to store the records is based largely on whether the records have been previously classified as active or inactive, long-term or temporary, a record or a nonrecord.

Records may be classified as active or inactive depending on how often they are used. A record is considered to be an **active record** if it is referenced (used) on a regular basis. For example, the personnel records of current employees are considered to be active records. Other examples of active records are invoices for the current fiscal period, correspondence, and creative works in progress. All of these would be referenced on a regular basis.

Long-term records have continuing value to the organization.

A record is considered to be an **inactive record** if it is referenced fewer than 10 times a year. A variety of records fall into the broad category of inactive records based on this reference rate criterion. For example, one kind of inactive record, the **semiactive record**, is classified as semiactive on the basis of its being referenced once a month. Examples of inactive records include personnel files of terminated employees, paid invoices for previous periods, completed projects, and cancelled cheques.

Records may also be classified as long-term or temporary. A **long-term record** has continuing value and is held indefinitely or for a specified period identified in the retention schedule. These records document organizational history, policies and procedures, and individual papers having historical significance—records having continuing value to the organization.

Records designated long-term may include documentation of organizational history, policies and procedures, and individual papers having historical significance. Also included in the category of long-term records are vital records (generally referred to as essential records in Canada). A **vital record** is essential to the operation of the organization at various points in time, the continuation and/or resumption of operations following a disaster, the recreation of legal and financial status of the organization at various points in time, or to the fulfilment of its obligations to shareholders and employees in the event of a disaster. Examples of vital records include accounts receivable, inventory lists, contracts, and creative works in progress. Based on their reference rates, long-term records may be either active or inactive.

Some long-term records are vital or essential to the organization.

For many years, records that had continuing value were classified as *permanent records* when, in fact, the records were not intended to be kept permanently. Records managers now recognize that few, if any, records are to be kept permanently—one day after forever. When asked about permanent retention of a record, one records manager inquired if 500 years would be adequate. The trend is to establish a record life in finite terms (20 years, for example) or to use the concept "life of the organization." The term "permanent" refers to the ability of the record to last for long periods of time rather than referring to retaining a record forever.

A **temporary record** does not have continuing or lasting value to the organization. Temporary records may also be referred to as *transitory records* or *transactional records,* indicating their temporary value to the organization. Temporary (transactional or transitory) records may include responses to letters, routine requests, memos for specific short-term activities, project control cards, or forms that are routine in nature and do not have continuing reference value.

Temporary records have short-term value to the organization.

A record may also be classified as a record copy or a nonrecord copy. A **record copy** is the official copy of a record that is retained for legal, operational, or historical purposes. For incoming records, the original copy is the record copy. For outgoing records, one copy is designated as the official record copy, which serves the documentation needs of the organization.

Nonrecord copy refers to a record not usually included within the scope of official records. This includes a copy of a document maintained in more than one location, not identified in the retention schedule, not required to be retained, or available from public sources.

Records are not limited to one classification. They are, however, active or inactive, long-term or temporary, and the record or nonrecord copy. Not only do records span classifications, but they may also change placement within the classifications over time. For example, most records move from active status to inactive status as the reference rates decrease. In general, it is unlikely that a record will change from long-term to temporary status and vice versa, or from record to nonrecord status and vice versa. Table 1-1 illustrates how the same record may have more than one classification.

Table 1-1

RECORDS CLASSIFICATION

Example	Active	Inactive	Long-term	Temporary	Record	Nonrecord
Current orders	X		X		X	
Last week's *Canadian Business* magazine	X			X		X
General correspondence	X	X	X	X	X	X
Personnel pay records for 1990–91		X	X		X	
Creative work in progress	X		X		X	

The current orders are considered active because they would be referenced more than 10 times annually; they are considered long-term records because they have continuing value to the organization, and they are record copies because they are the official company copy.

Last week's *Canadian Business* magazine is considered an active, though temporary, record because it will be read and then discarded. It has no lasting value to the organization.

General correspondence is considered either active or inactive, depending on how often it is referenced. It may also be either long-term or temporary depending on its value to the organization; and it is a record if it is the official organizational copy. Extra copies retained in various locations within the organization are nonrecord copies.

Personnel pay records for 1990–91 are inactive, long-term, record copies. They are inactive because of their limited reference rate, long-term because of their legal value to the organization, and a record copy because they are the original copies of the pay records. Disposition of these records will depend on the time specified in the records retention schedule. When unneeded records are allowed to accumulate, the cost of maintenance and storage rises accordingly.

Creative work in progress is active because it is in process; it is long-term because of its value to the organization, and it is a record copy because it is the original.

Discard or Destroy. The predetermined organizational plan (retention schedule) for records storage and disposition provides the organization with a timetable for records disposal. When a record reaches the disposition phase of its life cycle, the record may be either discarded or destroyed. The choice of disposition form depends largely on the type of document and its contents.

Every record may not proceed through each of the stages in the life cycle. For example, a memo may be created and distributed. A notation may be made by the user and the memo discarded, bypassing the maintenance or storage phases. An FYI (for your information) report may go from creation to distribution to maintenance, omitting the use phase.

The process portion of the records management system represents the life cycle of a record. During the process phase, input (information, equipment and supplies, money, and people) is processed through the system and is transformed into the output of the total records management system.

> Every record does not proceed through each stage of the life cycle.

 Learning Check: Can you describe the life cycle of a record as it relates to the process component of a records management system?

Output Component

The output of the records management system is information—information that has been processed through the system and is available in recorded form to the right person at the right time and at the lowest possible cost.

 Learning Check: Can you describe the output component of a system as it relates to records management?

TERMINOLOGY REVIEW

Review the terms listed below in the Glossary on page 521.

active record	record copy
electronic data interchange (EDI)	records management
file	retention schedule
inactive record	retrieval
life cycle	semiactive record
long-term record	system
nonrecord copy	temporary record
record	vital (essential) record

REVIEW AND DISCUSSION

1. Define record and records management.
2. Describe one piece of legislative action from each decade that you believe had a major effect on records management and give a rationale for your choice.
3. Explain five major reasons for establishing a systems approach to records management.
4. Describe the components of a records management system and the relationships among its components.
5. Describe the life cycle of a record.
6. State the methods for accomplishing each stage of the record life cycle.
7. Distinguish between active and inactive records, long-term and temporary records, and record and nonrecord copies.
8. How does filing differ from records management?

APPLICATIONS

1. Because records serve as the corporate memory, information must be accurate and complete. Unrecorded information is often unreliable, lost, or distorted as it is relayed from one person to another. The following activity illustrates this problem:
   a. Five participants will be selected from the class.
   b. One participant will be given a copy of an office scene and allowed five minutes to study the scene.
   c. Three of the remaining four participants will leave the room.
   d. The person who has studied the office scene will be instructed to describe the scene to the remaining participant. The person describing the scene should have the option of using any technique or combination of techniques to describe the scene, such as using a chalkboard or summarizing and repeating. The person to whom the scene is described may ask questions, ask to have information repeated, and so forth.
   e. The process is continued with each of the remaining participants in grapevine style; as the next participant is brought back into the room, the most recent participant describes the office scene.
   f. Student observers (the rest of the class) will identify
      (1) items omitted from the scene (never mentioned by the first participant).
      (2) items mentioned by the first participant but later dropped.
      (3) items that were modified to change their meaning or position within the scene.
      (4) items that were added by the participants.

(5) opinion statements by one participant that became facts; for example, "Two people were at the door; they may have been leaving" becomes "There were two people leaving the office."

  g. Discuss what you have learned about the importance of recording information.

2. Identify the many forms of records that are kept in a room in your home or dorm.

3. Classify the following types of records as active, inactive; long-term, temporary; record, nonrecord. Provide a rationale for your decisions.

  a. internal memos
  b. advertising brochures received
  c. Christmas party announcement
  d. current purchase order
  e. accounts receivable, current year

CONCLUDING CASES

A. The Country Music Sound

The Country Music Sound (TCMS) has been one of the leaders in country music recordings for over a decade. Recently, however, a new recording company has begun to make a name in the business, and TCMS is beginning to "feel the heat."

As the records manager for The Country Music Sound, Susan Martin, is aware of the pressure everyone is under. Susan is passing the vice president's office when she overhears the following conversation:

Bob S. (vice president): "We must have more current and accurate information about our market position. At this point, we receive sales reports at the end of the month only, and they are sometimes late."

Joan B. (marketing manager): "And I have no idea what new talent the agents have signed until well after the fact. It makes the marketing job much more difficult. We just don't seem to have any coordination of effort—or at least knowledge of what's going on in the other parts of the company."

Bob S.: "I am going to call a staff meeting for early next week to discuss this situation. If both of us see that problems exist, others probably have some problems they would like to 'put on the table,' too. We need a system around here."

Joan B.: "We also need to look at the entire approach to making information available. I think we should include Susan Martin in this meeting next week. Maybe she can help us to understand the records management function better. That system needs to be working for us, not against us!"

Susan hurries along to her office. She wants to be prepared when Bob or Joan calls her, so she begins to make notes.

1. What information should Susan provide to justify an improved records management system?
2. How can Susan explain to the group what a system is and how a systems approach can contribute to information availability?
3. What should Susan explain to the group about the life cycle of a record?

B. "But why do we keep the old stuff?"

Mark Simpson and Kim Okano are a part of a group of new college graduates who are management trainees at a bank. The procedure of the bank is to rotate the trainees through the major functions of the bank. Mark and Kim have just completed their rotation in the trust department and will begin on Monday to observe the activities of the records management department at the bank's main office.

Mark and Kim have discussed what they expect to see on Monday and Kim has expressed their feelings in a nutshell with "Why does the bank need to keep the old stuff? I can see keeping track of people's bank balances and all the new stuff, but that old stuff—toss it!"

You are the person in charge of the bank's records. How will you address the question, "But why do we keep the old stuff?"

SUGGESTED READINGS AND RESOURCES

Constantini, Jo Ann. "Survival Skills for Information Professionals in the Decade of Turbulence." *Records Management Quarterly,* Vol. 28, No. 1 (January, 1994), p. 26.

Goodman, Susan K. "Information Needs for Management Decision Making." *Records Management Quarterly,* Vol. 27, No. 4 (October, 1993), p. 12.

Internet Records Management Listserv: RECMGMT@LISTSERV.SYR.EDU.

Sanders, Robert L. "Document Distribution: The Neglected Link in the Life Cycle of Records." *Records Management Quarterly,* Vol. 30, No. 1 (January, 1996), p. 57.

Sanders, Robert L. "Record, Pre-record, Non-record?" *Records Management Quarterly,* Vol. 28, No. 3 (July, 1994), p. 52.

Skupsky, Donald S. "Legal and Operational Definitions of a Record." *Records Management Quarterly,* Vol. 29, No. 1 (January, 1995), p. 39.

Stephens, David O. "Records Management in the United Kingdom: Part I—Historical Developments." *Records Management Quarterly,* Vol. 29, No. 4 (October, 1995), p. 74.

Stephens, David O. "Records Management in the United Kingdom: Part II—Records Retention." *Records Management Quarterly,* Vol. 30, No. 1 (January, 1996), p. 76.

THE TERM PROJECT

The term project relates many of the records management concepts discussed in *Information and Image Management, Canadian Third Edition,* to what is being done in local organizations. Through visits with selected local organizations, you will develop in-depth profiles of records management programs. Your instructor will provide some guidelines for the term project, such as:

1. Establishing a due date for the project, with interim target dates, if necessary.
2. Requiring all students to submit for approval the name of an organization to be profiled. Some businesses may be too small or too new to have a fully developed records management program, and you would not benefit from selecting such a business. The approval process also prevents more than one student from profiling the same organization. With your instructor's approval, however, small groups may be assigned to profile a single organization.
3. Establishing a minimum and a maximum length for the profile. Length will be defined in terms of double-spaced, type-written pages. Additional pages may be allowed for photographs or sketches.

Important points that should be included in the profile are:

- Philosophy of the organization regarding its records management program.
- Placement of the records manager and staff within the organization. Show this with an organizational chart.
- Description of records inventory procedures. Include forms if available.
- Description of organization's records retention program. Include forms if available.
- Description and drawing of layout of facility(ies) for active and inactive records.
- Classification system(s) in use and rationale for selection.
- Description of filing and retrieval system(s) in place (manual, mechanical, or automated).
- Description of types of equipment in place; any plans for changes or additional equipment. (May use photographs from the organization or from vendor brochures to illustrate.)
- Types of microrecords used and specific applications; location of microforms processing.
- Description of vital records program.
- Description of archives program and archives facility.
- Control programs in use (correspondence, forms, reports, directives, copies, and microrecords).
- Extent of office automation and its effect on the records management system.
- Does the organization have an audit program? Describe and include forms if available.
- Description of the security system in place to protect records and their contents.
- Description of disaster prevention and recovery program in place.
- Development of records management manual(s).

Presentation of the content of the profile, correct use of grammar and punctuation, and eye-appealing quality of the profile are important.

In addition to the written report, your instructor may require an oral presentation of your findings.

The Records Manager and the Records Management Staff

Learning Goals

After completing this chapter, you should be able to:

1. Describe organizational staffing patterns that include a records manager and differentiate between the roles established by these patterns.
2. Describe the general education/training, experience, and personal characteristics required for entry into a records management staff position.
3. Match job responsibilities with job titles in the records management field.
4. List the duties of a records manager and explain how the size of the organization affects these duties.
5. Describe advancement opportunities available to the records management staff and the records manager and cite the actions that may be taken to prepare for advancement.

ROLE IN THE ORGANIZATION

Every organization operates within an established structure, which is usually outlined on an **organization chart**. This chart is a formal representation of the firm's hierarchical structure—a diagram showing task and functional responsibilities within an organization. Placement on this chart indicates the level of responsibility and authority of the records manager (and all other management personnel) and the ease with which those responsibilities can be accomplished.

Placement in the Organization

Organization size affects scope of responsibilities.

There are many organizational structures that include the position of records manager. The position designations (records manager, director of records management, and records and information manager) and patterns shown in Figures 2-1, 2-2, and 2-3 demonstrate the influence of organization size on the concept of the best operating structure. Smaller organizations tend to have more streamlined operations— fewer employees with each one performing a wider range of tasks. Larger organizations frequently have more specialized operations— more employees with each one performing only one task or a group of related tasks.

Figure 2-1
Organizational Structure—Retail Business

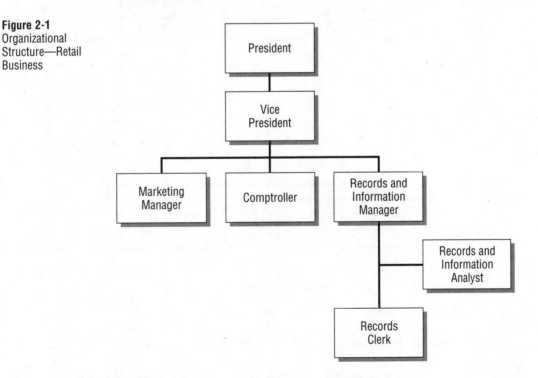

In small organizations, the records manager may have other management duties.

In many small organizations the smaller volume of records and the necessity for minimizing managerial positions force records management to be one of several tasks performed by a single manager. Some organizations may have records managers who perform some specific tasks of the records management program (such as forms analysis and management or the supervision of active and inactive records) in addition to their management duties. While small organizations may not find it cost-effective to employ a manager whose sole responsibility is the management of records, caution must be exercised to ensure that this important function receives adequate attention. No organization can afford to have its records—its memory—lost in the shuffle of administrative tasks.

Figure 2-2
Organizational Structure—Municipal Government

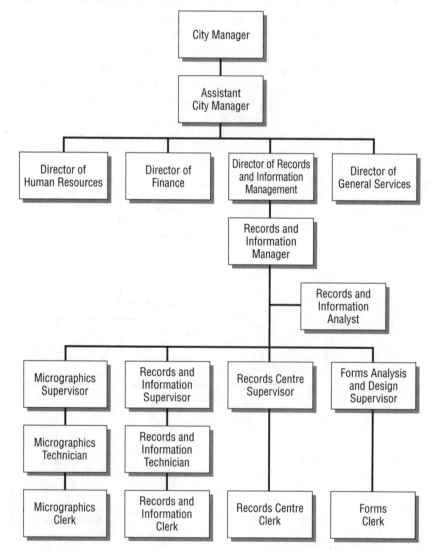

Figure 2-3
Organizational
Structure—
Manufacturing
Business

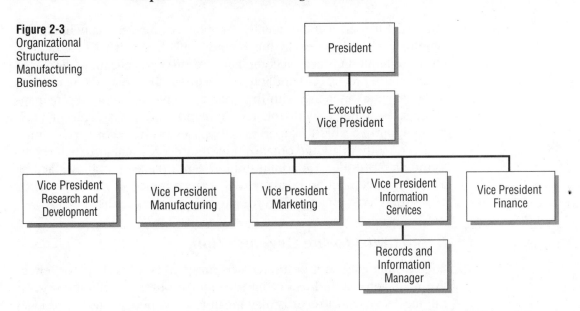

Note: The records manager's staff for this organization is shown in Figure 2-4, which is an extension of Figure 2-3.

In small to midsized businesses, the responsibilities of the records manager may include:

- Creating and maintaining a records retention and disposition schedule.
- Establishing written procedures for the timely destruction of records; conducting destruction according to the plan; and retaining proof of such destruction.
- Developing and implementing efficient filing systems, including written guidelines for using the systems.
- Locating and organizing records.
- Establishing and maintaining an organized storage system for inactive records; establishing guidelines for transferring records to inactive storage.
- Training office personnel in the use and function of established records management procedures.
- Integrating computer or microimaging applications with paper storage. Implementing programs where feasible and monitoring use.
- Updating records programs as required.
- Maintaining close links with other information systems personnel.

Large organizations have more specialized records operations.

Large organizations, because of the volume of records they generate and process, have more specialized records operations. The records manager is responsible for program planning and relies on other staff to perform the details of implementing and maintaining the system. Each employee in the records unit has a particular task or group of related tasks to accomplish, and this specialization allows for faster, more accurate handling of records. The records manager's responsibilities increase with the degree of specialization; the manager must be familiar with the requirements and procedures of each position and be able to supervise all phases of the records program.

Frequently in a large organization, the records manager will report to the vice president of administration. Such placement allows access to top management and usually reflects recognition of the importance of a strong, cost-effective records program to the organization.

Importance to the Organization

Effective management of the records program is the key to cost-effective management and use of information resources within the organization. Because lost records may mean lost business or increased legal liability, the records manager is a key employee.

The records manager recognizes organizational information needs.

To fulfil this critical role within the organization, the records manager must develop a thorough knowledge and understanding of the organization's information needs. A general knowledge of the nature of the organization's business activities is necessary, as well as specific knowledge of how the organization conducts its affairs. This knowledge can be developed through contact with key individuals (department heads, supervisors, and officers) within the organization and through a records inventory or a survey of problem areas (see Chapter 3). Combining information gathered in these ways with a previously developed, thorough knowledge of records management principles and procedures will allow the records manager to evaluate the existing records program and recommend changes to the improvement of information flows perceived to be necessary. The ability of the records manager to recognize needed changes in a consistent manner, to present logical, cost-effective proposals for achieving these improvements, and to maintain efficient records services will increase the organization's recognition of the importance of the records management function to overall operating efficiency.

Records managers themselves and others in this field agree that the records manager must be recognized by top management as an expert in information technology systems—knowledgeable in every aspect of information management from hard-copy manual systems to automated systems and integrated networks.

Learning Check: Can you explain how the roles of the records manager and the records management staff are affected by organization size?

CAREER PATHS FOR RECORDS MANAGEMENT STAFF

Career choice can be a very important influence on success and motivation on the job. The importance of a career decision should cause an individual to examine carefully the future of the industry and position to which he or she aspires and to examine the interests, aptitudes, and abilities that could be brought to the chosen position. Figure 2-4 shows some of the career paths available to those who are interested in a career in the records management field.

The information explosion has enhanced career opportunities.

The shift from an industrial society to an information society has caused records management to become an expanding technical information field, which is rapidly becoming more specialized. As organizations become more dependent on information and its rapid processing, effective control over records growth and efficient storage and retrieval become increasingly important. These factors have greatly enhanced career opportunities in records management. Not only do the number of positions in the information field continue to increase, but the advancement opportunities within and from these positions also increase.

Preparation

Entry into the records management field may be made at several levels and in several specific areas of expertise. While most positions in records management share some requirements, each has its own specialized requirements as well. The first step in successful preparation for a career in records management is to investigate types of positions available and qualifications required for each.

Entry may be made in a number of specialized areas.

As noted above, large, highly structured organizations usually have very specialized positions that offer many career opportunities. Smaller, less-structured organizations usually have fewer positions, less specialization, and include more of the overall records management responsibilities. These positions typically offer more limited career opportunities as well. The discussion in this chapter covers positions that may be found in a large organization's records unit under the direction of a records manager. A smaller organization that employs only a records manager and one or two records clerks may assign very different responsibilities to these individuals; however, those responsibilities are among those presented in this discussion.

Figure 2-4
Records and
Information
Management
Career Paths

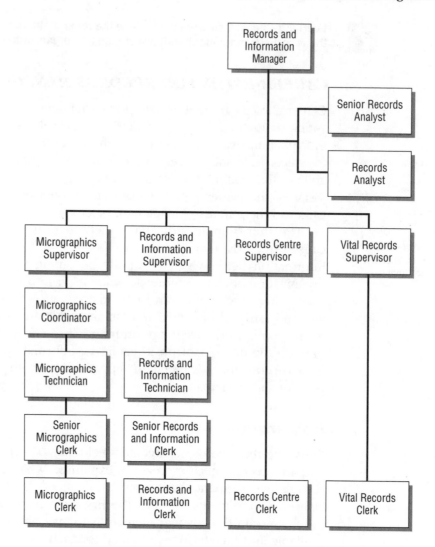

Job Qualifications

Job qualifications
are stated in terms
of education/train-
ing, experience,
and personal
characteristics.

In general, job qualifications are usually divided into three categories: education/training, experience, and personal characteristics. Each of these requirements varies somewhat from position to position and with the employing organization.

Education/Training

Formal education (such as graduation from high school, college, or university), specific course completion, and specific skills for each position may be required. In large organizations, most middle- and upper-level positions require a university degree and some experience in the field or some university course work and extensive experience. Most of the entry-level positions require at least a high school diploma or its equivalent.

Experience

Experience requirements vary from none for an entry-level position within the records unit to several years of related on-the-job experience for more advanced positions. Specific requirements for each position are shown in Figures 2-5 through 2-8.

Personal Characteristics

Personal characteristics contribute to success in any position. Good oral and written communication skills are crucial for most positions in records management. Staff members within the records unit must be able to relate well to other people, analyze data, and organize work. People who are detail- and service-oriented are more likely to find the records management field rewarding.

Career Paths

Three major career paths are available for records management staff.

Three major career paths in the field of records management have traditionally been available: active records, inactive records, and micrographics. These are shown on the Records and Information Management Career Paths in Figure 2-4. Each of these career areas contains both entry-level and advanced positions. Other associated areas are forms services, electronic records, reports, archives, vital records, disaster prevention and recovery, and library services, some of which may be under the broader umbrella of information management. This section gives a brief overview of the responsibilities and qualifications of positions in each of the main career paths. Increasingly, large organizations are outsourcing their inactive records and micrographics activities; forms design and reports are being handled by automated programs, reducing the need for specialized staff in these areas.

Active Records

The **active records staff** is responsible for controlling all records that are accessed at least once a month and for determining when records should be transferred to inactive status. The active records supervisor, sometimes called the records and information supervisor, is responsible for the efficiency and uniformity of filing procedures throughout the organization. Two or three levels of employees may report to the active records supervisor. Typical job responsibilities and qualifications in the active records department are shown in Figure 2-5.

Figure 2-5
Careers in the
Active Records
Department

Job Title	Duties and Responsibilities	Personal Characteristics	Education/ Experience	Advancement Opportunities
Records and Information Supervisor	Maintains uniform active records system and procedures throughout the organization Develops more efficient and economical methods of records maintenance Plans and conducts special active records projects Administers vital records program Selects and supervises staff	Works effectively with all levels of personnel Supervises effectively Coordinates available resources Has good organizational skills Has developed analytical skills Has strong oral and written communication skills	Minimum of 2 years college in records systems related work or equivalent work experience	Records Analyst Senior Records Analyst Other staff positions
Records and Information Technician	Maintains specialized records systems, such as medical or engineering records Conducts systems analysis in specialized area Assists in designing records retention schedules and monitors adherence to established schedule	Relates well to people Plans and organizes well Has developed analytical skills Has good oral and written communication skills	High school diploma 2 years' experience in records management or equivalent academic training	Records and Information Supervisor Other records management staff position
Senior Records and Information Clerk	Coordinates with records centre and other records areas to monitor files according to established standards Retrieves information for users Maintains logs and indexes summarizing status of information Oversees transfer of records according to retention schedule	Relates well to people Comprehends difficult questions and derives answers from records Plans and organizes well Possesses clerical and typing skills Has good oral and written communication skills	High school diploma 1 year's experience at Records and Information Clerk level	Records and Information Supervisor Records and Information Technician
Record and Information Clerk	Sorts, indexes, files, and retrieves all types of records Searches and investigates information in files Classifies materials and records Maintain charge-out system for records removed from files	Relates well to people Possesses mechanical aptitude Is able to analyze data for answers to questions Has good oral and written communication skills	High school diploma that includes some training in filing and retrieval Entry-level position	Senior Records and Information Clerk

Inactive Records

The **inactive records centre staff** is responsible for controlling all inactive records of the organization. The centre staff receives records that are transferred from the active records department and is responsible for the maintenance of the organization's vital records. The responsibilities of the records centre supervisor are very similar to those of the active records supervisor. Position responsibilities and qualifications in the records centre are described briefly in Figure 2-6.

Figure 2-6
Careers in the
Inactive
Records
Centre

Job Title	Duties and Responsibilities	Personal Characteristics	Education/ Experience	Advancement Opportunities
Records Centre Supervisor	Operates and maintains the records centre Is responsible for vital records protection, storage, and disposition Selects and supervises staff	Works effectively with all levels of personnel Supervises effectively Coordinates available resources Has good organizational skills Has strong oral and written communication skills	Minimum of 2 years college in records-systems-related work or equivalent work experience	Records Analyst Higher staff position
Records Centre Clerk	Assists in accession, reference, retrieval, and disposal activities of centre Assists with vital records Searches, sorts, and files records as required by users Maintains charge-out system for records removed from files	Relates well to people Possesses clerical and typing skills Possesses mechanical aptitude Is able to analyze data for answers to questions Has good oral and written communication skills	High school diploma that includes work in filing and retrieval May be entry-level position	Records Centre Supervisor Records and Information Technician

Micrographics

The **micrographics staff** is responsible for converting certain records or types of records to microforms. Microforms are miniaturized records produced on microfilm. The procedures used in this conversion and the microrecords control program are the responsibility of the micrographics supervisor. Usually both technicians and clerks serve as staff members. The number of persons employed in each position varies with the size of the organization and the number of micrographic applications used. Many organizations, especially smaller ones, often outsource their micrographic applications. Typical responsibilities and qualifications for the micrographics staff are shown in Figure 2-7.

Other Specialized Areas

Forms Services. Forms are used to collect and process data. The **forms staff** is responsible for establishing forms operating and analysis procedures, for establishing design and specification standards, and for controlling forms throughout the organization. Usually this function is assigned to the active records staff along with their other duties.

Reports. The **reports staff** is responsible for the development, implementation, and control of reports throughout the organization. Many smaller organizations have only one person in a reports position such as a records and information clerk responsible for maintaining the reports catalogue and operating the central reports library.

Electronic Records. Familiarity with automated systems and various types of electronic records is becoming an integral part of many jobs in records management. Staff from management information systems (MIS) could choose to move into higher level records management positions.

Figure 2-7
Careers in the
Micrographics
Department

Job Title	Duties and Responsibilities	Personal Characteristics	Education/ Experience	Advancement Opportunities
Micrographics Supervisor	Plans and controls central micrographics program Works closely with records and information analyst and other corporate members in development of micrographics applications Selects and supervises staff	Has developed analytical and organizational skills Supervises effectively Has strong oral and written communication skills	2 years' micrographic systems work experience 4 years' progressive related work experience	Records Analyst
Micrographics Coordinator	Sets priorities and schedules daily work Monitors human and operations resources Ensures quality control Trains micrographics personnel	Has ability to develop performance goals Has ability to supervise technical personnel Has strong oral and written communication skills	High school diploma or equivalent 3 years' experience in micrographics	Micrographics Supervisor
Micrographics Technician	Provides technical advice regarding new projects, equipment, and quality control Operates microfilming equipment Develops and maintains indexing and retrieval aids Monitors micrographics procedures manual and production statistics Monitors micrographics clerks	Relates well to people Plans and organizes work well Possesses mechanical aptitude Possesses knowledge of office procedures Has strong oral and written communication skills	High school diploma or equivalent 2 years' experience in micrographics	Micrographics Coordinator Micrographics Supervisor
Senior Micrographics Clerk	Receives and logs documents to be filmed Prepares documents for filming and operates equipment Handles special projects Monitors quality control Conducts routine equipment maintenance	Relates well to people Possesses mechanical ability Possesses filing, clerical, and typing skills Analyzes problems well Has strong oral and written communication skills	High school diploma or equivalent 1 year's experience in micrographics and/or training in micrographics	Micrographics Technician
Micrographics Clerk	Prepares documents for microfilming Operates microfilming equipment Prepares indexes and targets Searches, sorts, and files microforms	Relates well to people Possesses mechanical aptitude Possesses filing, clerical, and typing skills Has strong oral and written communication skills	High school diploma Entry-level position	Senior Micrographics Clerk

Archives. Staff may move in both directions between records management and archives positions. **Archives staff** select, appraise, and preserve those documents that have historical value. Many organizations maintain their own archives, and governments have extensive and varied archives employment opportunities.

Vital Records and Disaster Prevention and Recovery. The 3 to 5 percent of records essential to the continued life of a business need to be handled by a knowledgeable staff. Closely associated with this function are disaster prevention and recovery plans, which may be maintained by specialized staff.

Library Services. Rarely are library services included in records management, but, as with archives, staff may move in both directions because of the similarity of their functions.

Records Analyst Positions

In addition, beyond the career paths illustrated in Figure 2-4 are the positions of records analyst, senior records analyst, records and information manager, and top-level management positions responsible for the total information processing of the organization, such as chief information officer.

The **records analyst** acts as a sort of trouble shooter to create new systems, evaluate existing systems, and recommend improvements in all parts of a records management program (see Figure 2-8). In large organizations, analysts may be employed for specialized duties in the active records department or inactive records centre. Through systems analysis, they design new procedures for special projects involving active and inactive records, micrographics, forms, vital records, disaster prevention and recovery, and automated systems. To be successful in their jobs, records analysts need good analytical skills along with a thorough knowledge of records management techniques and computer technology. Since they work closely with staff at all levels, they must have excellent interpersonal and communication skills.

The **records analyst staff** are responsible for providing assistance in reviewing existing records systems and for making recommendations for improvement, as shown in Figure 2-8. With experience in all aspects of records and information management, the records analyst staff are able to move into higher level positions.

A typical advertisement for a records analyst might read as follows:

RECORDS ANALYST

Duties: Provide records management consulting services, training, and assistance to departments within the organization. You will deal with such issues as file classification schemes, automated records management, vital records, records retention, and archives.

Qualifications: You are a graduate of a recognized records management program or from a program in a related area and have two to three years of work experience in the information management field. Your strong communication and presentation skills enable you to work effectively with all levels of personnel. Time and project management abilities are essential. Familiarity with automated information systems and management of electronic records would be definite assets.

 Learning Check: Can you describe the general education/training, experience, and personal characteristics requirements for entry in a records management staff position?

Figure 2-8
Careers as
Records
Analysts

Job Title	Duties and Responsibilities	Personal Characteristics	Education/ Experience	Advancement Opportunities
Senior Records Analyst	Analyzes existing records systems and prepares proposals for change Designs manual and/or automated records systems Monitors retention programs Directs the establishment of a vital records protection program Directs and/or supervises other systems analysts	Relates well to people Has well-developed supervisory skills Has ability to analyze problems and seek solutions	College degree; or 2 years' college with specialized courses in records systems and a minimum of 2 years' work experience as a records analyst; or 4–6 years' experience in records systems with knowledge of automated technologies plus 2 years' work experience as a records analyst	Higher level staff position Supervisor
Records Analyst	Analyzes existing records systems and prepares proposals for change Designs manual and/or automated records systems Prepares or assists in preparing retention schedules Writes procedures Provides records staff training Assists in establishing a vital records protection program	Relates well to people Possesses organizational, planning, and motivational skills Has ability to analyze problems and seek solutions	College degree or 2 years' college plus courses in records systems; or 4–6 years' experience in records systems with knowledge of automated technologies	Senior Records Analyst

Advancement Opportunities

To advance in records management, staff members should take advantage of opportunities for growth and development.

Figures 2-5 through 2-8 provide an overview of advancement opportunities for records management staff positions. To prepare for these advancement opportunities, members of the records management staff should avail themselves of any opportunities for growth and development through on-the-job, purchased, or in-house training; by attending formal credit classes, seminars, or professional organizations' meetings; by reading professional publications; or by development through delegation and added responsibilities.

On-the-job training may be provided by other employees or through written, audio, or visual job aids. Purchased training can take the form of consultant services purchased by and designed for an organization or classes provided at educational institutions. In-house training is offered within the organization by its own personnel. The advantages of in-house training are that training, under the control of the records manager, can be tailored to the needs of the organization and its personnel, both in terms of time offered and content.

Educational institutions (both colleges and universities) offer a variety of courses that may be helpful to the records management professional. Courses in records management, business administration, information technology, and human relations should be considered. These courses may be particularly helpful to those starting at levels that do not require a college degree. Courses that earn credit toward a degree may not only add specific knowledge, but also help fulfil a requirement for advancement. Records management staff at all levels must be knowledgeable about computer applications.

Many opportunities exist for challenging employees with new activities and for delegating responsibility if the manager or supervisor is alert to discovering and utilizing them. As frequently as possible, the manager/supervisor should involve employees in making decisions relating to their work environment and procedures. This method of staff development is especially effective both for employees who are ambitious self-starters and for those who need to be given some direction.

THE RECORDS MANAGER

In the days of Alexander the Great (300 B.C.), a scribe had to answer the call to arms, hacking away with a sword at the enemy by day and with a stylus on a stone tablet by night. It was a prestigious job, but dangerous; Alexander lost 43 scribes during the Asian campaign alone!

The records manager's job requires diverse skills.

Today's records manager also has a challenging position: one requiring many and diverse skills. A sample advertisement for the position of records manager in Canada follows:

RECORDS MANAGER

This position is responsible for administering the company's records management program, which includes planning, organizing, monitoring, and coordinating the maintenance, protection, retrieval, and disposition of all information within the company. Budget preparation and monitoring are included. Information holdings consist of paper, microforms, and electronic records. This position requires extensive direct experience in planning, developing, implementing, and maintaining a records management program; excellent interpersonal, oral, and written communication skills; demonstrated knowledge of automated systems and applications; and superior planning and analytical skills. A bachelor's degree with five years' experience in a relevant management position is preferred. Certification in records management (CRM) would be a significant asset.

Job Qualifications for a Records Manager

Job qualifications for the records manager's position will vary somewhat with the organization; however, typical requirements are discussed briefly in this section.

Education/Training

Higher educational
levels are now
being sought by
organizations.

Education/training considerations include formal education requirements, such as a community college program or a university degree; specific course completion requirements—records management, computer science, automated systems, accounting, business law, and human relations; and specific skills required for the position. Many organizations now seek candidates for the records manager's position who have a bachelor's degree in business administration, library and information science, information management, or a related field. Preference is given to those who have five years' experience in records management or an advanced degree such as a master of library science or a master of archival studies. Some organizations with less sophisticated records programs may not require completion of a four-year program, but there is a trend toward a minimum educational requirement of the bachelor's degree for the position of records manager.

All organizations are interested in potential records managers who can demonstrate, through education or practical experience, knowledge of each area of the records program. Companies are also interested in hiring professionals—those who conduct their activities in accordance with established standards developed by a recognized professional organization in the field of records and information management, such as the Association of Records Managers and Administrators, Inc. (ARMA). Many business and government offices are using the **Certified Records Manager (CRM)** designation of the **Institute of Certified Records Managers (ICRM)** as a professional standard by which they measure the competence of applicants seeking records management positions.

Communication
skills are important
to success.

The records manager must possess effective oral and written communications skills. Poor communications skills may antagonize those whose cooperation is essential to the efficient operation of the records unit or impede the approval and implementation of needed changes. While the effectiveness of communications skills is difficult to determine from one's education/training or experience, many organizations will be especially alert to the demonstration of these skills in the application letter and the job interview. Some organizations require candidates for the records manager's position to submit examples of their writing as part of the application process. The level of skill demonstrated in the writing is weighted heavily among the selection criteria.

Experience

The requirements for the candidate for the position of records manager usually include at least one year of experience in each of one or more specific areas, such as micrographics, electronic records, or disaster prevention and recovery, and two or three years of experience in a supervisory position. Experience requirements generally increase as the responsibilities of the position increase. Because the records manager must supervise the many varied functions of the records unit, candidates for this position must demonstrate excellent leadership skills, as well as strong organization and planning skills.

Personal Characteristics

The records manager must work effectively with all levels of the organization.

Most positions have certain requirements in terms of personal characteristics. For the records manager, one of the most important personal characteristics is the ability to work effectively with all levels of personnel in the organization. Awareness of the role of each individual within the organization, the unique personal characteristics of each, and the importance of cooperating and of making requests easy to accept and complete are essential.

Other requirements include the ability to motivate employees to be efficient and effective in the performance of their duties, to delegate responsibility and authority, and to evaluate the performance of subordinates. Basic to a records manager's ability to motivate is an understanding of his/her employees and the ability to encourage them to work toward achieving their aspirations. Any attempt to motivate a person to perform at a high level must be tailored to the needs of that individual.

The records manager must be a self-starter—one who has the ability to identify and analyze problems, to determine alternative courses of action, to negotiate with others, and to implement solutions based on sound judgment and a thorough understanding of the records management profession.

Job Descriptions of Records Managers

Job descriptions and job specifications provide information about skills, knowledge, and abilities required for specific positions.

A **job description** is a written summary of the job that states (or lists) the tasks to be performed by the employee as well as identifying areas of responsibility. The records manager's job description will vary with the placement in the organization structure and the degree of specialization existing within the records unit.

Areas of responsibility frequently include supervision of records storage, retrieval, and security; forms and reports control; systems design for current records; floor plan/layout design, equipment selection, moving, and conversion; audit and litigation support; reprographics control; microrecords processing and control; development of technical manuals; human resources development; evaluation of performance and procedures; planning, negotiation, and implementation of changes based on better utilization of existing resources. Organizational structure may dictate that some of these responsibilities, all of these responsibilities, or these and additional responsibilities be included in a particular records manager's position.

The specific duties of the records manager also vary with the organization. These may, however, be expected to include planning records centre facilities; conducting or supervising the records inventory; planning or coordinating the development and revisions of the retention and disposition program; selecting the classification system(s); evaluating and selecting equipment and supplies; developing the records management manual; selecting, training, and evaluating the staff; working with department heads to establish controls on correspondence, reports, and copies; working with department heads to design forms; organizing disaster prevention and recovery plans; and establishing a records security program. Note the diversity of these tasks and the broad base of knowledge required to perform them successfully. Figure 2-9 is a typical job description and job specification for a records and information manager.

Figure 2-9
Job Description and Job Specification for Manager, Records Management

Title

Manager—Records and Information Management

Function

The primary responsibility of this function is to provide effective management, direction, and control of the organization's records and information management program and staff. Included are all the active records systems in the organization and an offsite inactive records centre. The records manager provides expertise and input into other functional areas connected with the recorded information of the organization such as copy practices, electronic information, privacy and access to information issues, and legislation. The individual works closely with the Computer Services Department to coordinate activities.

Duties

1. Records Management Program. Plans, implements, and maintains a comprehensive information and records management system.
2. Records Retention Schedule. Works with other departments to develop retention policies and guidelines. Publishes and implements the records retention schedule.
3. Active File Systems. Develops active file systems for microfilm, paper, and electronic records.
4. Inactive Records Systems. Develops guidelines and implements procedures for inactive records including transfer, storage, retrieval, and disposition in the inactive records centre.
5. Vital Records. Assists in identifying vital records and developing guidelines for their protection, including disaster prevention and recovery.
6. Automated Records Systems. Consults with users and Computer Services Department on automated records management applications and recommends solutions.
7. Magnetic/Electronic Records Systems. Develops and implements guidelines for management of magnetic and electronic records including retention, destruction, and archival storage requirements. Works with Computer Services Department to develop and implement this program.
8. Training and Education. Coordinates all records management educational and training programs within the organization.
9. Budget. Prepares and monitors departmental budget.

Position Requirements

Excellent oral and written communication skills. Strong interpersonal skills. Strong analytical and problem solving ability. Management skills of planning, organizing, leading, and motivating. Demonstrated expertise in records and information management.

Qualifications

Minimum educational requirement is an undergraduate degree in business administration, information management, computer studies, or a related discipline and five years of direct experience in records and information management. Certification in records management a significant asset. A thorough understanding of automated systems and applications is essential. Ability to function in French and English an asset.

 Learning Check: Can you cite the general education/training, experience, and personal characteristics required for a records management position?

Advancement Opportunities for Records Managers

Because the records manager is knowledgeable about the information requirements of each department within the organization and must work with each department to ensure the successful functioning of the records management system, this individual is in an excellent position to advance to the following positions: Director or Vice President of Information Services, Vice President of Information Resources, and eventually to Chief Information Officer.

To advance, the records manager must continuously upgrade skills and knowledge.

All records management personnel with the desire to advance must continuously upgrade skills and knowledge. This may be accomplished through in-house courses, classes offered through educational institutions, participation in professional organizations, reading and submitting articles for publication in the journals, and by preparing for and taking the Certified Records Manager Exam. To become a Certified Records Manager (CRM), an individual must meet experience and education requirements established by the Institute of Certified Records Managers (ICRM) and pass a six-part examination within a five-year period. Further information on this examination is presented in *Preparing for the CRM Examination: A Handbook,* available from ARMA.

The CRM designation recognizes the records manager as a professional in the field.

Participation in professional organizations such as the **Association of Records Managers and Administrators, Inc. (ARMA)**, the **Association of Canadian Archivists**, and the **Association for Information and Image Management (AIIM)** offers many opportunities for professional growth and development for all records management personnel. An organization similar to AIIM, the **Canadian Information and Image Management Society (CIIMS)**, has been actively involved in producing a new national Canadian standard for the use of microfilm and electronic images as documentary evidence. The

Canadian Information Processing Society (CIPS) and the **Information Technology Association of Canada (ITAC)** concentrate on information technology. Local chapters of these organizations provide monthly or bimonthly programs of technical interest to records managers and opportunities to meet other professionals and exchange ideas. Seminars and annual conferences present opportunities for experts to share new ideas and procedures, as well as a chance to see and evaluate new technology.

Many professional organizations also encourage and coordinate research into specific problems or procedures important to professionals in the field. Often records management personnel present results of research and the development and implementation of innovative procedures at annual conferences.

Professional publications are excellent sources of information on technical innovations or improvements in the records management field and provide a vehicle for sharing new ideas or for updating methods. Several journals and newsletters are published by professional organizations and by specialists in records management. Often these publications are available in the organization's library or public libraries. Members, of course, receive these publications with their membership. *The Records Management Quarterly,* an ARMA publication, and *Inform,* an AIIM publication, report studies of importance to records management personnel. The *IMC Journal,* the international publication of document imaging, also contains pertinent articles.

Records management personnel should be encouraged to submit their experiences to the professional journals. Writing for publication stimulates professional growth.

Participation in professional organizations offers development opportunities.

Learning Check: Can you describe the advancement opportunities available to records managers and cite actions that may be taken to prepare for advancement?

TERMINOLOGY REVIEW

Review the terms listed below in the Glossary on page 521.
active records staff
archives staff
Association for Information and Image Management (AIIM)
Association of Canadian Archivists
Association of Records Managers and Administrators, Inc. (ARMA)
Canadian Information and Image Management Society (CIIMS)
Canadian Information Processing Society (CIPS)
Certified Records Manager (CRM)
forms staff

inactive records centre staff
Information Technology Association of Canada (ITAC)
Institute of Certified Records Managers (ICRM)
job analysis
job description
micrographics staff
organization chart
records analyst
records analyst staff
reports staff

REVIEW AND DISCUSSION

1. Describe two organizational staffing patterns that include a records manager and differentiate between the roles established by these patterns.
2. Describe the general education/training, experience, and personal characteristics required for entry into a records management staff position.
3. Cite the general education/training, experience, and personal characteristics required for a records manager's position.
4. Select three duties performed by the records manager and explain how the size of an organization affects these duties.
5. Describe advancement opportunities available to the records management staff and the records manager, and cite the actions that may be taken to prepare for advancement.

APPLICATIONS

1. Obtain an organization chart that shows the placement of the records manager of your institution, local or provincial government, or a private business. Explain what the placement of the records manager reveals about the importance of that position within the organization you selected. Give a rationale for your answer.
2. Match each of the job responsibilities in Column B with the job titles in Column A. The items in Column B may be used as many times as appropriate.

A	B
1. Records and Information Supervisor	a. Sorts, indexes, and retrieves all types of records
2. Forms Clerk	b. Maintains micrographics procedural manual
3. Reports Clerk	c. Prepares documents for microfilming
4. Micrographics Clerk	d. Maintains uniform filing systems and procedures throughout the organization
5. Records and Information Clerk	e. Selects and supervises staff
6. Forms Supervisor	f. Determines when forms should be recorded
7. Records and Information Technician	g. Maintains catalogue of reports available for access
8. Micrographics Technician	h. Plans, implements, and coordinates a forms control program throughout the organization
9. Records Analyst	i. Monitors adherence to records retention schedule
	j. Analyzes records system and designs proposal for improvement

3. Explain how a records analyst would assist the forms supervisor and the records and information supervisor.

CONCLUDING CASES

A. SportsVision EyeGlass Company

SportsVision EyeGlass Company has expanded its sales territory into ski territory. Organizational goals call for expansion into three additional provinces over the next three years. Currently, records are maintained in each division by the secretaries. The president of SportsVision EyeGlass Company thinks that this expansion will require a more formal records program. The current organizational structure is shown in Figure 2-10.

1. Prepare a job description and job specification that highlights the function and qualifications that will be required for the position of records manager.
2. Assign a position on the organization chart shown in Figure 2-10 for the records manager. Explain the placement you selected.

B. Monarch Sports Equipment and Athletic Facilities, Inc.

Taylor Masters has been employed by the Monarch Corporation for eight years. Taylor has acquired experience in records centre operation, micrographics, forms analysis and design, and correspondence and reports management. Three years ago, Taylor was promoted to the position of records manager and joined ARMA. Taylor's education includes a two-year applied science program in data processing from Markham Community College.

Figure 2-10
Organization Chart

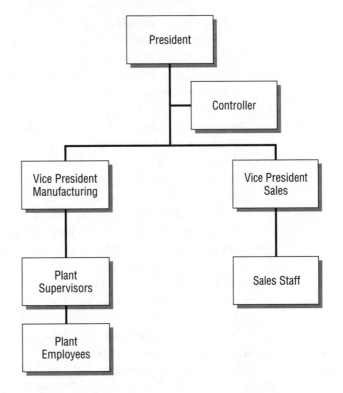

The records manager, to whom Taylor reports, was critically injured in an automobile accident last week and will not be returning to Monarch. The vice president of information services has formed a committee to find a qualified individual to serve as records manager.

1. Assume that you are Taylor Masters. Based on the information given in the case and any reasonable assumptions you may wish to make, draft a résumé for submission to the search committee. Emphasize your strengths for the position of records manager.

2. Assume the role of a member of the search committee charged with the responsibility of finding a corporate records manager. List weaknesses you find in this candidate's credentials for records manager. For each weakness identified, recommend a course of action that Taylor could pursue to overcome the deficiency.

SUGGESTED READINGS AND RESOURCES

ARMA International Standards Job Descriptions Task Force. *Job Descriptions—A Guideline,* Prairie Village, Kansas: Association of Records Managers and Administrators, Inc., 1991.

Boyd, Fraser. "Do Records Managers Manage?" *Records Management Quarterly,* Vol. 28, No. 2 (April, 1994), p. 14.

Hefner, Loretta L. "Resolving Conflicts Between Records Professionals and Managers: An Elusive Goal." *Records Management Quarterly,* Vol. 28, No. 4 (October, 1994), p. 14.

Information Associations Micro-Directory. *Records Management Quarterly,* Vol. 28, No. 4 (October, 1994), p. 60.

Pemberton, J. Michael. "High (Professional) Anxiety? Image and Status in Records Management." *Records Management Quarterly,* Vol. 30, No. 1 (January, 1996), p. 66.

Pemberton, J. Michael. "Professionals and Clerks: One Happy Family?" *Records Management Quarterly,* Vol. 28, No. 2 (April, 1994), p. 56.

Pemberton, J. Michael. "Records Management Education: In Pursuit of Standards." Vol. 28, No. 3 (July, 1994), p. 58.

Pemberton, J. Michael. "RIM: Navigating Through a Maze of Associations." *Records Management Quarterly,* Vol. 28, No. 4 (October, 1994), p. 56.

Pemberton, J. Michael, and Raymond R. McBeth. "Opportunities Out of Chaos: Survival Strategies in the Information Age." *Records Management Quarterly,* Vol. 29, No. 3 (July, 1995), p. 8.

Penn, Ira A. "Avoiding A Records Management Nightmare." *Records Management Quarterly,* Vol. 30, No. 1 (January, 1996), p. 26.

Penn, Ira A. "The Degeneration of the Work of Man." *Records Management Quarterly,* Vol. 29, No. 1 (January, 1995), p. 9.

Preparing for the CRM Examination: A Handbook, Prairie Village, Kansas: Association of Records Managers and Administrators, Inc., 1993.

Sanders, Robert L. "Disguised Office Saboteurs." *Records Management Quarterly,* Vol. 29, No. 1 (January, 1995), p. 47.

Profile
Director of Records Management and Archival Services

Jean K. Brown began her professional association with the University of Western Ontario in 1983 as a records management analyst in the university's archives. She has served as records management administrator, acting university archivist and director of records management, and currently as director of records management and archival services. The university employs 1,925; the department has four full-time employees and three part-time student employees.

The position of director of records management and archival services is described in the following way in the staffing manual:

The Director of Records Management and Archival Services reports to the Assistant University Secretary and is responsible for planning, developing, implementing, and administering records management policies and procedures designed to facilitate effective and efficient handling of University records and information in all media; for retrieving, analyzing and interpreting information for management and policy decisions; for serving as a principal information resource and advising senior management and the Trustees on University information through the University Secretary; for maintaining knowledge of legal matters which affect management decisions; and, for preparing documentation for legal counsel as assigned by the University Secretary.

The Director serves as Curator of archival collections and is responsible for the appraisal, organizing and processing of permanent records and historically valuable documents, researching archival materials and facilitating research by others, and, directing the safekeeping of archival documents and materials. The Director of Records Management and Archival services prepares and administers the Department budget; supervises staff, and also serves as Curator of the Permanent Art Collection of the University of Western Ontario for the office of the University Secretary.

Changes in duties and responsibilities have occurred as a result of records management program automation. The university archives is now responsible for monitoring electronic records management campuswide and has become more involved with the university's legal matters. Because of the increased resources needed in recent years to develop the records management program, fewer resources in the department have been devoted to archival processing, even though the archival collections are actively utilized. This has been a result of the impact on the department of the records management program's successful growth and development. In the future, closer contact with the university secretary's office on legal matters, increased work with electronic records management, and the development of a reports management program are expected to increase the effectiveness of the services provided by the university archives to the university.

Mrs. Brown is an active member of the Association of Records Managers and Administrators (ARMA). She has served as secretary, treasurer, newsletter editor, seminar chair, research chair, program chair, director, vice president and president of her local Region VIII chapter. She has been honoured four times by being selected Chapter Member of the Year. Mrs. Brown is also very active in the international association, having served on several association-level committees. She has had several articles published in records management publications and is a frequent speaker at workshops and seminars on a variety of records management topics. Mrs. Brown exemplifies the professional records manager.

Part 2
Records Evaluation

Records Inventory and Analysis

Learning Goals

After completing this chapter, you should be able to:

1. Define planning.
2. Explain the relationship among goals, objectives, and strategy.
3. Define records inventory.
4. Describe the goals of a records inventory.
5. Outline the steps in planning a records inventory.
6. Discuss the considerations in selecting personnel to conduct the records inventory.
7. Explain the advantages and disadvantages of the most common methods of conducting the records inventory.
8. Describe factors to be considered when selecting the records inventory form.
9. Describe the steps in conducting the inventory.
10. Define a records series and give examples of those found in most organizations.
11. State information that can be found in the records analysis.
12. Outline the steps in reporting the findings at the conclusion of the records inventory.

PLANNING THE RECORDS MANAGEMENT PROGRAM

Planning involves determining where the organization wants to go (goals) and how it will get there (strategy).

In *Alice in Wonderland,* Alice asked, "Cheshire-Puss ... Would you tell me, please, which way I ought to go from here?"

"That depends a good deal on where you want to get to," said the Cat.

"I don't know where I want to go," said Alice.

"Then it doesn't really matter which way you go," said the Cat.

Just as the Cat couldn't help Alice reach her destination until she knew where she ultimately wanted to go, an organization cannot develop a strategy to reach its goals until it determines what it hopes to accomplish.

Establish Goals and Objectives

Goals are established from highest to lowest levels.

The goals of an organization are established at the highest levels of management; **goals** reflect the philosophy and aspirations of management for the entire organization. Goals are established in all functional areas and at all levels of the company. The hierarchy of goals is top down, beginning with company-wide goals, then moving downward to the lowest management level, with each series of goals complementing the one above.

Objectives are more specific than goals.

Goals are usually stated in general terms. For example, one organizational goal might be to reduce the cost of administrative services. In keeping with this organizational goal, goals in records management might be to increase the capabilities and reduce the cost of providing information to managers. After the goal(s) have been defined, specific objectives relating to the goals are developed. An **objective** is a statement of how one step in reaching a goal is to be completed and measured. A specific objective for the organizational goal of a reduction in costs might be to reorganize the administrative services to streamline its operation to produce an 8 percent saving during the next two years. A specific objective of the records management goal of reducing the cost of providing information to managers might be to determine a more cost-efficient method of maintaining and storing records to result in a 10 percent saving in this fiscal year.

Determine Strategy

Strategy is a plan of action.

Once the goals and objectives have been established, action plans are then written to accomplish each of the objectives and consequently, to attain the goals. Given the records of management goals and one of the objectives as defined above, a plan for achieving the objective would be devised. The **plan** would include ways to accomplish the objective, a timetable for the planned action, and a cost projection. The records management department plan to accomplish the objective of cost reduction in providing information to managers might be similar to that shown in Table 3-1.

There are other actions that could be taken to accomplish this objective, and there are other goals and objectives that could be stated as a part of the total records management plan. The specific goals and objectives, as well as the action plan, have to be tailored to the particular needs of the organization. Plans serve as the foundation for all organizational achievements.

Table 3-1

COST REDUCTION PLAN

Goal: Increase the capabilities and reduce the cost of providing information to managers.

Objective	Action	Completion Date	Cost
5 percent cost reduction by using more cost-efficient storage and retrieval practices	Review retention schedule to determine if files are kept too long in active status	30 days	Labour only*
	Assess turnaround time to determine if clerks need additional training	30 days	Labour only
	Check files for overcrowding	10 days	Labour only
	Determine if files are being disposed of according to schedule	45 days	Labour only

*No additional labour costs. Tasks to be accomplished by staff members within the records management unit.

Obtain Authorization and Support

A firm commitment from top management is essential to achieving cooperation and promoting coordination among those involved in the implementation of plans for any major project, particularly if that project involves other departments. Support and commitment should be solicited at the beginning of the planning process and must be continued throughout the planning and implementation stages. Some of the ways to sell management include a special report, a one-on-one meeting with an executive, a presentation to a committee, and a well-planned test program for a single department.

Support and commitment must also be solicited from those who will be working with the project. To succeed in any endeavour, firm commitment and support from both upper management and those involved in the implementation must be obtained.

Management Support and Commitment

Management is primarily interested in the organization-wide benefits a records management program will provide. Top levels of management often do not recognize the need for a comprehensive program of records management. Basic education regarding the scope of records management is needed because too many managers equate records management with cabinets and boxes for housing paper records. Sometimes managers must be made aware of existing or potential problems in order to perceive a need for change. For some managers this knowledge comes late and is costly. Many organizations have become aware of the importance of records protection only after all of their records have been destroyed by fire.

Gaining management support may not start with the "grand design." Sometimes an elaborate plan scares off potential supporters. You may have to start with a single phase of a multiphase plan; for example, begin by instituting a program of records retention and disposition. Be prepared to present a well-designed plan for change.

Management support must be publicized. For example, if a study is to be conducted in any area of records management, a letter from management to all participants will convey the support required. In addition, the first item on the agenda at the orientation meetings should be a brief introduction of the project by a member of top management. This introduction should emphasize the importance of the study and the commitment of top management to its successful conclusion. Get support, then broadcast it.

User Support and Management Commitment

User support is achieved in two major ways: positive management attitudes and user involvement in the processes. Positive attitudes of top management tend to create positive user attitudes. The other tool used to gain user support—user involvement in the processes—has long been accepted as a successful supervisory technique. Promoting early user involvement; providing routine updates; welcoming, even soliciting, suggestions; encouraging participation; and making potential benefits known to the users are effective in gaining support.

Support for any program must be obtained from the people who will ultimately be responsible for the system's implementation and maintenance. In almost all instances, management and users share this responsibility.

 Learning Check: Can you explain the relationship among goals, objectives, and strategy?

RECORDS INVENTORY

To accomplish the overall goal of records management, "to provide the right record to the right person at the right time and at the least cost," records managers must first know what types of records are maintained, where the records are housed, and what volume of records is kept within the organization.

Definition

The **records inventory** is a detailed review of the quantity, type, function, and organization of records. Information from the records inventory, sometimes called the records survey, provides answers to these questions:

- What kinds of records do we have?
- Where are the records located?
- How many records do we have?
- Are the records active, inactive, or nonessential?
- Are the records vital?
- Which are record copies?

Goals

A records inventory provides a basis for many management decisions.

The records inventory has three major goals: to define the present scope and status of the records to be managed, to provide the database for the development of a records retention program, and to provide information for other decisions in the development of an effective records management program. For example, information provided by the records inventory provides a basis for determining what facilities, equipment, supplies, and staff are required to handle the organization's records; what training the staff needs; what controls should be placed on the creation and duplication of records; and what measures must be taken to protect the organization's vital records.

In some instances a complete records inventory is not necessary. A focus survey may be undertaken to target one particular problem area, such as poorly organized case records. This is a useful approach if an immediate solution is required.

✓ **Learning Check: Can you define records inventory and state the goals of a records inventory?**

PLANNING THE RECORDS INVENTORY

Records inventory should follow a plan.

A records inventory should only be undertaken with careful planning because the data provided affects most aspects of the records management program. The records manager is responsible for determining how to conduct this project. Steps in planning for the inventory should include obtaining authorization and support from top management and commitment from those who will be working on the inventory, selecting the personnel to conduct the inventory, determining the method to be used, selecting or developing the appropriate forms, and planning the schedule for the inventory.

Gain Commitment

Once management is committed to a total records retention program, the records manager begins the first task: conducting a records inventory. The staff should be informed in writing of the importance of this task in establishing a records retention program that will ultimately improve operations in all departments. The same communication should, if possible, name the project director and request support for that person in completing the task as expeditiously as possible.

Completion of a records inventory involves every department within the organization. Cooperation of staff members within each department is essential to obtaining an accurate and complete records inventory. Because taking an inventory causes some interruption of normal work flow and increases the responsibilities of key departmental personnel, these individuals must know that top management recognizes the importance of this task and expects their cooperation. Photos or slides showing unorganized and overflowing storage areas may help to make others aware of the need for the records inventory project.

Select Personnel

One of the first tasks in planning for the records inventory is selecting the people who will direct and implement the program. This includes selection of the project director and the members of the group who will actually conduct the survey.

Project Director

The project director may be selected from internal or external candidates.

The person selected as the project director must have a thorough knowledge of inventory techniques and of the importance of the records inventory as a basis for a sound records management program. Should someone on the staff be appointed to serve as the project director or should the organization hire an outside consultant for this position? Each choice has advantages and disadvantages.

Internal Director. If the organization employs a records manager, this person would be the logical choice to be appointed the project director. The records manager has an understanding of the goals and operating methods of the organization. In addition, the records manager is motivated to provide the best results.

If the records manager is unable to take on an additional project at this time, perhaps another member of the records management unit may be able to assume the responsibility. In this instance, the records manager may be required to give some assistance in carrying out the records inventory. This may cause some delay in beginning the inventory but should enhance the usefulness of the results.

External Director. When an organization hires an outside consultant or group of consultants, it is hiring an expert who has experience in doing a particular task or group of related tasks. The consultant knows the most up-to-date techniques and how these techniques have been applied in other organizations. A consultant also comes to the job with no bias toward any particular department or procedure within the organization.

A disadvantage to hiring consultants is the brief period of time the consultants are in the organization. Because of their limited knowledge of the organization's operating procedures, consultants may overlook some problem areas. As a result, the final report may not include all the details necessary for the staff to implement the recommended procedures.

The consultant should be asked to present a written proposal to the organization. This proposal should include a detailed list of activities to be completed, a schedule for completing the activities, and a cost estimate.

Inventory Group Members

The members of the group assisting in the inventory should be selected carefully.

Once the project director has been selected, the director will identify other members of the group who will assist in conducting the inventory. Unless the organization is very small with limited records, one person should not do the actual records inventory. The inventory might be conducted by a task force consisting of one person from each department to be inventoried, by a group selected from within the records management unit, or by a group contracted from outside the company. The decision is largely dependent on the availability of qualified personnel within the company and their other commitments.

Task Force. A task force composed of a member from each department to be inventoried yields consistent results because each department is inventoried following the same procedures. The representative from the department is familiar with the location of records and with the way in which they are maintained. Further, involving members of other departments provides an incentive for cooperation among departments. A training program in inventory procedures would have to be established with time set aside from routine duties for participation in the training.

Records Management Staff. If the records management unit has sufficient numbers of their staff who are familiar with inventory procedures and who can be spared to conduct the inventory, consistent results are obtained because the same people are conducting the inventory within each department. The members of the records management unit would also require less training than would members of a task force from the other departments and, because the records management staff is regularly engaged in maintaining records, they are already aware of the importance of an accurate inventory. They are, however, not as familiar with the location and storage of records in other departments as persons within the departments would be.

Contracted Services. The records inventory can be conducted by a group contracted by the organization for this project. This service would be beneficial when it is not feasible to pull workers off their assigned tasks to conduct the inventory or when time is essential. A contracted group has no other responsibilities except to render the service for which hired—to conduct the records inventory. If quick turnaround is essential and expense is not a consideration, this avenue should be considered. However, an outside group would not be familiar with the organization, its needs, or its records. A contracted group would need a detailed explanation of the desired outcome of the records inventory for a successful outcome.

Determine Method

The records inventory may be conducted by questionnaire, by a physical survey, or by a combination of the two methods.

Questionnaire

Questionnaires are used frequently to gather records inventory information.

Many organizations find the quickest way to complete a records inventory is to develop a survey form to collect the necessary data about volume and type of records in each department. These forms can be distributed to all departments simultaneously. Departmental personnel complete the forms and return them to the project director as requested.

Two problems frequently develop when this method is employed, however. First, departmental personnel may not be experienced in records inventory procedures. Instructions may be interpreted differently; if this occurs, the collected data will have little or no consistency. Meeting with the key departmental personnel prior to distributing the inventory forms—to explain their use and to answer questions—may minimize this problem. More training may be required, however, than simply a question-and-answer session.

Second, the departmental personnel who are assigned to complete the questionnaire may view it as one more job to be done. They may not see completing the questionnaire as an essential task. Departmental personnel may procrastinate in completing the inventory form and then do it in a haphazard manner. In addition, resentment may develop toward any effort to implement records controls within the organization. The commitment of the organization's key managers may help to alleviate these concerns. An enthusiastic project director who simplifies the task as much as possible also decreases the probability of having to deal with poorly prepared responses from resentful personnel.

Physical Survey

Physical inventories yield more accurate information.

A physical survey of all the active and inactive records of each department within an organization is time consuming; however, this method is the most accurate one for determining the current volume, types, dates, and locations of an organization's records. One person can usually survey 1,000 cubic feet of paper records (approximately 700 letter-size drawers) per week.

Training those who actually conduct the physical survey of the records provides consistency in the collected data and speeds the actual completion of the survey. In a small organization training may not be necessary, as the project director may be the only person involved in the survey. Specific steps in completing the physical survey are discussed in the section on conducting the inventory below.

Combination Physical Inventory and Questionnaire

In some cases it may be expedient to do a combination physical inventory and questionnaire, using a dual-purpose form. A preliminary physical inventory may be used, followed by a modified questionnaire that would ask a departmental member familiar with the files to complete the parts of the questionnaire that could not be completed based on the physical inventory.

A complete inventory covers *all* of an organization's records—including microforms, electronic records, optical media, drawings, plans, databases, video and audio tapes. Electronic records are particularly difficult to inventory since they may have no physical form. The best approach may be for each department to inventory its electronic records along with the paper and microforms. To be certain that the inventory covers all records, the team should ask if paper and microforms have electronic counterparts, and vice versa. Many offices share a central database or an electronic messaging system, and no one "owns" the records generated. The team should interview representative users to collect information about these records series.

Obtain Forms

Information required on the inventory form may vary somewhat from organization to organization. The form should reflect the unique requirements of the organization; therefore, the questions on the form should be those identified as important to the specific organization.

Forms should be easy to use.

The forms selected should be easy to use and should help to ensure that as much information as needed is collected the first time around. Second chances are difficult to get, so good use should be made of the first chance at gathering information by using a form that is inclusive enough to elicit all of the information required for future use in determining the records retention schedule.

Plan Schedule

A detailed schedule for the records inventory is a "must."

Before the records inventory is begun, a detailed schedule should be prepared, presented to key managers for approval, and published throughout the organization. Some records managers prefer to notify each department near the time of the survey to prevent departmental "clean-ups," which may destroy valuable records. The schedule cannot be prepared until the project director has identified the records to be inventoried, determined the locations of records within the organization, decided on the sequence in which records are to be inventoried, and estimated the time necessary to complete the inventory. An alternative is to select one part of the organization and start with the smallest unit and work each level until that part of the organization is complete.

Records

The project director must make a decision regarding the types of records to be inventoried. Is the inventory going to include both active and inactive records? If there is a small volume of records in one location, both active and inactive records could be inventoried at the same time. However, if this is a first-time, full-scale inventory or a large organization with enormous volumes of records, it might be prudent to begin with the active records, moving to the inactive only after the entire inventory of active records has been completed. The project director should keep the tasks "do-able," so that people inexperienced in inventory procedures are not overwhelmed by the magnitude of the task.

Locations

Location identified where records are stored.

The number of records locations varies according to the degree of centralization of the organization's records storage facilities. If all or most of the organization's active records are housed in a centralized area and most of the inactive records are housed in a records centre, the identification of locations is greatly simplified. In most organizations, however, the identification of storage locations is not so easy.

Records are often retained within each department (sometimes within each office). If this is the procedure, the project director may find it helpful to do a walk-through to assure a comprehensive inventory and to approximate the amount of time needed in each area. Unless the project director is familiar with the storage area for inactive records, a walk-through of that area is also helpful. The project director may want to sketch the approximate location of records and the storage equipment used in each area to save time in completing the actual inventory.

Records may be found in locations other than those normally associated with records. For example, sometimes they are found on top of cabinets, in or on desks, in closets, in boxes tucked away in corners, and in other locations. Therefore, the project director should be observant of other than traditional records files locations when conducting the walk-through.

Sequence

Sequence refers to the order in which the records will be surveyed.

The project director must also determine the order in which records are to be inventoried. A practical approach is to begin at the departmental level and move upward, completing all departmental inventories before inventorying records at the higher levels. One advantage of this approach is that records duplication is often easier to identify. Duplicate records can then be scheduled for shorter retention periods.

Time

Time estimates for completion must be made.

Once the order in which records are to be inventoried is determined, the project director must estimate the time to be spent in each location. Familiarity with the locations of records and the space required to contain them improves the accuracy of this estimate. The estimated time for completion should always provide for interruptions, which inevitably occur, and also take into consideration the level of expertise of the persons conducting the inventory.

When the elements of the schedule have been determined, the schedule can be presented to key managers for approval. After any suggested adjustments are made, key departmental personnel and others whose cooperation is needed should get the schedule. Orientation meetings and training sessions, if required, should be held for those assisting in the actual inventory, and the work can then begin.

 Learning Check: Can you describe the steps in planning an inventory?

CONDUCTING THE INVENTORY

If the records inventory has been properly planned, the implementation will be much more efficiently conducted and effectively concluded. Steps to be performed in each location when conducting the inventory include completing a preliminary purge, identifying the records series, developing the forms, and identifying the required space.

Complete Preliminary Purge

A preliminary purge shortens time required for the formal inventory.

While project directors would not want valuable departmental records destroyed, a preliminary purge of nonessential records will reduce the time required for the inventory. Assign employees specific files to purge so each knows which files are his/her responsibility. Set completion dates and follow through. Purging each file drawer or tier of paper records should take about 15 to 30 minutes of uninterrupted time. This is the time to identify duplicate records; keep the record copy or one duplicate and destroy or discard others.

During this preliminary purge, throw away as much as possible, without destroying essential records. If there is a question about keeping a record, keep it. File drawers are often catchalls for supplies and other nonrecord items. Remove them from the files and place them where they belong. One records management consultant estimates that this preliminary file purge should remove at least 30 to 40 percent of the materials in the files.[1]

Identify the Records Series

A records series may contain many files, all having a similar function.

In each records location, an inventory is completed for each records series identified. A **records series** is a group of records that is filed together as a unit and used as a unit and that can be transferred to inactive storage or destroyed as a unit. Examples of frequently used records series are paid vouchers, departmental correspondence, and personnel records. A personnel folder, while containing many types of forms and other records, is a single file within the personnel records series and should be inventoried as such.

A records series may contain many files (which may be on paper or other media); therefore, care must be exercised in determining the correct title for each records series and in deciding which files are to be included in each series. Defining records series titles and providing a list of definitions to the departments is helpful because similar titles sometimes contain different information.

When working with electronic media, such as computer tapes, one must identify the **data set** or group of data or information. It is important to determine the data set type. Is the data set a master file or a

---

[1]Mark Langemo, "How Long Must You Keep Your Business Records?" *Office Systems*, Vol. 5, No. 4 (April, 1988), p. 40.

backup? One must also identify the hierarchy of data sets. There may be redundant information, as daily, weekly, quarterly, and annual data sets are maintained for sales data, for example. Each type of data set and each level within the hierarchy will have different retention requirements. Is the same information contained in another form elsewhere (for example, on paper)? Do both need to be retained?

Develop the Forms

Some inventory forms are more inclusive than others.

Besides identifying the records series, the inventory form should indicate the value, locations, dates, types, and volume of the records; whether the record is a copy or a nonrecord copy; and the name of the person who surveyed the records, and the date on which they were surveyed. This information provides an audit trail. Audits and audit trails are discussed in detail in Chapter 15, "Records Control—Audits and Reports." The records series *value* indicates the business purpose for which the records are kept. *Location* refers to the physical place in which the records are housed; *dates* refer to the inclusive dates in this records series (for example, July 1–December 31, 1995). *Types* refers to the type of records media, such as paper, microfilm, 5 1/4-inch disks, 3 1/2-inch disks, and so forth. *Volume* refers to the amount of space the records series requires. Recall that *record copy* refers to the official copy of a record, while *nonrecord copy* refers to a duplicate record or a record such as one found in convenience files or reference materials.

In summary, for each record series, the forms should have space for gathering the following information:
- Record series title
- Brief description of value
- Location of records
- Volume of records
- Dates covered
- Records storage medium—microfilm, paper, floppy disk, etc.
- Storage equipment and supplies
- Records duplicated elsewhere
- Copy type—record copy, nonrecord copy, backup copy
- Vital records identified
- Type of technology—computer, audio, video
- Type of information—text, data, images
- Current retention procedures
- Current disposition practices

Figure 3-1
Records
Inventory
Worksheet
for Paper
and
Microfilm

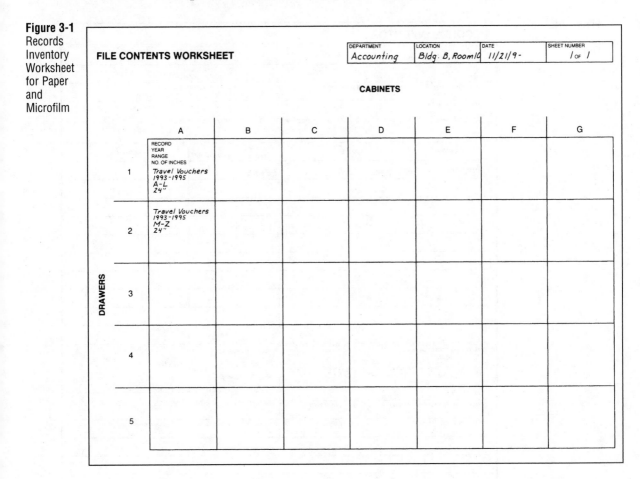

Sometimes an inventory worksheet is helpful to identify locations of paper records and microforms. Figure 3-1 illustrates such a worksheet.

A records inventory form is shown in Figure 3-2. Some companies may choose to use a dual-purpose records inventory and retention form, such as the one shown in Figure 3-3. The top half of the form should be used to inventory the records with the lower half to be completed when the records retention period is determined. The person completing the inventory fills in Questions 1 to 3; the one responsible for determining how long the records are to be retained would complete Questions 4 and 5.

Figure 3-2
Records Inventory
Form

RECORDS INVENTORY					

TITLE OF RECORDS *Travel Vouchers* — **FORM NO. (IF ANY)** 610 — **RECORD SIZE** *Letter* — **CURRENT RETENTION** *3 years*

DIVISION *Finance* — **DEPARTMENT** *Accounting* — **SECTION** — **LOCATION OF RECORD** *Bldg. B - Room 10*

IS THIS THE RECORD COPY? ☐ YES ☑ NO — **IF NO, WHERE IS THE RECORD COPY?** *Finance* — **IF YES, WHERE ARE OTHER COPIES?** *individual departments*

DESCRIPTION OF RECORD

travel vouchers for 1993-95 used to document travel reimbursement

YEAR(S)	RANGE	VOLUME (inches)	NO. OF DRAWERS	COMMENTS
1993-95	All travel vouchers	24"ea.dr.	2	
	TOTALS		TOTAL NO. OF FILE CABINETS	

PERSON RESPONSIBLE FOR FILES *M. Susken* — **TELEPHONE** 3512

NAME OF PERSON TAKING INVENTORY *M. Susken* — **TELEPHONE** 3512

DATE INVENTORY TAKEN 11-21-9—

DEPT. MGR. APPROVAL OF RETENTION — **DATE APPROVED**

RECORDS MANAGER'S APPROVAL — **DATE APPROVED**

IS RECORD MICROFILMED? ☑ YES ☐ NO

IF MICROFILMED:

TYPE OF MICROFILM *Microfiche*

HARD COPY RETAINED? ☑ YES ☐ NO

ORIGINAL MICROFILM STORED WHERE? *Finance* — **RETAINED HOW LONG?** *10 yrs.*

L E G A L — **STATUTE OF LIMITATIONS (IF APPLICABLE)** — **GOVERNMENT AGENCY REQUIREMENT (IF APPLICABLE)**

REMARKS

LEGAL APPROVAL — **DATE APPROVED**

FC-2559D

Source: *Adapted from Mary Lou Oliva, "The Nitty Gritty of Establishing Records Retention Schedules" (Presentation at ARMA Conference, October, 1987).*

Techniques that have proven helpful to both those experienced and inexperienced in inventory procedures are the use of a voice-activated recorder and the computerization of data. Using a voice-activated recorder permits the person doing the inventory to work through an entire set of records without having to stop to write the information.

Information can be transferred to its proper form at a later time. Because the voice-activated recorder does not require a constant on/off action, the hands are free to move quickly through the records.

Figure 3-3
Records Inventory/Retention Form

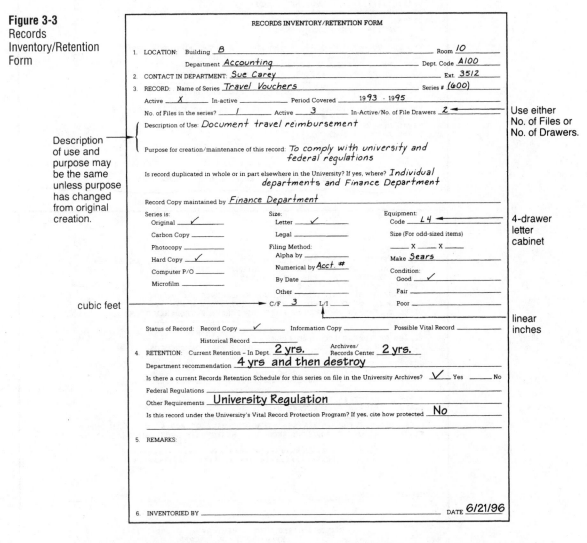

Description of use and purpose may be the same unless purpose has changed from original creation.

cubic feet

Use either No. of Files or No. of Drawers.

4-drawer letter cabinet

linear inches

Source: Adapted from Jean K. Crary. "So—You Want to Do an Inventory!" Records Management Quarterly, Vol. 17, No. 3 (July, 1983), p. 25.

Figure 3-4 illustrates computerizing the data at an early step in the records inventory. The top form has incomplete data obtained from a preliminary inventory. The question marks show the areas in which the data are unknown. These reports are returned to the departmental records representative, who fills in the missing data and reviews all information for accuracy. Computerizing the reporting will be discussed in the section below titled "Status Report."

Figure 3-4
Records Inventory
and Questionnaire
Computer Form

```
DEPARTMENT:  REGISTRAR          CODE:  R3
DATE:  11/12/9-     EQUIPMENT CODE: L4
TYPE OF DOCUMENTS:  45200     ACTIVE?:  ??     ORIGINAL?:  ??
TITLE:   CLASS ENROLMENT FORMS
DESCRIPTION:  ENROLMENT FORMS
PURPOSE:  ???
RELATED DOCUMENTS FOUND IN SERIES-    FIRST:  ADD/DROP FORMS
SECOND:  WITHDRAWAL FORMS           THIRD:
LESS THAN 1 REFERENCE REQUEST PER MONTH
SCOPE OF RECORDS: 1992-95     VOLUME:  14.00 LF
                   ----------------------------------
                       RETENTION RECOMMENDATIONS

YRS IN ACTIVE STORAGE:  ??          YRS IN INACTIVE STORAGE: ??
YRS AFTER WHICH TO MICROFILM:  ??
FINAL DISPOSITION:  ??
FINAL INACTIVE LOCATION: ??
                   ----------------------------------


              RECORDS INVENTORY WORKSHEET:  REGISTRAR
```

```
SERIES TITLE:  CLASS ENROLMENT FORMS                 CODE:  R3
CUSTODIAL DEPT:  REGISTRAR       INVENTORY DATE:  11/12/9-
SERIES DESCRIPTION:  ENROLMENT FORMS
TYPE OF DOCUMENTS:  45200
FUNCTION OF SERIES:  VERIFY CLASS ENROLMENTS
IS THIS SERIES COMPOSED OF RECORD COPIES? (Y,N,M):  Y
OTHER DOCUMENTS INCLUDED:  ADD/DROP FORMS, WITHDRAWAL FORMS
                   ----------------------------------
                           SUB SERIES DATA
FILING EQUIPMENT LOCATION CODE:  L4, RM 5
FIRST YEAR OF RECORDS:  1992       LAST YEAR OF RECORDS:  1995
LINEAR FEET OCCUPIED BY RECORDS:  14.00
CURRENT ACTIVITY STATUS:  A
FEWER THAN 1 REFERENCE PER MONTH
                   ----------------------------------
                           RETENTION DATA
YEARS TO MAINTAIN IN ACTIVE FILES:  04
YEARS TO RETAIN IN INACTIVE FILES:  06
YEARS AFTER WHICH THIS SHOULD BE MICROFILMED:  NA
FINAL DISPOSITION OF SERIES:  INACTIVE STORAGE FOR 6 YRS; THEN SHRED
FINAL LOCATION OF INACTIVE RECORDS:  REGISTRAR  ARCHIVAL VALUE (Y,N):  N

          ******************************************
          ******************************************


BUDGET MANAGER _____ DATE _____


            RECORDS MANAGEMENT INVENTORY AS OF 01/15/9-
                       DEPARTMENT:  REGISTRAR
```

Source: *Adapted from Robert L. Sanders, "Records Inventories and Scheduling for Small Organizations: A Case Study."* Records Management Quarterly, *Vol. 21, No. 3 (July, 1987), p. 24.*

Determine the Space Required

The inventory forms shown in Figures 3-2 and 3-3 and 3-4 ask for the volume of the records series being inventoried. The question may be asked in reference to volume of records, or to cubic feet, linear inches, or linear feet required to house the records. This information is critical for any facilities and equipment planning that may follow the completion of the records inventory.

Space can be estimated in linear or cubic measurements.

Two methods are used to measure the volume of records: a linear measure of the records series or an estimate of volume in cubic feet. A tape measure suffices for providing a linear measure; however, measures in cubic feet are more common especially when dealing with inactive records stored in boxes. When estimating the cubic feet used by a record series, allow 1.5 cubic feet for each letter-size drawer and 2 cubic feet for each legal-size drawer. Although Project ELF (Eliminate Legal-size Files), referred to previously in Chapter 1, is an ongoing effort, legal-size files still exist in many organizations.

Categorize Records as Active or Inactive

Identify active and inactive records.

While estimating the space requirements of a records series, the records analyst should identify records as active or inactive. Because of their decreased activity, those records identified as inactive should be moved from the office location to a storage area. Some of the records in storage may no longer be needed. These items within the record series should be noted by date, and a brief notation should be made in the "Description" or "Remarks" section of the inventory form. The note acts as a reminder to the records analyst of further action to be taken when the inventory is completed. The proper storage and disposal of records allows for more efficient utilization of locations and equipment.

The records analyst should also be alert to the presence of any vital records within the records series. Vital records should be removed immediately from office files and stored with other vital records in a maximum protection area. Vital records are the topic of Chapter 11.

Learning Check: Can you describe the steps in conducting the inventory?

RECORDS ANALYSIS

A records analysis provides managers with decision-making information.

When the inventory is completed, an analysis is made to identify records types common to most departments, those unique to certain areas, different records types that serve the same function, and the holder of the copy of record (record copy).

Standardize Terminology

Before beginning the analysis, the project director or the records analyst must review the inventory forms in order to standardize the terminology used from department to department. Careful staff orientation before beginning the inventory minimizes this problem; however, unless one person does all of the inventory, some similar records series may have very different titles. This review process also provides an opportunity to identify any records series that has been divided unnecessarily.

Standardized
terminology aids
in analysis.

Records common to most areas can be grouped under catchall headings, such as "general administrative" or "general financial." Sections can be established where specific records are identified. Records that serve the same function can be listed under a generic term with a specified records terms included in the brief description. For example, Form 745 and request for reimbursement can be maintained under the generic term *vouchers.*

Status Report

The records inventory is often the initial step in organizing a records management program. An inventory is critical in preparing a retention and disposition schedule and in planning facilities, equipment, and staff. Therefore, after completing the records inventory and analysis, reports of the findings should be presented to management. The computer should be used to aid in compiling and formatting the data to be presented. Many software packages are available for compiling and presenting data; the selection would depend on the type of information to be included in the report.

Interim status
reports keep
organizational
members
informed.

As the inventory progresses, the project director should prepare interim status reports to be presented to all involved in the inventory project. An interim status report is prepared to note progress and findings to date. The status report need not be long or detailed; a short report that notifies others of the current status is all that is required. For example, the status report might read as follows:

> *As of December 15, the records of the Personnel, Accounting, and Marketing Departments have been surveyed. With few exceptions, the inventories are complete in these departments. Preliminary purges have been completed in the Advertising, Manufacturing, and Finance Departments. These departments have a target date of February 1 for survey completion. Other departments not identified above will begin their preliminary purge in January. At this time, the anticipated date of completion of the records inventory for the company is June 15.*

Data Summary

The project director must give careful attention to the data summary and to the preparation of the data summary report. Several options are available for the presentation of data summaries. Usually, the project director summarizes the records inventory findings by department or other subgroup within the organization. Within the department, types, dates, and volume of records should be reported. Quantities of records that can be moved to storage or eliminated, and the amount of space that will be available for additional records as a result of these actions may be noted.

Report Preparation

A plan of action should be included in the report.

In preparing the status report, the project director should consider presenting departmental data in tabular form and summarizing the data for comparison by departments. A summary allows the top managers to see quickly the results of the records inventory and helps to identify those departments in critical need of records management assistance.

The final report should also contain a proposed plan of action based on the results of the records inventory. Preparing a retention schedule and planning for better utilization of facilities and equipment are two actions that will probably be included. The plan of action should include a proposed time schedule, an identification of required personnel, and the steps to be followed to accomplish the proposed plan of action.

If certain individuals or departments were especially helpful in completing the records inventory or certain staff members performed exceptionally well, the final report can provide a vehicle for commending these individuals or departments.

 Learning Check: Can you describe the contents of the records analysis and reports made to management following completion of the records inventory?

TERMINOLOGY REVIEW

Review the terms listed below in the Glossary on page 521.

data set	records analyst
goals	records inventory
objective	records series
planning	

REVIEW AND DISCUSSION

1. Define planning.
2. Explain the relationship among goals, objectives, and strategy.
3. Define records inventory.
4. What are the major goals of a records inventory?
5. Outline the steps in planning a records inventory.
6. What are the choices to be considered in determining who should conduct the records inventory? What factors should be considered in making this determination?
7. Explain the advantages and disadvantages of the most common methods of conducting the records inventory.
8. Describe the factors to be considered when selecting the records inventory form.
9. What information should be gathered on the inventory form?
10. Describe the steps in conducting the inventory.
11. What is a records series? Give at least two examples of records series other than those named in the text.
12. State information that can be found in the records analysis.
13. Outline the steps in reporting the findings at the conclusion of the records inventory.

APPLICATIONS

1. Identify at least five records series within your personal or family records. (You will be asked to use this information in an Application in Chapter 4.)
2. Complete an inventory worksheet for the records series identified in Application 1. Use the worksheet form shown in Figure 3-1 or one that you have developed that better suits your needs.
3. Michael Morris, chief information officer of a large bookstore chain, has just given his final approval to your plan for conducting a records inventory. The bookstore chain has never had a records inventory. As the records manager, you have chosen two records analysts from your staff to conduct the physical inventory. Outline the important procedures you will present to them in their orientation session on records inventories.
4. To make goal setting and objectives definition more realistic, define your personal and/or professional goals and specific objectives for the next 12-month period. Then write a plan for achieving one of the goals.
   a. My goal(s) for the next 12 months is (are) _____.
   b. My specific objectives are _____.
   c. My plan for reaching my goal of _____ is _____.

CONCLUDING CASES

A. *Your Computer Store*

Your Computer Store (YCS) is a rapidly expanding corporation with operations in two provinces. Jerry Fischer was recently promoted to records manager at YCS. Jerry graduated from the local university two years ago with a bachelor's degree in business administration. He has also completed several courses in records management, worked summers as a records clerk and a microfilm technician, and has been the records centre supervisor for the last two years.

Jerry has convinced YCS's top management that a more comprehensive retention program is needed, and has obtained approval to conduct a complete physical inventory of YCS's records. Jerry will serve as project director, but because he is so busy and is short-staffed, YCS has hired Janet Knight, a records consultant, to assist Jerry with planning and conducting this inventory.

1. How can Janet help Jerry with the records inventory?
2. What steps must Jerry be prepared to take to conduct a physical inventory of YCS's records?

B. *The Hoe-Down Place*

Ursula Chamberlin, a retired senior partner of Ontario Systems Management Corporation and an active member of SCORE (Service Corps of Retired Executives), has received a request from the Small Business Secretariat to provide assistance to Amy Leigh, owner of The Hoe-Down Place.

The Hoe-Down Place was opened in January 1994, and is having financial difficulties. Among other problems, Amy is inexperienced in planning. Her projections for future sales are always far too optimistic (as much as 36 percent above actual revenue), and her projections of expenses are always too low (as much as 32 percent below actual expenditures).

When Ursula contacted Amy, she asked Amy to have some information available to her when they met; a meeting was scheduled for two weeks later. Ursula asked Amy to have the documentation that she used in making her projections and to provide the goals and objectives for The Hoe-Down Place (both short-term and long-range).

At the meeting, it was obvious that Amy had little documentation for the activities of The Hoe-Down Place from the time of its opening in 1994. If you were Ursula Chamberlin, what advice would you give Amy regarding the importance of accurate records in her planning activities?

SUGGESTED READINGS AND RESOURCES

Couture, Carol, and Rousseau, Jean-Yves. (Translated by David Homel.) *The Life of a Document.* Montreal: Véhicule Press, 1987.

Gannon, Alice. "Know Your Merchandise: The Records Management Inventory." *Records Management Quarterly.* Vol. 26, No. 2 (April, 1992), p. 12.

Gannon, Alice. "Project Management: An Approach to Accomplishing Things." *Records Management Quarterly.* Vol. 28, No. 3 (July, 1994), p. 3.

Jones, Virginia A. "Put Records in their Place with a Retention Schedule." *Office Systems '86,* Vol. 3, No. 4 (April, 1986), p. 54.

Oliva, Mary Lou. "The Nitty-Gritty of Establishing Records Retention Schedules." Presentation at ARMA Conference, Anaheim, California (October 19–22, 1987).

Pelayo, Lisa. "Try a Records Plan for Efficiency." *Office Systems '89,* Vol. 6, No. 9 (September, 1989), p. 26.

Saffady, William. Chapter 4: Inventorying Electronic Records. *Managing Electronic Records.* Prairie Village, Kansas: Association of Records Managers and Administrators, Inc., 1992.

Sanders, Robert L. "In Search of the Purgeless Office." *Records Management Quarterly,* Vol. 29, No. 4 (October, 1995), p. 56.

Sanders, Robert L. "Records Inventories and Scheduling for Small Organizations: A Case Study." *Records Management Quarterly,* Vol. 21, No. 3 (July, 1987), p. 24.

Stephens, David O. "Making Records Retention Decisions: Practical and Theoretical Considerations." *Records Management Quarterly,* Vol. 22, No. 1 (January, 1988), p. 3.

Subject Filing Guidelines. Prairie Village, Kansas: Association of Records Managers and Administrators, Inc., 1988.

Records Retention and Legal Considerations

Learning Goals

After completing this chapter, you should be able to:

1. Define a records retention program and explain its goals.
2. Define records appraisal and the types of values that a records series might have to the organization.
3. Differentiate between organizational, legal, and archival requirements for records retention.
4. Outline the steps in implementing a records retention program.
5. Outline the factors necessary for a legally sufficient records retention program.

Source: Courtesy of Prime Learning International, Alpine, Utah

The cartoon is an exaggeration of the paperwork jungle many organizations face. However, this is exactly how office personnel feel when an important file cannot be found. A records retention program is a crucial element of a records management program. If every record were placed in the file and remained there indefinitely, files would become cumbersome and costly to maintain; they would lose their value as a means of organizing information for efficient retrieval. A **records retention program** provides a timetable and consistent procedures for maintaining the organization's records, moving the records to inactive storage when appropriate, and destroying records when they are no longer valuable to the organization. The development of a records retention program requires establishing goals and objectives, conducting a records inventory, completing a records appraisal, establishing a retention schedule, and implementing scheduled transfer and disposal of records. This chapter will cover the goals of a records retention program, completing a records appraisal, and establishing a retention schedule.

GOALS

A records retention program is developed and implemented under the direction of the records manager. During this process, the records manager must work closely with the organization's executives, division heads, and department heads in identifying and appraising the records of each office.

The first task in developing a records retention program is to determine the goals and objectives of the organization's retention program. A records retention program has two major goals: (1) to meet organizational needs and (2) to meet legal requirements.

Organizational Needs

An effective records management program has the right information for the right person at the right time at the lowest possible cost.

The major objective of a records management program is to have the right information in front of the right person at the right time at the lowest possible cost. An effective records retention program can help the organization meet this objective. The records retention program meets the organizational need by accomplishing cost reduction and retrieval efficiency and consistency.

Cost Reduction

A records retention program saves the organization money.

An established retention program reduces the cost of records maintenance in three ways. First, the destruction of unneeded records and the transfer of semiactive and inactive records to low-cost storage areas improve the use of expensive office space. Second, the equipment required for the storage of semiactive and inactive records (usually metal shelving and transfer boxes) is less costly than storage cabinets or shelves for office use. A third cost reduction is realized when the retention of duplicate records by various departments is eliminated. Only one copy, the record copy, needs to be retained during semiactive and inactive periods. The record copy should also be identified when identical information has been stored in more than one format, such as paper and electronic form.

Cost reductions must be balanced against the risks of not having records available if needed in the future. Since no one can be certain in advance which records will be needed, designers of the records management program weigh the probability of future use against the consequences to the organization of not having the information when it is needed.

Retrieval Efficiency and Consistency

Destroying unneeded records increases efficiency.

Sound management practices and the proliferation of information prohibit organizations from keeping all records indefinitely. In addition to storage costs, another (perhaps more important) need—retrieval efficiency—is sacrificed in an uncontrolled accumulation of records. In order to be used, records must be found. Time spent in searching through old documents is costly to the organization. An established retention program requires that semiactive and inactive records be transferred from the active files at scheduled intervals. Records that are no longer of value to the organization are destroyed at regular intervals.

This eliminates clutter and allows more rapid retrieval of those records with high accession rates. Proper transfer procedures allow semiactive and inactive records to be readily retrieved. These procedures are described in the section on records transfer in Chapter 7.

An efficient retention program must also address the fact that a file may contain records on more than one medium, for example, paper, computer disk, and microform. Links are established to maintain file integrity. **File integrity** refers to the accuracy and completeness of the file.

Standard retention procedures that are consistent throughout the organization provide control over employees who might be either "pack rats," who keep everything, or "nonsavers," who dispose of records too quickly. Top executives must be able to depend on the availability of similar types of records for each division or department during the periods that these records have value to the organization.

Legal Requirements

Fines, penalties, and large judgments are the prices that organizations have paid because they failed to make records management a priority by maintaining a legally acceptable records program. In fact, many organizations do not realize they have a problem until they are involved in litigation or there is a government investigation or audit. To be legally sufficient, a records retention program must adhere to government regulations and provide litigation protection and support.

Government Regulations

Records management staff have the responsibility to research federal, provincial, and municipal statutes that have an impact on the retention periods for business records. A **statute** is the same as an act or a regulation passed by Parliament or a provincial legislature. The statutes fall into three major categories: (1) tax records, (2) employment and personnel records, and (3) regulations related to specific industries.[1] The organization's accounting, sales, and tax records are important to the government to help establish the appropriate amount of tax due.

The second category includes employment and personnel records. The Canada Pension Plan Act and the Employment Insurance Act require employers to record employee deductions accurately. Provincial workers' compensation legislation and occupational health and safety legislation relate to employees' injuries in the workplace and protect workers' safety and health. Federal and provincial human rights acts prevent discrimination against employees because of age, sex, religion, or race.

---

[1]Donald S. Skupsky, *Recordkeeping Requirements* (Denver, Colorado: Information Requirements Clearinghouse, 1988), p. 11.

The third category of government regulations is statutes that apply to specific industries such as agriculture, banking and financial institutions, communications, transportation, and various professional groups like lawyers, physicians, and engineers. This category also deals with regulations concerning fair business practices, consumer affairs, the right to privacy and access to information, and other concerns for the general welfare. The federal Telecommunications Act covers businesses engaged in various types of communications. Records managers should be thoroughly familiar with Canada's Copyright Act and its copyright rules, for example, which cover the rights of creators of original works.

Many federal, provincial, and municipal statutes establish recordkeeping requirements.

Retention procedures must meet the statute requirements of the federal, provincial, and municipal governments, which establish a retention period for certain records, and make sure that the records are destroyed after the retention periods have been met. In the United States the case of Manville Corporation (formerly Johns Manville) is an example of records maintained too long and used against the organization. When the company began manufacturing products containing asbestos, its dangers were not known. However, after the dangers became apparent, the company was sued by a number of individuals who had developed lung disease, diagnosed as asbestosis. Manville assembled 16 million documents relating to these lawsuits. Although the company did have a records retention program, the files contained many documents that legally could have and should have been destroyed. As a result of all the litigation, the company was required to pay $2.5 billion into a trust fund over a 25-year period to cover the claims of asbestosis victims.

The records retention periods for records covered by the governmental statutes must be established so that the records are kept for the length of time specified by the statute. Since ignorance of a statute does not absolve the organization of its responsibility to keep the records for the stated time period, a great deal of research is often necessary. If one government entity requires the records to be maintained for a longer period of time than others do, the longest retention period should be used. In Canada, many statutes specify that certain records must be kept but do not specify for how long, further complicating the development of a retention schedule.

Litigation Protection and Support

While litigation (a lawsuit) is not as common in Canada as in the United States, it is imperative that legal counsel have the documentation to support the organization's position when it is involved in litigation. Records retention programs are used to help the organization maintain the records to protect itself in case of a suit by another party or to allow the organization to sue another party to protect its position. A records retention program helps to identify the records necessary for litigation and to locate the records needed as evidence in the courtroom.

A direct result of an effective records retention program is the knowledge of where all inactive records are stored. It is then easier for an organization to locate the records needed by counsel or to comply with subpoenas for records by opposing counsel. This saves the organization money by reducing labour costs involved with the assembly of documents.

An effective records retention program also helps ensure that records are destroyed when they are no longer useful. This is important during litigation because records that are destroyed according to an established records retention program *prior* to litigation cannot be used against the organization during litigation. The records retention program also helps the organization to identify copies of records and to make sure the copies are destroyed according to the retention program. Employees who keep personal copies at the office or at home may provide the opposing counsel with copies of records that could hurt the organization's position in court.

 Learning Check: Can you list and explain the two reasons for establishing a records retention program?

RECORDS APPRAISAL

A **records appraisal** is an examination of the data gathered through the records inventory to determine the value of each records series to the organization, based upon the main function or use of the records being evaluated. Basically, records fall into two main categories: those that are preserved permanently and those that are disposed of at some time. The records appraisal process ensures that proper retention and disposal of records are provided. The result of this appraisal process should be a records retention schedule. The steps to establish the records retention schedule are establish series value, establish retention periods, determine requirements, negotiate and finalize retention periods.

Establish Series Value

The value of each records series must be established.

Each of the organization's records series was identified and described as a part of the records inventory. The records manager must determine for each of these series whether its primary value to the organization is administrative (operational), fiscal, or legal. Many records also have a secondary historical (research) or archival value. These values are the basis for determining the retention period of each series.

Administrative Value

A records series has administrative value if it defines operating procedures.

The **administrative value** of a records series is the value it has to the creating office in performing its day-to-day business activities within the organization. Records that are used in determining organizational policy or in explaining operating procedures or departmental functions have administrative value. Such records might include an organization chart, policy statements, directives, and procedures manuals.

Fiscal Value

A records series has fiscal value if it documents use of funds.

A records series has **fiscal value** if it provides documentation of use of governmental funds necessary for audit or operational purposes, data necessary to compile the annual report or to complete the organization's tax return, or documentation of other financial transactions such as purchases and sales. Such records include financial reports and summaries of financial transactions.

Legal Value

A records series has legal value if it documents business transactions.

The **legal value** of a records series is established by the documentation it provides of business ownership, agreements, and transactions. Records having legal value include contracts, financial agreements, titles, and records that provide proof of compliance with regulatory requirements (such as environmental or safety standards).

Historical Value

A records series with historical or archival value documents the organization's accomplishments.

A records series may also have historical value. **Historical value** is based on the quality or content that causes a record of an event related to a particular project to be retained for purposes of history and not necessarily for business purposes. Future value to researchers with an interest in that organization, similar organizations, and prominent individuals within that organization is also important. Letters signed by nationally known figures such as politicians or scientists frequently have intrinsic value regardless of their content. Minutes of board meetings have historical value because they document changes in the direction of the organization or implementation of new procedures. Historical records are often housed in the organization's archives. If the organization does not maintain an official archive, historical records are housed in the most protected storage area.

 Learning Check: Can you list the four records series values that can be applied during the records appraisal?

Establish Retention Periods

Once the records manager has established the type or types of values for each records series, a retention period is recommended based on these values. As the retention periods are determined, several areas of the organization are involved. The originating department must determine the retention period to support the business activity; legal counsel must determine the retention period to meet the legal requirements of the records series; the fiscal officer must establish the retention period for the organization to maintain its fiscal responsibility; and the executive branch of the organization must also have input concerning the retention period of the record. The retention period can be based on the organizational need for the record to carry on business activity and/or to be maintained as a part of the history of the organization. The retention period may be the result of compliance with a government regulation concerning the length of time that particular records series must be maintained.

This retention information is usually placed on the lower half of the records inventory and retention form for each records series. The top portion was completed during the records inventory. Refer to Figure 3-3 in Chapter 3 for an example of a completed inventory and retention form. Figure 4-1 shows another example of a records inventory and retention form. Even though the forms are different, the same type of information is contained on both.

Determine Requirements

The length of time records are retained is based on two considerations: (1) support for business activity and (2) legal requirements. Recommended retention periods may be based on the records manager's experience with records of that type, knowledge of the manner in which other organizations are handling similar records, or information from sources such as published retention schedules. Additional requirements such as tax regulations, other government regulations, and legal requirements have an impact on the determination of retention periods. These requirements are usually categorized as organizational, legal (including government regulations and statutes of limitations), or archival.

Records must be maintained to support business activity of the organization.

Organizational Requirements. Organizational requirements are of two types: requirements of the originating office and requirements of the administrative policies of the organization. The manager of the originating office, also known as the office of primary responsibility, indicates the requirements of that office on the line beside *Originating Office* on the form in Figure 4-1. An officer of the organization indicates the retention requirements of organizational policies on the line beside *Executive* on this form.

Vital records need special attention. From 4 to 10 percent of an organization's records are usually labelled vital.

As a part of the originating office requirements, those records considered vital to the uninterrupted, efficient operation of each department are determined objectively by the department manager. Vital records are defined in Chapter 1 as essential to the operation of the organization, the continuation and/or resumption of operations following a disaster, the re-creation of legal or financial status of the organization, or to the fulfilment of its obligations to shareholders and employees in the event of a disaster. A balance between retaining everything and retaining nothing is desirable. Estimates of the percentage of records that should be considered vital range from 4 to 10 percent. When significantly more than 10 percent of the records have been classified as vital, a re-evaluation of the records or the process is in order.

One of the major responsibilities of the records manager is to review the recommendations of the department managers regarding which records are vital and, therefore, must receive maximum protection.

Figure 4-1
Records Inventory
and Retention
Form

RECORDS INVENTORY AND RETENTION SHEET			

Department Human Resources **Records Series Title** Annual Performance Appraisals **Date** 1/10/--

INVENTORY

Inventoried by: Jane Smith

☒ Record Copy ☐ Computer Tape
☐ Duplicate ☐ Computer Printout
☒ Letter Size ☐ Microfilm ☐ Microfiche
☐ Legal Size ☒ Other (specify) Paper

Description: Annual Performance Appraisal of each employee.

Location	Volume	Inclusive Dates	Retention Period
Office	5 cu. ft.	1/3/91 to 12/31/92	5 years
Storage	2 cu. ft.	1/2/93 to 1/10/96	5 years

REQUIRED RETENTION PERIOD

APPROVALS	YEARS
Originating Office Charles Johnson	5
Fiscal Officer R. T. Greene	1
General Counsel M. A. Anders	5
Executive Sharon E. Turner	5

FINALIZED SCHEDULE

Office 3	Storage 2	Destroy After 5 years

Authorized by: E. Harrison   Date 1/31/--

Special Instructions
Confidentiality to be maintained in storage location as well as in the office.

P110: 5/86

On those occasions when the records manager and the department manager disagree, they should meet and discuss the differences. If the disagreement is not resolved, the records manager has the authority and the responsibility for the final decision. (Procedures for protecting vital records are discussed in Chapter 11.)

Legal Requirements. The legal requirements of the records retention program must serve two purposes. First, business records must be maintained in compliance with federal, provincial, and municipal statutes and rules and regulations established by government regulatory agencies. Second, the statute of limitations for certain business activities must be considered when records retention periods are established. The **statute of limitations** is the period of time during which a person or organization can bring action in a lawsuit or be sued.

Government Regulations. Several distinctly Canadian factors make the task of compliance with government statutes more difficult in Canada. The first factor concerns varying federal and provincial jurisdictions, based on the Constitution Act of 1867. Provinces look after property and civil rights and thus generally regulate business activities (with some exceptions). The federal government looks after regulating international and interprovincial trade, commerce, transportation, communication, navigation and shipping, plus certain intraprovincial activities like banking. A second factor concerns the two major legal systems in effect in Canada: the civil code of Quebec and the common law system in the rest of the country. In addition, some records must be maintained in both official languages—French and English. Companies doing business in Quebec must comply with that province's requirement to maintain records in French. Those doing business in more than one province comply with the statutes of each province. Different parts of the same business may be subject to the jurisdiction of different levels of government.

Researching records retention requirements is an important part of a records manager's job.

Records managers must establish retention periods for the records covered by the federal, provincial, and municipal statutes so that the records are maintained for the period of the statute. This is particularly important when the organization is subject to a governmental audit. Before establishing retention periods, however, the records manager or analyst must research the necessary legislation to determine the statutes and other recordkeeping requirements that apply to the types of records maintained by the organization. As described in Chapter 2, a **records analyst** is a specialist in systems and procedures used in creating, processing, and disposing of records. Although Canada does not have a single source listing all government statutes and regulations, many reference books can be used to help the records manager or analyst research the requirements for records retention. There are also government and private publishers of guides to records retention requirements to help in locating and adhering to records retention regulations. An excellent example is *Records Retention: Statutes and Regulations,* which documents all the legal and statutory/regulatory records retention requirements in force in Canada and the provinces and keeps them up to date.[2] Another publication by the same publisher is *Records Retention: Law and Practice.*[3] Experts recommend that researchers read the acts and regulations as well.

Statutes of Limitations. Records managers must establish a records retention program that will support the organization in case the organization is involved in litigation. The possibility of litigation and the need to support the firm's position require that certain records be retained until the statute of limitations expires on that particular activity. The statutes of limitations do not state records retention requirements but rather designate the time period during which an organization can sue or be sued. The most common types of litigation in business concern contracts and wrongs known as torts. The general rule is that actions for breach of contract must be brought within six years after the cause of action arose. Let's assume that an organization entered into a written contract on January 15, 1995, and the other party to the contract breached the contract on January 1, 1996. The organization would have six years from January 1, 1996 (the date the contract was broken), to sue the other party to require compliance with the contract or to collect damages. Sometimes the date on which the limitation period begins to run may be years after the record was created, which presents a further problem for records managers. Obviously, the organization would want to maintain the documents to support its position for the period of time during which a suit could be brought or until any lawsuit is resolved.

Prior to submission to the executive officer of the organization, the retention form should be submitted to the fiscal officer and to the organization's general counsel. The fiscal officer is responsible for noting retention requirements related to taxes or other financial reports. These notations are made on the line beside *Fiscal Officer* (see Figure 4-1). The general counsel is responsible for noting any requirements for retaining these records to support possible litigation and/or to meet statutory requirements at any level of government. Counsel notes these requirements on the line beside *General Counsel* on the records inventory and retention sheet (see Figure 4-1).

Statutes of limitations affect records retention policies.

---

[2]*Records Retention: Statutes and Regulations* (Scarborough, Ont.: Carswell, Thomson Professional Publishing, 1993) p. 1.

[3]Ronald M. Anson-Cartwright, et al. *Records Retention: Law and Practice* (Scarborough, Ont.: Carswell, Thomson Professional Publishing, 1994).

Archival Requirements

The records
manager usually
identifies records
with archival
requirements.

Archival requirements (for long-term retention) usually apply to approximately 5 percent of records and are identified by the records manager. Archival retention may be based on legal, fiscal, or historical reasons. Archives are used to preserve corporate memory; provide production information, policy direction, personnel information, and financial information; maintain public relations activities; provide legal advantage and research service; and prepare commemorative histories. Records should be labelled for long-term retention at the time they are created.

✓   **Learning Check: Can you explain why statutes of limitations are not records retention requirements?**

Finalize Retention Periods

When the records manager receives the records inventory and retention sheets with all the required signatures (or secures the same information using other forms), a records retention schedule can be finalized. Retention periods include the length of time records are to remain in the originating office, the length of time they are to be housed in the records storage area, their final disposition (archives or destruction), and the date the records are scheduled for destruction. To maintain efficient operations, every effort is made to retain records in the originating office as long as the records are active—referenced (used) on a regular basis. When records are no longer active, they should be transferred to the storage area. The records inventory and retention sheets shown in Figure 4-1 include space to designate each of these dates—in office, in storage, and destruction.

Some records are superseded or become obsolete, such as a new policy replacing a previous one. Other records have no such natural end to their active life and require a decision by the records manager about how long they are likely to be referred to regularly. Often these records series, for example, correspondence files, are kept as active files for the fiscal year plus one additional year before transfer to inactive storage. Efficiencies can be realized by using as few retention periods as is reasonable and by keeping the schedule as simple as possible. For example, a records series may have a short active life of one to two years; a medium life of five to seven years; or a long-term life of up to 30 years. Series having to do with federal taxation and basic legal matters are usually active for seven years; however, legal materials which may involve a statute of limitations could require an active life of 30 years.

Final retention periods may include the amount of time the record will remain on its original medium, the medium to which it should be transferred for further retention, and the time on the new medium. For example, most magnetic tapes must be copied periodically even with proper maintenance in order to maintain readability. If lengthy retention of information on magnetic tape is necessary, a special note (such as "Dump to computer output microfiche and retain 10 years") may appear on the retention schedule. It is important to note that the retention period is based on the records series, not the type of medium on which the record is stored. Even though the record may be dumped to computer output microfiche, the total retention time period is not affected.

PROGRAM IMPLEMENTATION

After records retention periods have been determined, several steps must be completed to implement the retention program. These steps include schedule preparation, schedule dissemination, schedule review and revision, and the development of a manual of retention policies.

Schedule Preparation

The retention schedule is summarized into a retention timetable.

The established retention periods must be summarized in a list or a retention schedule for distribution within the organization. Records series are usually listed in alphabetic order or grouped in alphabetic order by division or function on the retention schedule (also referred to as the retention timetable) along with the number of years the records series is to be retained. Some organizations also include an indication of the authority that established that particular retention period. Many formats can be used; however, the retention schedule must include at least the name of the records series and the retention period. One retention schedule is shown in Figure 4-2. To save space on the retention schedules, many codes are used; however, studying Figure 4-2 clearly reveals the retention period for each of the records series.

Schedule Dissemination

The records retention schedule cannot be used, and the retention program cannot function if the organization's employees are not informed. The schedule should be disseminated to each office that deals with records as soon as it is printed. A department may receive the entire schedule or only those sections that apply to that department. Some organizations designate one employee within each office as the records liaison person. The designated individual receives the retention schedule and is responsible for compliance with the established retention periods. This includes responsibility for transferring records when appropriate.

Figure 4-2
Retention
Schedule

PERSONNEL/HUMAN RESOURCES

Function Code	Title / Description/Cross Reference	Legal Group Code	Retention of Official Records			Retention of Copies	Office of Record
			Legal	User	Total		
PER1000	**Personnel/Human Resources Benefits**	EMP110	ACT+06	ACT+01	ACT+06	SUP	Benefits
	Records related to company sponsored benefit plans including insurance, pension, disability, etc.						
PER1010	**Personnel/Human Resources Benefits Pension Plan Reporting**	EMP100	06	03	06	01	Benefits
	IRS Form 5500 under ERISA						
PER1020	**Personnel/Human Resources Benefits Contributions/Benefits Provided**	EMP100	06	03	06	01	Benefits
	Records related to contribution and participation in company sponsored benefit plans including insurance, pension, disability, etc.						
PER2000	**Personnel/Human Resources Employee Records Detailed Records**	EMP300	03	03	03	01	Personnel
	Records regarding specific employees including hiring, promotion, performance appraisals, transfers, termination, training, etc.						
PER2010	**Personnel/Human Resources Employee Records Summary Records**	EMP300	03	ACT+03	ACT+03	ACT	Personnel
	Summary records for individual employees.						

ACT: while active
SUP: until superseded

Schedule Review and Revision

The records retention schedule must be reviewed and revised periodically.

An organization is unlikely to repeat the entire inventory and schedule development process more than once every 20 to 30 years, but adjustments to the schedule will likely be required during that time. An effective retention program must provide for review and revision of the retention schedule at planned intervals. Some records series may be subject to immediate revision of their retention periods. Due to changes in governmental regulations, some records series may be destroyed earlier or held longer. Other records need periodic review in order to discover the need for new forms of storage, to accommodate records series that have been added or deleted, or to adjust the retention time for records already in storage. The rate of reference shown by charge-out records would be evidence of this latter need. If records are seldom referred to after storage, the organization may be able to destroy them at an earlier time. If the reference rates are heavy until scheduled destruction dates the retention periods may need to be extended.

Manual Development

Many organizations develop a records retention manual to disseminate policies and procedures on records retention, transfer, and disposal. Other organizations prefer to have one records policies manual, which includes policies and procedures for all aspects of the records program. Regardless of the type of manual used, the policies and procedures of the retention program should be prepared for dissemination and distributed along with the retention schedule. These policies and procedures should also include information on how the schedule was developed and contain provisions for revising the schedule. Procedures for transferring records covered in Chapter 7 and procedures for destruction of records covered in Chapter 17 should also be included. Specific details of manual development are presented in Chapter 16.

LEGALLY SUFFICIENT RECORDS RETENTION PROGRAM

The focus of this chapter has been to explain the records retention program, give guidelines on the establishment of records retention periods, and explain the final implementation of the records retention program. However, the implementation of a records retention program is not legally sufficient unless certain factors are included. **Legal sufficiency** refers to the requirement for a records retention program to adhere to government regulations and to provide litigation protection and support. Every effort must be made to operate the records retention program properly.

The following factors, as outlined by Donald S. Skupsky, must be included in a records retention program to make the program legally sufficient.[4] These factors apply in Canada as well as in the United States.

The records retention program must be part of the ordinary course of business.

1. The records retention program must be developed in a systematic manner. The program must be established as a part of the usual and ordinary course of business. It cannot be seen as a way of destroying documents that might be detrimental to the organization if used as evidence in litigation or an investigation by a government agency. Establishing the records retention program over a period of time beginning with the records inventory and including appraisal of records, establishing records retention periods, and implementing the program through procedures and manual development provide evidence that the program was conceived as a course of business and not as a cover-up for destroying records that may be unfavourable to the organization.

---

[4]Ibid., pp. 113–116.

Many copies of certain records are produced.

2. All records must be covered in the records retention program. Many records retention programs schedule retentions for the original or record copy of a document only. Because there are copies other than the record copy of documents filed and maintained, the records retention program must schedule the destruction of other copies of the documents as well. Although courts in Canada prefer the original record, a copy may have the same legal significance as the original. Unless the records retention program includes copies of documents, these copies may be used against the organization during litigation or government investigations.

Many business records are maintained on media other than paper.

3. Records maintained on media other than paper must be included in the records retention program. All records maintained by the business must be included in the records retention program. This is true of microform records, data processing records, electronic records (5-inch and 3-inch disks, hard disks, E-mail, etc.) or any other types of records maintained by the organization. With microform records, the original paper document is destroyed; however, the records retention schedule should include a destruction date for the microform record also. Electronic records present a serious problem because of the way the records are stored and the automatic backup procedures used by many organizations. The electronic records must be included in the records retention schedule.

Key personnel must approve records retention schedules.

4. Records retention schedules must have written approval by key personnel of the organization. As outlined early in the chapter, all records retention schedules must be signed by the head of the originating department, the legal counsel, and the fiscal officer. The signed approvals for each series must be kept indefinitely.

Records retention schedules must be followed.

5. Records must be systematically destroyed according to the records retention program. Simply implementing a records retention program is not legally sufficient if the provisions of that program are not carried out. Once the destruction times have been designated, the records must be destroyed according to the schedule. Of course, instructions will be given to halt destruction of records that relate to current litigation or investigations in which the organization is involved (see 7 below). Provisions must also be included that would halt the destruction of records that are still needed by the organization for ordinary business activity.

The systematic destruction of records according to the records retention schedule further establishes the records retention program as a part of the ordinary course of business for the organization. The destruction of records cannot be selective or haphazard but must be systematic according to the procedures provided in the records retention program.

One person should be in charge of the records retention program.

6. The records retention program must be managed. One person in the organization should be given the responsibility for managing the records retention program. This person's responsibility would be to see that the program is up to date and that destruction of records takes place according to the retention schedule.

7. Procedures must be in place to suspend destruction of records involved with litigation and government investigations. If an organization receives a notice of pending or actual litigation or government investigation, records management personnel must cease the destruction of all records immediately. If destruction of records does not cease, the organization may be charged with obstruction of justice or contempt of court or may face other legal problems. Information concerning litigation or investigations of any kind received by any member of the organization should be given immediately to the legal counsel or chief executive officer. This information should then be given to the records manager, and the destruction of all records ceased immediately.

Litigation or government investigation will stop the destruction of records.

As facts of the litigation or investigation become clearer, the destruction of some records outside the scope of the litigation or investigation may continue. After suspension of the destruction of all records, the legal counsel and fiscal officer should be involved in the approval of any requests to destroy records in order to make sure the records being destroyed are not involved with the legal action.

Accurate documentation of the records retention program must be maintained indefinitely.

8. Documentation relating to the destruction of records must be maintained indefinitely. All documentation relating to all phases of the records retention program must be retained indefinitely to prove that the program was developed and operated in a systematic manner. The documentation should include records relating to the development of the program, the signed retention schedules, and the lists of destroyed records. These documents provide evidence that the records were destroyed in the ordinary course of business.

Proof of legal research performed during the process of establishing the retention period for business records is also important. This documentation will help prove that the organization used its best effort to comply with records retention requirements. Because many legal requirements are difficult to locate and/or interpret, this documentation may help the organization prove that research was done but the statutes or regulations were not located after a reasonable search. This documentation of legal research may prove to be a satisfactory defence even if the organization does not adhere to statutes and regulations not located.

 Learning Check: Can you name the eight factors that must be included in a records retention program to make the program legally sufficient?

TERMINOLOGY REVIEW

Review the terms listed below in the Glossary on page 521.

administrative value

file integrity

fiscal value

historical value

legal sufficiency

legal value

records appraisal

records retention program

retrieval efficiency

statute

statute of limitations

REVIEW AND DISCUSSION

1. What is a records retention program? Explain the goals of a records retention program.
2. Define records appraisal.
3. Define the four types of values that a record series might have to an organization.
4. Explain the importance of records retention in relation to the support of organizational, legal, and archival requirements.
5. Explain the two purposes of the legal requirements of the records retention program.
6. What are statutes of limitations and how do they affect records retention policies?
7. What are the steps taken by records managers or analysts to research the records retention requirements of federal, provincial, and municipal governments?
8. Why is it important that the records retention schedule for each records series be shown to the originating department head, legal counsel, and the fiscal officer of an organization?
9. List the steps necessary to implement a records retention program.
10. Name and explain the eight factors that help establish a records retention program as legally sufficient.

APPLICATIONS

1. For the five records series identified in Application 1, Chapter 3, establish a series value, suggest a retention period and give a reason for establishing same.
2. You have just been hired as the records and information manager for the Brevard Manufacturing Corp., a three-year-old firm on the Prairies, which has never had a records or information manager or a records or information management program. Outline your presentation to Eric Gordon, chairman of the board, on the functions of a records retention program.

3. You have just completed the records inventory for Midlands Chemicals and are ready to establish retention periods. Outline the procedures and the reference materials you would use to help determine the retention periods for records maintained by Midlands Chemicals.

CONCLUDING CASES

A. Productive Power Service, Inc.

Susan Stokes is the records manager for Productive Power Service, Ltd. (PPS), an electrical service company based outside Toronto, Ontario. PPS has been in business for 45 years. While some revisions in its retention program have been necessitated by changes in governmental regulations over the years, Susan can find no documentation of when the last records inventory was completed or of any major reconsideration of the retention schedule.

Susan has been employed by PPS for six weeks. During this time she has been familiarizing herself with the records procedures employed by the major divisions of the organization. She decides that before any other aspects of the records management program can be centralized and refined, the retention program must be completely overhauled.

1. What basis can Susan use to convince top executives that such an investment of time and effort is necessary and will produce positive results for the company?
2. How can Susan obtain the support of the other employees for this undertaking?
3. What steps must be completed in planning and conducting the records inventory?
4. What are the major considerations in performing the records appraisal?
5. What additional steps are necessary to revise and implement the retention schedule?

B. Coastal Manufacturing Co.

Jody Smith is the records manager for Coastal Manufacturing Co., which has just been purchased by a new group of investors, who will take key positions on the board. The investors have replaced key executive positions with new personnel. The new executive officers are looking for ways to cut the budget. They are not familiar with the records management program and its importance to the organization and have targeted the records management program to be phased out of the organization structure.

Jody is upset that the new officers have targeted the records management program and thinks it is because they do not understand the importance of the program to the organization. She has requested permission to make a report at the next board meeting.

1. What specific areas should she include in her report?
2. What information should she include concerning the records retention program and why?

SUGGESTED READINGS AND RESOURCES

Anderson, John C. "Dance to the Music: Records Management and Litigation in Canada." *Records Management Quarterly,* Vol. 27, No. 2 (April, 1993), p. 12.

Anderson, John C. "Legislative Interpretation When Developing a Records Retention Programme." *Records Management Quarterly,* Vol. 26, No. 4 (October, 1992), p. 16.

ARMA International's Standards Records Retention Task Force. *Developing and Operating a Records Retention Program—A Guideline.* Prairie Village, Kansas: Association of Records Managers and Administrators, Inc., 1986.

Bishop, Patsy G. "If Saber Saws Were Information Systems." *Records Management Quarterly,* Vol. 29, No. 4 (October, 1995), p. 32.

Benmergui-Perez, Marlene. "Playing It Safe." *Office Management and Automation,* August, 1988, p. 27.

Gannon, Alice. "Project Management: An Approach to Accomplishing Things." *Records Management Quarterly,* Vol. 28, No. 3 (July, 1994), p. 3.

Montana, John C. "It Can Make You or Break You: The Importance of Records Management in Litigation." *Records Management Quarterly,* Vol. 29, No. 1 (January, 1995), p. 3.

Phillips, P. Fern. "Case Law and the Evidence Acts in Canada." *Records Management Quarterly,* Vol. 29, No. 2 (April, 1995), p. 3. (This article also provides an excellent case law review and bibliography on pages 10 to 11 and 28.)

Skupsky, Donald S. "Developing and Operating a Records Retention Program: Legal Requirements for Records and Information Management Programs." Presentation at ARMA International Conference, Calgary, Alberta (March 3, 1992).

Skupsky, Donald S. "Establishing Retention Periods for Electronic Records." *Records Management Quarterly,* Vol. 27, No. 2 (April, 1993), p. 40.

Skupsky, Donald S. "Legal Requirements for Microfilm, Computer and Optical Disk Records—International Perspectives." *Records Management Quarterly,* Vol. 25, No. 1 (January, 1991), p. 32.

Skupsky, Donald S. "The Functional Records Retention Schedule ... An Alternative That Works!" *Records Management Quarterly,* Vol. 23, No. 4 (October, 1989), p. 37.

Stephens, David O. "Recordkeeping Provisions of International Laws." *Records Management Quarterly,* Vol. 29, No. 3 (July, 1995), p. 60.

Profile
Records Manager

Mona Carstairs, the records manager of a large mortgage company in eastern Canada, has been in her position for two years. The company employs 1,800 people, and the records management department has three employees. The positions in the department include the records manager, clerk I, and clerk II.

Education and experience requirements for the manager's position include a thorough knowledge of mortgage procedures and organization, familiarity with statutes for federal and provincial record retention requirements, and computer expertise, particularly in the area of electronic databases. Supervisory and communication skills are also important for this position. Ms. Carstairs attended university for four years and received a business administration degree.

The major duties and responsibilities of the records manager are to manage the records management department including interviewing and hiring new employees, disciplining employees, establishing the budget for the department, communicating with other departments, and preparing reports for other departments and upper management of the company. The records manager also serves as the liaison with the legal department to decide on retention periods for records series. When establishing records retention periods, it is the records manager's responsibility to coordinate the needs of the department and the legal requirements so that the correct retention period is determined for each records series. The records manager helps the computer department design and establish new reports.

The major changes in the records management department in the last few years have resulted from computer technology. The retention schedule is an electronic database using dBase IV. As the database grows and newer technology is available, changes are made to accommodate the growth. Micrographics is not used in the records management department currently; however, as space becomes more costly, micrographics will merit consideration.

Advancement opportunities in the company are limited for the records manager unless she goes to another department. Ms. Carstairs is not active in professional organizations at this time.

Part 3
Active Records
in Manual Systems

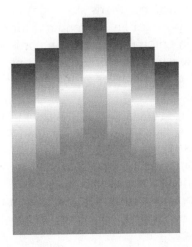

Manual Systems of Active Records Management, Equipment, and Supplies

Learning Goals

After completing this chapter, you should be able to:

1. Explain the difference between centralized, decentralized, and combination active records storage systems.
2. Explain the physical layout required for an active records facility.
3. List selection criteria for manual records storage equipment and explain how each affects the purchasing decision.
4. Define and give examples of manual and mechanical storage equipment.
5. Describe appropriate storage equipment for audiovisual materials, magnetic and electronic media, maps, engineering drawings, and publications.
6. List selection criteria for storage supplies and explain how each affects the purchasing decision.
7. Describe appropriate supplies for a manual records system.

After the records an organization holds are identified and a retention program has been developed, facilities must be planned for the two basic types of records—active and inactive. This chapter is about the choices of active records facilities, equipment, and supplies for manual records storage and retrieval. Chapter 9 will address the storage and retrieval needs for magnetic and electronic records, which must be combined with the manual systems.

ACTIVE RECORDS FACILITIES

As a rule, only 25 percent of an organization's records need to be in the active files.

Facilities must be planned to house two basic types of records—active and inactive. Some practitioners have advocated that, as a general rule:
- 10 percent of an organization's records could be retained for long-term value;
- 25 percent of an organization's records could be maintained in active files;
- 30 percent of an organization's records could be maintained in inactive files; and
- 35 percent of an organization's records may be useless and should be destroyed.

Active records must be organized for rapid retrieval of information.

This categorization, then, classifies 40 percent of an organization's records as inactive (30 percent inactive and 10 percent long-term—which are usually inactive), and only 25 percent are classified as active (see Figure 5-1). Since these active records are used in the daily operation of the organization, they are the ones that provide managers with the necessary information on which to base current business decisions. Because active records are such a vital part of the decision-making function, they must be available to managers when they are needed. Fast turnaround time from request to retrieval is essential and is met by having the active records housed near to the people requiring the information.

Figure 5-1
Distribution of
Records Status

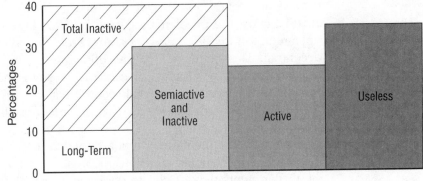

Types of Facilities

Active records may be housed in a centralized, decentralized, or a combination system. Each system has distinct advantages and disadvantages.

Centralized

A **centralized records storage system** provides for the housing of all active records in one location within the organization. All records that need to be retained are forwarded by each department to a central records area. Large organizations do not find a totally centralized system efficient because placing the central records in a location convenient for all departments is virtually impossible. For many smaller organizations, however, a centralized records system is appropriate.

A centralized records storage system provides a uniform approach.

Centralization provides a uniform approach to the records system. All records are stored by the same rules and retrieved by the same procedures, which is advantageous in terms of:

- Providing consistency in procedures,
- Identifying responsibility and accountability,
- Keeping related records together,
- Training new clerical personnel,
- Providing uniform service to all departments,
- Minimizing duplicate records,
- Providing better utilization of space, equipment, and personnel,
- Allowing greater security of records, and
- Providing one-stop retrieval of records.

 Learning Check: Can you name three advantages of the centralized records storage system?

Decentralized

A **decentralized records storage system** is one in which the records of each major department or office are housed within that area. Many managers prefer this system because it allows them to retain control over and have immediate access to their own records. Accessible records and total control over the department's records must be balanced against the problems incurred by allowing each department to operate autonomous records systems. Problems associated with some decentralized systems include the following:

A decentralized records storage system provides immediate access for each department.

1. Each department has its own records system; therefore, a lack of uniformity exists in the total records system.
2. Each department houses its own records; not all related records are housed together.
3. Several departments may retain copies of the same record; this practice encourages duplicate records.
4. Departments may duplicate equipment or maintain underutilized equipment; maximum equipment utilization will not be realized.

5. Each department tends to secure records in a different manner; therefore, records security may be haphazard and inadequate.

When information must be immediately available with multiple references to records made by only one department, and when individual departmental records control is necessary, a decentralized system is appropriate.

 Learning Check: Can you name two disadvantages of the decentralized records storage system?

Combination

A combination records storage system combines decentralized files under centralized control.

The **combination records storage system** is a system that allows many departments to maintain their own records under a centralized system of control. Typical records maintained in a decentralized records system include personnel, payroll, credit, financial, and sales records. Under the combination approach, responsibility for the system is assigned to the records manager or to the person operationally responsible for maintaining the organization's records. This person establishes the network for the control system and for the operational procedures of the system.

The combination approach provides the individual control, the accessibility, and the immediacy of a decentralized system as demanded by many managers. It also provides the controls and uniformity of a centralized system. Advantages of a combination system with centralized control include

- Providing a uniform system of storage and retrieval,
- Minimizing misfiles and lost records,
- Minimizing duplicate records,
- Providing for centralized purchasing, which results in better cost efficiency,
- Facilitating records movement according to the records retention and disposition schedules and,
- Providing the structure to assist managers in administering the records management program.

However, many of the problems inherent in each of the systems are transferred to the combination system. The problems of not having related records housed together and lack of flexibility resulting from uniform, organization-wide procedures may still occur. Nevertheless, the combination system is now chosen more often than the other two because of its many advantages.

In general, the records storage system selected—centralized, decentralized, or combination—should be the system that most closely fits the needs of the particular organization, its subunits, and its personnel.

 Learning Check: Can you explain the system in use when the organization uses the decentralized records storage system with central control?

Floor Load Capacity

Because active records are located in prime office space, the area should be planned for maximum efficiency at minimum cost. A discussion of the advantages and disadvantages of various types of equipment is presented later in this chapter since, in many instances, the available space dictates the type of equipment and the layout.

Floor load capacity must be considered when planning the active records files.

One factor to be considered is the weight of the storage equipment and load stress on floors. This is particularly true in older buildings, although newer construction should also be checked to establish weight capacity. If this is a concern, the use of alternative equipment may produce the storage capacity required at less total weight. Floor load capacity is the weight of records and equipment that a floor can safely accommodate. **Floor load capacity** may be calculated by multiplying the weight the floor can stand (measured in pounds per square foot) by the amount of available space (measured in square feet). For example, if a floor is able to stand 50 pounds per square foot and the room contains 300 square feet of floor space, a total weight of 15,000 pounds (50 multiplied by 300) may be safely stored in that room.

Of course, different types of equipment vary considerably in their empty weight, known as *nonproductive weight*. Their contents are known as *productive weight*. When the capacity of the equipment measured in filing inches and the weight per filing inch of the contents are known, the productive weight can be determined. For example, paper files weigh two pounds per filing inch; microfiche files weigh 14 ounces per filing inch. With the floor load capacity and the productive weight of various types of equipment calculated, the quantity of equipment needed to house the records can be determined.

Layouts

Whether four- or five-drawer vertical cabinets, open-shelf files, or mobile files are selected will depend on the organizational needs, the selected storage system (decentralized, centralized, or combination), the available storage space, and the floor load capacity.

Decentralized Records Storage

Typical cabinet arrangements in a decentralized system are illustrated in Figure 5-2.

Traffic aisles must be considered when planning active files.

Guidelines for more efficient layout include the following:

1. Avoid opening cabinets into a traffic aisle. If this arrangement is unavoidable, allow four feet for drawer opening and an additional 18 to 24 inches for aisle traffic (assuming a one-person traffic pattern).

2. If the aisle is not a traffic aisle, allow four feet for each drawer opening and for one records clerk.
3. Allow four feet for each drawer opening and each records clerk where cabinets on each side of the aisle open facing each other.

Figure 5-2
Decentralized Storage Cabinet Arrangements

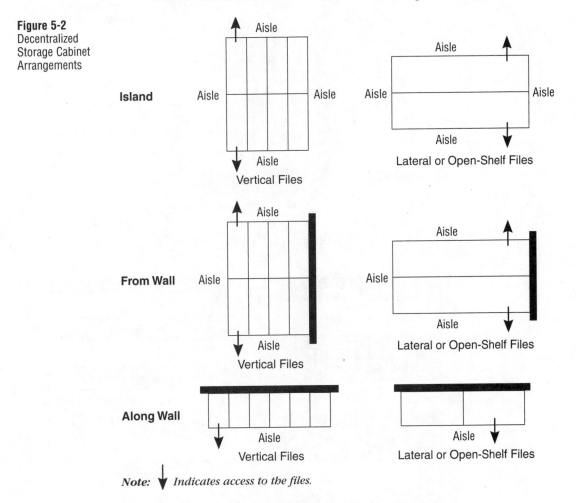

Note: ▼ Indicates access to the files.

Centralized Records Storage

Centralized records storage, depending on space available, may be arranged in various ways. Ample aisle space should be allowed—a minimum of 3 feet; 4 feet if cabinets open into aisle space; 5.5 feet if allowing for cabinet opening and passageway; 8 feet if cabinets open face to face; 9.5 feet if cabinets open face to face and passageway is required (see Figure 5-3).

Figure 5-3
Centralized
Storage Cabinet
Arrangements

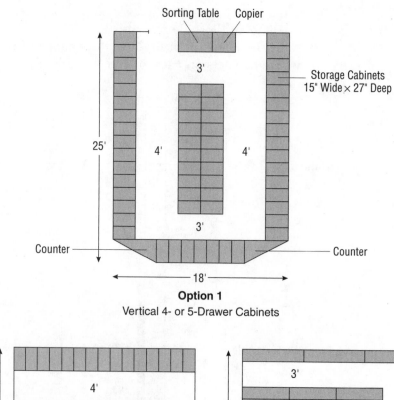

Option 1
Vertical 4- or 5-Drawer Cabinets

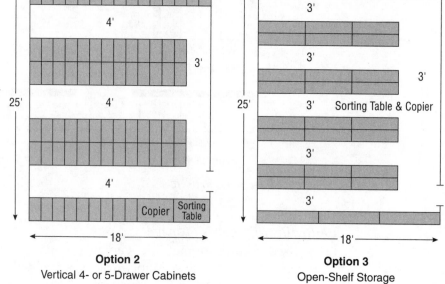

Option 2
Vertical 4- or 5-Drawer Cabinets

Option 3
Open-Shelf Storage

Note that the wide aisle provides enough room for two workers in a single aisle. With the two-aisle system, four employees can comfortably work in the file system. This means increased speed and efficiency in filing (see Figure 5-4).

Figure 5-4
Centralized
Records Storage

Cross aisles should be provided every 25 feet if rows are long. Outlets for convenience, efficiency, and safety in case of an emergency are provided. Several arrangements for centralized records storage are possible. The important point to remember is that these records must be efficiently arranged to save space (because of their high-cost location) and to save time (because of their labour-intensive function).

Learning Check: Can you explain the factors used in determining the types of equipment and layouts needed in decentralized and centralized storage cabinet arrangements?

MANUAL STORAGE EQUIPMENT AND SUPPLIES

Different record
forms require
different types of
storage.

Proper selection of storage equipment and supplies is one of the keys to efficient storage and retrieval of information. Multiple options exist for the storage of all forms of records—documents, cards, microforms, magnetic, and electronic media. Vendors are constantly upgrading their products in this very competitive and rapidly changing field. Most vendors offer consultative services to assist in the selection of storage equipment and supplies. A basic knowledge of available options is still, however, essential for selection of equipment and supplies to meet the needs of individual organizations.

Selection Criteria for Equipment

Selection criteria vary in importance with each organization. Certain criteria are important and should be considered (then eliminated if not appropriate for specific needs) before any purchases are made. Some criteria are applicable to both equipment and supplies. Because of differences in the way the criterion is applied or in the importance of each criterion to the individual organization, selection criteria for equipment and supplies will be discussed separately.

There are eight selection criteria for choosing equipment.

Equipment selection criteria can be categorized as (1) ergonomic considerations, (2) storage and retrieval requirements, (3) space requirements, (4) security requirements, (5) equipment costs, (6) operation costs, (7) number of individuals regularly accessing the records, and (8) physical characteristics of the records.

Ergonomic Considerations

For a safe and healthy workplace, equipment must conform to the people who use it.

Rather than making people conform to the equipment they use, **ergonomics** is the applied science that fits the working environment and equipment to the people. Ergonomic factors include design, lighting, colour, acoustics, security, safety, and accessibility. Serious injuries could result from improperly designed equipment that forces workers to reach awkwardly for files, lift heavy files or books, or make continuous repetitive movements. Increased productivity results from the use of well-designed equipment in an ergonomically friendly environment.

Storage and Retrieval Requirements

Storage and retrieval speed must be considered.

Determining storage and retrieval requirements involves defining the basic storage needs of the organization. The types of records to be stored—paper, cards, microforms, oversize documents, audiovisual materials, magnetic and electronic forms, or other media—need to be considered. Equipment may need to be mobile or adaptable to more than one location or function. The storage and retrieval speed required by the organization should also be taken into consideration. The speeds obtainable with different types of manual equipment vary; with some automated equipment, a record can be stored or retrieved in just seconds. Faster speeds are usually required for more active records or situations in which a large volume of records must be stored or retrieved.

Space Requirements

Space requirements vary according to the equipment chosen.

Office space is expensive; therefore, the amount of space required for various types of storage equipment is an important consideration. Compare floor space ratios when evaluating equipment space requirements. Floor space ratios represent the storage capacity per square foot of floor space occupied by the storage equipment. Table 5-1 shows the square feet required for various types of storage equipment.

Table 5-1

COMPARISON OF SPACE REQUIREMENTS FOR DIFFERENT TYPES OF STORAGE EQUIPMENT

Type of Housing	Square Feet Required Per Unit	Square Feet Required to House 10,000 Filing Inches
8-shelf open shelf	6 3/4	250
5-drawer lateral (letter size)	13 1/2	810
5-drawer vertical (letter size)	7	588
4-drawer vertical (letter size)	7	728
8-shelf mobile aisle	3 3/4	141

When calculating the space requirements for different types of storage equipment, consideration must also be given to the space required for aisles. As already discussed, typical aisle space required for vertical and lateral storage cabinets is 18 to 24 inches, not including the space necessary to pull the drawer out to access the records.

Security Requirements

Security features are available when needed.

Security requirements will vary within an organization. Some records may be accessed by all employees; others, such as personnel records protected by the Freedom of Information and Privacy Acts, require very limited access. Storage equipment may have no security features (open shelves) or may have various security features, such as locks or security codes, for access. Because of the higher cost, secure equipment should be purchased only as required to protect the records from unauthorized access.

Equipment Costs

In addition to purchase price, capacity should be considered.

For most organizations, cost should not be the overriding factor in the equipment selection process. All types of equipment that meet the first three selection criteria and are available from local vendors should first be identified. Then the costs of these types of equipment should be compared. Item costs should be adjusted so that equal volumes of storage space are being compared in price. For example, if one four-drawer cabinet with a lock costs $385 and a five-drawer cabinet with a lock costs $465, the five-drawer cabinet, which costs approximately 21 percent more, is actually less expensive because it provides 25 percent more storage capacity in the same floor space.

Storage capacity may be measured in cubic feet (1.5 cubic feet per letter-size drawer or 2.0 cubic feet per legal-size drawer) or in linear filing inches (using a tape measure to determine actual storage inches available). Storage capacity is most often measured in cubic feet for inactive records and linear filing inches for active records. The calculations for the storage capacity of a vertical storage cabinet drawer are illustrated in Figure 5-5. Note that the height and width measurements of the container are greater than the height and width of the documents. This allows for ease of storage and retrieval.

Figure 5-5
Storage Capacity of a Letter-Size Vertical Storage Cabinet Container

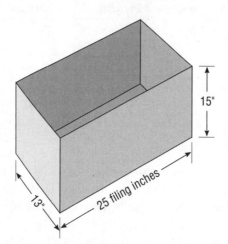

Height of stored documents: 9.0"
Width of stored documents: 11.5"
Length of stored documents: 25.0"
Volume of records drawer:

9.0" × 11.5" × 25.0" = 2587.5"
÷ 1728" = 1.5 cu. ft.

Operation Costs

Many other factors are included in the cost of operations.

Operation costs include the costs of personnel to store and retrieve information, the cost of compatible supplies, maintenance costs, and the cost of the space required to house the equipment. Personnel costs will be determined by the number of employees required to process the volume of records, the frequency of requests for materials or information, and the storage and retrieval speed of the equipment. The total personnel costs are then calculated by multiplying the number of employees required by the salaries of these employees.

The cost of compatible supplies may be a very important consideration if the equipment vendor is the sole source of these supplies. If the equipment is adaptable to standard sizes of supplies, cost of supplies becomes a much less important consideration. It is, however, important to determine before equipment is purchased whether special supplies are required. If additional space must be purchased or leased to accommodate additional equipment, this cost is considered to be an operational cost. Because of such additional costs, space requirements are a priority consideration in equipment selection.

Number of People Regularly Accessing the Records

The number of people who regularly access the records is an important consideration. If access is limited to one or two people, then there is a wider choice of equipment because there is not the same concern for having to wait to be able to store or retrieve a record in a cabinet drawer. If a number of people will be accessing the records, the records must be dispersed so that waiting is minimized.

Physical Characteristics of the Records

Obviously, index cards require different storage equipment than do letter-size documents; microfiche has different requirements than disks; and maps require different storage than do computer tapes and disk packs. Therefore, consideration must be given to the physical characteristics of the records that will be housed before making an equipment selection decision.

 Learning Check: Can you list the criteria for selecting equipment and describe how each affects the purchasing decision?

Manual Storage Equipment

Storage equipment may be classified as manual, mechanical, or automated. This chapter deals only with manual and mechanical storage equipment. Equipment options will be presented for all forms of records: documents (records in paper form), cards, microforms, magnetic media and electronic media, audiovisual records, publications, and maps and engineering drawings.

Many types of manual storage equipment are available.

Manual storage equipment provides a stationary storage space for records where the records user must go to the files to store or retrieve records. Types of manual storage equipment described in this section are (1) conventional (vertical) cabinets, (2) shelf files, (3) lateral files, (4) card files, (5) microrecord files, (6) centre hook files, and (7) other media files.

Conventional (Vertical) Cabinets

A **conventional (vertical) cabinet** is a storage unit in which file access is vertical (from the top); records must be dropped into the unit for storage or lifted out for use. Vertical cabinets are available in one- to five-drawer sizes. One-drawer units may be on casters to provide mobility. Two-drawer cabinets are often used at desk side so that the user can remain seated. Three-drawer units are frequently used as counter areas and may have a simulated wood top to provide attractive working space. The four-drawer cabinet has traditionally been the most frequently used piece of equipment for document storage; however, the five-drawer unit has gained in popularity because of the 25 percent increase in storage capacity in the same floor space. Conventional (vertical) storage cabinets are recommended for personal use, paper-based files in smaller work spaces. Most new equipment purchases are lateral storage cabinets. The reference rate for conventional cabinets is 25 to 35 file actions per hour. Examples of file actions include placing a document in a file folder and retrieving a document from a file folder. One employee may complete as many as 280 actions per day.[1]

---

[1]The Spacesaver Group, Brochure SCC-79.33 from Spacesaver Corporation.

Open-Shelf Files

Open-shelf files provide faster retrieval than do drawer files.

An **open-shelf file** is a lateral file container consisting of horizontal open shelves similar to open bookshelves. Records are accessed from the side; guide and folder identifiers are on the side. Shelf units are usually 36 inches wide (width may vary from 32 to 42 inches) and may be from two to eight tiers high. Although many shelf files are open, both large and small units are available with roll-back fronts. Documents are stored in folders, which are placed on shelves in the same manner as in drawer files (bottom edge of the folder down). However, guides and folders with side tabs are necessary for proper identification. Because there are no drawers to open or close, storage and retrieval speeds are faster with shelf files. Open-shelf files are recommended for work spaces with large amounts of paper-based records where space is at a premium, multi-user access is required, and the reference rate is below 320 file actions per day. One employee may reference 30 to 40 records per hour.[2] Another space saver offered by open-shelf files is the additional space available due to the added height such systems make possible. A shelf system can have seven or eight rows of shelving, an advantage not possible with drawer files.

Lateral Files

Lateral files require less aisle space than do vertical files.

A **lateral file** is a storage unit in which files are accessed from the side (horizontally). (See Figure 5-6.) The most frequently used type of lateral file is the roll-out cabinet. Lateral file cabinets are similar to conventional cabinets except that lateral drawers are wider and not as deep. Because of this construction, less aisle space is consumed by the open lateral drawer—about 13 inches compared with 25 inches for the vertical drawer cabinet. Lateral files are available in two- to five-drawer sizes. Frequently the upper tiers of a large lateral unit are used for less-active records prior to their transfer to the records centre. Lateral cabinet storage is often used in work spaces that require closed file units for paper-based files or for the design effect. Typical reference rates are 25 to 35 file actions per hour. One employee may complete as many as 320 file actions per day.[3]

Unit box lateral files provide protection for records.

A **unit box lateral file** is a shelf filing system that uses specially designed boxes that hang from rails. The rails are affixed to heavy posts along the shelves. Each box holds about four inches of material and hangs at a slight angle (see Figure 5-7). The slant of the boxes provides fast reference and usually eliminates the need to completely remove a folder from the box before storing or retrieving information. Typical storage and retrieval speeds using unit box lateral files are slightly higher than for open-shelf storage.

---

[2]Ibid.
[3]Ibid.

Figure 5-6
Lateral Storage
Cabinet

Source: Courtesy of TAB Products

Figure 5-7
Unit Box Lateral
Files

Source: Supreme Equipment & Systems Corp.

Card Files

A **card file** is a file that accommodates card stock in varying sizes. Card files are used in many organizations to provide (1) quick reference to frequently used information, (2) an index of specific items or of other files, and (3) a record of activities (such as accounts receivable payments and charges). Cards used in card files are usually one of three types: (1) index cards (5 by 3, 6 by 4, or 8 by 5 inches), (2) aperture cards (7 3/8 by 3 inches), and (3) ledger cards (5 by 8 inches) used to record accounts receivable and accounts payable activities.

Special types of manual storage equipment are available for cards. These types of equipment include cabinets with drawers of special heights (sometimes partitioned to store two rows of cards per drawer), boxes, trays, and card visible cabinets, which allow one edge of each card to be viewed to identify the information found on the card (see Figure 5-8).

> Special types of storage equipment are available for cards.

> **Figure 5-8**
> Card Visible
> Cabinet

Source: Photograph courtesy of Gaylord Bros.

Microrecord Files

A **microrecord file** is a vertical storage container with shallow drawers to accommodate the size of the microforms. With the use of drawer dividers, the same cabinet can be used to house microfiche, aperture cards, or microfilm (see Figure 5-9). These cabinets are constructed of various materials and may contain from 4 to 11 drawers.

Trays constructed in various sizes and of materials ranging from high-impact plastic to metal are also used to store microrecords. Most trays have optional protective covers. Fiche trays are frequently stored in specially designed cabinets, which may be modular, mobile, or permanent units (see Figure 5-10).

Microfiche are also stored in ring binders with loose-leaf pages; each of these pages will house from 4 to 10 microfiche. Many of these are easel binders, which stand on the desk for easy use.

> Microforms may be stored in cabinets, trays, or binders.

Figure 5-9
Microform Storage

Source: Courtesy of Luxor Corporation

Figure 5-10
Microfiche Tray

Centre Hook Files

Increased use of information stored on a variety of media has increased the need for equipment that allows information that is used together to be stored together. A **centre hook** file is a method of storage that allows various media to be hung on bars similar to hangers in a closet. Printouts, microfiche, diskettes, magnetic tapes, letter and legal-size papers, and audiovisual media may be hung on hanger bars (see Figure 5-11).

Centre hook filing can be installed in shelf units or on walls over workstations for easy access and efficient space utilization. The media filed are housed in binders, folders, or containers that provide space for labelling contents.

Centre hook files allow for mixed-media storage.

 Learning Check: Can you describe various types of storage equipment used for manual records storage?

Figure 5-11
Centre Hook Filing
Equipment

Source: Haworth, Inc.

Other Media Files

Many organizations also need to store and retrieve information from other media, such as audiovisual media, magnetic media, maps, engineering drawings, and publications. Each of these media types has some special storage requirements.

Films, filmstrips, tape recordings, records, and optical disks may be housed in cabinets similar to those used for roll microfilm stored in cartridges. Canisters of film are usually stored on open shelves; filmstrips and tape recordings are usually stored in cabinets. Records and optical disks are placed in protective envelopes and then stored in boxes or trays.

Electronic media must be protected from dust.

Disks used in word processing applications, computer tape reels, cartridges, and other disks must be protected from dust. Disks are placed in protective pockets to minimize danger from handling or environmental factors. These pockets may then be stored in boxes, albums, or binders (see Figure 5-12). Computer tapes may be stored in lateral files or in open-shelf files, which use canister racks or hanging racks (see Figure 5-13).

Maps may be stored flat, in rolls, or hanging.

Maps and engineering drawings present unique storage requirements because of their large size. These media may be stored flat in specially designed cabinets (see Figure 5-14), roll-stored in either vertical or horizontal units, or placed in hanging files (see Figure 5-15). Documents in flat or roll files are usually numbered and indexed by location for easy reference. Oversize documents in hanging files may be identified by a clip attached to the rod; these documents should also be indexed for efficient access.

Figure 5-12
Disk Storage

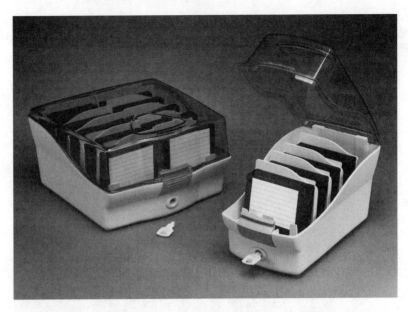

Source: Fellowes®

Figure 5-13
Computer Tape
Storage

Publications include all types of printed matter prepared for distribution; however, periodicals present unique storage requirements.
Periodicals require open, slanted shelves or literature racks (see Figure
5-16) for the display of current issues; and open shelves or unit boxes
are used to display past issues until they are bound. Books and bound
copies of periodicals may be stored on open shelves.

Figure 5-14
Maps/Engineering
Drawings Storage

Source: Fellowes®

Figure 5-15
Hanging File

Source: Azon Corp.

Figure 5-16
Periodicals
Displayers

Source: Photograph courtesy of Gaylord Bros.

Multimedia storage
is cost-efficient.

The vast amounts of media and paper being used in the office to accumulate and record information have necessitated that equipment manufacturers provide more flexibility for multimedia storage. However, diversity is not the only factor when considering mixed-media equipment. Space limitations require that companies make the best use of their space, and they can no longer afford to give different types of media individually protected shelves or files. Processed information may now be stored in shared spaces to economize on both the storage equipment and the office space. Figure 5-17 shows one type of multimedia storage equipment.

Figure 5-17
Mixed-Media
Storage

Source: Supreme Equipment & Systems Corp.

 Learning Check: Can you describe methods of housing records in various media?

Mechanical Aids to Manual Storage and Retrieval

Mechanized
equipment aids
storage and
retrieval.

Mechanical aids to manual storage and retrieval are pieces of mechanized equipment used to speed access to records. Most mechanical storage equipment saves space and reduces storage and retrieval time. Types of mechanical storage equipment described in this section are (1) mobile aisle systems, (2) rotary files, (3) power elevator lateral equipment, and (4) conveyor systems. The last three systems eliminate much of the nonproductive time normally consumed by walking to the files. The records, however, are still manually placed in the storage equipment and manually removed from the storage equipment.

Mobile Aisle Systems

A **mobile aisle system** is a space-conserving high-density cabinet of shelves or trays that move on track (either manually, mechanically, or electrically) to create aisles for accessing records (see Figure 5-18). With a manual system the user physically slides the units along the track to open the appropriate aisle. For small collections of records, a manual system is satisfactory. A mechanical system provides a mechanism that allows the user to move the units with minimal effort. An electrically powered system allows the user to press a button, and the shelves move electronically to create an aisle at the appropriate spot.

Optional safety precautions such as locking carriages, safety stops, and "in-use" lights are available with the electrically powered units. Much of the space in central records locations has traditionally been consumed by the aisles, which provide access to conventional cabinets or shelves. Rapidly increasing costs for office space have caused many organizations to seek ways to eliminate the unproductive space consumed by aisles.

Figure 5-18
Mobile Aisle
Storage

Source: Kardex Systems, Inc.

Mobile aisle
storage is
compactible.

Mobile systems are sometimes called compactible units because they can be positioned together to form a closed unit. This compactibility also provides additional security because the system can be closed and locked, thereby restricting access to the records.

Mobile aisle systems offer a storage alternative that can increase the storage capacity of existing space 100 percent or more or can accommodate existing records in 50 percent or less of the space required for conventional cabinets. The floor space requirements to house comparable filing inches of records in conventional vertical cabinets, static shelves, and a mobile aisle system are compared in Figure 5-19. The reduced floor space requirement and the subsequent reduction in cost of floor space for records storage significantly reduce records system operating costs.[4]

---

[4]Ibid.

Rotary Files

A **rotary file** is a storage unit in which records are attached to a centre wheel that is turned for access. Rotary files may be single- or multiple-tier units in which each tier turns individually for rapid storage and retrieval of records. Rotary files allow multiple access to stored materials and provide efficient use of storage space. They are used to house documents, cards, and microforms. One multiple-tier unit designed to house several types of media is shown in Figure 5-20.

Figure 5-19
Floor Space Requirements and Savings with Mobile Aisle Storage

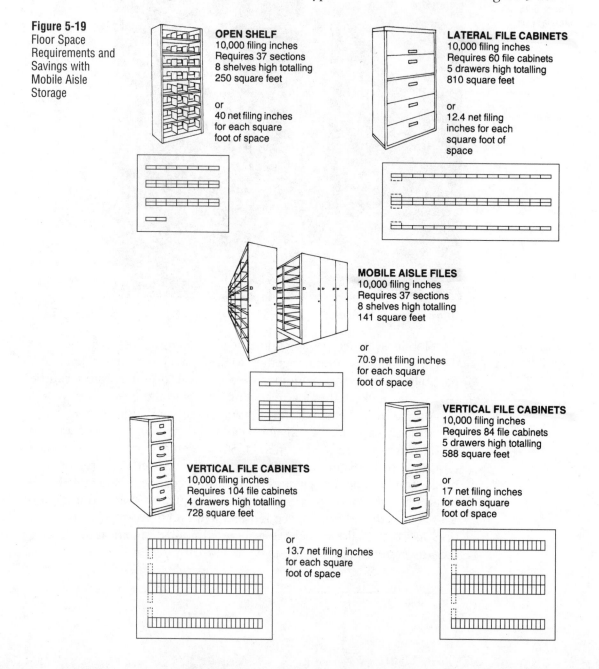

OPEN SHELF
10,000 filing inches
Requires 37 sections
8 shelves high totalling
250 square feet

or
40 net filing inches
for each square
foot of space

LATERAL FILE CABINETS
10,000 filing inches
Requires 60 file cabinets
5 drawers high totalling
810 square feet

or
12.4 net filing
inches for each
square foot of
space

MOBILE AISLE FILES
10,000 filing inches
Requires 37 sections
8 shelves high totalling
141 square feet

or
70.9 net filing inches
for each square
foot of space

VERTICAL FILE CABINETS
10,000 filing inches
Requires 84 file cabinets
5 drawers high totalling
588 square feet

or
17 net filing inches
for each square
foot of space

VERTICAL FILE CABINETS
10,000 filing inches
Requires 104 file cabinets
4 drawers high totalling
728 square feet

or
13.7 net filing inches
for each square
foot of space

Figure 5-20
Rotary File

Source: Courtesy of Delco Associates, Inc.

Power Elevator Lateral Files

Power lateral files work like a Ferris wheel.

A **power elevator lateral file** is a multiple-tier unit that utilizes a Ferris wheel approach to electrically bring the desired shelf to the user when needed. The shelves may be constructed to employ the sideways position of files used in other lateral storage equipment; however, the conventional forward position is also widely used. Power elevator lateral files may house documents, cards, or microforms.

Although these are expensive units, a primary feature of this equipment is improved efficiency in storing and retrieving documents or other media because the shelf or drawer comes to the user as needed (see Figure 5-21). Many systems have a numeric keypad for directing the appropriate shelf to the access position. The operator may perform all filing functions from a seated position; this eliminates time lost in walking from the desk to the files and back.

Figure 5-21
Power Elevator
Lateral File

Source: Kardex Systems, Inc.

Power Carousel Files

A **power carousel file** is a circular storage unit that rotates (see Figure 5-22). Files are accessed horizontally on one or more levels. The rotating shelving sections are operated by a bidirectional foot pedal, optional microprocessor keypad, or PC-based software. The carousel can bring the desired section to the operator in seconds. This equipment allows for storage of either magnetic tape reels or cartridges or both. Modular sections make this automated carousel file suitable for changing records storage needs.

Figure 5-22
Power Carousel
File

Source: White Office Systems

Conveyor Systems

Carousel files have modular sections to suit changing needs.

A **conveyor system** is a mechanical storage system that brings the desired folder to the user in response to dialling or keying in the folder number. A conveyor system is similar to the conveyor system found in many dry cleaning businesses, where an attendant pushes a button and a rack of clothes turns to the desired location. Similarly, the records user pushes a button and a rack of records moves around to the desired location for access. These systems are used for documents, cards, and microfiche.

 Learning Check: Can you describe mechanical records storage equipment that aids in manually storing or retrieving records?

Selection Criteria for Supplies

The five selection criteria for supplies are (1) equipment compatibility, (2) efficiency, (3) quality, (4) economy, and (5) environmental considerations.

Equipment Compatibility

Supplies such as guides and folders must be compatible with the equipment purchased. For example, open-shelf files require guides and folders with side tabs rather than top tabs; visible index or other card files may accommodate cards of only one size. Any such restrictions should be considered before the equipment is purchased in order to avoid higher operating costs. The person responsible for purchasing supplies must be aware of any restrictions to avoid stocking quantities of unusable supplies or causing work slowdowns because needed supplies are not in stock.

Efficiency

Manufacturers are conscious of increasing storage and retrieval efficiency through special features of their supplies. For example, preprinted folders are available for alphabetic, numeric, and alphanumeric classification systems. These folders are especially helpful when an organization or department establishes its records system or converts to a new type of storage equipment. The use of colour coding (discussed in Chapter 7) also contributes to the efficiency of a records system through rapid identification of records locations and misplaced records.

Quality

The quality of supplies may be determined by weight or type of materials used in construction. For example, file guides, which are discussed below, require a heavier material than file folders because of their more frequent use and greater length of time within the drawer or on the shelf. In addition, some organizations are setting up systems with file folders that last for many years. Selection should be based on the quality necessary to do the job economically.

Economy

Minimizing costs is a consideration in most organizational operations. However, purchasing the least expensive item may not always be the most economical move. Buying a lesser grade of material for file guides or folders (which will be in active use for long periods of time) often results in costly replacement purchases. Savings can often be realized through quantity supplies purchases. First, purchase small lots of supplies from a vendor to determine the quality of supplies and the ability of the vendor to provide needed sizes and weights. If the initial purchase is satisfactory, larger quantities should be considered for frequently used items or for supplies with long shelf lives.

Environmental Considerations

Many organizations are now recycling guides and file folders when they are worn out. Plastic strips and metal reinforcements can present problems in recycling. File folders in certain colours cannot be recycled with other materials.

Supplies for Manual Systems

The active files in a manual filing system are normally stored in filing cabinets, most commonly, vertical files and open-shelf or lateral file units. Because of their space-saving characteristics, mobile storage units are now often being used for active records. In order to organize the files stored in these filing cabinets, guides and file folders are used.

Guides

Guides are signposts in the file system.

Guides are heavy press board or cardboard used to separate the file drawer or shelf into sections that enable searchers to locate specific records by drawing the eye to a certain area. In a file drawer, the guides also stabilize the records and prevent them from sagging or sliding to the bottom of the file drawer.

Figure 5-23
OUT Guide with Insertion

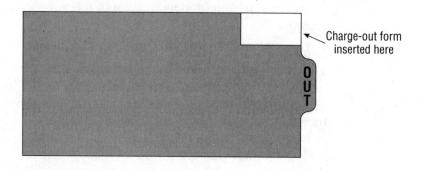

Charge-out form inserted here

Out Indicators

OUT indicators show where items have been removed from the files.

Out indicators made of plastic or cardboard are used to show where materials have been taken from the file and remain there until the materials are returned to the file. They are available in the form of an OUT guide, an OUT folder, or an OUT sheet. See Figure 5-23 for an illustration of an OUT guide.

Tabs

A **tab** is a projection from the top or side of a guide or folder used to identify the contents. The tab contains a **caption**, which identifies the range of records to be stored behind the guide. The caption may be printed directly on the guide tab or on a label affixed to the tab. The width of the tab is determined by the cut of the guide or folder. For example, a one-fifth cut means the tab is 1/5 the width of the guide or folder. The position of the tab is determined by the location of the tab along the edge of the guide or folder. Guides and file folders may be purchased in a variety of cuts and tab positions.

Labels

A **label** identifies the contents of a file folder, a drawer, a shelf, or a box. It may be used on a guide to identify a section of a file. Labels may be purchased in a variety of colours and styles such as rolls, strips, or continuous forms for generation by computer. They may also contain a bar code for computer scanning.

 Learning Check: Can you explain the purpose of guides, tabs, and labels?

File Folders

File folders store documents in the files.

File folders are containers used to store correspondence or other documents in the files and are made of heavy paper known as manila or kraft paper. Plastic folders are also available in many colours. A tab extends at the top of the file folder used with vertical files and at the side of the folder when used with lateral files. Score marks at the bottom of the folder allow the user to expand the folder as the number of documents increases. Figure 5-24 shows some commonly used file folders. Other kinds of file folders are the hanging (suspension) type; bellows (expansion) folders; and pocket folders when more folder capacity is needed.

Figure 5-24
Types of File
Folders

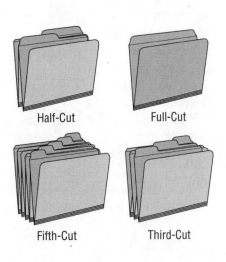

Half-Cut   Full-Cut

Fifth-Cut   Third-Cut

 Learning Check: Can you explain the uses of the various file folders?

TERMINOLOGY REVIEW

Review the terms listed below in the Glossary on page 521.

caption	guides
card file	label
centralized records storage system	lateral file
centre hook file	microrecord file
combination records storage system	mobile aisle system
conventional (vertical) cabinet	open-shelf file
conveyor system	out indicators
decentralized records storage system	power carousel file
ergonomics	power elevator rotary file
file folder	tab
floor load capacity	unit box lateral file

REVIEW AND DISCUSSION

1. Define centralized and decentralized active records storage systems. What are the advantages and disadvantages of each system?
2. Explain the advantages of using a combination of centralized and decentralized records storage systems.
3. Explain floor load capacity and how it is calculated.
4. List seven of the eight selection criteria for storage equipment and explain how each affects the purchasing decision.
5. Define and give at least two examples of manual and mechanical document storage equipment.
6. Describe two storage equipment options for each of the following:
   a. audiovisual materials
   b. magnetic media
   c. maps and engineering drawings
   d. publications
7. State four of the five selection criteria for supplies and explain how each affects the purchasing decision.
8. Explain the types of guides and folders in an active filing system.

APPLICATIONS

1. Identify the problems in space requirements and layout in the stacks area of the following records centre sketch.

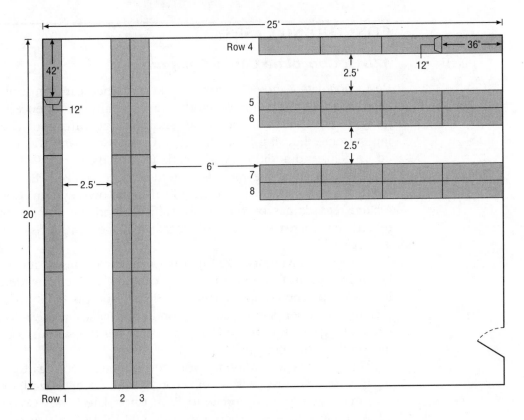

2. Rearrange the layout in Application 1 to eliminate the problems identified. Describe how the new arrangement accomplishes this goal.

3. In groups of five or six people each, prepare a two- to four-page summary of one of the following topics: manual storage equipment, mechanical storage equipment, or records storage supplies. Each summary should be accompanied by several brochures and cost data. On the assignment due date, each group should be prepared to make a three- to five-minute oral report summarizing its findings.

4. Compare the square feet of storage space and the cost of floor space to store 6,000 filing inches of paper documents in (a) four-drawer letter-size file cabinets, (b) eight-tier open-shelf units, (c) five-drawer lateral cabinets, and (d) eight-tier mobile aisle storage units. The cost of floor space is $45 per square foot. (The information in Table 5-1 and Figure 5-19 may be helpful.)

CONCLUDING CASES

A. Best Chocolate Candy Company

Best Chocolate Candy Company is an established candy manufacturer, celebrating its 75th anniversary. The company experienced steady growth until 1988, when it had an enormous growth spurt. The building currently housing Best Chocolate Candy Company was constructed in 1946, and additions were made to it in 1964 and 1988.

The current active records system is decentralized. Each department maintains its own records and uses its own system. Compiling related records has become more difficult, and the number of "lost" records has increased to the point that management decision making is impaired.

A records inventory identified 9,000 linear inches of records now being housed in four-drawer vertical cabinets 15 inches wide and 27 inches deep. The company has investigated the possibility of making a change to open shelves and has indicated its willingness to authorize that expenditure if the task force studying the system documents the need for this change.

1. What factors will influence your recommendation regarding the type of active records system (centralized, decentralized, or combination) most appropriate for Best Chocolate Candy Company?
2. Assuming there is a room measuring 27 by 15 feet that could be made available for active records storage, design a layout for a central storage facility. Also calculate the floor load capacity. The room has been rated at 65 pounds per square foot of space.
3. State your recommendation for Best Chocolate Candy Company's active records system, giving the rationale for that decision.

B. Saskatchewan Dermatology Associates

Saskatchewan Dermatology Associates has maintained patient records by patient number since it opened 20 years ago. The records are stored in a spare room at some distance from the office staff. The same four-drawer traditional vertical cabinets that the office began with are still being used for the records. However, space is becoming an increasing problem as the numbers of physicians and patients increase and as office staff turnover occurs.

Kim Ing, SDA's records manager, must do something to control the situation, as the company is running out of space in the records room. File folders are becoming dog-eared from being stuffed into drawers that are already full. Folders are not returned to their proper location when staff are too busy to make the trip to the spare room. Sometimes a patient's missing folder is only found after searching everyone's desk. Kim's first thought was to hire another records clerk; however, she would like to avoid the cost of additional personnel.

1. Should Kim consider another location for SDA's patient files? Explain.
2. Should Kim consider other equipment options to store the patient files? Explain.
3. Should Kim consider other supplies options? Explain.

SUGGESTED READINGS AND RESOURCES

Diamond, Susan Z. "Colour Speeds Filing." *Office Systems* '88, Vol. 5, No. 2 (September, 1988), p. 66.

Diamond, Susan Z. "Save Time and Space with Central Filing." *Office Systems* '85, Vol. 2, No. 2 (February, 1985), p. 62.

Fernberg, Patricia M. "The Economics that Drive Mobile Storage." *Modern Office Technology,* Vol. 32, No. 6 (August, 1987), p. 50.

Gannon, Alice. "Project Management: An Approach to Accomplishing Things." *Records Management Quarterly,* Vol. 28, No. 3 (July, 1994), p. 3.

Johnson, Mina M., and Norman F. Kallaus. *Records Management,* 5th ed. Cincinnati: South-Western Publishing Co., 1992.

LaFollette, Larry L. "Help: We Can't Breathe in Here!" *Records Management Quarterly,* Vol. 25, No. 2 (April, 1991), p. 24.

Mims, Julian L. "An Outline for Files Control." *Records Management Quarterly,* Vol. 22, No. 1 (January, 1988), p. 18.

Phillips, John T. "Managing Project Records." *Records Management Quarterly,* Vol. 26, No. 3 (October, 1992), p. 36.

Wells, Janet H., and Elisabeth Novakovich. "Bringing the Paper Files into the Family." *Records Management Quarterly,* Vol. 23, No. 1 (January, 1989), p. 22.

Indexing Rules and Classification System Selection

Learning Goals

After completing this chapter, you should be able to:

1. Learn standardized indexing rules and explain their importance.
2. Determine when cross-references are necessary when indexing personal and business names.
3. Prepare cross-references in the correct form.
4. Define alphabetic classification system and identify applications for which an alphabetic classification system—by name, by subject, or by geographic location—is appropriate.
5. Define numeric classification system and identify applications for which a numeric classification system—by serial or duplex—is appropriate.
6. Explain the differences between middle- and terminal-digit arrangements.
7. Define alphanumeric classification system and describe its arrangement.
8. Define chronologic classification system and identify applications for which a chronologic classification system is appropriate.
9. Describe the advantages of a Uniform Classification System.
10. Explain the importance of determining the basic file groups of an organization's records prior to selecting a classification system.
11. Explain the importance of determining the filing segments and identifying user requirements of an organization's records prior to selecting a classification system.

INDEXING RULES

Business records stored in electronic form represent 3 to 4 percent of all currently stored information.

Computers have changed many facets of business in the past decade, and the area of records management is no exception. However, there is a misconception that simply because computers are used to store part of business records that the skills and abilities to deal with hard-copy records are no longer needed. The truth is that electronic and micrographic files account for a small percentage of business records today and the majority of business records are still maintained in hard-copy form. Of the information currently stored, business records stored in electronic form, while growing, represent only 3 to 4 percent, micrographic records only 4 percent, and the remaining 92 to 93 percent are retained in hard-copy paper form. Office personnel must learn the proper procedures for classifying and storing hard-copy records.

Indexing is the process of determining the filing segment.

The basis of the major classification systems is alphabetic organization. The records may be filed by name, subject, location, or number, or a combination; but all of these systems rely on a set of alphabetic indexing rules. **Indexing**, the process of determining the segment of each record to be used for filing purposes, will be discussed in Chapter 7 as one of the steps in the filing process. In this chapter, indexing rules are discussed with regard to the **filing segment**—the entire name, subject, or number that is used for filing a record. These indexing rules establish the procedures for choosing filing units, which are then placed in alphabetic order so that records can be found when needed.

Each organization or part of an organization could establish a set of alphabetic indexing rules that would work for the records stored in that organization or part of it. But it is highly recommended that the organization use a standard set of rules so that everyone is using the same indexing rules. In 1986 the Association of Records Managers and Administrators Inc. (ARMA), the professional organization for the records management field, published their *International Standard for Records and Information Management Alphabetic Filing Rules*. By using these rules or rules based on ARMA's filing rules, all records would be indexed in the same way.

ARMA recommends using Simplified Filing Standard Rules for consistency in filing.

ARMA recommends the following Simplified Filing Standard Rules for consistency in filing. Each word, abbreviation, and initial is a separate **filing unit**, unless otherwise defined in a specific rule.

1. Alphabetize by arranging files in unit-by-unit order and letter-by-letter order within each unit.
2. Each filing unit in a filing segment is to be considered. This includes prepositions, conjunctions, and articles. The only exception is when the word *the* is the first filing unit in a filing segment. In this case, *the* is the last filing unit. Spell out all symbols; e.g., change &, $, # to *and, dollars,* and *number,* and file alphabetically.

✳ 3. File "nothing before something." File single-unit filing segments before multiple-unit filing segments.

4. Ignore all punctuation when alphabetizing. This includes periods, comma, dashes, hyphens, apostrophes, and so on. Hyphenated words are considered one unit.

5. Arabic and Roman numbers are filed sequentially before alphabetic characters. All Arabic numerals (1, 2, 3) precede all Roman numerals (I, II, III).

6. Acronyms, abbreviations, and radio and television station call letters are filed as one unit.

7. File under the most commonly used name or title. Cross-reference under other names or titles that might be used in an information request.

The following alphabetic indexing rules provide more detailed directions for filing personal, business, and government names.

The units in the Indexing Order sections below are in capital letters to emphasize that file folder label captions are in capital letters.

RULE 1: Indexing Order of Units

A. Personal Names

A personal name is indexed in this manner: (1) the surname (last name) is the key unit, (2) the given name (first name) or initial is the second unit, and (3) the middle name or initial is the third unit. If determining the surname is difficult, consider the last name written to be the surname.

A unit consisting of just an initial precedes a unit that consists of a complete name beginning with the same letter—*nothing before something*. Punctuation is omitted. In these examples, the key letter determining the index order is underscored.

Examples of Rule 1A

INDEX ORDER OF UNITS IN NAMES

Name	Key Unit	Unit 2	Unit 3
1. Victoria L. Cintron	CINTRON	VICTORIA	L
2. Victoria Lois Cintron	CINTRON	VICTORIA	LOIS
3. Martha M. David	DAVID	MARTHA	M
4. Carmen Garneau	GARNEAU	CARMEN	
5. John Mark	MARK	JOHN	

B. Business Names

Business names are indexed *as written* using letterheads or trademarks as guides. Each word in a business name is a separate unit. Business names containing personal names are indexed as written.

Examples of Rule 1B

INDEX ORDER OF UNITS IN NAMES

Name	Key Unit	Unit 2	Unit 3	Unit 4
1. Air Port Limousine Service	AIR	PORT	LIMOUSINE	SERVICE
2. Airport Newsstand	AIRPORT	NEWSSTAND		
3. Central Trust Company	CENTRAL	TRUST	COMPANY	
4. Dale Perkins Construction	DALE	PERKINS	CONSTRUCTION	
5. Mid Atlantic Transportation	MID	ATLANTIC	TRANSPORTATION	
6. New Brunswick Lottery	NEW	BRUNSWICK	LOTTERY	
7. Overton Real Estate Company	OVERTON	REAL	ESTATE	COMPANY
8. Southeastern Fitness Centre	SOUTHEASTERN	FITNESS	CENTRE	
9. Zoological Society	ZOOLOGICAL	SOCIETY		

RULE 2: *Minor Words and Symbols in Business Names*

Articles, prepositions, conjunctions, and symbols are considered separate indexing units. Symbols are considered as spelled in full. When the word *The* appears as the first word of a business name, it is considered the last indexing unit.

Articles: A, AN, THE

Prepositions: AT, IN, OUT, ON, OFF, BY, TO, WITH, FOR, OF, OVER

Conjunctions: AND, BUT, OR, NOR

Symbols: &, ¢, #, $, % (AND, CENT or CENTS, NUMBER or POUND, DOLLAR or DOLLARS, PERCENT)

Examples of Rule 2

INDEX ORDER OF UNITS IN NAMES

Name	Key Unit	Unit 2	Unit 3	Unit 4	Unit 5
1. A Place In The Sun	A	PLACE	IN	THE	SUN
2. $ Off Discount Furniture	DOLLAR	OFF	DISCOUNT	FURNITURE	
3. Down to Earth Construction	DOWN	TO	EARTH	CONSTRUCTION	
4. Hundred % Savers	HUNDRED	PERCENT	SAVERS		
5. The Lite House, Inc.	LITE	HOUSE	INC	THE	
6. Nice & Natural Foods	NICE	AND	NATURAL	FOODS	

RULE 3: *Punctuation and Possessives*

All punctuation is disregarded when indexing personal and business names. Commas, periods, hyphens, apostrophes, dashes, exclamation points, question marks, quotation marks, and slash marks (/) are disregarded, and names are indexed as written.

Examples of Rule 3

INDEX ORDER OF UNITS IN NAMES

Name	Key Unit	Unit 2	Unit 3	Unit 4
1. Advo-System, Ltd.	ADVOSYSTEM	LTD		
2. The Basil Pot	BASIL	POT	THE	
3. Bits 'N Pieces	BITS	N	PIECES	
4. Boyd Sharpe's Capital Appliance	BOYD	SHARPES	CAPITAL	APPLIANCE
5. Camelot In-The-Hills Apts.	CAMELOT	INTHEHILLS	APTS	
6. Gus & Associates Architects/Planners	GUS	AND	ASSOCIATES	ARCHITECTS-PLANNERS
7. Hall's Auto Sales	HALLS	AUTO	SALES	
8. Johnson's Tailoring & Alterations	JOHNSONS	TAILORING	AND	ALTERATIONS
9. Mary Ellen Morris	MORRIS	MARY	ELLEN	
10. Mary-Ellen Morris	MORRIS	MARYELLEN		
11. Tri-City Heating Co.	TRICITY	HEATING	CO	

RULE 4: Single Letters and Abbreviations

A. Personal Names

Initials in personal names are considered separate indexing units. Abbreviations of personal names (Wm., Jos., and Thos. for William, Joseph, and Thomas) and nicknames (Liz, Bill) are indexed as they are written.

B. Business Names

Single letters in business and organization names are indexed as written. If there is a space between single letters, index each letter as a separate unit. An acronym (a word formed from the first, or first few, letters of several words) is indexed as one unit regardless of punctuation or spelling. Abbreviated words (Mfg., Corp., Ltd.) and abbreviated names (IBM, CAI) are indexed as one unit regardless of punctuation or spacing. Radio and television station call letters are indexed as one unit.

Examples of Rule 4

INDEX ORDER OF UNITS IN NAMES

Name	Key Unit	Unit 2	Unit 3	Unit 4	Unit 5
1. A & S Electric Co.	A	AND	S	ELECTRIC	CO
2. A O Smith Electric Motors	A	O	SMITH	ELECTRIC	MOTORS
3. ABC Driver Training School	ABC	DRIVER	TRAINING	SCHOOL	
4. ACTA-FAX Business Machines	ACTAFAX	BUSINESS	MACHINES		
5. ARMA	ARMA				
6. E-B-E Service Centre	EBE	SERVICE	CENTRE		
7. EZ Limousine Service	EZ	LIMOUSINE	SERVICE		
8. HC Enterprise Inc.	HC	ENTERPRISE	INC		
9. IBM	IBM				
10. WIS TV	WIS	TV			

RULE 5: Titles and Suffixes

A. Personal Names

A title before a name (Dr., Miss, Mr., Mrs., Ms., Prof., etc.), a seniority suffix (II, III, Jr., Sr., etc.), or a professional suffix (CRM, DDS, Mayor, M.D., Ph.D., etc.) after a name is the last indexing unit. Numeric suffixes (II, III, etc.) are filed before alphabetic suffixes (Jr., Mayor, Member of Parliament (M.P.), Sr., etc.). If a name contains both a title and a suffix, the title is the last unit.

Royal and religious titles followed by either a given name or a surname only, such as Father Leo, are indexed and filed as written.

Examples of Rule 5A

INDEX ORDER OF UNITS IN NAMES

Name	Key Unit	Unit 2	Unit 3	Unit 4
1. Brother Joseph	BROTHER	JOSEPH		
2. J. Lloyd Edwards	EDWARDS	J	LLOYD	
3. J. Lloyd Edwards, II	EDWARDS	J	LLOYD	II
4. J. Lloyd Edwards, III	EDWARDS	J	LLOYD	III
5. J. Lloyd Edwards, Jr.	EDWARDS	J	LLOYD	JR
6. J. Lloyd Edwards, Sr.	EDWARDS	J	LLOYD	SR
7. Miss Susan T. Fuller	FULLER	SUSAN	T	MISS
8. Ms. Susan T. Fuller	FULLER	SUSAN	T	MS
9. Mr. J. M. Kane	KANE	J	M	MR
10. Mrs. Mary Louise Kane	KANE	MARY	LOUISE	MRS
11. Sister Mary Louise Kane	KANE	MARY	LOUISE	SISTER
12. Dr. Jill Martin	MARTIN	JILL	DR	
13. Jill Martin, M.D.	MARTIN	JILL	MD	
14. Prof. Jon Martin, Ph.D.	MARTIN	JON	PHD	PROF
15. Queen Mary	QUEEN	MARY		

B. Business Names

Titles in business names are indexed as written.

Examples of Rule 5B

INDEX ORDER OF UNITS IN NAMES

Name	Key Unit	Unit 2	Unit 3	Unit 4
1. Doc's Shoe Repair	DOCS	SHOE	REPAIR	
2. Doctors Weight Loss Centre	DOCTORS	WEIGHT	LOSS	CENTRE
3. Dr. Tire of Columbia	DR	TIRE	OF	COLUMBIA
4. Major Bud's Gallery	MAJOR	BUDS	GALLERY	
5. Rev. R. E. Major	MAJOR	R	E	REV
6. Mister Donut	MISTER	DONUT		
7. Mr. David's	MR	DAVIDS		
8. Mrs. Deli	MRS	DELI		

RULE 6: Prefixes—Articles and Particles

A foreign article or particle in a personal or business name is combined with the part of the name following it to form a single indexing unit. The indexing order is not affected by a space between a prefix and the rest of the name, and the space is disregarded when indexing.

Examples of articles and particles are: à la, D', Da, De, Del, De la, Della, Den, Des, Di, Dos, Du, El, Fitz, Il, L', La, Las, Le, Les, Lo, Los, M', Mac, Mc, O', Per, Saint, San, Santa, Santo, St., Ste., Te, Ten, Ter, Van, Van de, Van der, Von, Von der.

Examples of Rule 6

INDEX ORDER OF UNITS IN NAMES

Name	Key Unit	Unit 2	Unit 3	Unit 4
1. Dr. M. L. D'Adamo	DADAMO	M	L	DR
2. Mr. Robert T. De Loache	DELOACHE	ROBERT	T	MR
3. El Dalaw Service Bureau	ELDALAW	SERVICE	BUREAU	
4. Mercedes El Shazly	ELSHAZLY	MERCEDES		
5. FitzGerald Garage	FITZGERALD	GARAGE		
6. Rhonda Fitzgerald	FITZGERALD	RHONDA		
7. Barry McCall	MCCALL	BARRY		
8. Carmen C. O'Neal	ONEAL	CARMEN	C	
9. Jerry L. Saint Clair	SAINTCLAIR	JERRY	L	
10. Van De Grift Animal Clinic	VANDEGRIFT	ANIMAL	CLINIC	
11. Von Kleist Mfg Co.	VONKLEIST	MFG	CO	

RULE 7: Numbers in Business Names

Numbers spelled out (seven) in business names are filed alphabetically. Numbers written in digit form (7) are filed before alphabetic letters or words (B4 Photographers comes before Beleau Building Co.). Names with numbers written in digits in the first units are filed in ascending (lowest to highest) order before alphabetic names (229 Club, 534 Shop, Bank of Nova Scotia). Arabic numerals are filed before Roman numerals (2, 3; II, III).

Names with inclusive numbers (33–37) are arranged by the first digit(s) only (33). Names with numbers appearing in other than the first position (Pier 36 Cafe) are filed alphabetically and immediately before a similar name without a number (Pier and Port Cafe).

When indexing numbers written in digit form that contain *st, d,* and *th* (1st, 2d, 3d, 4th), ignore the letter endings and consider only the digits (1, 2, 3, 4).

Examples of Rule 7

INDEX ORDER OF UNITS IN NAMES

Name	Key Unit	Unit 2	Unit 3	Unit 4	Unit 5
1. 3rd and Main Auto Sales	3	AND	MAIN	AUTO	SALES
2. 7 to 11 Convenience Store	7	TO	11	CONVENIENCE	STORE
3. 600–612 Gervais Associates	600	GERVAIS	ASSOCIATES		
4. 1720 Main St. Associates	1720	MAIN	ST	ASSOCIATES	
5. A1 Auto Sales	A1	AUTO	SALES		
6. Over Thirty-Nine Club	OVER	THIRTYNINE	CLUB		
7. Route 66 Restaurant	ROUTE	66	RESTAURANT		
8. Route Six Garage	ROUTE	SIX	GARAGE		

RULE 8: *Organizations and Institutions*

Banks and other financial institutions, clubs, colleges, hospitals, hotels, lodges, magazines, motels, museums, newspapers, religious institutions, schools, unions, universities, and other organizations and institutions are indexed and filed according to the names written on their letterheads.

Examples of Rule 8

INDEX ORDER OF UNITS IN NAMES

Name	Key Unit	Unit 2	Unit 3	Unit 4	Unit 5
1. Amalgamated Clothing & Textile Workers	AMALGAMATED	CLOTHING	AND	TEXTILE	WORKERS
2. Association of Citizens for Justice	ASSOCIATION	OF	CITIZENS	FOR	JUSTICE
3. Chamber of Commerce	CHAMBER	OF	COMMERCE		
4. Columbia Sailing Club	COLUMBIA	SAILING	CLUB		
5. Council of Native Canadians	COUNCIL	OF	NATIVE	CANADIANS	
6. Daily News (Belleville)	DAILY	NEWS	BELLEVILLE		
7. Daily News (Riverton)	DAILY	NEWS	RIVERTON		
8. Federation Centre of the Blind	FEDERATION	CENTRE	OF	THE	BLIND
9. Food Retailers Association	FOOD	RETAILERS	ASSOCIATION		
10. Good Shepherd Lutheran Church	GOOD	SHEPHERD	LUTHERAN	CHURCH	
11. The Green Leaf Inn	GREEN	LEAF	INN	THE	
12. Royal Bank of Canada	ROYAL	BANK	OF	CANADA	
13. Sarah's School of Dance	SARAHS	SCHOOL	OF	DANCE	
14. Sir Wilfred Laurier High School	SIR	WILFRED	LAURIER	HIGH	SCHOOL
15. University of Western Ontario	UNIVERSITY	OF	WESTERN	ONTARIO	
16. Working Woman	WORKING	WOMAN			

RULE 9: *Identical Names*

When personal names and names of businesses, institutions, and organizations are identical (including title as explained in Rule 5), filing order is determined by the addresses. Compare addresses in the following order:

1. City names.
2. Province or state names (if city names are identical).
3. Street names, including *Avenue, Boulevard, Drive, Street,* (if city and province names are identical).
   a. When the first units of street names are written in digits (18th Street), the names are filed in ascending numeric order and placed together before alphabetic street names.
   b. Street names with compass directions are considered as written (South Park Avenue). Numbers after compass directions are considered before alphabetic names (East 8th, East Main, Sandusky, SE Eighth, Southeast Eighth).
4. House or building numbers (if city, province, and street names are identical).
   a. House and building numbers written as figures (912 Riverside Terrace) are considered in ascending numeric order and placed together before alphabetic building names (The Riverside Terrace).
   b. If a street address *and* a building name are included in an address, disregard the building name.
   c. Postal and ZIP Codes are not considered in determining filing order.

Examples of Rule 9

INDEX ORDER OF UNITS IN NAMES

(Names of Cities Used to Determine Filing Order)

1. General Construction Chilliwack, British Columbia	GENERAL	CONSTRUCTION	CHILLIWACK	BRITISH	COLUMBIA
2. General Construction Courtenay, British Columbia	GENERAL	CONSTRUCTION	COURTENAY	BRITISH	COLUMBIA

(Names of Provinces and States Used to Determine Filing Order)

1. Bartlet Hotel Overton, Alberta	BARTLET	HOTEL	OVERTON	ALBERTA	
2. Bartlet Hotel Overton, Ontario	BARTLET	HOTEL	OVERTON	ONTARIO	
3. First Choice Cab Denton, Manitoba	FIRST	CHOICE	CAB	DENTON	MANITOBA
4. First Choice Cab Denton, Nova Scotia	FIRST	CHOICE	CAB	DENTON	NOVA	SCOTIA

(Names of Streets and Building Numbers Used to Determine Filing Order)

1. Market Restaurant 43-12 Street Calgary, Alberta	MARKET	RESTAURANT	CALGARY	AB	43	<u>12</u>	STREET	
2. Market Restaurant 12-23 Street Calgary, Alberta	MARKET	RESTAURANT	CALGARY	AB	12	<u>23</u>	STREET	
3. Market Restaurant 345 Akers Street Calgary, Alberta	MARKET	RESTAURANT	CALGARY	· AB	345	AKERS	STREET	
4. Market Restaurant 975 Akers Street Calgary, Alberta	MARKET	RESTAURANT	CALGARY	AB	<u>975</u>	AKERS	STREET	
5. Market Restaurant 475 NW 15th Street Calgary, Alberta	MARKET	RESTAURANT	CALGARY	AB	475	<u>NW</u>	15	STREET
6. Market Restaurant 13 NW Ninth Street Calgary, Alberta	MARKET	RESTAURANT	CALGARY	AB	13	NW.	<u>NINTH</u>	STREET
7. Market Restaurant 132 Perkins Avenue Calgary, Alberta	MARKET	RESTAURANT	CALGARY	AB	132	<u>PERKINS</u>	AVENUE	

RULE 10: Government Names

Government names are indexed first by the name of the governmental unit—country, province, county, or city. Next, index the distinctive name of the department, bureau, office, or board. The words *Office of, Department of, Bureau of,* etcetera, are separate indexing units if they are part of the official name.

Note: If *of* is not a part of the official name as written, it is not added.

A. Federal

In the past, the first three indexing units of a Canadian (federal) government agency name were *Canada, Government of* followed by the agency name. In 1995 a number of federal departments and agencies were restructured and given new names. The names of departments now have *Canada* as a part of the name, for example, *Agriculture and Agri-Food Canada* (formerly Agriculture Canada) or *Fisheries and Oceans Canada* (formerly the Department of Fisheries and Oceans).

Examples of Rule 10A

Names	Indexed Order
1. Food Production and Inspection Branch Agriculture and Agri-Food Canada	CANADA GOVERNMENT OF AGRICULTURE AND AGRI-FOOD CANADA FOOD PRODUCTION AND INSPECTION BRANCH
2. Environmental Protection Branch Environment Canada	CANADA GOVERNMENT OF ENVIRONMENT CANADA ENVIRONMENTAL PROTECTION BRANCH
3. Hydrography Branch Fisheries and Oceans Canada	CANADA GOVERNMENT OF FISHERIES AND OCEANS CANADA HYDROGRAPHY BRANCH

B. Provincial and Local

The first indexing units are the names of the province (or state), county, parish, city, town, township, and village. Next index the most distinctive name of the department, board, bureau, office, or governments/political division. The words *Province of, County of, City of, Department of, Board of,* and so on are added only *if needed* for clarity and in the official name, and are considered separate indexing units.

Examples of Rule 10B

Names	Indexed Order

1. Kent County
   Water Treatment Plant
   Richibucto, New Brunswick
	KENT COUNTY
	WATER TREATMENT PLANT
	RICHIBUCTO NEW BRUNSWICK

2. Emergency Measures Organization (Nova Scotia) Halifax, Nova Scotia	NOVA SCOTIA PROVINCE OF EMERGENCY MEASURES ORGANIZATION HALIFAX NOVA SCOTIA

3. Department of Municipal Affairs
   Province of Nova Scotia
   Halifax, Nova Scotia
	NOVA SCOTIA PROVINCE OF
	MUNICIPAL AFFAIRS DEPARTMENT OF
	HALIFAX NOVA SCOTIA

4. Department of Health Town of Yarmouth, Nova Scotia	YARMOUTH TOWN OF DEPARTMENT OF HEALTH YARMOUTH NOVA SCOTIA

C. Foreign

The distinctive English name is the first indexing unit for foreign government names. This is followed, if needed and in the official name, by the balance of the formal name of the government. Branches, departments, and divisions follow in order by their distinctive names. States, colonies, provinces, cities, and other divisions of foreign governments are followed by their distinctive or official names as spelled in English.

Examples of Rule 10C

Names	Indexed Order
1. Kongeriget Danmark	DENMARK KINGDOM OF
2. Nippon	JAPAN
3. Jamhuri ya Kenya	KENYA REPUBLIC OF
4. Kongeriket Norge	NORWAY KINGDOM OF
5. United States	UNITED STATES OF AMERICA

Note: *The World Almanac and Book of Facts,* updated annually, includes facts and statistics on many foreign nations, and is helpful as a source for the English spellings of many foreign names.

Learning Check: Can you explain why it is important to have a set of standardized indexing rules?

CROSS-REFERENCING BUSINESS RECORDS

Cross-references
help locate records
called for under
alternate names.

Since cross-referencing is closely related to the classification system selected, the rules for cross-referencing are discussed in this chapter. Many individuals who do not work with the storage of records retrieve records from filing systems. These individuals may call for records under a name or classification other than the one under which the record is filed. Consequently, the records staff must prepare cross-references for the records that could be called for under another name or classification. The cross-reference can be a form entitled *cross-reference sheet.* Sometimes a photocopy is used for the cross-reference; however, photocopying is discouraged because of the resulting duplication of paper. Figure 6-1 illustrates an original document and a cross-reference sheet. The original document is filed under the most obvious name or classification, and the cross-reference sheet is filed under the alternate name or classification. On the original document, the records staff should place an *X* next to the name used to file the cross-reference sheet. If a photocopy is used as the cross-reference, it should be marked clearly as the cross-reference.

Cross-reference guides and cross-reference cards are also used. A cross-reference guide serves as a permanent cross-reference in a correspondence file. A cross-reference card refers a searcher to an original card in a card file.

The following rules cover the cross-referencing of personal names and business names.

Cross-Referencing Personal Names

Cross-references should be prepared for the following types of personal names:

1. **Unusual Names.** When determining the surname is difficult, index, as the surname, the name that appears last on the original record. Prepare a cross-reference with the name that appears first, just in case this may be the surname. Examples are Harold George and Rinji Akita.

Original Index Order	Cross-Reference
GEORGE HAROLD	HAROLD GEORGE SEE GEORGE HAROLD
AKITA RINJI	RINJI AKITA SEE AKITA RINJI

2. **Hyphenated Names.** Examples are Lydia B. Thomas-Scott and Mr. Ichiro Mitsui-Dazai.

Original Index Order	Cross-Reference
THOMASSCOTT LYDIA B	SCOTT LYDIA B THOMAS SEE THOMASSCOTT LYDIA B
MITSUIDAZAI ICHIRO MR	DAZAI ICHIRO MITSUI MR SEE MITSUIDAZAI ICHIRO MR ICHIRO MITSUIDAZAI MR SEE MITSUIDAZAI ICHIRO MR

Figure 6-1
Original Document and Cross-
Reference Sheet

```
                                    Vancouver, City of
                                    Zoning and City Planning

                                            FILE COPY

                    March 12, 19--

        Mr. Thomas Nogaki
        Sherwood, Nogaki, and Rivers
        955 Park Street
        Vancouver, BC
        V8R 4N4

        Dear Mr. Nogaki:

                    BUILDING CODE X

            I am glad to be able to report that last evening
        the City Council passed the necessary ordinance creating
        an approved building code. A copy of the new code will
        be mailed to you in a day or two.

            Immediately following the adoption of this code, I
        presented applications for the necessary permits to build
        the Conference Centre and the Pavilion, and both of these
        permits were immediately granted.

                        Very truly yours,

                        A. E. Hibbard

                        A. E. Hibbard

        ce

        pc Ms. Lee
           Mr. Gallagher
           Miss Fallon
```

```
        Records Management Manual
        Part I

                            CROSS-REFERENCE SHEET

        NAME _____ DATE March 12, 19--
        SUBJECT  Building Code
        FILE NUMBER _____

        REGARDING  Permit granted by the City Council to build the
                   Conference Centre.

                                SEE

        NAME _____ DATE _____
        SUBJECT  Vancouver, City of Zoning and City Planning
        FILE NUMBER _____

        HOW TO USE CROSS-REFERENCE SHEET
        Attach a copy of the first page of the original document being cross-
        referenced and file under NAME/SUBJECT/NUMBER shown at the top of this
        sheet. Document in its entirety will be filed under NAME/SUBJECT/NUMBER
        shown under "SEE."

        Form 18
        5-90
```

3. *Alternate Names.* Examples are Mrs. Lydia B. Scott and Mrs.
   Edward Scott; Marlene Markham-Turner and Mrs. Marlene Turner;
   Susan Fuller and Mrs. Susan Horton; Joseph Leon Thomas and Joe
   Thomas.

Original Index Order	Cross-Reference
SCOTT LYDIA B MRS	SCOTT EDWARD MRS
	SEE SCOTT LYDIA B MRS
MARKHAMTURNER MARLENE	TURNER MARLENE MRS
	SEE MARKHAMTURNER MARLENE
FULLER SUSAN	HORTON SUSAN MRS
	SEE FULLER SUSAN
THOMAS JOSEPH LEON	THOMAS JOE
	SEE THOMAS JOSEPH LEON

4. *Similar Names.* Examples are Able, et al. SEE ALSO cross-references are prepared for all possible spellings.

Cross-Reference	Cross-Reference
ABLE	ABEL
SEE ALSO ABEL ABELL ABEEL	SEE ALSO ABLE ABELL ABEEL
ABELL	ABEEL
SEE ALSO ABLE ABEL ABEEL	SEE ALSO ABLE ABEL ABELL

Cross-Referencing Business Names

Cross-references should be prepared for the following types of business names: The original name is the name appearing on the letterhead.

1. ***Compound Names.*** When a business name includes two or more individual surnames, prepare a cross-reference for each surname other than the first. For example, Daniel Horn & Laura Bennett Mfg. and Mayfield, Mace, and McCulloch Lawyers.

Original Index Order	Cross-Reference
DANIEL HORN AND LAURA BENNETT MFG	LAURA BENNETT AND DANIEL HORN MFG SEE DANIEL HORN AND LAURA BENNETT MFG
MAYFIELD MACE AND MCCULLOCH LAWYERS	MACE MCCULLOCH AND MAYFIELD LAWYERS SEE MAYFIELD MACE AND MCCULLOCH LAWYERS MCCULLOCH MAYFIELD AND MACE LAWYERS SEE MAYFIELD MACE AND MCCULLOCH LAWYERS

2. ***Abbreviations and Acronyms.*** Examples are IBM (International Business Machines Corp.), CAI (Canadian Airlines International Ltd.), and KFC (Kentucky Fried Chicken).

Original Index Order	Cross-Reference
IBM	INTERNATIONAL BUSINESS MACHINES CORP SEE IBM
CAI	CANADIAN AIRLINES INTERNATIONAL LTD SEE CAI
KFC	KENTUCKY FRIED CHICKEN SEE KFC

3. ***Popular and Coined Names.*** Examples are Parkland (Parkland Seafood House) and Sears (Sears Canada Inc.).

Original Index Order	Cross-Reference
PARKLAND	PARKLAND SEAFOOD HOUSE SEE PARKLAND
SEARS	SEARS CANADA INC SEE SEARS

4. ***Hyphenated Names.*** An example is Robinson-Humphrey Investments.

Original Index Order	Cross-Reference
ROBINSONHUMPHREY INVESTMENTS	HUMPHREYROBINSON INVESTMENTS SEE ROBINSONHUMPHREY INVESTMENTS

5. ***Divisions and Subsidiaries.*** Examples are Aiken Business Forms, a Subsidiary of Applied Industries, Inc.; and Allendale Distributors, a branch of Eastern Wholesale Group that gives to each branch the name of the city in which the branch is located.

Original Index Order	Cross-Reference
AIKEN BUSINESS FORMS	APPLIED INDUSTRIES INC SEE AIKEN BUSINESS FORMS
ALLENDALE DISTRIBUTORS	EASTERN WHOLESALE GROUP SEE ALLENDALE DISTRIBUTORS LANCASTER DISTRIBUTORS WATERBORO DISTRIBUTORS

6. ***Changed Names.*** An example is Allegheny Airlines to US Air.

Original Index Order	Cross-Reference
US AIR	ALLEGHENY AIRLINES SEE US AIR

7. ***Similar Names.*** An example is Northwest.

Original Index Order	Cross-Reference
NORTHWEST	NORTH WEST SEE NORTHWEST

8. ***Foreign Business Names.*** An example is L'Aluminum Beige Societe Anonyme.

Original Index Order	Cross-Reference
ALUMINUM CORPORATION OF BELGIUM THE	LALUMINUM BELGE SOCIETE ANONYME SEE ALUMINUM CORPORATION OF BELGIUM THE

9. ***Foreign Government Names.*** An example is Republica Oriental del Uruguay secretario de Educacion Publica.

Original Index Order	Cross-Reference
URUGUAY REPUBLIC OF PUBLIC EDUCATION SECRETARY OF	REPUBLICA ORIENTAL DEL URUGUAY SECRETARIO DE EDUCATION PUBLICA SEE URUGUAY REPUBLIC OF PUBLIC EDUCATION SECRETARY OF

 Learning Check: Can you give three examples of when cross-reference might be needed during the storage of records?

TYPES OF CLASSIFICATION SYSTEMS

There are four basic classification systems.

Selecting the appropriate classification system is a function common to all records programs. By definition, a **classification system** is a logical, systematic ordering of records that uses numbers, letters, or a combination of numbers and letters for records identification.

There are four basic systems for classifying records: (1) alphabetic, (2) numeric, (3) alphanumeric, and (4) chronologic. Each of these basic systems has variations; however, the principle of alphabetic, numeric, alphanumeric, or chronologic order is consistent within each system.

Alphabetic

Alphabetic classification systems are those that arrange records alphabetically by letter, word, and unit. There are three primary types of ordering within an alphabetic classification system: (1) by name, (2) by subject, and (3) by geographic location.

Ordering by Name

Records arranged in **name order** are filed according to names of people, organizations, agencies, and businesses. The name filing order is a simple alphabetic system and is the easiest system to create and use. An alpha name filing order groups records pertaining to the same individual or organization, keeping these records together. However, name ordering does not group records of related subjects together. Because alpha name files may be accessed directly, no index is required.

Name ordering does not group records with related topics.

Records filed in alpha name order are most appropriate for correspondence or case files in which the volume is small and the need for expansion is limited. In general, if records exceed 1,000 files, alpha name filing is inefficient.

Some problems associated with filing records by name are:

1. Handwritten correspondence and signatures are sometimes difficult to interpret, causing misfiles.
2. Congestion often occurs under common names. For example, in a normally distributed file arranged by name, almost half of the names will be under six letters of the alphabet—*B, C, H, M, S,* and *W.*
3. Similar or identical names may cause the person searching the files to go through numerous records to obtain the requested file or information.
4. Larger volumes of records cannot be accommodated.
5. File expansion is difficult.
6. Files are difficult to purge because the alpha system does not correspond to age of record, as compared with straight numeric systems that are in chronologic order.

Alphabetic systems have a built-in provision for general files not provided by other classification systems. In Figure 6-2, the general files are separate A, B, and C folders at the end of each section.

Ordering by Subject

Subject order is an arrangement of records by their content subjects. The subject arrangement is the most difficult to classify because different people tend to see records in different ways. One person classifying records involving leased automobiles may conclude that the subject is *Automobiles—Leased,* while another may judge *Vehicles—Leased Cars* as the primary subject. In pure subject filing, the subject topic is based on the record content. Some organizations do not follow this guideline, and the result is a topic mix of informational content (record subject), record-centred topics (for example, the name of the department originating the record), or a record characteristic (for example, press releases). One method of minimizing this problem is to establish a subject files manual (or incorporate this information into the organization's records management manual) to control general correspon-

Subject arrangement is the most difficult.

An index is imperative with a subject filing system.

dence filing. A subject files manual includes a written reference list, or relative index, of subjects within the files. The index is alphabetically arranged and serves as a control list for classifying records. A portion of a subject files relative index is shown in Table 6-1.

Figure 6-2
Alpha Name
Arrangement

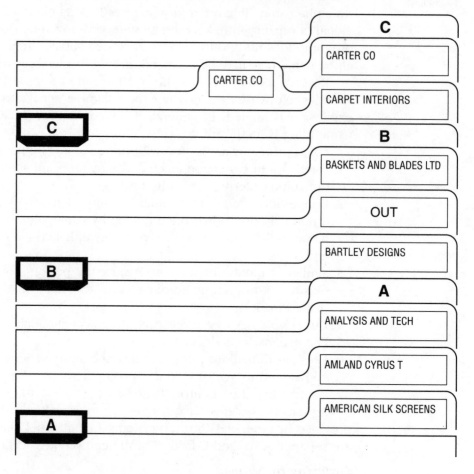

Table 6-1

RELATIVE INDEX TO SUBJECT FILES

Subject		Filed Under
	A	
Account Balances		ACCOUNTING
Activities—Employees		HUMAN RESOURCES
Administrative issuances		ADMINISTRATION
	B	
Benefits Administration		EMPLOYEE BENEFITS
Brokers and Agents		INSURANCE
	C	
Claims and Loss		INSURANCE
Compensation		HUMAN RESOURCES
Corporate Law		LEGAL

Dictionary order is
referred to as
topical order.

Subject files may be arranged in **dictionary order** in which records are in alphabetic order by subject with no real attempt made to file related subjects together. Dictionary order is often referred to as topical order.

Encyclopedic order
groups related
subjects.

Subject files may also be arranged in **encyclopedic order**—filed by subject alphabetically. However, unlike dictionary order, the subjects are grouped as they would be arranged in an encyclopedia—by major subject areas with subgroupings. The major subject areas should be broad and of relatively equal importance, sometimes a difficult task. Encyclopedic order moves from the general to the particular.

A comparison of dictionary and encyclopedic orders shown in Table 6-2 illustrates the difference in handling the same subjects in two subject ordering systems.

Filing arrangements of dictionary and encyclopedic orders are shown in Figure 6-3.

Though encyclopedic order is better suited for larger volumes of records than is dictionary order, it is still limited to small numbers of records that can be processed efficiently, with the exception of functional order, which is noted below. Subject ordering is dependent on an alphabetic relative index that is both logical and comprehensive. The use of a relative index assures consistency when more than one person handles the records.

Subject filing is
suitable for
individual executive
files.

Subject filing is particularly suitable for manager or executive individual files. These files, which are based on the records of a particular manager or department, are largely personalized. Subject files save time for executives requiring immediate reference to all information on a particular topic prior to making a decision. Flexibility and expansion are provided by adding subdivisions to a main file. However, unless extreme care is taken, subdivisions may grow until the system becomes inefficient.

Table 6-2

EXAMPLES OF DICTIONARY AND ENCYCLOPEDIC ORDER

Dictionary Order	Encyclopedic Order
Bids and Quotes	ADMINISTRATION
Employee Activities	Office Services
Grievance Procedures	Security
Housing Assistance	Visitors
Office Services	EMPLOYEES RELATIONS
Purchase Orders	Employee Activities
Security	Grievance Procedures
Specifications	Housing Assistance
Visitors	PURCHASING
	Bids and Quotes
	Purchase Orders
	Specifications

Figure 6-3
A Comparison of
Dictionary Order
and Encyclopedic
Order

Dictionary Order   Encyclopedic Order

Selection of subject topic is time consuming because each document must be read prior to coding; and topic selection, as mentioned earlier, is sometimes difficult. In theory, subject files should not require the use of general folders because every record has a subject. In application, however, general folders may be used at the end of each primary or secondary topic to collect generally related items. General folders may be used when there is not enough correspondence or subjects to justify individual folders.

Coding of subject records and preparation of folder labels are made more efficient through the use of subject codes. Subject codes consist of numbers, letters, or a combination of numbers and letters used in designating and arranging subject headings for storage and retrieval. The subject codes must be placed on the folder labels, the storage equipment labels, and the records.

There are many coding systems that may be used with subject files. The most often used methods are alphabetic, alphanumeric, and decimal-numeric. Using the alphabetic coding system, the records may be coded two ways. The code may contain an entire subject heading, or the code may include an abbreviation created using the primary subject heading. The primary subject heading ACCOUNTS RECEIVABLE would be coded

ACCOUNTS RECEIVABLE or ACCREC

The alphanumeric coding system combines letters and numbers. The decimal-numeric code consists of the number of the first subdivision followed by a decimal and one or more digits. Examples of the alphanumeric and decimal-numeric coding system are shown in Table 6-3.

Ordering by Function

Students interested in records management employment and staff already employed in federal or provincial records management positions should be knowledgeable about their government's records system. Initiated by the federal government and adopted with appropriate changes by many provincial governments for their records, ordering by function has developed into a powerful system for large volumes of records. It is known as the **block numeric system** because a block of numbers is assigned to each of the major functions of government. The two main groups of functions are identified as administrative (housekeeping) functions common to most government departments and agencies and operational functions specific to a particular department or agency. This division of activities makes it possible to prepare guidelines for all administrative records that will apply to every department, while allowing for unique activities to be included within each department's system.

Table 6-3

EXAMPLES OF ALPHANUMERIC AND DECIMAL-NUMERIC CODING SYSTEMS

Alphanumeric	Decimal-numeric
PRSNL PERSONNEL DEPARTMENT	600 PERSONNEL DEPARTMENT
PRSNL-01 BENEFITS	601 BENEFITS
PRSNL-01-01 ANNUITIES	601.1 ANNUITIES
PRSNL-01-02 DENTAL INSURANCE	601.2 INSURANCE
PRSNL-01-03 HEALTH INSURANCE	601.2.1 DENTAL
PRSNL-01-04 LIFE INSURANCE	601.2.2 HEALTH
	601.2.3 LIFE
PRSNL-02 OFFICE EQUIPMENT	602 OFFICE EQUIPMENT
PRSNL-02-01 CALCULATORS	602.1 CALCULATORS
PRSNL-02-02 COMPUTERS	602.2 COMPUTERS
PRSNL-02-03 TELEPHONES	602.3 TELEPHONES
PRSNL-02-04 TYPEWRITERS	602.4 TYPEWRITERS
PRSNL-03 TRAINING	603 TRAINING
PRSNL-03-01 CONSULTANTS	603.1 CONSULTANTS
PRSNL-03-02 INHOUSE PROGRAMS	603.2 INHOUSE PROGRAMS
PRSNL-03-03 ORIENTATION	603.3 ORIENTATION

The steps in setting up a block numeric system for both administrative and operational records are:

1. Identify the broad main functions.
2. Assign titles and number blocks to each main group. These are the primary subjects and primary numbers in the system.
3. Provide a short description, with an example, of what is included in each of the primary groups. These descriptions are also known as *scope notes.*
4. Break down primary subject areas into secondary subjects with their corresponding numbers. These represent specific files.
5. If necessary, secondary subjects and numbers may be subdivided again into tertiary subjects and numbers, although the third level is not usually needed.

As an example of how the block numeric system works, Table 6-4 shows the federal government's primary groups with their descriptions and the number blocks (100 to 1399) assigned to administrative records.

Table 6-4   **ADMINISTRATIVE—HOUSEKEEPING—RECORDS OF THE FEDERAL GOVERNMENT**

SECTION	TITLE	DESCRIPTION	NUMBER RANGE
1	ADMINISTRATION	Covers a wide variety of subjects relating to administrative and managerial services, acts and legislation, associations, committees, conferences, meetings, etc.	100–499
2	BUILDINGS AND PROPERTIES	Involves acquisition of accommodation through purchase or rental of existing buildings and land, or through construction of new buildings; includes fire prevention, utilities, etc.	500–699
3	EQUIPMENT AND SUPPLIES	Covers functions of procurement, storage, and warehousing, issuing, maintaining, and repairing, and disposal or write-off of obsolete or surplus materials.	700–849
4	FINANCE	Covers the receipt, control, and expenditures of public funds, including accounts and accounting, allotments, audits, claims, and other fiscal details.	850–999
5	PERSONNEL	Covers subjects relating to the employment of members of the Public Service of Canada including attendance, establishment, leave, holidays, salaries and wages, promotions, training of staff, etc.	1000–1399

Source: Subject Classification Guide, Records Management Series, Public Archives Canada, 1980.

Operational records are covered by the numbers 2000 to 9999, leaving sufficient gaps in the numbering system to allow for expansion where needed. Since operational functions are specific to each department, those setting up this system must analyze the records, talk to the users, and inventory the records to learn about the department's needs.

The main advantage of the block numeric system is that it covers all government records, both general administrative and unique departmental records. Flexibility allows the system to be easily expanded or contracted; and there is consistency throughout the government in the way records are handled. An extensive alphabetic index including cross-references must be available to all users. A numeric index listing all file numbers in use is also needed.

Ordering by Geographic Location

Geographic order is an arrangement of records in alphabetic order by place or location. Locations may be grouped in various arrangements, as is shown in Table 6-5.

Geographic files are particularly appropriate for sales records filed by district; real estate property information filed by address; customer files for specific types of similar institutions or businesses, such as banks, schools, churches; market surveys; branch offices; or other kinds of information that may be referenced according to geographic location.

Table 6-5

EXAMPLES OF LOCATION GROUPINGS FOR GEOGRAPHIC ORDER

Location	Example
<u>County or Province</u>	
Province, City	Alberta, Medicine Hat
Company or	Addison-Daniel Manufacturing
Person	Dan Dorchester, Treasurer
<u>Region or District</u>	
Region	Western Division
City	Edmonton
Company or Person	RV Dealers
<u>City</u>	
City	Victoria
Company or Person	McAfee Bagpipes
<u>Street</u>	
Individual Address	Duquesne Avenue, 106

Figure 6-4 shows a portion of a geographic file arrangement.

Figure 6-4
Geographic
Arrangement

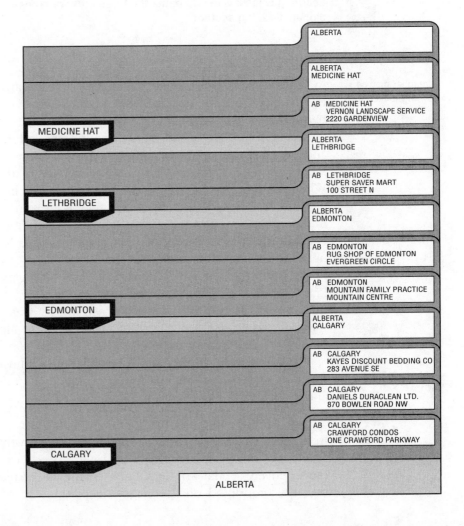

An alphabetic index
is essential to
geographic filing.

An alphabetic index is essential to geographic filing. Reference is commonly made to an individual name or a company name rather than to place or location. The alphabetic file includes the name of the person or organization and the complete address for that correspondent. When an address is unknown or misplaced, the alphabetic index provides a quick reference.

Geographic filing systems have certain advantages. A visual estimate of the file activity within any geographic area can be made quickly. Files may be added, deleted, or rearranged easily. However, more time is required to establish and use a geographic file because two files must be established—the geographic file and the alphabetic file. Also, two locations may have to be referenced when locating an individual file. Misfiles may occur because many cities having the same names are located in several provinces; sometimes there are several locations with the same name within a province.

 Learning Check: Can you name the three primary types of ordering in an alphabetic filing system?

Numeric

A number may be
part of the record.

In a **numeric classification system** records are arranged in order by number. Numeric file numbers may originate in several ways: the number may be a part of the record itself, as in invoices, cheques, or social insurance numbers; or the number may be added to make processing and retrieval easier. When numbers are a part of the original document, reference will generally be made to the document number. When the number has been added to the record internally, reference will usually be made to subject or name. For example, a cheque has a number that is part of the record (cheque) itself, and when an inquiry is made regarding the cheque, that inquiry is usually made by cheque number. On the other hand, if a number is assigned within the organization to a case history, a person outside the organization would not know the assigned case number, and the inquiry would be made by the name of the individual whose case history was being referenced. Internally, then, reference would be made to an alphabetic index to obtain the case history number.

A number may be
assigned to the
record.

There are two primary types of ordering within the numeric classification system: (1) serial (consecutive) and (2) duplex (numbers separated into parts).

Serial

In a **serial order** records are arranged consecutively, such as 1, 2, 3, 4, and so forth. Numbers may begin with 01, 10, or 100 and increase consecutively. Serial arrangement is particularly suitable when numbers are preprinted on the original record, such as the numbers on purchase orders, tickets, or cheques. When the organization has control over issuance of numbers, a simple sequential numbering system can be developed. Missing numbers within a file allow for quick identification of lost or misfiled documents. Because a serially numbered file is also chronologic (last number issued is most current), files can be purged in large blocks.

Expansion of serial files is relatively simple; additional numbers are added at the end of the file. The ease of adding files, however, creates congestion of new files in one area and slows retrieval if more than one person accesses the file at the same time. Serial order is recommended for files with volumes of 1,000 to 10,000 records. Figure 6-5 shows a serial number file arrangement.

Figure 6-5
Serial Number
Arrangement

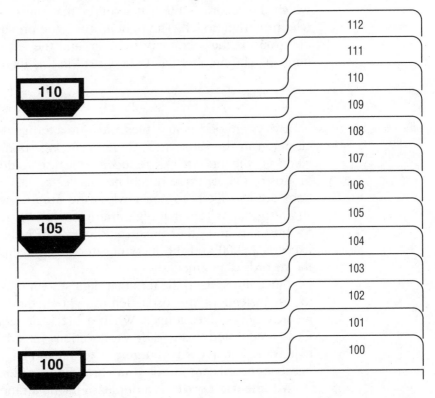

Duplex

Duplex order
provides more
even distribution of
files than serial
order.

The **duplex order** uses duplex numbers consisting of two or more parts, separated by a dash, space, or comma. Because files are arranged by different parts of the number, new files are evenly distributed throughout the file series. A duplex arrangement is advantageous when large numbers of records—generally more than 10,000 records—are to be filed. Two variations of the duplex-numeric system include terminal- and middle-digit.

In terminal- and middle-digit filing, a number is divided into three groups. Zeros are added to the left of the number to create three groups; for example, 76214 becomes 07 62 14. The parts or groups of numbers comprising the duplex number are referred to as the primary (first), secondary, and tertiary (final) numbers. The primary number is the guide to the file section, drawer, or shelf; the secondary number indicates the guide location within the file system; and the tertiary number indicates the order in which the file is located behind the secondary guide. Because you are working with groups of numbers rather than one long number, there is less chance of misfiling.

Terminal-digit order is a duplex-numeric arrangement in which the last two or three digits of each number are the primary digits under which the record is filed. It requires that the groups of numbers be read from right to left. The right group is the primary number, the middle group is the secondary number, and the left group is the tertiary number. The number 04 10 25 is read in this manner:

04	10	25
Tertiary	Secondary	Primary
(Folder Number)	(Guide Number)	(File Section, Drawer, or Shelf Number)

Terminal-digit order is appropriate for records in excess of 10,000.

By system design new files added to a terminal-digit system are not clustered in the same area; therefore, congestion of users or records clerks in the file area is reduced. Because folders are divided into groups of two or three numbers, misfiles are also reduced; transpositions are less likely to occur when the number is broken down into shorter groups. Terminal-digit arrangement is particularly appropriate for hospitals and other organizations in which the volume of records exceeds 10,000 and the incoming records are rapidly turned over to the records department.

Since numbers in the terminal-digit system must be read from right to left instead of the usual left-to-right method, training users and records clerks takes longer. When a block of sequentially numbered files is requested, many different locations must be accessed in order to retrieve the records. Purging a terminal-digit system takes longer because records are not filed in chronologic order.

Middle-digit order is a duplex-numeric arrangement in which the middle two or three digits of each number are the primary digits under which the record is filed. The middle numbers are the primary digits under which the record is filed. The number 04 10 25 is read in this manner:

04	10	25
Secondary	Primary	Tertiary
(Guide Number)	(File Section, Drawer, or Shelf Number)	(Folder Number)

Middle-digit order distributes records in blocks of 100.

Middle-digit arrangement distributes records through the files in blocks of 100; records consecutively numbered 702500–702599 would be in the same sequence. Therefore, a user or records clerk must look in only ten places for 1,000 consecutively numbered records in order to purge the files. **Block integrity**—all records related to one subject being filed together—is maintained with the middle-digit arrangement. For example, a real estate agency may file all records relating to one tract of properties together, or an insurance company may retain all active policies written by one sales representative in one block. However, training people to read the numbers in a middle-digit arrangement requires additional training time before a high level of proficiency is reached.

A comparison of serial, middle-digit, and terminal-digit file arrangements is shown in Table 6-6.

Table 6-6

COMPARISON OF SERIAL, MIDDLE-DIGIT AND TERMINAL-DIGIT ARRANGEMENTS

If you were filing vouchers numbered			16207 16204 16206 16205 16208

	In a Serial Number System	In a Middle-Digit System	In a Terminal-Digit System
Drawer/shelf	16200-16299	62 62 62 62 62	04 05 06 07 08
Guide		01 01 01 01 01	62 62 62 62 62
Folder	16204-8	04 05 06 07 08	01 01 01 01 01

There are advantages and disadvantages with each of the three previously described numeric systems—serial, middle-digit, and terminal-digit. These factors should be considered when making a selection of the most appropriate system for your particular needs. The filing tasks for each of the three numeric systems are compared in Table 6-7.

Table 6-7

TASK COMPARISONS FOR SERIAL, MIDDLE-DIGIT, AND TERMINAL-DIGIT ORDERING

Filing Task	Serial	Middle-Digit	Terminal-Digit
Sorting	Slow	Fast	Fast
Work Distribution	Difficult to divide work evenly	Easy to divide work evenly	Easy to divide work evenly
File guide preparation	Constantly updated	Guides prepared once	Guides prepared once
Records transfer and destruction	Easy	Easy	Difficult
Pulling 100 consecutively numbered records	Easy	Easy	Difficult
Placing new records in the file	All placed at open end of file	Last 100 records evenly distributed	All evenly distributed

Learning Check: Can you explain the difference between consecutive and duplex numbering systems?

Numeric filing arrangements are indirect access systems.

Each numeric system has standard components that must be in place for efficient use of numeric ordering. Numeric arrangements are indirect access systems—the person accessing the files must first consult an alphabetic index to determine the code number for the record, correspondent, or subject. This is in contrast to an alphabetic system, which is a direct access system. The person accessing the alphabetic file goes directly to the file without first having to consult an index to determine the location of the file.

An accession log is used to list the numbers assigned.

Numeric files require (1) an accession log, (2) an alphabetic index, (3) a general alphabetic file, and (4) a numbered file. The **accession log** is a serial listing of numbers assigned to correspondents and subjects, and numbers available for assignment. When a record is accessed, reference is not made to the accession log to obtain the number; the accession log simply provides information regarding previously assigned numbers and numbers available for assignment to new records. The accession log lists only the name assigned to a particular number. All other pertinent information may be obtained from the alphabetic index. Therefore, to obtain the number assigned to Super Charger Engines, first look in the alphabetic index and then go to the numeric file to pull the record. A partial page from an accession log and a sample alphabetic index are shown in Figures 6-6 and 6-7.

Figure 6-6
Accession Log

		Page 105
Number	Name	Date
2000	Super Charger Engines	8/16/--
2001	Marine World	8/16/--
2002	Recreational Vehicles, Inc.	8/17/--
2003	Thomas Martin	8/17/--
2004	Jerome Cozens	8/17/--

Figure 6-7
Alphabetic Index

NAME	NUMBER	DATE
COZENS JEROME	2004	8/17/95
MARINE WORLD	2001	8/16/95
MARTIN THOMAS	2003	8/17/95
RECREATIONAL VEHICLES, INC.	2002	8/17/95
SUPER CHARGER ENGINES	2000	8/16/95

In a numeric filing system a general alphabetic file must be maintained for correspondents and subjects not active enough to warrant a separately numbered folder. Usually when documents for a particular correspondent or subject exceed five, these materials are removed from the general (G) file, assigned a number, and placed in an individual folder. If fewer than five records were filed under the name of Jerome Cozens, the alphabetic index would have a G instead of the 2004 file number.

In a numeric filing system, cross-referencing is done in the alphabetic index.

Cross-references are prepared for most filing systems—alphabetic, subject, or any other system in which a relative index is not maintained. Cross-references are maintained in the correspondence files when using an alphabetic system. When a numeric system is used, the cross-references are placed in the alphabetic index. The cross-references merely note other places where information might be located. For example, if Jerome Cozens were president of Recreational Vehicles, Ltd., the cross-reference would note "See also Recreational Vehicles, Ltd." Cross-referencing makes finding records easier when reference might be made to a record in more than one way.

> ✓ **Learning Check: Can you name the four components of a numeric filing system?**

Alphanumeric

Alphanumeric classification systems are arrangements of records based on a combination of alphabetic and numeric characters. These alpha codes should provide some information about the contents of the file.

Subject names and numbers arrangements are the most often used alphanumeric classification system. Subject alphanumeric follows an encyclopedic arrangement; related materials are filed under major headings and subheadings. Subject titles are assigned numbers that indicate major divisions and subdivisions. For example, a file on OFFICE EQUIPMENT, a major division, might include headings of *Computers, Facsimile Machines, Photocopiers, Telephone System*. Each major heading would be assigned a number indicating that it is a major division. Each major division may be divided into subdivisions *(Computers, Facsimile Machines, Photocopiers, Telephone System)* and assigned numbers that indicate these are subdivisions of a major division (OFFICE EQUIPMENT). A subject-numeric system is most appropriate for volumes of 1,000 to 5,000 files.

Chronologic

Chronologic classification systems are arranged in date order.

A **chronologic classification system** is an arrangement in which records are filed in sequence by date. Records are filed in chronologic sequence by day (date) of the month. Chronologic arrangements have three accepted applications: (1) for suspense files, (2) for transaction files, and (3) within individual files. Suspense files are often referred to as pending, or tickler, files. The term *tickler* is used because reference to the file tickles your memory, and you are reminded to take certain action. As information that requires future action is received, the record (or a copy) is filed in the folder that corresponds to the date action should be taken. Such material should never be filed in an individual file until action is completed. Similarly, interoffice records that require a response should not be filed in individual files until the response has been received. Placing these records in a suspense file eliminates the need for a "pending list." Each morning the suspense file is checked for possible required action. If action is required, the record is removed from the suspense file, and appropriate action is taken before releasing the record for filing.

Transaction files organize records by date of the transaction. This type of file is most appropriate for documenting transactions that occur on a day-to-day basis. Transaction documents may include purchase and sales records, personnel records, shipping records, and so forth.

Chronologic files requested by name require a physical search.

A chronologic arrangement does not use an index; therefore, if a record is requested by name, a physical search of the file is required. If frequent reference is made by information other than date, other file systems should be considered.

Within all files, records should be arranged in reverse chronologic order—that is, the most recent (last) record in the front of the folder and the first record at the back of the folder. Records are arranged in the order of their occurrence, with the most recent transaction being the first record the user sees.

Surveys have shown that alphabetic by name, straight numeric, and subject classification systems are the most commonly used classification systems. Geographic and subject-numeric systems are also used frequently. Because most organizations have a variety of types of records that are referenced in different ways, many organizations use more than one classification system.

UNIFORM CLASSIFICATION SYSTEM

A Uniform Classification System improves communication.

Communication cannot flow easily between individuals when inconsistent and nonstandard vocabulary is used in the records of an organization. A **Uniform Classification System (UCS)** is a standard classification system used throughout an organization. It is an attempt to bridge this communication gap through the use of standardized business vocabulary in records classification. Companies that are geographically separated, multilingual, or experience heavy staff turnover suffer particular difficulties when exchanging records and information. A UCS is a way to minimize these difficulties through a consistent and standardized subject classification system that is communicated and used throughout the organization.

In their efforts to implement a UCS, many organizations have developed comprehensive manuals, complete subject indexes, and comprehensive relative indexes. In addition, preprinted folder labels are furnished and used in all departments and units throughout the company. A partial subject-numeric index is shown in Figure 6-8, along with a preprinted folder label corresponding to one of the categories in the index.

Figure 6-8
Subject-Numeric
Index

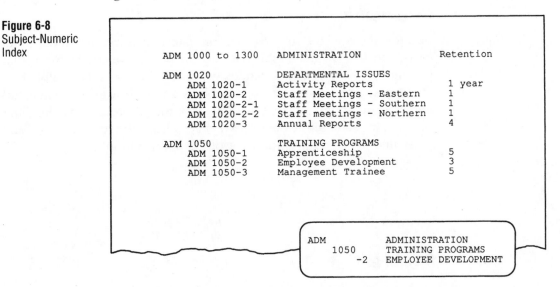

ADM 1000 to 1300	ADMINISTRATION		Retention
ADM 1020	DEPARTMENTAL ISSUES		
ADM 1020-1	Activity Reports	1 year
ADM 1020-2	Staff Meetings - Eastern	1
ADM 1020-2-1	Staff Meetings - Southern	1
ADM 1020-2-2	Staff meetings - Northern	1
ADM 1020-3	Annual Reports	4
ADM 1050	TRAINING PROGRAMS		
ADM 1050-1	Apprenticeship	5
ADM 1050-2	Employee Development	3
ADM 1050-3	Management Trainee	5

```
ADM            ADMINISTRATION
     1050      TRAINING PROGRAMS
       -2      EMPLOYEE DEVELOPMENT
```

 Learning Check: Can you explain the importance of a Uniform Classification System?

FOLDER LABELS

Folder label captions are in capital letters. When labels are generated using a computer, they can be easily set up in a consistent fashion. Examples of alphabetic, subject, geographic, and numeric label captions follow.

Alphabetic

The alphabetic letter(s) behind which a folder is filed is (are) keyed two spaces from the left edge of the label. The name is keyed five spaces to the right of the letter(s).

```
A              ABBOTT PAUL JR
M              MANCHESTER BELINDA
MC             MCCAULEY NEAL R
```

Subject

The subject code is keyed two spaces from the left edge of the label. Key any additional information five spaces to the right of the code or of the abbreviation.

ADM	ADMINISTRATION
	CONTRACTS

Geographic

Because the spelled-out province or state names require more label space, the two-letter abbreviations are recommended. Note that province, territory, or state names will not be in spelled-out alphabetic order when using the two-letter abbreviations; however, storage and retrieval are more efficient with use of the abbreviations. Key the province or state abbreviation two spaces from the left edge; key the city name five spaces to the right of the abbreviation.

BC	VANCOUVER
	BC HYDRO
GA	ATLANTA
	BANK OF ATLANTA
YT	YUKON TERRITORY
	GOLD RUSH DAYS

Numeric

Numeric captions begin two spaces from the left edge of the label.

1993
1994
1995
123-95-456
123-95-457
123-95-458

CRITERIA FOR CLASSIFICATION SYSTEM SELECTION

As defined earlier, a classification system is a logical, systematic ordering of records. The basic records groups within the system and the manner in which individual records are most frequently referenced must be determined in order to establish the most appropriate records classification system for the organization.

Determine Basic File Groups

There are nine basic file groups.

A **file group** consists of a collection of records with similar characteristics that should be separated from other groups of records in the office. There are nine basic types of file groups: general correspondence; transitory correspondence; case records; case working papers; technical reference materials; convenience copies (nonrecords); film, tape, or disk records; cartographic materials and drawings; and cards.

General Correspondence

The general correspondence file consists of letters, memorandums, enclosures, reports, and miscellaneous materials usually kept longer than six months. Such records are usually arranged by subject.

Transitory Correspondence

The transitory correspondence file consists of routine materials and may be authorized for disposal within a six-month period or less. If these records account for 5 percent or more of the correspondence, they should be kept in separate folders for ease of disposition. If fewer than 100 papers a month are involved, they may be kept in a single folder in chronologic order; if the volume is much larger, subject filing may be required to facilitate reference.

Case Records

Case record files consist of records such as purchase orders, invoices, contracts, investigations, requisitions, loans, research projects, construction projects, and personnel records. The case record file group contains material relating to a specific action, event, person, organization, location, product, or thing. Typically, a case record handles a transaction or relationship from its beginning to end. Case records are always filed by name or number or a combination as in alphanumeric systems.

Case Working Papers

In order to reduce the size of the case records file, case working papers should be differentiated from case records. Case working papers have short-term use and comprise the background, preliminary papers, drafts, and routine reminders, requests, or correspondence regarding a particular case file. Working papers should be kept in a separate folder from the case records so that later screening for disposal can be avoided. Generally, these two folders (distinguished from one another by labelling) are retained together while the case file is active.

It is important to distinguish between case working papers and transitory correspondence. Working papers are related to case records; transitory correspondence is related to general correspondence. Intermixing case working papers and transitory correspondence complicates disposal. Transitory correspondence is normally disposed of within six months after creation or receipt; case working papers are generally disposed of after a specified time following the conclusion of the transaction or working relationship.

Technical Reference Materials

Technical reference materials include printed reports, periodicals, research studies, and internal instruction and information manuals. As a general rule, when more than one file drawer of the general file contains reference materials, separate filing should be arranged.

Convenience Copies

Maintaining extra copies results in cluttered, inefficient files. These copies should never be filed unless some action needs to be documented. If extra copies are retained for the convenience of users, the copies should be kept in separate folders identified by the name of the originating office. Copies should not be interfiled with general correspondence or case records.

Many organizations keep a day file of letters or memos originating from an office; papers are arranged in date order. This convenience file is circulated to allow others within the organization to be informed.

Tape, Film, Disk, and Microrecords

These records are easily identifiable, unlike some other records groups. Tape, film, disk, or microrecords may require special handling and storage. When sound recordings are converted to paper records, the recording may be discarded or reused.

Cartographic Materials and Drawings

This file group contains maps (including field survey notes, geodetic surveys, and astronomic readings, as well as what are traditionally called maps); charts (including graphic presentations and nautical, weather, and aeronautical charts); and engineering drawings (including blueprints, diazo prints, pencil sketches, and tracings). Many materials may be reduced to a standard 8 1/2-by-11-inch size and filed with related information. If more than 10 percent of this category of materials is oversized, separate filing is warranted.

Cards

Cards have a physical size and format that logically separates them from other file groups. Cards include common sizes used as indexes, catalogues, or summaries; punched cards; and aperture cards.

Separating records into basic types facilitates referencing by reducing the search area. Separation also keeps essential documents apart from short-term papers, allowing more efficient disposition. Different retention periods are accommodated more easily when record groups are established.

The quantity of records involved affects the file grouping. If less than a file drawer of case records or technical reference materials is involved, little advantage is gained by separating them from general correspondence.

Determine Requested Filing Segment

Before choosing a classification system, determine filing segments.

Once the basic file groups within the organization have been identified (most often accomplished during the records inventory), a system must be selected for arranging the records for each separate file group. Records series are also identified during the records inventory. Records series indicate groups of records related by content; file groups indicate categories of records by function.

To select an appropriate classification system, first determine how the users will most often request that particular record—which *filing segment* will most likely be used.

When a user requests correspondence, the request is made by one of the following filing segments:
1. Surname of individual or organization name.
2. Name (title) of project, product, transaction, or thing—for example, the name of a project (text revision); name of product (IBM computer); transaction (blouse returned for credit); or thing (poster).
3. Location (geographic or political division—county, province, parish, and so forth).
4. Number (symbol) assigned to transaction, commodity, location, project, individual, or organization unit.
5. Date prepared or used.
6. Subject/topic describing the content.

Forms are usually requested by:
1. Title of form (subject),
2. Surname of individual or organization name,
3. Number (symbol assigned for transaction control or other identification), or
4. Date.

Because forms are often used in case files, they are usually filed by name or number. See Chapter 14, "Forms and Reports Management," for more information about forms and reports.

Reports may be requested by:
1. Title of report (subject),
2. Subjects in addition to the main subject,
3. Surname of author,
4. Name of originating organization,
5. Number of project or contract with which identified,
6. Number assigned for control, or
7. Date of issuance.

Some file systems place recurring or periodic reports under a reports category subarranged by report title or form title (if the report is a form).

The primary task, then, is to identify which filing segment will be requested most frequently by users. Are the users more likely to request information by name, by assigned number, or by other identifying elements?

Determine Additional User Requirements

Unique user needs must be considered.

In addition to determining the file groups within the organizational records and the filing segments most often used, consideration must be given to any additional user needs. These requirements vary from organization to organization or from department to department; therefore, any unique needs that were not previously considered must be identified. For example, the need of records users for complete information should not be overlooked. If photographs and correspondence are separated, either both files are searched when records are requested, or the office runs the risk of the user taking action without having complete information. Usually the physical characteristics of papers, such as the size of engineering drawings, require materials that might preferably be filed as a unit to be filed separately.

Should the files be continuous or should they be separated into individual file groups? A guide to systems for arranging files is shown in Figure 6-9. This guide summarizes operating considerations under each of the filing segments of records. It is important that the classification system(s) that best fit(s) the needs of the users be selected and implemented. An efficient records system with logical filing arrangements allowing for fast retrieval will provide the user with the requested information to be used in the decision-making process.

Conversion from Manual to Electronic Systems

Computers provide huge opportunities to increase the efficiency of alphabetic filing systems, especially with indexing and cross-referencing. However, those involved in the changeover must understand how the alphabetic system is designed and what changes are needed in the sorting capability. Section III of the *ARMA International Standard for Records and Information Management Alphabetic Filing Rules* contains excellent guidelines for automating alphabetic systems.[1]

---

[1]ARMA *International Standard for Records and Information Management Alphabetic Filing Rules* (Prairie Village, Kansas: Association of Records Managers and Administrators, Inc., 1986), p. 21.

Figure 6-9   Guide to Classification Systems

Filing feature of record	Usual filing sequence	Most suitable file groups	Need for index file (by second filing feature)	Need for cross-referencing a record within the file	Likelihood that record description used in request will pinpoint file location	Likelihood of file designation being shown on record when originated	Likelihood of file designation being expressed the same on records to be filed together	Ease and accuracy in marking a record for filing	Ease and accuracy in sorting and filing
Names of people, organizations, or firms.	Alphabetic by name.	Case. Case working papers. Technical reference.	Normally not needed except for precedent cases.	If more than one name involved.	Usually. Foreign, organization, and unusual names may be troublesome. The larger the file, the greater the problem.	Nearly always.	Usually, except for misspellings. Exchanging personal and organization names causes inconsistency.	Fast and easy, if names can be underlined. Fairly slow if names must be written. Spelling errors may occur in unfamiliar names. Adherence to filing rules required.	Slow and difficult. Eye must scan each letter of each word to determine sequence; words and titles vary widely in length. The larger the file, the greater the problem, and the greater the need for rigid adherence to filing rules.
Names or titles of projects, publications, products, or things.	Alphabetic by name.	Case. Case working papers. Technical reference.	Normally not needed, except for precedent cases.	If more than one name or title involved.	Sometimes. Project titles may be troublesome. The longer the name or title, the less chance of agreement. The larger the file, the greater the problem.	Usually.	Usually. Difficulties may occur with project and other long titles.	Fairly slow. Key words to be underlined may be buried in long titles. Incomplete titles may have to be completed by handwriting. Adherence to filing rules required.	Slow and difficult. Eye must scan each letter of each word to determine sequence; words and titles vary widely in length. The larger the file, the greater the problem, and the greater the need for rigid adherence to filing rules.
Geographic areas or locations.	Alphabetic by name (often subarranged by people, things, etc.)	Case. Case working papers. Technical reference.	Frequently needed as location is not always known.	If more than one area or location involved.	Sometimes. Record may be requested by city but filed by province, or may be requested by people, organizations, or things without the location given. The larger the file, the greater the problem.	Usually. Location is shown, but not subarrangement file designation.	Depends on consistent choice of locational level for each record.	Fast, if location can be underlined. Subarrangements often require handwritten designations.	Fairly difficult, depending on number of breakdowns and subarrangements. Precise filing required. The larger the file, the greater the problem.
Numbers or symbols.	By number or symbol.	Case. Case working papers. Technical reference.	Name index needed to obtain number or symbol, not known or incorrectly shown.	If more than one number or symbol involved.	Depends upon widespread use of the numbers or symbols within the office and extent of use on records from the outside.	Nearly always—but sometimes omitted.	Nearly always.	Fast, if numbers or symbols are short or segmented. Numbers or symbols susceptible to transportation and other errors.	Easy, if numbers or symbols are short or segmented. Transposition and other errors likely.
Dates.	By date prepared or used.	Convenience. Transitory. Suspense.	Not needed unless large volume filed only by date.	Not needed.	Usually for suspense. For convenience or transitory files, exact date often not known.	Always.	Always.	Fast and accurate. Marking rarely needed.	Easy and accurate.
Subject topics.	Alphabetic by subject topic; or by numeric or alpha-numeric file code.	General correspondence (may include cases subarranged by names or numbers). Technical reference.	Occasionally an index by names of people, firms, and organizations needed.	If more than one subject involved, or record is brought forward.	Unlikely. Request may be vague, and differing terms may be used to describe same record. Relative index may be needed to determine proper subject topic.	Unlikely, since subject, if shown, rarely matches subject topics of receiving organization.	Unlikely.	Slow, as content must be read. Use of file code speeds writing, but may require reference to subject outline or relative index. Faulty decisions and errors in writing may occur.	Difficult, if alphabetically filed by word topics. Easier if filed by short file codes. The more complex the code the more difficult the accuracy.

Source: Adapted from Files Operations: Managing Current Records. General Services Administration, National Archives and Records Service, Office of Federal Records Centers, 1981.

TERMINOLOGY REVIEW

Review the terms listed below in the Glossary on page 521.

accession log
alphabetic classification system
alphanumeric classification
   system
block integrity
block numeric system
chronologic classification system
classification system
dictionary order
duplex order
encyclopedic order
file group

filing segment
filing unit
geographic order
indexing
middle-digit order
name order
numeric classification system
serial order
subject order
terminal-digit order
Uniform Classification System (UCS)

REVIEW AND DISCUSSION

1. Explain the importance of having standardized indexing rules.
2. List three situations in which a cross-reference might be used.
3. Define alphabetic classification system and identify the three common types of ordering used in an alphabetic classification system.
4. Define numeric classification system and identify the two major types of ordering used in a numeric classification system.
5. Explain the differences between middle- and terminal-digit arrangements.
6. Define alphanumeric classification system and describe its arrangements.
7. Define chronologic classification system and list two applications of the chronologic arrangement.
8. What are the advantages of a Uniform Classification System?
9. Prior to selecting a classification system, why is it important to:
   a. Identify basic file groups?
   b. Identify filing segments?
   c. Identify additional user requirements?

APPLICATIONS

1. Given the following limited information, which of the classification systems would you recommend to the users? Justify your recommendation.
   a. Small (800) volume of client records
   b. 26,000 insurance policy files in a branch office
   c. Patient records in a large medical complex

     d. Personal files of the president of Northern University

     e. Incoming purchase orders for a grocery wholesaler

     f. Routine correspondence—transitory

     g. Home office of a large department store with branches in 21 cities

     h. Invoices for purchasing department of a parts manufacturer

     i. 1,000 active files for a law office with three lawyers

     j. Records on which future action must be taken

2. a. Index and ~~code~~ the following names and place them in the correct folders (shown below) using an alphabetic order by name:

       1. James D. DeLiso, Sr.

       2. Delio Construction Company 1/15/95

       3. Jan Delio

       4. Delio Construction Company 2/14/95

       5. Donna C. Delsey 2/26/95

       6. James D. DeLiso, Jr.

       7. Daniel Davidson, MD

       8. Deleo's Deli

       9. Danielle Evans

      10. Water Dept. of Kent County, New Brunswick

      11. Donna C. Delsey 3/3/95

      12. Donna C. Delsey 4/7/95

      13. Rodger Dempsey

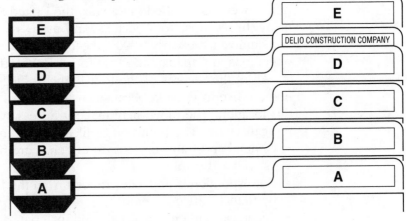

     b. Place the names below in dictionary order; then place the names in encyclopedic order.

Rusty Tub	Hairdynamics
Bathroom Boutique	Hairstyles Unlimited
Aspen Tile Company	John's Barber Shop
Mosaic Tiles	Johnson Hairworks
The Bathtub Ltd.	The Lion's Mane

c. Place the following numbers in correct order using terminal-digit, middle-digit, and serial arrangements:

27114, 27410, 27001, 16754, 27119, 27117, 17456, 27118, 21327, 27115, 26000, 27110, 29175

d. Place the following records in chronologic order. This is November.

Memo dated 11/21/95, received 11/29/95
Letter dated 8/18/95, received 8/22/95
Letter dated 11/22/95, received 11/26/95
Memo dated 8/13/95, received 8/23/95
Memo dated 8/12/95, received 8/22/95

3. Prepare a suggested relative index for the following records used in a large discount department store.

junior dresses	men's sport coats	women's shoes
junior sportswear	men's suits	purses
rings	pearl necklaces	wallets
watches		

CONCLUDING CASES

A. Radisson Division, Language Laboratories

Radisson Division of Language Laboratories is a multinational corporation selling both hardware and software to organizations and individuals for use in developing competency in a second language. The company experienced phenomenal growth in the 1980s, and branch offices were established in Canada, the United States, France, and Germany. In response to a decrease in business and a general recessionary slump in the early 1990s, the decision was made to consolidate operations in Canada and close four branch offices.

All of the records of the four branch offices will be moved to the home office in Canada because customers will now be serviced from this location. The move may make it necessary to recommend a files reorganization. The home office files records in several ways:

- General and transitory correspondence are filed together by client as well as by subject.
- Correspondence and sales reports from the branch offices are filed by branch office location.
- Technical reference manuals and materials are in stacks.
- Case records are filed according to function:
  - Purchase orders are filed serially by prenumbered series.
  - Invoices are filed by vendor name.
- Total volume housed in the home office exceeds 100,000 records.

Branch office records are filed differently at each branch. Branch No. 1 files all records alphabetically by name of individual or organization. Volume of records totals 22,000.

Branch No. 2 files all account records serially by account number. Correspondence is filed with the account record. Volume of records totals 7,000 active accounts.

Branch No. 3 has only been in operation for eight months. Their system is still in the organizational stage because of a turnover of staff. An estimated 4,000 records are in the files.

Branch No. 4 has an office manager who is a stickler for detail. All records have been identified and are filed by file group. Although the volume of some file groups is very small, the office manager requires that the records be separated into the appropriate file groups. Volume of records totals 18,700.

You are asked to recommend a classification system for the consolidated home office records. Provide support for your recommendation.

B. Special Occasion Leasing

Six months ago Sandy Davis was hired as the office manager of Special Occasion Leasing, a limousine leasing agency in a large metropolitan area. She has noticed many problems with the alphabetic-by-name classification system for client records. Some of the problems she has found include (1) many clients have more than one folder under different names, (2) information concerning credit and previous service is difficult to locate quickly, and (3) files are not filed in the correct order in the system because all employees have access to files and most employees are not familiar with correct filing procedures.

Sandy is aware that she has other choices among classification systems for the client records. She thinks a numeric system with a computer-generated index would work. Do you agree? If so, how should she set up the system? If not, what system would you recommend? How can she eliminate the problem of incorrect filing by the employees?

SUGGESTED READINGS AND RESOURCES

ARMA *International Guideline for Records and Information Management:* Filing Procedures. Prairie Village, Kansas, 1989.

Association of Records Managers and Administrators, Inc. *ARMA International Standard for Records and Information Management Alphabetic Filing Rules*. Prairie Village, Kansas, July, 1986.

Association of Records Managers and Administrators, Inc. *Numeric Filing Guideline*. Prairie Village, Kansas, 1989.

Association of Records Managers and Administrators, Inc. *Subject Filing Guideline*. Prairie Village, Kansas, 1988.

Daum, Patricia. "Implementing Administrative File Systems." *Records Management Quarterly,* Vol. 19, No. 2 (April, 1985), p. 36.

O'Shea, M. "Information Management: Making Your System Work." *Office,* Vol. 118, August, 1993, p. 26.

Perks, Denis G. "Uniform File System for the Multinational, Multilingual Corporation." Presentation, 30th Annual Conference, Association of Records Managers and Administrators, Inc., New York, (September, 1985).

Supply and Services Canada. *Subject Classification Guide.* Records Management Series, Public Archives Canada, Ottawa, Ontario, 1989.

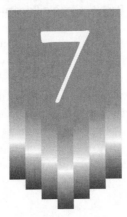

Manual Records Storage and Retrieval

Learning Goals

After completing this chapter, you should be able to:

1. Define the manual filing procedures applicable to most records systems.
2. Describe specific procedures for maintaining manual file operations.
3. Describe the use of indexes in accessing files.
4. Determine when cross-references are necessary and prepare them in the correct form.
5. Explain how colour coding increases storage and retrieval efficiency, and describe applications in which colour may be used.
6. Describe the use of colour coding in alphabetic, numeric, and alphanumeric classification systems.
7. Describe procedures for retrieving and tracking records.
8. Describe the types of transfer periods.
9. Explain how to determine which records are to be transferred.
10. Describe how records are prepared and transferred to the records centre.

The goal of an effective records management system is to reduce the time it takes to file and retrieve records. One way to achieve this goal is to use an alphabetic, numeric, or combination file arrangement, as discussed in Chapter 6. As well, procedures for filing and retrieving records must be set up, adhered to, and known to everyone involved in these activities. The files must be maintained through the use of guides, labels, and file folders. Although this chapter emphasizes the storage and retrieval procedures for active, paper-based records, the material is equally applicable to electronic records and microforms, as well as to inactive records.

MANUAL STORAGE PROCEDURES

"It's not my filing, it's my finding ..." is a familiar saying when problems are experienced in locating records. The saying is inaccurate because the storage procedures affect the finding: records properly stored according to established procedures will be easily retrievable by anyone familiar with the system. **Manual storage and retrieval** refers to the process of storing and retrieving records without the aid of mechanical or automated devices. Anyone placing a record in its appropriate folder in a storage cabinet, on a shelf, or in a disk box is using a manual system. As discussed in Chapter 5, records may be stored or retrieved by manual, mechanical, or automated methods. Studies indicate that, although many organizations are using more automated retrieval systems, the majority of small and mid-sized organizations still rely on manual retrieval. The trend, however, is toward more efficient, less labour-intensive systems of records storage and retrieval. The general procedures for records storage are shown in Figure 7-1.

Figure 7-1
General Procedures
for Record Storage

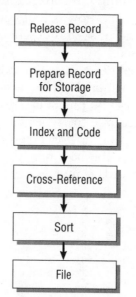

Release the Record

A release mark may be an initial or the word *file*.

The first step in the procedure is to check for a release mark on the record. A **release mark** is a notation that the immediate need for the record has passed and the record may now be stored. The record recipient has the responsibility for making that decision. The release mark may be an initial or the simple notation "file." The mark is usually made on the upper- or lower-right-hand corner of the document, if it is a hard copy. In any case, the release mark authorizes the record to be stored.

Prepare the Record for Storage

Paper Records

Remove unnecessary attachments from records before filing them.

Paper records should be checked for filing condition. Paper clips are removed; related records are stapled together or punched so that they may be fastened to folders; torn papers are mended with transparent tape; and small papers are taped on standard-sized paper. Oversized material to be filed must be folded separately; this reduces the amount of filing space required and allows each record to be retrieved individually. Unnecessary attachments such as envelopes, routing slips, receipt acknowledgments, or duplicate copies (unless considered a part of the record) should be destroyed.

Source Documents

Prepare source documents that are to be microfilmed or stored on other media. The documents should be unfolded, paper clips and staples removed, and wrinkled papers straightened.

Magnetic Media

Magnetic media must be handled and stored with care. Microcomputer disks must not be bent, folded, creased, or mutilated in any way. Manufacturers of these disks will not guarantee performance of the disks unless measures are taken to file each disk completely pressure free. Hair, dust, or fingerprints on the read-write head may damage or erase stored data. Exposing magnetic media to extreme heat, cold, or light may also result in lost data. To avoid data loss on magnetic media, keep disks in their jackets when not in use, store disks on edge, handle disks by jackets only, and write on labels *before* placing them on the disks. Also, when storing magnetic disks, avoid stacking disks, attaching paper clips or rubber bands to disks, or placing magnets near disks. Disks should not be placed near motors, transformers, power cords, chemicals, or liquids.

Index and Code

Indexing is the mental process of deciding by which filing segment a record is to be filed.

Filing segments are marked on the record during the coding process.

Coding meant marking the filing segment on a record to be filed.

Indexing is the mental process of deciding by which filing segment a record is to be filed based on the classification system used. The entire name, subject, or number that is used for filing purposes is called the **filing segment** (see Chapter 6). Determining the name, subject, or caption by which a record is to be stored is a mental process that takes place prior to coding.

Coding refers to marking the filing segment on a record. Proper coding follows alphabetic indexing rules and the procedures for the specific classification system used. There are various methods of coding, depending on the record medium. They include underlining or circling key words, names, or subjects and writing a subject or numeric code at the top of (or other prominent place on) the record. Complete coding of magnetic and film media is essential. Paper documents contain visible information, and a reasonable chance of locating and identifying misplaced records exists. Because disks, tapes, and film do not have this visible advantage, their contents should be marked with identical codes on the media as well as on the storage containers. This code is repeated on the locator index.

 Learning Check: Can you explain the difference between coding and indexing?

Cross-Reference

A cross-reference directs the searcher to another possible location of the record.

If records may be requested in more than one way, indicate that fact and prepare a cross-reference for the record. Cross-referencing is accomplished at the same time as the indexing and coding procedure. A **cross-reference** directs the person looking for the record to another location where the record or information may be found. Cross-referencing is also used when related material is in another location or when the location of the record within the system has been changed. The rules for cross-referencing business records are contained in Chapter 6, "Indexing Rules and Classification System Selection."

The cross-reference notation appears on a paper document. The person doing the coding may mark an *X* next to the related name or subject within the document to indicate a cross-reference. If the related subject (cross-reference topic) is inconsistent with the relative index to subject files, an *X* is written at the top of the record followed by the subject under which the cross-reference should be made. Figure 7-2 shows these cross-reference notations.

 Learning Check: Can you explain the importance of cross-referencing in correspondence files?

Figure 7-2
Cross-Reference Notations

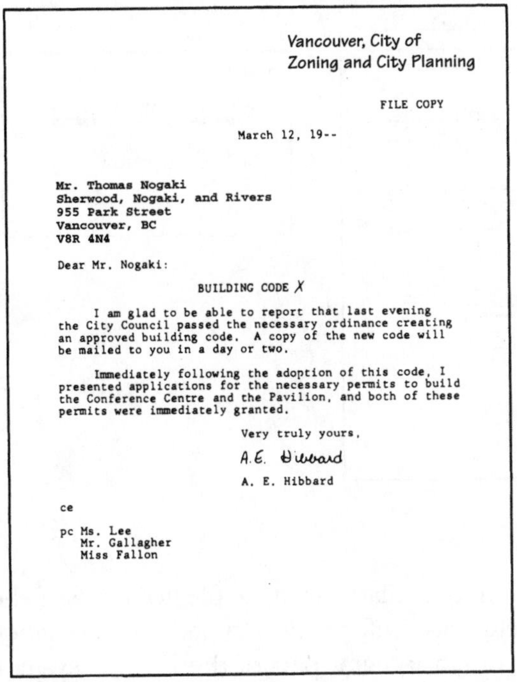

```
                    Vancouver, City of
                    Zoning and City Planning

                             FILE COPY

             March 12, 19--


Mr. Thomas Nogaki
Sherwood, Nogaki, and Rivers
955 Park Street
Vancouver, BC
V8R 4N4

Dear Mr. Nogaki:

           BUILDING CODE X

     I am glad to be able to report that last evening
the City Council passed the necessary ordinance creating
an approved building code.  A copy of the new code will
be mailed to you in a day or two.

     Immediately following the adoption of this code, I
presented applications for the necessary permits to build
the Conference Centre and the Pavilion, and both of these
permits were immediately granted.

                    Very truly yours,

                    A.E. Hibbard

                    A. E. Hibbard

ce

pc Ms. Lee
   Mr. Gallagher
   Miss Fallon
```

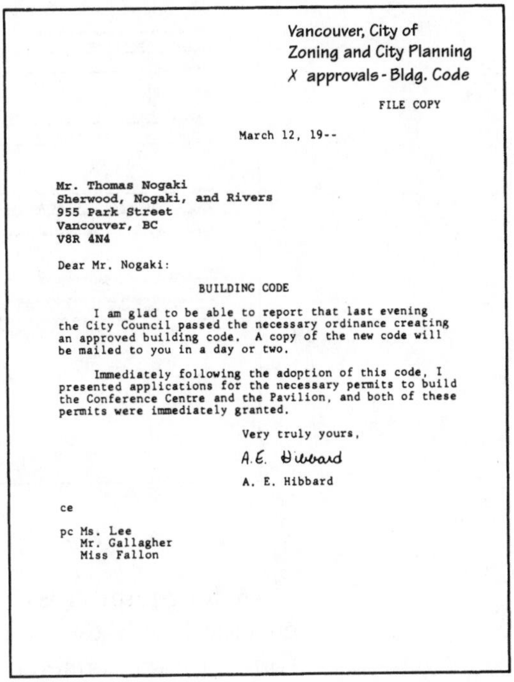

```
                    Vancouver, City of
                    Zoning and City Planning
                    X approvals - Bldg. Code

                             FILE COPY

             March 12, 19--


Mr. Thomas Nogaki
Sherwood, Nogaki, and Rivers
955 Park Street
Vancouver, BC
V8R 4N4

Dear Mr. Nogaki:

                BUILDING CODE

     I am glad to be able to report that last evening
the City Council passed the necessary ordinance creating
an approved building code.  A copy of the new code will
be mailed to you in a day or two.

     Immediately following the adoption of this code, I
presented applications for the necessary permits to build
the Conference Centre and the Pavilion, and both of these
permits were immediately granted.

                    Very truly yours,

                    A.E. Hibbard

                    A. E. Hibbard

ce

pc Ms. Lee
   Mr. Gallagher
   Miss Fallon
```

A long-term cross-reference provides a trail for the record.

The cross-reference may take several forms: (1) photocopy of the original record, (2) cross-reference sheet, (3) long-term cross-reference, or (4) index card (see Figure 7-3).

Long-term cross-references are used to provide a trail or forwarding address for the record when one or more of the following factors are present:

- Names of people or organizations are filed in more than one place.
- Related material is stored in multiple locations.
- Filing is contrary to standard indexing rules.
- Names have been changed.
- Entire file is moved to a new location.
- Records are reclassified from one file arrangement to another.
- Divisions and subsidiaries of a large corporation are to be identified.

Figure 7-3
Cross-Reference
Forms

Records Management Manual
Part I

CROSS-REFERENCE SHEET

NAME _____   DATE March 12, 19--

SUBJECT Building Code

FILE NUMBER _____

REGARDING Permit granted by the City Council to build the
                  Conference Centre.

SEE

NAME _____   DATE _____

SUBJECT Vancouver, City of Zoning and City Planning

FILE NUMBER _____

HOW TO USE CROSS-REFERENCE SHEET

Attach a copy of the first page of the original document being cross-
referenced and file under NAME/SUBJECT/NUMBER shown at the top of this
sheet. Document in its entirety will be filed under NAME/SUBJECT/NUMBER
shown under "SEE."

Form 18
5-93

Building Code

SEE: VANCOUVER CITY OF
         ZONING AND CITY PLANNING

A long-term cross reference is made from a file folder or fiche envelope with the cross-reference information typed on the label. Long-term cross-references are an integral part of the records system. These references are microfilmed if the records are filmed or transferred with the other folders to inactive storage at the appropriate interval. Long-term cross-reference folders should be marked with a shoulder label or other labelling device, such as a distinctive colour or type style, to facilitate replacement of the cross-reference when the existing cross-reference is microfilmed or transferred (see Figure 7-4).

Figure 7-4
Long-Term Cross-
Reference with
Shoulder Label

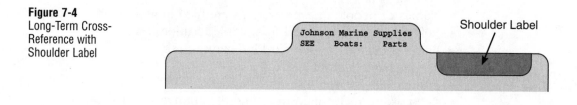

Johnson Marine Supplies
SEE   Boats: Parts

Shoulder Label

Learning Check: Can you explain the reasons a record may have a long-term cross-reference?

Sort

Sorting is arranging records in filing order according to the classification systems used. Records to be microfilmed, as well as records that are manually or mechanically placed in files, must be in the desired sequence. Records placed in an automated system do not require sorting prior to storage.

Fine sorting puts records in strict order according to the system used.

If large numbers of records are to be sorted, a rough sort is made first. Depending on the number of items to be sorted, the rough sort may first be block sorted. **Block sorting** is the process of rough sorting records into groups of alphabetic letters *(A, B, C, D, E, F)* or in groups of numbers *(1–10, 11–20)* and so forth. If a numeric system is used, block sorting is done in multiples of 10 or 20. Geographic sorting is done first by province. If the number of records to be sorted is small, rough sorting is usually accomplished by placing all the *A*s, *10*s, or cities alphabetically (depending on the system) in one stack; *B*s or *20*s in another stack; and so on. Fine sorting is then done by putting the records in order within the alphabet, digits within the numeric system, and cities alphabetically within the province.

When sorting is performed manually, horizontal or vertical sorters may be used to aid the sorting process. Horizontal sorters are flat, in either a long and narrow or a circular style. They are most efficient for sorting single papers and offer savings of as much as 60 percent over desktop sorting. Vertical sorters have self-supporting dividers or an adjusting track. These sorters can be used for folders, jackets, and single documents. Because several inches of material can be placed behind a divider, the vertical sorter is appropriate when a horizontal sorter cannot be used.

File

Filing is actually placing records in file folders.

Filing is the action of storing the record. The record may be stored on hard copy in an appropriate storage area; on microfilm, microfiche, magnetic tape/disks, or optical disks; or within the memory of a computer.

FILES MAINTENANCE

Filing systems remain efficient only if they are properly maintained and if established maintenance procedures are followed on a regular basis. The following are standard procedures to maintain filing efficiency.

Drawer/Shelf Files

Overcrowded storage cabinet drawers cause slowed records retrieval. A properly maintained vertical file drawer should use 23 to 24 of the 27 available storage inches, allowing 3 to 4 inches for work space.

Microfiche filed in drawer cabinets should have 1 to 2 inches of work space. Shelf files should be full enough to allow files to stand upright but loose enough to allow folders to be easily stored and retrieved.

Labels

To narrow a search, all drawers/shelves should be clearly labelled with the records title, years covered, the arrangement followed, and the segment of the particular file included in that drawer/shelf. Labels are also used with guides and top- or side-tab file folders. They should be typewritten or computer generated with uniform format, should be applied in a consistent position, and should provide current information. Two drawer label samples are shown in Figure 7-5.

Figure 7-5
Sample Drawer
Labels

INVOICES JULY 1-DEC. 31 19-- #1200-1650	#1200-1650 7/1 - 12/31, 19-- INVOICES

 Learning Check: Can you explain the need for labels?

Guides

File guides provide
eye targets.

Guides or dividers allow storage and retrieval to be accomplished more quickly by providing eye targets, which narrow the search to several folders. Too few guides are inefficient; too many guides waste storage space. Guides should be provided for every 6 to 8 folders in a very active drawer/shelf file and for every 10 to 15 folders in a less active drawer/shelf file. This translates to 15 to 25 guides per file drawer/shelf for very active files and 10 to 15 guides per file drawer/shelf for less active files. Card files require a file guide for every 20 cards in very active files; for less active card files, one guide per 30 cards is sufficient.

Guides may be primary guides or special guides. A **primary guide** is used to begin the major divisions and subdivisions of files in each file drawer or shelf. A **special guide** is used to highlight sections that are used frequently because of a common name, a special topic, or a particularly active client or account. OUT guides are another type of special guide. The OUT guide is used to indicate materials that have been taken from the file, and it remains in the file until the materials are returned.

 Learning Check: Can you explain the purpose of the primary guide?

Folders

Folders may be general, individual, or special folders. General folders have the same caption as the primary guide that begins each division or subdivision of the file. A **general folder** at the end of each of these divisions is used to store any documents that do not have their own individual or special folder. The **individual folder** is used to store correspondence to and from or about one individual person or company. After four or five documents have accumulated in the general folder about one individual or company, an individual folder is created for that material. The **special folder** is used to store correspondence concerning a special subject or topic, such as letters of congratulations.

Folders must be clearly labelled to reduce retrieval time. Like drawer/shelf labels, folder labels should be typed or computer generated using a uniform format. Folder labels narrow the search to the contents of one folder. Labels and folders must be replaced when their condition slows storage or retrieval. In order to minimize wear, folders should be handled by the sides—not by the tabs. All folder labels should be clearly visible. When folders become filled with papers, the scoring at the bottom of the front folder leaf should be creased to allow papers to rest squarely on the bottom of the file drawer. Folders should not be overcrowded—three-fourths of an inch of material is the maximum one folder should house, even if the folder is scored. Noticeably thick folders should be subdivided into separate folders either by date or subtopic.

 Learning Check: Can you explain the purpose of the individual folder?

When a paper record is filed, the record is inserted facing forward with the top of the page to the left. Documents should be arranged chronologically within the folder; the latest record should be placed on top. This placement makes the most recent information available first.

Using file backers with the documents attached to the backer by an ACCO fastener reduces file folder wastage considerably. A **file backer** is a document-sized file folder weight sheet to which the one- or two-hole punched documents are attached at the top. A label on the file backer matches the label on the file folder. When the contents of the file folder are to be transferred, only the documents and the file backer are transferred to the records centre. As a result, replacement file folders and labels need not be created until the folders are worn out, yet inactive files can still be identified. Figure 7-6 illustrates a file backer.

A straight-line guide/folder arrangement (all guides at left and all folder labels at right) allows additional guides and folders to be inserted without causing a confusing arrangement. If the file arrangement is consecutive and fixed, with no additional guides or folders to be added, staggered positions may be used.

Figure 7-6
File Backer with
Label on Back Side

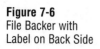 **Learning Check: Can you explain the usage of guides and folders in files maintenance?**

Figure 7-7
Alphabetic
Correspondence
File

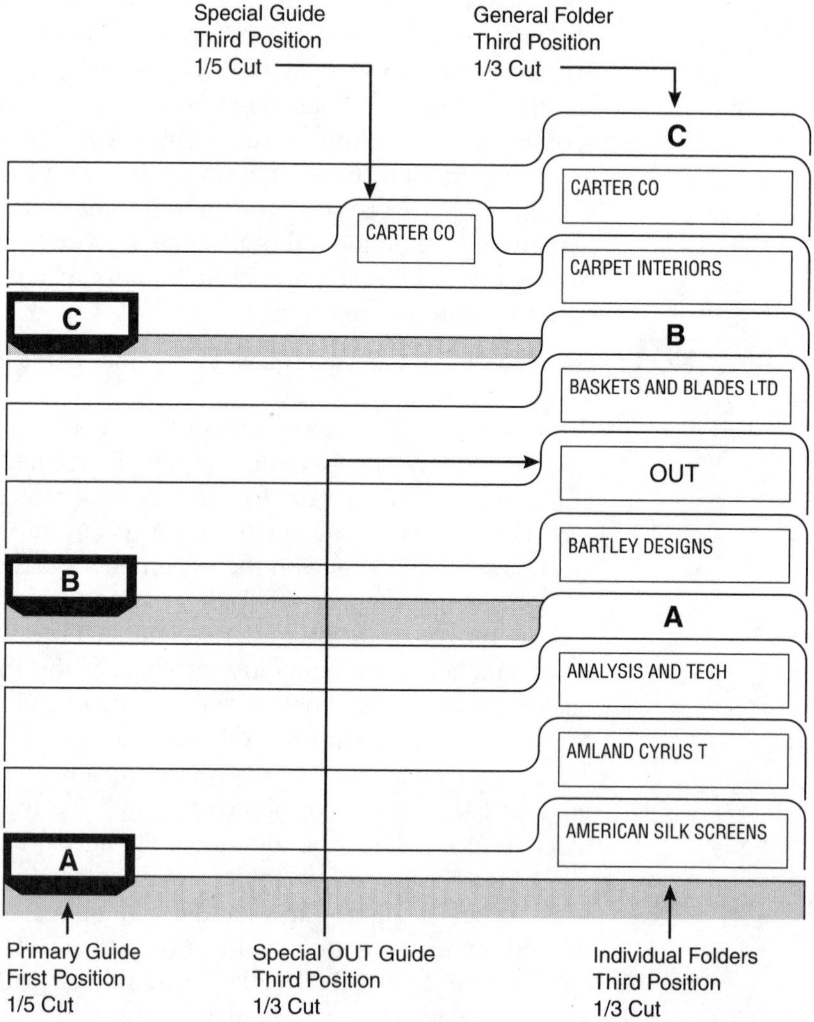

Special Guide
Third Position
1/5 Cut

General Folder
Third Position
1/3 Cut

C

CARTER CO

CARTER CO

CARPET INTERIORS

C

B

BASKETS AND BLADES LTD

OUT

BARTLEY DESIGNS

B

A

ANALYSIS AND TECH

AMLAND CYRUS T

AMERICAN SILK SCREENS

A

Primary Guide
First Position
1/5 Cut

Special OUT Guide
Third Position
1/3 Cut

Individual Folders
Third Position
1/3 Cut

Guides and folders, with their labels, are used to construct the files so that their contents can be located as efficiently as possible. Figure 7-7 is an example of an alphabetic correspondence file. Alphabetic and other file systems are discussed in greater detail in Chapter 6.

In Figure 7-7 the primary guides are in first position, one-fifth cut. The general folders are in third position, one-third cut. The special guide is in third position, one-fifth cut. The individual folders are in the third position, one-third cut. Also included in this example is an OUT guide, which occupies the third position—the same as the individual folders. Organizing the guides and folders in this way, makes it easy to locate the appropriate file for each record to be stored.

ACCESSING THE FILES

To maintain files efficiently and to provide ready access to records, the person accessing the files must have knowledge of the record system (whether it is direct or indirect access) and must follow established steps for requisitioning and charging out records.

Direct and Indirect Access

Records may be accessed directly or indirectly. **Direct access** requires no intermediary steps—one goes directly to the storage area and retrieves the record. **Indirect access** requires the use of an index to direct the person accessing the record to the appropriate storage area.

Indexes

An index is a location tool and guide for code selection.

An **index** is a location tool. Just as an index in a book directs the reader to a page within the book, a records index directs the researcher or records clerk to the particular file where the required information may be located. The index also provides the person coding documents with a guide for code selection. Indexes can be prepared in two formats: a simple list of headings in straight alphabetic sequence or an alphabetic list of headings with subheadings listed below each heading. An index can be stored in three different forms: alphabetically arranged index cards, a typewritten list arranged alphabetically, or, as is increasingly the case, a list stored electronically.

The index must include all headings and cross-references contained in the filing system. This is imperative for efficient retrieval. The index accomplishes three objectives in a subject filing system where it is most often used: (1) provides a complete list of headings to speed retrieval, (2) eliminates the possibility of duplicate headings being created in the file, and (3) simplifies cross-referencing by having the cross-references in the index. The manual index is based upon the classification system used by the organization and the manner in which information is normally requested.

The indexes may be comprehensive, sophisticated systems or simple listings as required to meet the needs of the organization and the user. Essential in most offices is a **classified index**, in which the entries are not arranged in one straightforward alphabetic sequence, but in which the subject of the work is divided into a number of main headings and these in turn are subdivided as necessary, each sequence of entries being arranged alphabetically (as in the Yellow Pages). A **relative index** shows all possible words and word combinations by which the material may be requested. Each index to stored material should be kept current by making new entries for additional classifications as they occur. An example of one type of index is shown in Table 7-1.

Table 7-1

RELATIVE INDEX TO SUBJECT FILES

Subject		Filed Under
	A	
Account Balances		ACCOUNTING
Activities—Employee		HUMAN RESOURCES
Administrative Issuances		ADMINISTRATION
	B	
Benefits Administration		EMPLOYEE BENEFITS
Brokers and Agents		INSURANCE
	C	
Claims and Loss		INSURANCE
Compensation		HUMAN RESOURCES
Corporate Law		LEGAL

✓ **Learning Check: Can you explain the purpose of indexes in a filing system?**

MANUAL RECORDS RETRIEVAL

Manual retrieval refers to finding and retrieving records without the aid of automated devices. Although mechanical storage equipment does speed records retrieval and reduce worker fatigue, the method of actually retrieving the record is still manual.

Retrieving Varied Record Types

Regardless of its form, manual retrieval requires the user to go to the record.

Paper records are stored in folders and housed in cabinets or shelves. Anyone requiring the record must go to the cabinet or shelf and, with the aid of guides and labels, retrieve the record from its folder. Microfiche, roll film in jackets, and aperture cards are retrieved similarly. Codes or identification numbers on the fiche headers, fiche envelopes (if used), jackets, and aperture cards are used to locate these records.

Roll film, cartridges, and cassettes may be manually located by referring to their indexes for location information. These microforms are then manually placed on readers or reader-printers to obtain the required information.

Roll film may be manually retrieved from storage. A reel of film that fits in the palm of your hand is more easily misplaced than a drawer of paper records. Care must be exercised to replace film in the proper carton, particularly when several reels are used at the same time. Using colour signals on film cartons and reels is one way of preventing misfiling.

Using Colour Coding

Colour coding is the use of colour and colour patterns on file folders, labels, tabs, or cards. It has gained wide acceptance for improving efficiency for records storage and retrieval and aiding in the identification of misfiles. The human eye can read colours and colour patterns much faster and from greater distances than it can read alphabetic or numeric characters or groups of characters. Colour may be added to the system through colour file folders, colour labels, colour bars or bands on labels or folders, colour OUT cards, or colour signals.

Colour File Folders

The substitution of colour file folders for manila folders is particularly useful in designating files by date or identifying specific departments or functions. For example, yellow folders might identify the finance department, blue folders the human resources department, green folders the planning department, and so forth. Colour folders are not limited to these applications; however, the advantages of coloured folders must be weighed against the increased cost of purchasing. Some colours such as red create problems for recycling projects.

The use of colour speeds storage and retrieval.

Colour Labels

Colour labels may have a stripe across the top edge or be all of one colour. Solid colours are usually fairly light in tint to allow printed information to be readable.

Colour Bars or Bands

Colour bars or bands are placed uniformly on folders. A misplaced folder labelled with a colour bar or band is quite evident with even a cursory inspection. Colour bands can be used on film cartons and reels as a way of preventing misfiling. Reels of different series can be assigned different colours. A diagonal line drawn end to end across the tops of all storage cartons in a drawer or on a shelf is particularly effective for cartons maintained in numeric sequence. A visual scan quickly reveals missing or misfiled cartons.

Colour OUT Cards

Colour OUT cards are vivid reminders that a file has been borrowed and not returned. These cards may also be used to denote the day, week, or month of the out-of-file material.

Colour Signals

Colour signals are usually plastic clip-on or pressure-sensitive signals. These signals are attached to records that require special attention. For example, a colour signal could draw attention to significant dates.

 Learning Check: Can you explain how colour coding increases storage and retrieval efficiency and describe applications in which colour may be used?

Colour Coding Filing Systems

Colour coding can be used in most filing systems. Methods of using colour coding in alphabetic, numeric, and alphanumeric systems are included in this section. An illustration of colour coding using each of the systems is shown in Figure 7-8.

Alphabetic Systems

The use of colour coding reduces the number of misfiles.

In alphabetic systems colour coding is assigned to the first and second letters of the surname. The second letter is coded because that is where most misfiles occur. Most colour-coded alphabetic systems use between 10 and 13 colours.

Numeric Systems

In numeric systems colour may be used to speed storage and retrieval by using 10 colours to represent the digits 0 to 9. By adding colour labels (which represent the digits in a numeric file), a band of colour is produced throughout the storage system. When a folder is out of place, this band will be interrupted with a different colour, which will easily identify the misfiled folder.

Terminal-Digit Systems

In terminal-digit systems colour is used to represent the numbers. By adding colour labels representing fields of 10 (0–9, 10–19, etc., to 99), locating a file is made easier. With this system, three sets of numbers would be used—one representing the last two digits, one representing the middle digits, and one representing the first two digits in the filing code.

Alphanumeric Systems

Colour coding is equally effective in enhancing alphanumeric systems. In this type of arrangement, letters are assigned a numeric value; and each number, or both letter and numeral, is colour coded.

Figure 7-8
Colour Coding

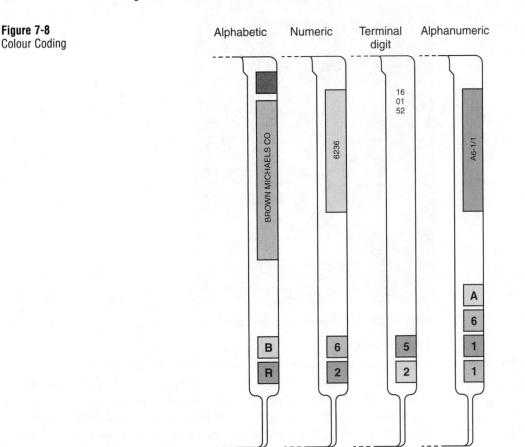

Using colour to aid storage and retrieval speed and efficiency is not limited to paper copy. Colour may be used for all types of records media. Microfilm rolls, jackets, magnetic tapes, and disks can be colour coded (see Figure 7-9). Colour coding is available for nearly all styles and types of records.

Procedures for Records Retrieval

A procedure for retrieving and tracking records activity should be followed.

A method for recording activity and tracking records is essential to the total records management system. The method includes procedures for requesting records and data, for charging out requested records, and for follow-up and return of the records. A number of computer programs are available for tracking records, and these will be discussed in Chapter 10, "Integrated Information Systems."

Figure 7-9
Colour Coding for
Mixed Media

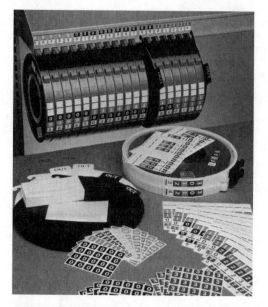

Source: Tabbies, Division of Xertrex International, Inc.

Requisition

Records may be
requested in
person, by
telephone, by
interoffice mail, or
by computer.

Records may be requested in written form, by telephone, or by computer. All requests, however, should be recorded. If the organizational policy allows telephone records requisitions, the documentation responsibility rests with the records clerk who receives the telephone call. The same format may be used for either telephoned or written requests (see Figure 7-10).

Figure 7-10
Records Retrieval
Request

RECORDS RETRIEVAL REQUISITION			
REQUESTED BY	EXT	DATE REQUESTED	
DEPARTMENT	LOCATION	RECEIVED (DATE/TIME)	
RECORD TYPE ☐ BOX ☐ FILE ☐ OTHER:			
TITLE	ROW	SECTION	SHELF
REQUEST TAKEN BY			
Form 55 5/31/87			

Charge-Out

A multipart form
may be used for
requisition and
charge-out.

After completion or receipt of the record requisition, the record is then charged out to the requester, who is responsible for its return. A multiple-part requisition form may be used for charging out a record as well, with one copy of the form inserted in the pocket on the plastic

OUT guide (see Figure 7-11), the second copy inserted in the tickler file, and the third copy attached to the folder. One copy of this form may be used to prepare management reports.

Figure 7-11
OUT Guide with
Insertion

Charge-out form
inserted here

An OUT guide, OUT folder, or OUT sheet may also be used to indicate that a file/record has been removed. Colour coding materials for computer disks are shown in Figure 7-9. An OUT guide replaces a folder removed from the files when other documents will not need to be filed in the folder during its absence from the file. An OUT guide provides space to fill in information regarding the name of the folder, the date the folder was removed, who requested the folder, and the date the folder should be returned. Of course, if the system of inserting a copy of the requisition or charge-out form in the pocket of the guide is used, the necessary information will be included on that form and not on the OUT guide (see Figure 7-12).

Figure 7-12
OUT Guide

OUT			
Subject	Charged To	Date	Return Date
~~Marshall file~~	~~Todd~~	~~6/21/--~~	~~6/26/--~~
~~Tompson file~~	~~Patterson~~	~~6/24/--~~	~~6/26/--~~
Car Rental file	Simpson	7/3/--	

An OUT folder replaces the requested folder as it is removed from the files and serves as a holding device for incoming papers until the return of the original folder to the file. Folder name, removal date, and requester name should be filled in on the form printed on the outside of the OUT folder. An OUT sheet is used to replace a document that has been removed from a folder. An OUT sheet identifies the docu-

ment (by subject, date, and originator when applicable), who requested the document, when the document was requested, and date the
document is to be returned. Since an OUT sheet is placed within the
folder as a substitute for a removed document, it should be placed in
the same chronologic position within the folder as the removed document. The charge-out form must be removed from the files upon
return of the charged out material. A line is drawn through the notation on the OUT form or OUT folder (as shown in Figure 7-12), and
the form or folder is ready to be reused.

Follow-Up

Follow-up is
important in the
retrieval process.

Records are not always returned on the specified date, and follow-up
is often necessary to maintain complete files. A reasonable period for
charging out is a week to 10 days. However, accommodation must be
made if records are needed for a longer period. Confidential records
usually may not leave the premises. If the policy of the organization
allows confidential material to be borrowed, this material should not
be charged out for longer than overnight.

The manual system used for follow-up is usually a tickler or suspense file. This file is arranged chronologically with the current month
guide in front followed by 31 day guides. Guides for the remaining
months are at the back of the file. One efficient way to indicate records
that have been charged out and require follow-up is to place a copy
of the requisition form behind the month guide to show the due date.
Another efficient follow-up method is the use of follow-up folders.
These folders have a plastic protected edge with a visible sliding signal, which can be set to indicate the date of follow-up.

Each day the file is checked for records charged out and not yet
returned. Records still outstanding require a follow-up, which may
take the form of a phone call or a fill-in form (see Figure 7-13) sent to
the person who charged out the material. The longer the time that files
are allowed to remain out, the more difficult they are to recover.

Figure 7-13
Request for Return
of Records

REQUEST FOR RETURN OF RECORDS		NO.	
To: *Miss Jane Matsumi*	Mail Sta. *148*	Date: *2/17/--*	
We like to give good service to everyone. Please cooperate with us by returning either the material listed below or this form showing the expected date of return. Thank you.			
		Records Center Supervisor	
Record Title/Description *Cash Voucher*		Charge – Out Date *2/2/--*	
CV 14763			
Remarks:		Expected Return Date: *2/16/--*	
☐ Continued Over	By *Trudy Masters*	Date *2/17/--*	
FORM 32-3/15/86			

RECORDS TRANSFER

Records transfer should be completed according to the schedule.

Records transfer is the physical movement of records from expensive office space to a records centre or other designated storage area. The steps in the transfer process are (1) determining when records are to be transferred, (2) determining what records are to be transferred, (3) preparing records for transfer, and (4) arranging the transfer.

Determine Transfer Method

Transfer methods may be periodic or perpetual.

Transfer periods are usually determined by organizational policy rather than by individual departments or offices. Records transfer depends on the active retention periods listed in the retention schedule. Some records are identified as inactive and transferred as a result of the records inventory. After the inventory, records are transferred on a periodic or perpetual basis. **Periodic transfer** means that records are transferred at regularly scheduled intervals. One entire period of records is transferred at one time; many organizations do this at the end of their fiscal year. RCA Corp. has an established policy of designating one week each year as Records Review Week. During this week each office of each division reviews its records, destroys records no longer needed, transfers all inactive records to their records centres, and ensures that all records that were scheduled for destruction at the end of the previous calendar year have been destroyed. This activity is widely publicized in the company and receives support from its top executives. Each office is required to complete a report indicating the volume of active records reviewed, transferred, and destroyed, as well as the number of drawers or shelves emptied and placed in storage.

A variation of periodic transfer is known as the **maximum-minimum method**, in which all records are kept in the active files for a specified minimum and maximum period of time, for example, a minimum of six months and a maximum of 18 months. This method is useful for keeping at least six months of ongoing files such as correspondence records near the users, on the assumption that records older than that will not likely be referenced.

If the file folders are transferred with their contents, a replacement set of folders with labels must be prepared at the designated transfer date. This is where file backers become useful: the documents that have become inactive go to the records centre attached to their file backer with its label, and the current records are left to accumulate with a new backer and label in their file folder.

Perpetual transfer allows the division or office to transfer records to storage when there is a natural end to activity of a file. This method is also known as continuous transfer or the flagging method. (A signal or flag is added to a file folder that has become inactive.) This method could be used for files containing information about clients, patients, or customers such as in hospitals, prisons, law offices, and universities. The perpetual transfer method must be monitored, however, because of possible forgetfulness, neglect, or lack of time.

Learning Check: Can you describe types of transfer periods?

Determine Records to Be Transferred

Many records will have been identified as inactive during the records inventory and should be transferred as rapidly as possible to the records centre. After this initial transfer, records to be transferred are identified from the retention schedule. Regardless of the transfer period, all records eligible for transfer must be transferred. Careful identification of all records scheduled for transfer enhances the effectiveness of the retention program.

Learning Check: Can you explain how to determine which records should be transferred?

Prepare Records for Transfer

There are two steps in preparing records for transfer to the storage area. These steps are completing the necessary forms and packaging the records for storage.

Forms

A transmittal form accompanies records being transferred.

The originating office should prepare a records transmittal form to send with the records being transferred to the storage area. In addition to the records transmittal form, some organizations require that detailed labels be prepared for each transfer carton. Other organizations simply require boxes to be numbered and their contents described on the records transmittal form. A records transmittal form and instructions for completion are shown in Figure 7-14.

Packaging

Transfer boxes are available for various sizes and types of records.

Space for retrieval should be left in filled boxes.

Records being packaged for storage should be placed in corrugated fibreboard transfer cartons, which are described in Chapter 17, "Inactive Records." Cartons are available for both letter- and legal-sized records and for top- and side-tab folders.

About three inches of space should be left in each box for ease of retrieval. To facilitate destroying records when the time comes, many organizations request that all the records in a box have the same disposal period. If records with different periods of retention are packed in one box, typically the whole box will be retained until the last date mentioned for destruction. Project files that span more than one year should be packed in the same box so they will be destroyed at the same time.

Figure 7-14
Records
Transmittal
Form

FOR ASSISTANCE CONTACT RECORDS MANAGEMENT X-5478

RECORDS TRANSMITTAL

ASSIGNED BY RECORDS MANAGEMENT
BOX/CONTROL NO. _____

COMPLETED BY TRANSMITTER	TEMPORARY BOX NUMBER _____			PAGE _____ OF _____	
DEPARTMENT		DATE			
PREPARED BY		TITLE			
RECORD SERIES TITLE	DESCRIPTION	YEAR		RETENTION	BOX NO.
		FROM	TO		
1	2	3		4	5

COMPLETED BY RECORDS MANAGEMENT			
RECEIVED BY	DATE	MEDIUM	
RETENTION PERIOD	DESTRUCTION DATE	NOTIFY	

DISTRIBUTION
WHITE - Organization File
GREEN - Control No. File

CANARY - Retention File
PINK - In Box
GOLD - Transmitter (after Control No. Assigned)

How to complete this form:

1. *RECORD SERIES TITLE:* Indicate the type of document, such as correspondence, reports, invoices, brochures, etc.
2. *DESCRIPTION:* If the records in the box are in one continuous sequence, either alphabetic or numeric, list the title of the first and last folder only. If the box contains more than one group of records, list the first and last folder title of each group.
3. *YEAR:* Indicate the date(s) of the documents. This may be only one year, such as 1991, or a range (from-to), such as 1992-1995.
4. *RETENTION:* Indicate how long the records should be held. The retention period begins on the date mentioned on the records themselves, not the day the records are transferred to storage.
5. *BOX NO.:* Label the group of boxes you are sending to the records centre *1, 2, 3,* etc., to help the records centre staff determine which box contains what documents.

Arrange Transfer

Plans must be made for records transfer.

The records storage area may be located offsite, sometimes several miles from the originating office. Advance planning is necessary to ensure that personnel and equipment are available for physically moving the records from one area to another. In addition, the records centre personnel must be notified of the planned shipment so that they can coordinate their schedules and be prepared to receive the records upon arrival.

Learning Check: Can you describe how records are prepared and transferred to the records centre?

TERMINOLOGY REVIEW

Review the terms listed below in the Glossary on page 521.

block sorting	individual folder
classified index	long-term cross-reference
coding	manual storage and retrieval
colour coding	maximum-minimum method
cross-reference	periodic transfer
direct access	perpetual transfer
file backer	primary guide
filing	records transfer
filing segment	relative index
general folder	release mark
index	sorting
indexing	special folder
indirect access	special guide

REVIEW AND DISCUSSION

1. What storage procedures are applicable for most records systems?
2. Explain the purpose of guides in an active filing system.
3. Name two types of guides and give the purpose of each type.
4. Name three types of folders and explain the type of material stored in each.
5. Describe specific procedures for maintaining manual file operations.
6. Explain the use of indexes in accessing files.
7. How does the use of colour coding increase storage and retrieval efficiency?
8. Describe two applications in which colour is used.
9. Describe the use of colour coding in alphabetic, numeric, and alphanumeric classification systems.
10. Describe manual retrieval procedures for various types of media.
11. Describe procedures for retrieving and tracking records.
12. Describe two methods of transferring records to inactive storage.

APPLICATIONS

1. Visit an office that uses colour coding in its filing system. Submit a two-page summary to your instructor describing how the office uses colour for increased efficiency.

2. Visit a business office and study the guide/folder arrangement in the correspondence files. Evaluate the arrangement. If the arrangement is inefficient, prepare a suggested arrangement.

CONCLUDING CASES

A. Whitehall Business College

Whitehall Business College's enrolment for the current college year is 1,200 students. Enrolment has been steadily increasing during the school's 15 years of operation.

Student records are maintained in 20 four-drawer vertical file cabinets in the registrar's office. There is no space in the registrar's office for any additional file cabinets, although there is a little room in some of the drawers. Student records are filed by eight-digit student numbers in one continuous file without the use of guides. However, a label on each drawer identifies its contents.

The registrar is concerned about the increasing volume of records, the increasing demand for information from the student records, and the slowness of responses to requests. Dr. McPherson, Whitehall's president, ordered a freeze on hiring six months ago, which means the problems cannot be solved by hiring more staff.

1. Based on the information in this chapter, suggest improvements in the components of the student records system that should result in more efficient retrieval of information.
2. Are there other options Whitehall should consider to improve its student records function? Explain briefly the advantages and disadvantages of the options you suggest.

B. Manitoba Physiotherapy Associates

Manitoba Physiotherapy Associates has maintained patient records by patient number arranged in a terminal-digit system since it opened 12 years ago. The records are stored on open shelves. Misfiles have become an increasing problem as the numbers of therapists and clients increase and as the turnover in office staff occurs.

Kim Ing, MPA's records manager, must do something to control the number of misfiles. Often clients (and therapists) have to wait while the client records are located. Some of the physiotherapists have become impatient and started to ask the client for information again, rather than waiting for the records to appear. Some clients have chosen to go to other physiotherapists, and the effect on business is beginning to be evident. Further, the financial records are based on the client charts, so it is possible that some statements for services rendered are not being sent.

Kim's first thought was to hire another records clerk; however, she would like to avoid the ongoing cost of additional personnel.

1. Should Kim consider changes in procedures? Explain.
2. Should Kim consider other supplies options? Explain.

SUGGESTED READINGS AND RESOURCES

Diamond, Susan Z. "Colour Speeds Filing." *Office Systems* '88, Vol. 5, No. 2 (September, 1988), p. 66.

Fernberg, Patricia M. "Filing Fundamentals." *Modern Office Technology,* Vol. 34, No. 8 (August, 1989), p. 60.

Langemo, Mark. "Colour-Coded Filing." *Office Systems* '89, Vol. 6, No. 9 (September, 1989), p. 54.

Mims, Julian L. "An Outline for Files Control." *Records Management Quarterly,* Vol. 22, No. 1 (January, 1988), p. 18.

Sanders, Robert L. "The Quest for the Lost Record: A Records Management Myth." *Records Management Quarterly,* Vol. 27, No. 4 (October, 1993), p. 52.

Wells, Janet H., and Elisabeth Novakovich. "Bringing the Paper Files into the Family." *Records Management Quarterly,* Vol. 23, No. 1 (January, 1989), p. 22.

Zielinski, Janet M. "Color Coding Basics." *Records Management Quarterly,* Vol. 24, No. 3 (July, 1990), p. 34.

Profile
File Clerk

Robin Ross is a clerk/typist in the reception and docketing area of the Metropolitan Family Court and has been in the position for one year. There are 14 employees in the Family Court Section and six of them are in the Reception and Docketing area. The position titles in the family court are clerk/typist I, clerk/typist II, deputy clerk, docketing clerk, and receptionist.

Education and experience requirements for the clerk/typist I position include a high-school diploma plus a business/commercial course and keyboarding skill of 35 words per minute with accuracy. Excellent communication and interpersonal skills, and ability to deal tactfully with clients, court officials, and the general public are also required in this position. Familiarity with computers is also required.

Major duties include retrieving files for judges and checking the files in and out on the computerized tracking system. There are approximately 6,000 files maintained in the system. Robin also makes sure that all signed motions and abuse and neglect reviews are sent to the docketing clerk and unsigned orders are sent to the appropriate judges. Robin types summonses and correspondence, makes sure the flow of court activities is maintained through liaison with the court reporter, and checks in clients,

police officials, and lawyers. She processes the paperwork for young offenders and for taking in clients who have not been to family court before. It is her responsibility to check the documentation for peace bonds, assaults, Children's Aid cases, and child welfare. Robin fields requests from judges, lawyers, law clerks, and clients.

A colour-coded system has just been implemented. This will help to eliminate misfiles and speed up retrieval of records. During the implementation of the colour-coded system, new procedures were established for retrieving files. A centralized system for pulling files was established. Only authorized personnel may retrieve files from the system, and the movement of each file from location to location must be entered into the computerized tracking system. Because of the confidential nature of the family court records, privacy of information is a major concern, and the records must be kept secure at all times. Robin makes sure that unauthorized people do not have access to the files.

The advancement opportunities in this area are from clerk/typist I to clerk/typist II to docketing clerk to deputy clerk.

Robin recognizes the need for computer skills in her job and continues to upgrade her skills by attending classes in the area of computer software at the local community college.

Part 4
Imaging and Document Management Systems

Microfilm Technology

Learning Goals

After completing this chapter, you should be able to:

1. Define microforms and micrographics.
2. List and define the types of microforms.
3. Describe the general preparation of documents for filming.
4. Describe standard camera film.
5. Define reduction ratio.
6. Define the modes of microfilm image orientation.
7. Describe the types of microform cameras and list an application of each type.
8. Describe the types of microfilm coding.
9. Describe the types of film processors.
10. List the factors that affect film development.
11. Explain the functions of a light box, densitometer, resolution test, and methylene blue test in the inspecting process.
12. Define the types of film used in duplicating microforms.
13. Explain the importance of readers and reader-printers to the use of microforms.
14. Describe automated microimage storage and retrieval.
15. Explain the uses of computer output microfilm (COM).
16. Explain the process of computer-assisted retrieval (CAR) using microforms.
17. Describe general microform production requirements.
18. State the advantages and limitations of using microforms.
19. Evaluate the future of microfilm use.

MICROFILM IN IMAGE TECHNOLOGY

Image technology is the storage of documents or other data that includes text, graphics, tables, and pictures. Once this data is stored, it can be retrieved on a reader or a monitor or printed on paper. Three technologies are considered image technology in the office today. They are micrographics, optical disk, and facsimile. However, only two, micrographics and optical disk, are true storage and retrieval technologies. Facsimile technology is mainly used to transmit information (text, graphics, and pictures) from one location to another. Therefore, it is more a communication tool than a storage medium and is discussed in the communication subsystem section in Chapter 10. Recent advances in facsimile technology that allow the fax to function as an input device are discussed in Chapter 9 "Electronic Records Management."

Imaging is the process of recording an image of a document on microfilm or optical disk. Of course, both technologies are capable of storing text, but both also have the capability of storing graphics and pictures. The technology of micrographics has been around since the early 1800s; whereas, the optical disk technology is a new one.

Microforms

Demand for rapid storage and retrieval speeds, and the spiralling costs of storage space resulted in the popularity of microforms as a medium for storing records. Therefore, the records manager must have an in-depth knowledge of microfilm technology in order to make intelligent choices in the management of records. A **microform** is any medium that contains miniature or "micro" images. The records stored on microforms are often called **microrecords**. **Micrographics** is the term that refers to the procedures for creating, using, and storing microrecords. This is a mature industry, but one which is still experiencing growth because of some significant advantages microfilm has over other imaging technology.

Six types of microforms will be discussed in this section. These are (1) roll film, (2) microfiche, (3) jackets, (4) aperture cards, (5) nonstandard microforms, and (6) computer input microfilm. Microopaques, which in the past have seen limited use, are no longer chosen as an option (see Figure 8-1).

Roll Film

Roll film in 100- or 200-foot lengths is the most economical and frequently used microform. Roll film may be 16mm, 35mm, or 105mm and may be made from filming source documents or from computer output. Roll film may be stored on an open reel or encased in a cartridge or cassette. Documents such as correspondence, cheques, and sales records are filmed on 16mm film or 35mm film; oversize documents such as maps and engineering drawings are filmed on 35mm or 105mm film. The 105mm film is used with step and repeat cameras (described in the section on types of cameras below). Computer output microfilm is imaged directly from the computer mainframe or indirectly from magnetic computer tape. The direct process has the advantage of allowing the film to be imaged without the intermediate step of recording on magnetic tape. CRT (cathode ray tube—the picture tube of a video display terminal) recorders are being replaced by laser technology to capture computer output on microfilm.

Figure 8-1
Microforms

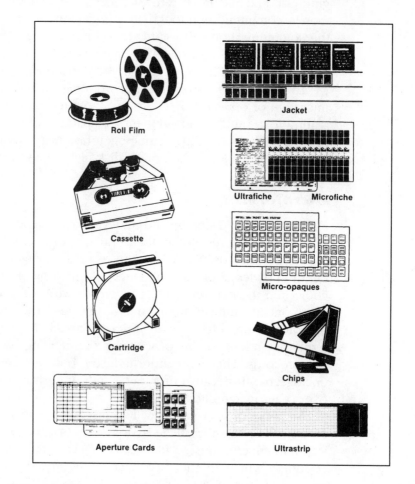

Roll Film

Jacket

Cassette

Ultrafiche　　Microfiche

Cartridge

Micro-opaques

Chips

Aperture Cards

Ultrastrip

Microfiche

One microfiche can store 98 document pages with a reduction ratio of 24x.

A **microfiche** is a sheet of film containing multiple miniature images in a grid pattern. Microfiche are available in various sizes; however, the most common sizes are 6 by 4 inches and its close metric counterpart, 105mm by 148mm. This size accommodates 98 document pages per fiche (using a 24x reduction ratio, which is explained below in the subsection on image size). Fiche that are manually stored and retrieved have an eye-readable header (line containing title information) that *legal, Equipment To read it*

identifies the content. Fiche that have very high reduction ratios (90x or greater) are referred to as ultrafiche. One 6-by-4-inch **ultrafiche** may contain 4,000 or more pages. The lower right corner frame (or frames) of the grid usually contains an index of either that particular fiche or an entire set of fiche. Microfiche (105mm film) may also be imaged directly from computer tapes or on-line from electronic impulses producing another form of computer output microfilm (COM).

Jackets

A **jacket** is a transparent plastic carrier for strips of microfilm cut from reels. The horizontal area into which the strip of film is placed is called a channel. Jackets may be of several sizes and may contain either 16mm or 35mm film. Individual frames or additional strips of microfilm may be added to the jacket at any time. The plastic carriers are stored on cards. These cards are often preprinted to accommodate specific information (such as personnel files or bank accounts) and provide channels for one or more strips of microfilm as may be necessary to keep the file current. The microfilm stored in the jacket can be duplicated so that the duplicate becomes a form of microfiche. The duplicate copy of the jacket (microfiche) cannot be updated, however.

Jackets provide channels for one or more strips of microfilm.

Aperture Cards

An **aperture card** is a 7 3/8-by-3 1/4-inch card into which (an) opening(s) has (have) been cut to accommodate the insertion of a frame(s) of microfilm. Aperture cards are widely used for a single large item, such as a blueprint or map on 35mm film, or multiple images on 16mm film. Indexing information may be punched into the card and printed across the top.

Nonstandard Microforms

Some additional microforms (chips, scrolls, and strips) are in limited use in custom-designed microrecords systems. A **chip** is a piece of film containing a microimage and optical or magnetic coding for automated retrieval. A **scroll** is a roll of extra-wide film (105mm) found in some automated retrieval systems. **Strips** are short lengths of film (105mm) that are stored in containers and coded for use in an automated retrieval system.

Computer Input Microfilm

Computer input microfilm (CIM) is microfilm containing images that are converted to electronic signals for storage on magnetic tape to be input into a computer. CIM has great potential as a low-cost method of rapidly introducing information from large microfilm files (such as medical, insurance, or census data) into a computer for processing.

MICROFORM PROCEDURES AND EQUIPMENT

Each of the steps in producing and using microrecords requires special procedures and equipment. Required procedures and equipment options are discussed in this section.

Filming

When the records to be filmed have been identified, the documents must be prepared. Film, image size, image orientation, and type of camera also must be selected.

Document Preparation

Before documents can be filmed, they must be prepared for the camera. The details of preparation are different for different types of cameras. However, these preparations are not always necessary, particularly for the planetary camera (described in the section on types of cameras below). General preparations may include:

1. All paper clips and staples must be removed since these may cause camera malfunctions.
2. Torn papers should be mended with transparent tape.
3. Small papers should be attached to standard-sized paper by using transparent tape or rubber cement.
4. Unnecessary attachments such as envelopes, routing slips, receipt acknowledgments, or duplicate copies (unless considered part of the record) should be destroyed.
5. Computer printouts can be processed in batches by using a pin-fed method (pins on a machine fit into the punched holes on the sides of the computer printouts) to feed the printouts onto the camera bed.
6. Forms do not need to be separated for filming.

Camera Film

Standard camera film uses silver halide emulsion to capture details.

Microfilm is either camera film or copy film. (Copy film is discussed in the section on duplicating below.) All microfilm is made of an acetate, triacetate, or polyester base material. Standard camera film is often called silver film because of its silver halide emulsion coating. This coating makes the film extremely light-sensitive and, thus, able to capture the detail essential to microimages.

Image Size

A reduction ratio compares film image size to original document size.

The use of microforms requires reduction of document size to a miniature image on film and the magnification of that image for reading. Image size is usually stated as a reduction ratio. A **reduction ratio** is the size of the film image as compared with the size of the original document. Reduction ratios are expressed as 24x, 30x, or 24:1, 30:1, and so forth. A reduction ratio of 24x, for example, means that the film image is 1/24th the size of the original document.

Image Orientation

Image orientation is the positioning of images on the film and depends on the kind of camera being used. Single images may be placed across the width of the film in either the cine or comic modes (see Figure 8-2). The **cine mode**, which takes its name from cinema film, is achieved by feeding the document into the camera horizontally, with the heading or top of each sheet entering the camera first. The **comic mode** of image orientation, which takes its name from the manner in which frames of a comic strip are presented, is achieved by feeding the document into the camera with the heading to the left or to the right.

Figure 8-2
Modes of Image
Orientation

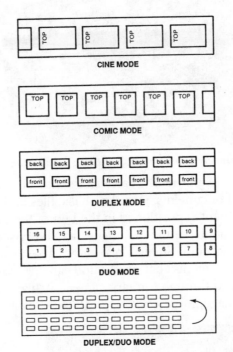

Two images may be placed across the width of the film in either the duplex or the duo mode (see Figure 8-2). The **duplex mode** is a method of microfilming both sides of the document simultaneously with the images presented side by side. The **duo mode** is a method of microfilming in which images are placed in consecutive order down one half of a strip of film and back up the other half. Duo mode filming allows the filming of more documents per roll of film at high reduction ratios than the duplex mode. There is also a film that provides for **duplex/duo mode**.

Types of Cameras

Several types of cameras are used in microfilming source documents. Special filming equipment is required to produce computer output microfilm or microfiche.

A **rotary camera** uses rotating belts to transport documents through the machine and advances the film at the same relative speed to create the effect of a stationary image (see Figure 8-3). A rotary camera is used to film high-volume records (such as cheques, invoices, and sales slips), which require fast, efficient, and economical procedures. Filming rates depend on the skill of the operator and the condition of the documents to be filmed.

A rotary camera is used to film high-volume records.

Figure 8-3
Rotary Camera

Source: Photo courtesy of Bell & Howell Document Management Company

Planetary cameras are flatbed cameras.

A **planetary camera** is a flatbed camera used to microfilm all types of documents, including basic files and engineering drawings. The document is positioned in the bed of the camera (see Figure 8-4). The film unit above the document may be raised or lowered to vary the reduction ratio. Smaller planetary cameras are available for filming smaller documents that are bound, are of varying sizes, or are too brittle to feed through a rotary camera. A planetary camera produces a superior image, more control, and better resolution than a rotary camera.

Figure 8-4
Planetary Camera

Source: Courtesy of Minolta Corp.

The step and repeat camera is used in micropublishing applications.

A **step and repeat camera** is also a flatbed camera with an overhead film unit. The step and repeat camera is designed to expose images in uniform rows and columns for preparing microfiche (see Figure 8-5). Images are positioned on the microfiche by the programmed movement of the film over a stationary aperture. The film is stationary when the exposure is made.

The step and repeat camera is used in micropublishing books, catalogues, parts lists, and specifications. A step and repeat camera is particularly appropriate for these applications because of the simplicity of its operation and because it allows the precision alignment necessary to prepare an index of images and to locate a particular frame. Since a step and repeat camera produces a better-looking product, it is used if many duplicates will be made of the original. The product is also more expensive to create. Special characteristics of step and repeat cameras are now being incorporated into other planetary cameras and so, they are not as much used as they once were.

Figure 8-5
Step and Repeat
Camera

Source: Photo courtesy of Bell & Howell Document Management Company

A **COM recorder** records electronic data from computer output onto microfilm or microfiche. The units may be either on-line or off-line. On-line units interface with the host computer; they do not require the intermediate step of computer tape input. Off-line units operate only with computer tape input. Formerly COM recorders used standard COM film, which was processed outside the recorder in a separate processing unit. New highly automated systems are designed with the recorder, processor, and duplicator in the same unit and function largely without human intervention.

 Learning Check: Can you name and describe four types of cameras?

Figure 8-6
COM Recorder,
Processor, and
Duplicator Unit

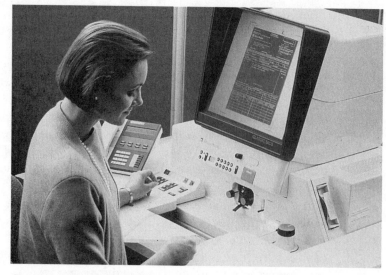

Source: Courtesy of Bell and Howell

Coding

Coding on roll film
identifies segments
and locations.

During the filming process, microforms may be coded or indexed for
automated retrieval. The coding may utilize either (1) flash targets, (2)
bar coding, (3) odometer indexing, or (4) blip coding. Blip coding is
the predominant method. The four coding methods are illustrated in
Figure 8-7.

Figure 8-7
Microforms Coding
Techniques

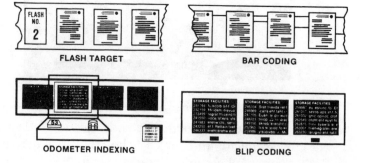

Flash Targets

Flash targets are used to divide a roll of film into batches of information. A flash card, which identifies a batch, may be used as a title
page to begin a roll of film, a section of roll film, or a row or channel
of a microfiche. Such a target would be positioned to indicate each
change in subject matter. When such a coding system is used in producing computer output microfiche, the final frame of the microfiche
may contain an index of its contents.

Bar Coding

Bar coding is another method of coding microforms. **Bar coding** is a pattern of clear and opaque bars between images on roll film. Its appearance is similar to that of the pricing code on many food items. Bar coding requires additional space on the film and for retrieval requires a special terminal to advance the film, interpret the code, and stop the film at the desired group of images. The operator must then advance the film frame by frame to the desired image.

Odometer Indexing

Odometer indexing indicates the distance of each image from the beginning of the roll of film. This system requires that processed film pass through a viewer with an odometer to record these index codes. A contents index may appear on the first frame of the roll of film.

Blip Coding

Image-count marking or **blip coding** is accomplished by placing a blip (an opaque or nonopaque optical rectangle) below each image to identify it. A microimage terminal equipped with logic and a computer interface counts blips until it reaches the requested frame.

 Learning Check: Can you name and describe four methods of coding or indexing microforms?

Processing

Although many smaller organizations now outsource their microfilming for commercial processing, noncommercial processors available today process film to archival quality standards, do not require darkrooms, and are relatively simple to operate. Such advantages make it feasible to develop and process microfilm on site when an organization does a good deal of microfilming or needs fast turnaround. These processors develop 16mm or 35mm film at a rate of 5 to 10 feet per minute.

Types of Processors

A roller transport processor uses rollers to move the film in a serpentine path.

The three types of processors—deep tank, roller transport, and straight film path—are shown in Figure 8-8. In a deep tank processor, the film is supported by bottom and top rollers and is pulled through the developing chemicals by a lead document moving in a serpentine path. A roller transport processor uses rollers to move the film in a serpentine path through the developer. A straight film path processor uses rollers to move the film in a straight line through the developing solution.

Reversal Processing

Reversal processing is a procedure that changes the polarity of the film. **Polarity** refers to the light to dark relationship of a film image and can be either positive or negative. Positive polarity (image) produces

Figure 8-8
Types of
Processors

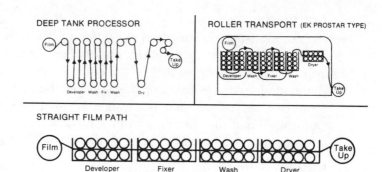

black characters on a clear background; negative polarity produces clear characters on a black background.

Reversal processing was developed for use in conjunction with COM, which has positive polarity. Because a positive image produces a glare from light passing through the clear background in a reader, and also magnifies dirt and dust on the film, positive polarity may be undesirable, thus creating a need for reversal processing.

Developing

The higher the temperature of the developer, the less time the film is required to be in the solution.

The four factors affecting film development are (1) the temperature of the developer, (2) the length of time the film is in the solution, (3) the condition of the developer, and (4) the agitation of the film. The higher the temperature of the developer, the less time the film is required to be in the solution. If the film is transported through the solution at a fixed speed, the only way to control development is to control the temperature.

The fixing solution dissolves any silver bromine not reduced to metallic silver during processing.

Since the developer becomes less effective with repeated use, it must be replaced as used and in accordance with the manufacturer's recommendations. Film agitation is provided automatically as the film moves through the processor. Upon leaving the developer, the film is submerged in a fixing (hypo) solution to stop development and harden the emulsion. This fixing solution dissolves any silver bromine that was not reduced to metallic silver during processing. (Some organizations find it advantageous to reclaim this silver from the fixing solution for resale.) After being submerged in the fixing solution, the film is washed and dried.

Inspecting

Established quality standards for microfilm can only be maintained through frequent inspections. An inspection may include checking with a light box, taking densitometer readings, making comparisons with a resolution test chart, and performing a methylene blue test.

Light Box

Film is cranked over the glass top of a light box and read with a magnifying glass or jeweller's loupe. The purpose of this initial inspection is to determine that the documents were captured on the film without any distortion, such as improper positioning or blurred images.

Density

Density is a numeric measurement, obtained from a densitometer, of the amount of light that passes through the black background of negative microfilm. The standard density measurement for film is 1.0 to 1.2; measurements outside this range indicate that the film images have poor contrast. Lower readings indicate that insufficient light was used in filming; higher readings indicate that too much light was used in filming or that the film was overexposed.

Resolution

Resolution is the sharpness of the image.

Resolution measures the degree of sharpness or acuity of the film, which refers to the ability of the film to satisfactorily record fine details, such as separate but closely placed lines. The resolution or sharpness of the image becomes increasingly important with enlargement since any blurred image will become increasingly fuzzy. Good resolution results from good film and lens quality. Resolution is usually expressed as the maximum number of line-pairs per millimetre the film system (camera, microfilm, and development process) can satisfactorily resolve, with measurement made using a microscope.

The National Bureau of Standards Resolution Test Chart 1010, the most frequently used test chart, consists of 21 identical test patterns in varying sizes (see Figure 8-9). Each pattern on the chart is assigned a numeric value from 1.0 (largest pattern) to 18 (smallest pattern). The resolution test consists of determining the smallest pattern of five lines in each direction that can be distinctly recognized under the microscope. Values below 120 lines per millimetre (LPM) indicate substandard resolution.

Methylene Blue Test

Because hypo (fixing solution) residue affects the longevity of film images, a methylene blue test is performed to test for this residue. Commercial processors perform this test routinely once a day or every other day on each processor. The test can be performed in-house by trained personnel using test kits and following the manufacturer's instructions.

 Learning Check: Can you distinguish between density and resolution?

Figure 8-9
Microcopy
Resolution Test
Chart

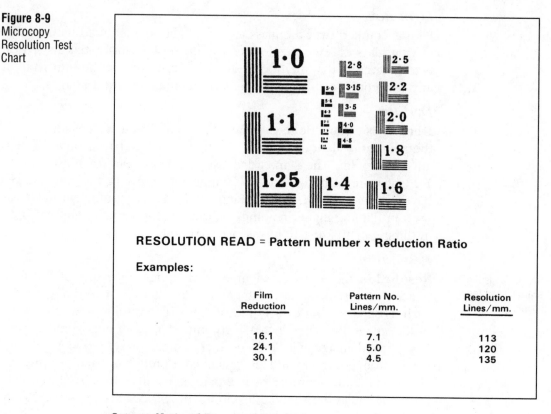

Source: National Bureau of Standards

Duplicating

Duplicating is the process of producing multiple copies of microforms, so that one of the great advantages of microfilm—low distribution costs—may be realized.

Duplication of microfilm can be accomplished by simultaneously exposing two rolls of film in the film unit of the camera. Multiple copies of microfilm are, however, most frequently made by contact printing. **Contact printing** is achieved by placing the emulsion side of the original developed camera film in contact with the emulsion side of the copy film and directing a light beam through the original image to the copy. The copy film is then developed to produce the duplicate microfilm.

Each type of copy film—silver print, diazo, and vesicular—has different characteristics.

There are three types of copy film, each with different characteristics: (1) silver print film, (2) diazo film, and (3) vesicular film. Silver print film may be either reversal or nonreversal film. Reversal film will produce a positive copy from a negative-image original; nonreversal film produces a copy with the same polarity as the original film. (If the original film has a positive image, the copy will have a positive image.) Duplication of silver print film requires darkroom conditions. After exposure, the film is developed using the same procedures as for the original film.

Diazo film is a nonsilver film, consisting of an acetate or polyester base coated with diazonium salts and a dye. This coating is light sensitive. Diazo film is developed through exposure to ammonia vapours in a development chamber. If the film is underdeveloped, the process can be repeated until the film is fully developed. Thermal diazo film, which can be developed by heat in the same type of equipment used to process vesicular film, is also available. Diazo duplicates always have the same polarity as the original film.

Vesicular film is developed by a heat process. Most vesicular film will produce duplicates having the reverse polarity of the original film. The development of vesicular duplicates does not require darkroom conditions.

Reading

Magnification of microimages should match reduction ratio.

Utilization of microforms depends on the ease with which the stored information can be read. Microimages are usually read using a reader (viewer) that magnifies the microimages to eye-readable sizes. When the magnification of the reader matches the reduction of the camera used in filming, an image will fill the viewing screen and, consequently, be easier to read. If the reader magnification is less than the reduction, the image will be smaller than the screen, may be difficult to read, and may cause eyestrain. If the magnification is greater than the reduction, only a part of the image will be visible on the screen at any given time.

Some microform readers have screens that allow the simultaneous viewing of two pages. Readers are available in varying sizes from freestanding models to hand-held models (see Figure 8-10). Reader-printers have the ability to produce a hard copy of a document shown on the screen.

Learning Check: Can you name and describe the three types of copy film?

AUTOMATED MICROIMAGE STORAGE AND RETRIEVAL

There are many sources of microimages.

Microimage storage and retrieval is the process of storing and retrieving records that have been reduced in size and stored on roll film, fiche, aperture cards, and jackets. Manual storage of microfilm follows the same guidelines as paper storage. Today, however, a wide range of choices is offered for automated storage and retrieval of information in microform format and a huge potential exists for combining micrographic systems with electronic imaging systems. All of these choices require physically coding the film, fiche, jacket, or aperture card in some way. The generic term for these approaches is Automated Document Storage and Retrieval (ADSTAR) systems.

Figure 8-10
Microform Reading
Equipment

Source: Canon U.S.A., Inc.

Source: Photo courtesy of Bell & Howell Document Management Company

Information Capture

Information is captured on microforms by filming source documents or computer printouts, by converting machine-readable computer tapes to microimages by input from a word processor into the computer, by facsimile input through a computer, or by direct input from a computer's memory. When source documents are filmed, an operator prepares the documents for the camera, using the same techniques that are used to prepare documents for filing.

COM is an integration of computer and microform technology.

Computer output microfilm (COM) is an integration of computer and microform technology that converts the information on computer tapes or from computer memory into a microform, without a paper intermediary. A COM recorder, or COM unit, records the information on special film and performs a similar function to the laser printer's output of hardcopy (paper) printouts from the computer. The output may be roll film or fiche, whichever is the more appropriate medium for a particular organization.

Some sophisticated word processors have the capability of providing input to COM. Word processing disks are translated into computer tapes that the COM recorder converts into computer output microfilm (COM). This provides paper copies for the general public and microfilm copies for internal use or record storage. Figure 8-11 illustrates components of an integrated micrographics system.

Figure 8-11
Components of an
Integrated
Micrographics
System

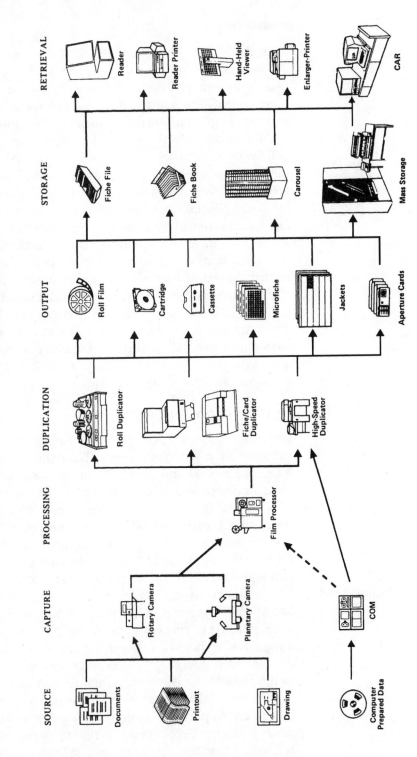

Source: International Information Management Congress, Bethesda, Maryland

Indexing

Records that are filmed are assigned descriptors (date, author, recipient, key words) along with their film addresses. The film addresses usually include roll number, frame number, and any other identifying number that will assist in locating the records. A sequential number may be assigned to provide a visual verification that the located record is the one that was requested. Indexing may be accomplished in several ways. Computer indexing of source documents may be accomplished during the filming process by having the microfilmer assign the descriptors from the hard copy. Source document indexing may also be accomplished after filming. The operator places the roll of microfilm into a retrieval terminal and advances to the first document image. From this image, the operator assigns descriptors, which are keyed into disk memory along with the sequential number assigned to the record. Indexing may also be accomplished automatically with very sophisticated computer equipment and software.

With computerized indexing, records may be filed randomly. The computer can automatically cross-reference—some systems incorporate dictionaries that automatically reference documents under appropriate synonyms. These complex systems allow indexes to be updated and, at the same time, retain the old index (identified as such) as an audit trail.

Information Retrieval

Computer-assisted retrieval (CAR), using microforms, capitalizes on the strengths of two technologies—the ability to store images on microforms at low cost and the ability of the computer to make logical decisions under programmed control. At one time, all documents had to be arranged in the desired order before filming took place. **Computer-assisted retrieval (CAR)** uses microfilming techniques to film documents in random order and the computer to index the documents for fast, precise retrieval. CAR serves all types of microforms, both roll film and unitized formats such as jackets and microfiche.

Computer-assisted retrieval can be operated either off-line or on-line to the computer. Off-line retrieval has indexing and retrieval as separate functions. The operator, using the computer terminal, keys in information to begin the search for the record. In response to the operator-provided information, the computer screen will display the location of the record. The operator is then responsible for finding that record.

On-line CAR has retrieval connected to the computer. The computer may respond in several ways, depending on the level of assistance given by the computer program. Minimum computer assistance is given when the operator keys in information; the computer then responds by displaying the roll of film that the operator should insert. After the operator inserts the appropriate roll of film, the computer

Computer-assisted retrieval can be either off-line or on-line.

advances the film until it finds the information that has been requested. The maximum level of computer assistance is given when the
operator keys in the search parameters and the record image is displayed on the screen without further operator intervention.

Fiche and other microforms may be retrieved through automated
systems that combine a computer database, image processing, and
communications technologies to capture, store, manipulate, and
retrieve both computer-based and microfilmed source document information. An operator can enter a descriptor using a keypad. The microprocessor then scans the fiche or fiche carrier to locate the record, and
the information is delivered to the user quickly and efficiently. Often
a robotic autoloader, more commonly known as a **jukebox**, is used to
store large numbers of film magazines or cartridges. When jukeboxes
are linked to the system, an operator at a workstation can instruct the
computer to retrieve a particular image or file. Under computer control, the autoloader automatically retrieves the cartridge or magazine,
loads it at a scanning station, and threads and advances the film to the
desired frame. The computer then scans and digitizes the image for
transmission to a workstation.

Charge-out cards should be used for fiche or reels to maintain file
integrity. The charge-out card should be a distinctive colour to flag the
absent reel or fiche and large enough to write the user's name, location of the reel, and date the film was removed on it. Automated document retrieval and control systems (as shown in Figure 8-12) are also
used to maintain file integrity.

Figure 8-12
Automated
Document Retrieval
System

Source: Courtesy of Bell and Howell

Learning Check: Can you discuss the strengths of computer-assisted retrieval using microforms?

Image Transmission System Example

An example of the successful combination of CAR microfilm with magnetic and optical disks in the same imaging system is Quebec's income tax system, which is administered by the province's Ministry of Revenue. It is one of the largest imaging systems in North America. With the cooperation of Imnet Corporation and Bell and Howell, the income tax returns of Quebec citizens are microfilmed and prepared in cartridge format. The Ministry loads the 16mm-microfilm cartridges into any one of eight microfilm jukeboxes. Each of these jukeboxes contains 1.8 million microfilm images. In less than 10 seconds, the jukebox selects the appropriate cartridge of microfilm, locates the requested image, scans it, and, using the Ministry's local area network (LAN), sends the image to the person who requested it. The LAN allows access to the microfilm database from several remote locations around the province. Other Ministry of Revenue files recorded on optical disk are also available through the same LAN and an optical disk jukebox. Both types of images are displayed on the same electronic image display monitors throughout the network.

PLANNING THE MICROFORMS CONTROL PROGRAM

After the decision has been made to implement a micrographics program, consideration must be given to a microrecords control program. Control decisions must be made regarding where to locate the micrographics system and how to control the microfilming operation.

Examine Microforms Production Requirements

Offsite locations are usually operated by a service bureau.

Microforms can be produced either in-house or offsite. An in-house facility is operated within the company location; offsite locations are usually operated by a service bureau. Regardless of where the microfilm production takes place, however, certain general requirements for production efficiency and effective use must be met. These requirements are discussed in the following subsections.

Quality Assurance

Quality of output is the most important consideration.

The quality of the output is one of the most important considerations in the production of microfilm. Quality may be measured in terms of clarity, density, eye-readable headers, and film thickness. Poor quality film that is difficult to read or deteriorates is unacceptable regardless of the superiority of any or all other criteria. Minimum quality standards must be established, monitored, and enforced. This is often more easily accomplished by an in-house operation.

Legal Acceptability

The Canadian Information and Image Management Society has been involved both in producing a new national standard for the use of microfilm and electronic images as documentary evidence in legal cases and in proposing amendments to the federal and provincial evidence acts. The October 1993 edition of *Microfilm and Electronic Images as Documentary Evidence,* available from the Canadian General Standards Board in Ottawa, provides guidelines for establishing an image management program and includes evidentiary requirements as well.[1] In order to be legally acceptable, the quality of the original film and all copies must be maintained. If certain elements are controlled, microfilm records are usually acceptable in the courts.

Production Turnaround Time

Turnaround time is the time required for processing.

Turnaround time requirements differ according to the needs of the individual users within the organization. For some applications, fast turnaround time is not essential. It may be necessary to know only that the microform will be delivered at the requested, specified intervals. Other applications, however, may require very quick turnaround in order for employees to perform their jobs in a timely manner. In either case, users should expect to receive microforms within the same time frame as they currently receive hard copy.

When an off-premises service bureau is contracted to perform the processing, equal consideration must be given to each client. However, a service bureau off-premises cannot afford to be as responsive to the needs of the individual user as can an in-house staff operation.

File Integrity

File integrity refers to the accuracy and completeness of the file. For an in-house operation, responsibility for lost or misfiled records lies with the organization's staff. When an outside agency is employed to produce microfilm, tracking misplaced records is more difficult because more people are handling the records, and organizational control over the integrity of the files may be considerably diminished or lost altogether.

Information Control

In an in-house operation, data never leaves the premises for processing. Any required information is always accessible to users; there is no dependence on an outside agency. Many users see this complete control over information as vital to the information processing function.

---

[1] *Microfilm and Electronic Images as Documentary Evidence* (Ottawa: Canadian General Standards Board Sales Centre), Can/CGSB-72.11-93.

Data Security

Information security is a major concern to all organizations. The current emphasis on legislation and enforcement of individual privacy and freedom of information forces organizations to be especially careful of the security of their documents. In-house operations provide better control over the physical security of information as well as better control over employees responsible for maintaining information security.

Standards Consistency

Quality checks must be made often so that any deviation from the desired standards can be immediately detected and corrective action taken. Service bureaus also actively seek to maintain consistent standards and stress the importance of uniformity to their employees.

Equipment Required

The equipment required in microforms production varies according to the needs of the organization, the input to be processed, and the output desired. Input may be source documents or computer output film; output may be in the form of computer output microfilm or microfiche. Therefore, equipment must be selected after analyzing the needs, input, and desired output. Companies may not wish to spend their resources to properly equip a facility. The additional cost considerations of maintenance and equipment downtime must also be considered.

Training Required

Trained personnel are required to run the microfilm production operation. Consequently, the provision for training and regular updating of the staff is an important consideration.

Many companies do not have the trained microfilm staff, nor do they have the expertise necessary to train inexperienced personnel. An additional cost incurred by inexperienced microfilming staff is the cost of refilming during the learning curve.

Space Needed for Facility

Some companies do not have the space required to house the equipment and staff for a complete microfilming operation. Other companies may not want to reallocate space currently used for other company operations.

Determine Production Location

Microforms can be produced in-house as an organizational operation or by an offsite service bureau on a contracted basis. Each approach to microforms production has benefits and limitations. These benefits and limitations must be identified and carefully evaluated prior to making the decision regarding in-house or service bureau microfilming.

However, many organizations are now outsourcing their microfilming requirements.

Cost Benefit Analysis

A **cost benefit analysis** compares the benefits of a new procedure, system, or technology with its costs. In this instance, the analysis should be conducted to determine which microform production location is more appropriate for the individual organization. The benefits must at least equal, if not exceed, costs. Some benefits are not tangible, but they must still be considered in the determination. For example, the confidence and security an executive might feel by having all records processed in-house is an intangible benefit—one that cannot be measured in dollar value.

Service bureaus spread overhead expenses over many users, so the cost is often significantly less than for an in-house facility. Long-term costs should be considered as well as initial start-up costs.

IMPLEMENTING THE MICROFORMS CONTROL PROGRAM

After the decision regarding in-house microrecords operation or service bureau processing is made, the microrecords control system is implemented.

Analyze Microforms Conversion Requests

Additional requests for microform applications should be evaluated.

After the original conversion from paper to microforms, any additional request for a microforms application must be evaluated to determine if the application is appropriate and within the cost-benefit parameters set by the organization. A formal procedure should be established for evaluating these requests.

Establish Storage and Retrieval Controls

Any effective records management system, regardless of the method of storing and retrieving records (manual, mechanical, or automated) or the form of the record (electronic, magnetic, microform, or hard copy), must have controls for storing and retrieving records. Some storage and quality controls are unique to microfilm applications.

Quality Assurance Procedures

Resolution and density checks are a daily routine.

Since the ability to extract information from a microform depends on the quality of the product, a daily routine should be established for making resolution and density checks to ensure that all microfilm produced is to specification. Documents such as job status logs, microfilm inspection reports, and source document microfiche inspection reports provide an audit trail.

Special Film Targets

Special film targets of the same size as the documents being filmed are used when filming to indicate unique filming procedures or to identify particular sequences on the film. Some of these special targets are:

- **Cross-reference targets**, which provide information regarding the location of related records;
- **Missing document targets**, which document the fact that certain records were missing when the records were received for filming;
- **Substandard document targets**, which show that the original record was not completely legible and that the quality of the microimage is below standards;
- **Correction targets**, which testify that the preceding document has been remicrofilmed to assure legibility;
- **Camera operator targets**, which provide identification of the camera operator and the date of the filming; and
- **Organization of information targets**, which state the order in which the records were received and filmed.

Selected film targets are shown in Figure 8-13 in reduced size.

✓ **Learning Check: Can you explain the function of special film targets and give three examples?**

Determine Charge-Back to Users

Accountability is essential.

One of the controls exercised is a system of accountability for the costs of converting paper documents to microforms; the user is charged for the costs involved in the conversion, which may be calculated in several different ways. This charge-back system provides the basis for monitoring and evaluating microforms use.

Maintain File Integrity

File integrity refers to the accuracy and completeness of the record. Updatable microfilm jackets allow all of the file information to accumulate on one record and provide a master jacket from which copies may be made. It eliminates the necessity of sending a number of microfilm records to a user because one single record contains all of the information (see Figure 8-14).

An additional protection of file integrity is a dated **certificate of authenticity** or **identification**. This target, signed by the operator, may be imaged on each fiche or at the beginning of every roll of film. If any question arises regarding the record, validation may be made with the operator who processed the record.

Figure 8-13
Special Film
Targets

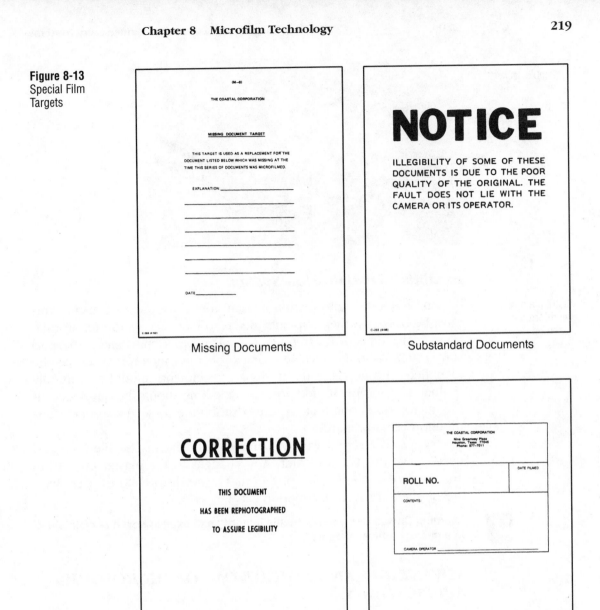

Missing Documents   Substandard Documents

Correction   Camera Operator

Source: The Coastal Corporation, Houston, Texas

Figure 8-14
Updatable Jackets

Establish Distribution System

Distribution of microforms is based on recipient needs.

As with any other information system, the distribution of microforms must be based on the recipients' needs to have access to the information. At the time of the request for microforms conversion, the person(s) who should receive copies of the microform should be identified. The needs of the designated recipients should be carefully evaluated; appropriate additions or deletions should be suggested. If the microform is one that requires distribution to several users, a distribution list is prepared.

Master copies are usually maintained in the master file area and never leave this central point. Any changes to the master microform are made centrally. Copies of the master are distributed to users who are on the approved distribution list.

 Learning Check: Can you define file integrity and explain how it is maintained in a micrographics system?

ADVANTAGES AND LIMITATIONS OF MICROFORMS APPLICATIONS

The decision to use microrecords must be based on an organization's specific needs and records applications. Consideration of a new microrecords application usually arises from a specific records problem, such as limited storage space or the need for faster storage and retrieval speeds. When a conversion to microrecords seems to be an appropriate solution to a records problem, the organization must examine the advantages and limitations of using microrecords and complete a feasibility study to determine whether the benefits outweigh the costs of such a conversion. A **feasibility study** is an examination of the practicality of implementing new or modified procedures, methods, or technologies.

As with every records management tool, the use of microrecords has both advantages and limitations. Each of these should be weighed carefully in evaluating the potential benefits of using microforms within an organization.

Advantages

The most obvious advantage of using microforms is the floor space saved for uses other than records storage. Records reduced to microimages may require as little as 2 percent of the storage space the original records required. The reduction in records size also means fewer storage cabinets, which will produce savings in storage equipment and supplies purchased.

Microrecords improve file integrity; individual film images cannot be separated or misplaced as sheets of paper might be. This advantage increases in significance as the number of pieces of paper per file increases.

As the demand for up-to-date information increases, improved productivity resulting from the use of microrecords becomes more important. Also, information stored as microimages can often be retrieved in a few seconds from an automated file system. No longer is valuable time wasted in walking to the file room while customers or managers wait for a response.

Microforms stored under proper conditions will last for 100 years or more. Thus storing records in microform is an excellent means of protecting vital and archival records. As a solution to protect vital records, the original microfilm can be stored offsite while copies are stored in the office. For archival records, microfilm's very long life and lack of dependence on hardware and software to access the information make it a good option for long-term record storage. The low cost of making diazo duplicates and of mailing duplicate microrecords enhances the practicality of their use. In addition, producing paper copies of microimages when required is easy. Also, microforms are (in most cases) admissible as primary evidence in court.

Limitations

One major limitation of using microforms continues to be that microimages are unfamiliar to many users. While familiarity is increasing, users need to be trained in the use of readers and reader-printers and in how to locate the desired image. Sophisticated integrated systems require even more training. In addition, the floor space required for equipment and storage facilities does add to the costs.

Microforms use is also limited by the turnaround time needed to produce microimages. During preparation and filming, the original

Microforms improve file integrity.

records are inaccessible. Further, the inability to annotate or change information on microrecords makes the production of microrecords impractical for high-activity records (any records that are modified frequently). Other imaging solutions are now competing with microfilm and will be discussed in Chapter 9.

THE FUTURE OF MICROFILM

Upon the arrival of optical disks with their huge storage potential, some experts predicted that microfilm would soon disappear. However, micrographics today appears to have a solid niche in the imaging market. Hybrid systems are available that combine the best features of microfilm and imaging technology, allowing users to add technological improvements while maintaining their past investment in microfilm. In addition, the following features of microfilm make it attractive:

- Microfilm takes up approximately 2 percent as much space as equivalent paper records.
- The film itself has a permanence of from 100 to 500 years.
- Microfilm can be read with the human eye; it is not totally dependent on specific hardware or software for access.
- It is a mature product with well-proven uses.
- The legality of microfilm is well established.

Because of these factors, microfilm will continue to be used for the foreseeable future as an excellent solution for storing large volumes of records for long periods—fulfilling archival needs. It also has a place in disaster planning by functioning as a backup for an organization's records.

TERMINOLOGY REVIEW

Review the terms listed below in the Glossary on page 521.

aperture card	contact printing
bar coding	cost benefit analysis
blip coding	density
certificate of authenticity/	duo mode
identification	duplex mode
chip	duplex/duo mode
cine mode	feasibility study
comic mode	file integrity
computer-assisted retrieval (CAR)	flash targets
computer input microfilm (CIM)	imaging
computer output microfilm	image orientation
(COM)	image technology
COM recorder	jacket

jukebox
microfiche
microform
micrographics
microimage storage and retrieval
microrecords
odometer indexing
planetary camera
polarity
reduction ratio

resolution
reversal processing
roll film
rotary camera
scroll
special film target
step and repeat camera
strips
ultrafiche

REVIEW AND DISCUSSION

1. Define the terms microforms and micrographics.
2. List and define five types of microforms.
3. What are the general preparations that may be required of documents prior to filming?
4. Describe standard camera film.
5. Define reduction ratio.
6. Define five modes of microfilm image orientation.
7. Describe four types of microform cameras and list one application for each type.
8. Describe four types of microfilm coding.
9. Describe three types of film processors.
10. List four factors that affect film development.
11. Explain the function of a light box, densitometer, resolution test, and methylene blue test in the inspection process.
12. Define three types of film used in duplicating microforms.
13. Explain the importance of readers and reader-printers to the utilization of microforms.
14. How is information captured for and retrieved from automated microimage storage?
15. Explain the uses of computer output microfilm (COM).
16. Explain the process of computer-assisted retrieval (CAR) using microforms.
17. Describe seven general microform production requirements.
18. State three advantages and three limitations of using microforms.
19. Evaluate the factors that will affect the future of microfilm.

APPLICATIONS

1. Using ads in periodicals in your college library, compare the advertised features of three brands of one of the following types of equipment: microfilm cameras, COM recorders, readers,

reader-printers, duplicators, or computer-assisted retrieval systems. Prepare a grid (similar to the one below) to report your findings. Use a ✓ to indicate which brands have which features.

Type of Equipment _____			
	Manufacturer		
Feature	Name_____ Model No._____	Name_____ Model No._____	Name_____ Model No._____

2. Visit an organization that has a micrographics department and write a report on the visit. Include the following information in the report:
   a. Training provided employees
   b. Types of equipment used
   c. Procedures established to process microforms
   d. Types of documents filmed
   e. Use of in-house or service bureau processing
   f. Procedures used to evaluate the microforms process
   g. Any additional important information

3. You are the records manager of Jewel Insurance Corp., a company that has used a manual filing system for all documents since the company was founded in 1983. The company is running out of filing space and is considering using micrographics to conserve space. What factors should be considered before a final decision is made?

CONCLUDING CASES

A. H & M Insurance Company

Anita Hoffman is the records manager of H & M Insurance Company. H & M has had a micrographics department for the past five years. The jacket system is being used, and the film processing is done in-house. The volume of records to be microfilmed has increased rapidly during the last two years. The manager of the department was replaced a year ago, and staff turnover has increased steadily with the new manager.

Anita has noticed a decline in productivity in the micrographics department in the last six months and is concerned about its effectiveness. Agents and other company personnel have complained that files are not current and the staff is not responding to requests as quickly as they should.

You recently completed a course in records management, and Anita has asked you to list the areas that should be evaluated to determine the problems in the micrographics program. List at least five areas that you would recommend be evaluated to determine the problems that exist in the micrographics program at H & M.

B. Maxwell Schools

You have just graduated from college and taken a position with the Maxwell Schools as the manager of the micrographics department. You are excited about the chance to use the knowledge you gained in your records management courses in college. As you become familiar with your job, you discover that not only are the staff members poorly trained, but the microforms are not of acceptable quality. On closer examination, it is evident the equipment is outdated, the training is inadequate, and the procedures are inappropriate. Many student files are either lost or unreadable because of the quality of the processing. What steps would you take to improve the micrographics department?

SUGGESTED READINGS AND RESOURCES

Avedon, Don M. "Selecting a Microform Reader Is a Matter of Application." *Office Systems,* Vol. 2, No. 8 (August, 1985), p. 66.

"Buyer's Guide to Micrographic Readers and Reader-Printers." *The Office,* Vol. 117, No. 3 (March, 1993), p. 39.

D'Alleyrand, Marc R. "Producing Microforms with Your Imaging System." *IMC Journal,* Vol. 29, No. 6 (November/December, 1993), p. 16.

Fruscione, James. "A Blueprint for the Evaluation of Computer Output Microfilm Applications." *Records Management Quarterly,* Vol. 19, No. 3 (July, 1985), p. 44.

Jones, Virginia A. "Micrographics: Still a Hit in the Office Market." *The Office,* Vol. 117, No. 3 (March, 1993), p. 36.

Hallerman, Dennis M. "Why Microfilm?" *Records Management Quarterly,* Vol. 19, No. 2 (April, 1985), p. 30.

Naukam, Lawrence W. "Buying a CAR and Making It Run." *Records Management Quarterly,* Vol. 19, No. 4 (October, 1985), p. 36.

Oris, Michael. "A Case for Micrographics." *The Office,* Vol. 102, No. 3 (September, 1985), p. 84.

Saffady, William. *Optical Disks vs. Micrographics.* Westport, Connecticut: Meckler Publishing, 1993.

Settani, Joseph A. "Micrographics Applications: Safe, Secure, & Cost Effective." *Office Systems '86,* Vol. 3, No. 6 (June, 1986), p. 78.

Siragusa, Gail. "Archival Records Storage—Microfilm vs. Paper." *Administrative Management,* Vol. 46, No. 12 (December, 1985), p. 56.

Wise, Joseph. "In-House or Service Bureau? Seven Factors to Consider." *Administrative Management,* Vol. 47, No. 3 (March, 1986), p. 20.

Wise, Joseph. "Micrographics: When Is It Right for You?" *Administrative Management,* Vol. 47, No. 1 (January, 1986), p. 59.

Profile
Microfiche Supervisor

Morton Fine is the microfiche supervisor for the Saskatchewan Farm Bureau Mutual Insurance Company located in Regina. He has been in this position for over seven years. The company employs 220 people, and the Operations Department in which the microfiche supervisor works has approximately 27 employees. Positions in this department include trainer, supervisor, and department manager.

Education and experience requirements for the microfiche supervisor's position include five years' experience in records management and demonstrated supervisory skills or experience as a supervisor. An additional requirement is the ability to work well with people.

The major duties and responsibilities of this position are to oversee microfilm quality control and to supervise the preparation of documents to be filmed, including vital records microfilmed as a method of protec-tion. Mr. Fine's ability to handle his job was tested when the office experienced a major disaster. The procedures he had initiated allowed the office to continue business without interruption. Other offices in the company began to request his assistance in setting up similar systems. Currently six other offices have been converted to Mr. Fine's system. In addition, recent changes in the in-house system of requesting microfiche have created a need to modify many procedures and to communicate the changes to those who use the microfiche.

Advancement opportunities in this company are from Mr. Fine's present position as microfiche supervisor to department manager. He has been active in the local chapter of the Association of Records Managers and Administrators. In 1993 he received the Chapter Member of the Year Award from the local chapter.

Electronic Records Management

Learning Goals

1. Describe what is meant by electronic records management.
2. Describe text, data, and image files.
3. Describe the three types of magnetic media and their uses.
4. Describe the three most common optical disk media: WORM, rewritable, and read-only memory (CD-ROM).
5. Describe the care and maintenance of removable electronic media.
6. List and explain six elements of an electronic records management program.
7. Describe procedures for organizing electronic media.
8. Explain how to prepare filenames.
9. Define a document imaging system.
10. Describe the basic components of a document imaging system.
11. Explain the steps in the imaging process.
12. Define bit-mapping and explain its place in image capture.
13. Describe compression and explain its advantages.
14. Explain resolution as it applies to imaging technology.
15. Define COLD technology.

ELECTRONIC INFORMATION SYSTEMS

Electronic
information
systems process
information with
the aid of
computers.

Computers are able to generate and store enormous quantities of records. Records managers realize that these records-creation devices also present a powerful tool for managing huge amounts of information effectively. Studies estimate that the volume of information retained by businesses is increasing at a rate of about 20 percent a year and is expected to continue at that rate. **Electronic records management systems** use computer technology to process information.

Records managers in large organizations with mainframe systems or client/server networks are not likely directly involved in managing the entire information system. In order for the organization to function effectively, however, records managers must share with management information system (MIS) departments the planning and implementing of records management programs. In small organizations, the records manager may be responsible for managing all records, no matter what their form. Therefore, it is important for records managers to know as much about electronic records as they know about paper records and microfilm.

Information is stored on a variety of media—paper, microforms, disks, and tapes. Each storage medium has its strengths and weaknesses. As concluded in Chapter 8, microfilm is best suited for long-term, compact storage of archives and as backups in disaster prevention plans. Paper is still by far the most commonly used medium in day-to-day operations that do not require multiple or simultaneous access. Electronic media are best suited where access speed is critical, volumes of information are large, and simultaneous access is vital. Figure 9-1 shows the percentage use of each storage medium in the early 1990s. Some experts suggest that by the year 2004 information will be 50 percent paper and 50 percent electronic, compared to about 90 percent paper today.

Unless *all* information, regardless of its form, is managed together, valuable resources may be inaccessible to decision makers. This chapter will focus on the processing of information electronically, an area that is expected to grow substantially. No one storage medium, however, is ever likely to totally replace the others.

TYPES OF ELECTRONIC RECORDS

Electronic records
contain
machine-readable
information.

Electronic records are those that contain machine-readable, in contrast with human-readable, information like paper and microfilm. Most computers create, store, retrieve, and (by means of networks) distribute electronic records, of which there are three main categories: text files, data files, and image files. The word *file,* as in traditional records management terminology, refers to a collection of electronic records.

Figure 9-1
Use of information
storage media in
the 1990s.

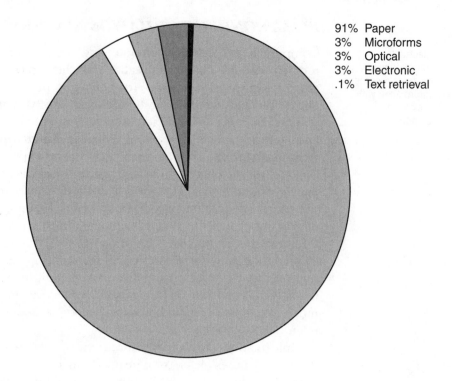

91% Paper
3%   Microforms
3%   Optical
3%   Electronic
.1% Text retrieval

Text Files

Text files consist of character-coded letters, digits, punctuation marks, and other symbols in material created by keyboard entry through word processing programs, text editors, or typesetters. They may also be created through optical character recognition (OCR) programs. Since many printers are able to print only 95 to 100 characters, the capabilities of the printer limit the sophistication of the text file output. Individual characters are represented by a predetermined number and sequence of *bits* (a combination of zeros and ones), depending on which coding system is employed by the computer. Most text files use the **ASCII (American Standard Code for Information Interchange)** format; however, some use IBM's **EBCDIC (Extended Binary Coded Decimal Interchange Code)** coding scheme. Because ASCII files are so basic, it is possible to transfer ASCII text files from one computer to another. Text files with long retention periods should be stored in ASCII format so that full-text retrieval in the future is not dependent on availability of particular hardware or software. However, retrieval of complex documents from long-term storage can present problems even if ASCII coding is employed.

Data Files

Data files store numbers, along with some textual information, as quantitative values that can be manipulated arithmetically in data processing functions. A **data file** is a collection of records with each record containing the same fields of data. A record is a group of related fields describing one occurrence in the file. A field, or data element, is a group of characters combined to create one unit of data. For example, an organization may have a personnel data file that contains records of each employee. Each record will have the same fields, such as Name, Home Address, Social Insurance Number, Salary, and so on. The proper data items are stored in each field, which is typically a character field, a numeric field, a date field, a logical field, or a memo field. An example of a data file is shown in Figure 9-2.

Figure 9-2
Example of a
Database File

ONE FIELD
NAME

NAME	SIN	SALARY	MARRIED
JAN COOK	123-456-789	60000.00	F
HAROLD SMITH	234-567-890	45000.00	T
DAN COLEY	345-678-901	55000.00	F

DATA ITEM
IN FIELD

ONE
RECORD

Image Files

Image files are electronic records consisting of digitally coded "pictures" of documents, drawings, graphics, and so on. They are created by document scanners, graphics programs, computer-aided design (CAD) programs, and other methods. Because they store all the information needed to reproduce the original document, image files take considerable storage space. Optical disks are, therefore, often the medium of choice for image files, although magnetic media can also be used.

 Learning Check: Can you describe the three main types of electronic records?

ELECTRONIC RECORDS STORAGE MEDIA

Electronic records are stored on magnetic or optical media.

Two general types of media are available to store electronic records—magnetic media and optical media. Magnetic disks and tapes have been on the market since the 1950s, while optical media are a relatively recent application dating from the 1980s.

Magnetic Media

Magnetic media are so named because information is recorded on the medium using magnetic impulses. Disks, diskettes, and tapes have a ferromagnetic coating that accepts the electromagnetic impulses and retains them after the magnetic field is removed.

Magnetic Disks

Magnetic media are either fixed or removable.

Magnetic disks, which are shaped like platters, store and retrieve information. They are usually fixed but some may be removed from the computer. Fixed disks generally range in size from 2- to 14-inch diameters, although 9- to 12-inch sizes are most common. The trend over the years has been toward smaller sizes and increased capacity. Storage capacities now range from 500 megabytes to 5 gigabytes. In microcomputers, 5.25-inch fixed magnetic disk drives are the norm. Larger, high-capacity fixed disk drives are mainly encountered in mainframe and minicomputers where rapid, on-line access is required.

Diskettes, also known as floppies or flexible disks, are the prime example of removable magnetic storage media because of their use in personal computers. The 3.5-inch size introduced in the 1980s has replaced the older 5.25-inch diskettes and offers 720 kilobytes of storage capacity and up to 1.44 megabytes for double-sided, high-density diskettes. Diskettes provide the distinct advantage over fixed disks of portability.

Magnetic tape is a removable magnetic storage medium of ribbon or a plastic film strip coated with a magnetic recording material. The usual application encountered is .5-inch-wide, 2,400-foot-long reels in mainframes and minicomputers for duplicating on-line files as backup protection and data archiving for off-line storage. Their function is limited because the information is recorded in a serial fashion and thus access is slower. Figure 9-3 shows the two main types of magnetic media—disk and tape—and some categories of disks.

Optical Storage Media

Optical disks have very large storage capacities.

Optical disks, another primary technology for the storage of images, are record-like devices for writing and reading information by means of laser beams with a storage capacity that far surpasses other storage media. The major advantage of optical disks is the amount of information that can be stored on one disk. Optical disks may be used as replacements, supplements, or complementary additions for magnetic media. Any information that can be stored on magnetic media can be stored on optical media, but the storage capacity of one compact disk can be more than one hundred times the storage capacity of a magnetic disk of the same size and may surpass the storage capacity of microfilm as well. Because optical disk technology is random access, the speed of retrieval is very fast.

Figure 9-3
Magnetic Storage
Media

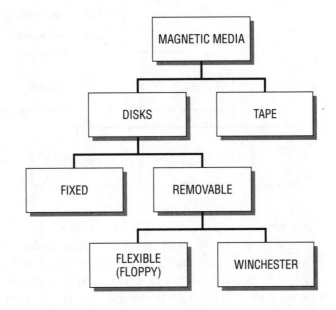

By a relatively expensive method, compared with micrographics and paper systems, information is recorded on the platter-shaped medium by means of a highly focused laser beam, which explains the word *optical*. Through a heat process, the energy from the laser beam creates microscopic holes, pits, bumps, or bubbles in a thin coating on the disk. Immediately after it has been recorded, information can be retrieved and read by optical reader equipment. The legal admissibility of documents stored on optical disk is gradually gaining acceptance by the courts. The use of optical media in the regular course of business is a major factor in court decisions to admit the electronic records as evidence.

There are three main types of optical disk storage: Write-Once/Read Many times (WORM); rewritable optical disks; and read-only disks such as the Compact Disk, Read-Only Memory (CD-ROM). Multifunctional disks may combine optical disks into one package to suit a specific purpose such as a training program. Figure 9-4 shows the main types of optical media—disks, cards, tape, and multifunctional—along with some choices of disks.

Figure 9-4
Optical Storage
Media

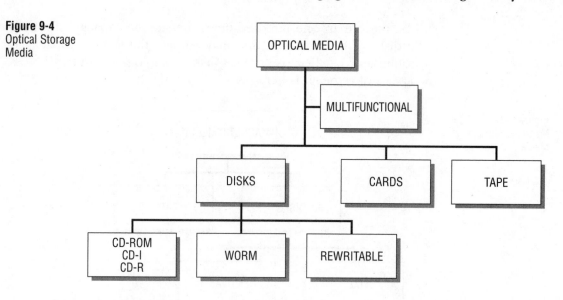

WORM

The information on
a WORM disk can
be read many
times, but it cannot
be erased.

Available since the early 1980s, **WORM disks** are a form of optical disk on which information is written once and may be read many times. Depending on the use to which they are put, the disks come in several sizes from 5.25 to 14 inch as in diameter, and their capacity varies from about 230 megabytes to 10 gigabytes. The data may be recorded on a WORM disk by a laser that burns microscopic pits into the surface of the disk, although there are several different recording technologies. A disk can be updated by adding a newer version of a document to it, but previously recorded areas cannot be reused. Because these disks cannot be erased, the older versions stay on the disk, and are either simply ignored or the file identification in the computer index is purged from the database and the newest version is retrieved when the document is requested.

However, since a newer version can be added to the disk, this technology is ideal when both data integrity (accuracy) and the ability to update the data are important. Write-once disks are utilized to store databases, text files, document images, archival information, and backup data. Figure 9-5 shows an optical disk system.

Rewritable Optical Disks

When information
must be changed
frequently,
rewritable disks
may be the
solution.

Rewritable optical disks are optical disks used for recording, erasing, and reading data. Where data must be changed on a continual basis, erasable optical disks may be the solution. This technology has been available since the late 1980s and employs magneto-optical recording technology. As the name implies, these disks are a blend of two technologies: information is stored magnetically and retrieved optically by means of a laser beam. Rewritable disks come in 3.5-inch- and 5.25-

inch-diameter sizes, can be double-sided, and store approximately 130 megabytes. They are mainly intended for small computer applications.

Figure 9-5
Optical Disk
System

Source: An example of a stand-alone imaging system with WORM optical drives from Adaptive Information System, a U.S. subsidiary of Hitachi.

Read-Only Optical Disks

The compact disk, read-only memory (CD-ROM), the most common type of read-only optical disk, is capable of storing audio, video, digital, and digitized data. The disk, first introduced in 1980, comes in 3.5- and 4.75-inch sizes and requires a special laser disk drive for playback. The disks store approximately 180 to 540 megabytes of permanently recorded information. Once the master CD-ROM is produced and copies made, it cannot be altered with a PC; it cannot be updated or erased.

CD-ROM disks are the most common type of read-only optical disks.

The CD-ROM is best suited for situations in which several hundred copies of unchangeable data are needed, such as distribution of databases and reference materials. Software on CD-ROM reduces the time and effort required to install packages that occupy megabytes of disk space. Documentation, manuals, and tutorials can be put on the disk so that users can refer to them on the screen as needed. Vendors are also using CD-ROMs to let potential buyers try out their product before purchasing it.

Other forms of compact disks with specialized applications are the CD-I (interactive) and CD-R (recordable). The CD-I combines sound, text, graphics, and video and is becoming popular in a variety of innovative applications, including the diagnosing of illness, explaining the complexities of investment portfolios to investors, and providing the public with interactive presentations at museums. CD-R disks are blank and with the proper equipment allow do-it-yourself recording.

Optical Cards and Tape, and Multifunctional Media

Optical memory cards, also known as optical digital data cards, are the size of a credit card and can be used for recording a wide variety of information. Their advantage is in the portability of the two to four megabytes of information they can contain. They are found in electronic publishing, identification systems, insurance data systems, and medical applications such as an individual's medical history.

Optical tape is a very new technology, first available in 1990, which offers huge storage capabilities. Ribbons of film coated with an optical recording material can hold one terabyte (one trillion bytes) of information. This technology appears to have the limited use of replacing very large magnetic tape libraries in mainframe and minicomputer data processing installations.

Multifunctional media combine several types of optical disks for specialized applications such as instructional materials prerecorded on a CD-ROM, packaged with a blank WORM disk on which to add one's own documents.

 Learning Check: Can you describe the various kinds of electronic and optical storage media and explain their uses?

CARE AND MAINTENANCE OF REMOVABLE ELECTRONIC MEDIA

Electronic media must be protected from magnets, heat, dampness, and other hazards.

Since inadequate storage conditions can adversely affect the stability and the life of electronic media, it is important to provide a proper storage environment for them. One danger is magnets, which, if placed near magnetic media, can cause the data on them to be corrupted, or lost. The media must also be protected against high temperatures and humidity. A constant temperature of about 18°C and relative humidity of 35 to 45 percent are required for an optimum storage environment.

As described in Chapter 11 with regard to vital records, magnetic media also need to be protected against fire, water, and human threats, such as theft and vandalism. Because magnetic tapes may develop creases or stretch in storage, the should be checked carefully and rewound regularly at normal speeds with constant tension. Sometimes material must be recopied to new media so that the information will be preserved.

Standards have not yet been established for storing optical media, and it may not be wise to rely on the manufacturers' recommendations. However, magnetic media storage standards are conservative and may be applied to optical media as well. As with long-term storage on magnetic media, optical media may have to be recopied to prevent losing the information they contain. Dust, heavy objects, liquids, and heat—even sunlight—can damage both magnetic and optical media. They should be stored vertically, in proper containers, and handled carefully to preserve their effective life.

 Learning Check: Can you explain how to care for and maintain removable electronic media?

ELECTRONIC RECORDS MANAGEMENT PROGRAMS

Organizations already have a variety of electronic records they must manage daily. If they use computers, they probably have a word processing program by which records can be created, named, stored, and retrieved. Database management programs have a component that allows the creation, storage, reporting, and retrieval of information in the database.

Most organizations have an organized records management program for their paper records, but a truly comprehensive records management program must incorporate all of an organization's records from creation to disposition. Setting guidelines covering the creation of electronic records and identifying electronic records throughout the organization are the first steps toward integrating information holdings into one records management program. A comprehensive electronic records program therefore consists of (1) identifying all electronic records including vital electronic records; (2) carrying out an inventory and appraisal; (3) expanding the retention schedule to cover records in any form; (4) developing guidelines for active records storage and retrieval; (5) handling inactive electronic records through long-term storage and disposition; and (6) updating the records management manual.

Identify All Sources of Electronic Records

Some characteristics of electronic records make the job of identifying them more difficult than for paper records. These records may not even exist in paper form; for example, electronic mail may have been created and deleted without ever having been printed. This "invisibility" makes it easy to overlook them. In the absence of organization-wide procedures, staff will develop their own methods of naming, labelling, backing up, and deleting records. As a result, records are difficult to find and important ones may disappear. Some electronic records are shared among users but are not the responsibility of any one department; they may even be located a considerable distance from the users. All of these factors contribute to the difficulty of identifying certain electronic records. Therefore, to identify all the sources of electronic records, the staff should search the following locations:

- Electronic mail systems
- Shared databases
- Word processing records
- PC-based records

Conduct an Inventory and Appraisal

An inventory should include all records of an organization, no matter what storage medium is involved.

Conducting an inventory of electronic records is similar to conducting one for paper and microfilm records, although probably more difficult, and it is the means to an end—preparing retention and disposition schedules. In his book *Managing Electronic Records,* William Saffady suggests that conducting inventories by program unit (division, department, office) and integrating the electronic records inventory with the paper and microfilm records inventory often gives better results than separate inventories. He cautions that those conducting the inventory should check for interrelationships and redundancies, for electronic counterparts of paper records, for overlaps among media, and for records that have no paper or photographic counterparts.[1] The individual users of microcomputers actually create and manage their own records. They should be consulted for estimates on the size of their disk files and the functions performed.

Saffady also suggests that to obtain a comprehensive inventory, complete information should be collected about each records series (a group of records that have a similar function and that can be handled as a unit)—the functional title of the series and a brief description; the storage medium, size, manufacturing and media recording dates; associated hardware and software; records volume; physical storage; reference activity; active and inactive life; relationship to human readable records; and vital records status.[2] Developing a checklist beforehand makes the task simpler and ensures that all relevant information will be gathered. The inventory data should be analyzed to make certain that all records have been covered and that nonrecords can be identified and eliminated.

Develop the Retention and Disposition Schedule

Guidelines for the retention and disposition of electronic records are similar to those for paper and microfilm.

The same principles discussed in Chapter 4 for retaining and disposing of paper and microfilm records by series also apply to retaining and disposing of electronic records. Retention periods are negotiated based on the administrative, fiscal, legal, and historical values of each records series. In addition to retention periods, the schedule should

---

[1] William Saffady, *Managing Electronic Records* (Prairie Village, Kansas: ARMA International, 1992), p. 72.

[2] Ibid, p. 77.

indicate the physical storage medium for each records series; more than one medium and location may be specified. For example, a school's database for current students may be stored in the office on fixed magnetic disks for the school year, then transferred to magnetic tapes or other removable media for off-line storage after the school year has ended.

Legal considerations about the admissibility of electronic records are not as clear as for paper or microfilm records, which places an additional burden on the records manager. The criteria outlined in Chapter 4 for a legally sufficient records retention program should be followed for electronic records as well. Some electronic records are particularly susceptible to tampering and need the protection discussed in Chapter 12, "Records Security and Information Privacy."

Choosing an appropriate storage medium is affected by the retention periods required for the records series. Electronic records media generally have limited storage stability and are dependent on hardware and software that may become obsolete before the retention period expires. Therefore, electronic media are not a good choice if very long retention periods are required.

Where electronic records have been identified as vital records, the considerations discussed in Chapter 11 with regard to vital records become important.

Learning Check: Do you know how to carry out an inventory and prepare a retention schedule for electronic records?

Develop Procedures for Storage and Retrieval

The importance of established procedures to index and code manual records has been addressed in Chapter 6. Without the classification system established with a manual filing system, it would be impossible to locate records when they are needed. Just as important is establishing procedures to maintain control over the electronically stored information. Every situation where there is no organizational control over individuals' ability to create records using the keyboard, store them on hard drives and removable diskettes, retrieve them, and dispose of the records is a potentially dangerous situation. Searching for electronic files on a hard disk or on external disks can be a very time consuming, frustrating task and an unnecessary one. Directories and indexes are a means of locating information stored on magnetic media; therefore, establishing directories and naming files when using software becomes a very important tool. Tips on establishing directories and subdirectories and naming electronic files follow.

Create Directories and Subdirectories

Computer systems are run by an operating system, such as MS-DOS, Macintosh, OS/2, or UNIX, which is the system's fundamental software. Microsoft's Windows 95 operating system (new, at the time of this writing) offers many improvements in its previous Windows offerings and new features. Operating system commands boot the system (get it started), format disks (get them ready to accept data), copy files from one disk to another, erase files from disks, set up directories and subdirectories, and so forth. Although they vary somewhat from one system to another, commands have the common purpose of organizing directories and subdirectories and of naming files.

Disks are partitioned into segments called volumes, with single volumes on low-capacity disks and multiple volumes on high-capacity disks. A comparison is often made with manual storage, in which the disk and its volumes are roughly equated with a filing cabinet, the contents of subdirectories with file drawers and folders, and data files with individual documents.

The directories and subdirectories of a hard disk look like an upside-down tree, with the root directory as its base.

Directories contain a summary of the contents of the electronic medium. Some media such as removable diskettes have only one directory; others have a main or root directory and a number of subdirectories containing groups of files logically related by function. Depending on the operating system's capabilities, subdirectories may be further divided. All systems provide user manuals with clear directions for organizing disks and naming files. The main directory of a hard disk is called the **root directory**, which should be limited to a small number of files. The directories shown in the root directory can have their own subdirectories. Figure 9-6 illustrates one method of organizing directories and subdirectories of a hard disk. Notice the root directory has five levels in this example and the administrative function of the organization has been divided into five subfunctions. Using the human resources department as an example, this subdirectory has been split into Employee Files, Payroll, Training, and Job Classification. Under Employee Files, each employee has a separate file with the associated data files including various file types such as word processing, images, and spreadsheets.

Develop Guidelines for Filenames

Follow ARMA International's *Filing Procedures Guideline* for subdirectory filenames.

Since lack of consistency can be a real problem in retrieving information from electronic media, the individual filenames within each subdirectory should follow a standard, predesigned coding system, and everyone in the organizational unit should use it. DOS, for example, allows each name to have up to eight characters and a three-character extension. Windows 95 has the ability to accept long filenames of up to 255 characters. As the hard disk organization is being developed, the following concepts, outlined in the *Filing Procedures Guideline* prepared by ARMA International's Filing Systems Subcommittee, should be followed:

1. Start with the root directory.
2. Maintain a hierarchical structure by placing related files together and limiting the number of files in one directory.
3. Place a word processing program and its spell-check and thesaurus programs in the same directory.
4. Recognize that a filename is like an abbreviated document title. A filename should be meaningful, coherent, and consistent. It should reflect a file's contents.
5. Diagram your plan and add to it when creating subdirectories.[3]

Figure 9-6
Directories and Subdirectories on a Hard Disk

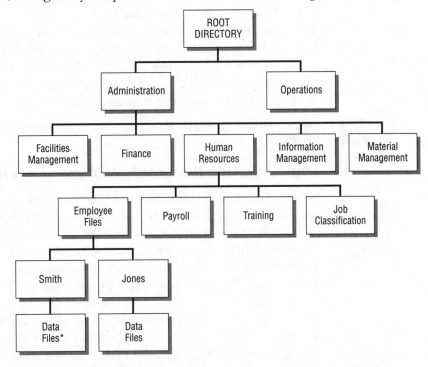

Data files may include various file types such as word processing, images, spreadsheets, etc.

Label Removable Media

Electronic files stored on removable disks can also be divided into directories and subdirectories for convenience in locating files, although removable magnetic diskettes usually have only one directory. When working with external disks, it is important to label the outside of the disk to identify the information it contains. Labels should

---

[3] *Filing Procedures Guideline* (Prairie Village, Kansas: ARMA International, 1989), p. 9.

indicate the general file type such as data or text files and include the broad title (project, case study, or subject), name of application software used, file code, and equipment on which the disk runs.[4]

Consider Colour Coding

A specific colour may represent a special project.

Colour coding is as helpful in locating disks as it is in locating file folders in a manual filing system. By establishing a colour-coding system for the external disks maintained in the office, users can locate specific disks quickly. Special colour strips may be added to identify the information contained on the disk. For example, one colour could be used for program disks, another colour for an individual's work, and so forth.

Use Utility Programs to Find Files

It can be extremely difficult to find lost files; **utility programs** can help with this problem by automatically searching for specific information through a hard-disk drive. The length of time required to carry out these searches can be reduced by limiting the search to the most likely areas containing the requested information.

 Learning Check: Can you set up directories and assign filenames to your electronic records?

Store Inactive Electronic Records Carefully

When electronic records become inactive, they must be treated carefully and checked regularly according to the guidelines already discussed. As many people know, it is easy to destroy a file inadvertently but very difficult to recover it. Hard-disk crashes, viruses, sudden losses of power, even inattention can have disastrous results. To protect information, backups are made by creating copies of the data and information on removable media that can be stored in another location. Large computer system and network server backups are often automatic. Microcomputer users should also protect the records they create by regularly backing up their information holdings. A variety of software and storage media is available for backups. Licensing agreements usually allow only one backup copy of the software application for each licensed user. Therefore, organizations should maintain the original software copy and keep at least one backup in a safe place.

Update the Records Manual

Since the records management manual covers all forms of records, it should be updated by incorporating guidelines to handle the elec-

1)

2) Users should know how to use the new system

[4] Ibid., p. 5.

tronic records of an organization. The preparation of records management manuals is discussed in Chapter 16. Policies and procedures followed consistently will go a long way toward creating a successful records management program.

 Learning Check: Can you explain why system backups are important?

DOCUMENT IMAGING SYSTEMS

Document imaging systems are often promoted as an alternative to microfilm.

Document imaging systems are a subset of electronic information processing. First promoted in the 1980s as a solution to the paper explosion and as an alternative to microfilm, entire systems are being developed based on the storage capabilities of electronic media. These useful imaging and document processing technologies are variously referred to as electronic imaging, electronic image management, document management, and even as optical disk systems. They are part of a much larger workflow management system, in which documents are routed in the sequence of activities most logical to the employees who process transactions, perform designated operations, or complete other specific activities.

A **document imaging system** employs computer hardware and software components to store, retrieve, transmit, process, and manage pictorial copies (images) of documents. These documents can include handwritten and machine-written text, graphics, drawings, completed forms, and so on. All the characteristics of the original document are preserved—the visual and spatial characteristics and appearance. A computer index allows image retrieval in seconds. Optical disks, with their ability to store large volumes of information, are particularly appropriate storage media in these systems.

Components of an Imaging System

An imaging system may range from a relatively simple stand-alone setup to one that requires workstations and local area or wide area networks. However, the basic components are similar in any imaging system: a central processing unit, application software, scanner, video monitor, keyboard, laser printer, optical disks, and an index. Large systems may require jukeboxes or autochangers to store the optical disks.

Central Processor

Depending upon the complexity of the imaging application, the central processor might be any size from a microcomputer to a minicomputer or a mainframe.

Application Software

The application software may be purchased as part of a packaged system or developed by the user, a much more difficult method. This software provides a file management program that acts as an index and performs cross-referencing functions. Specialized software addresses the unique needs of the legal, insurance, financial, and medical industries where imaging solutions are very appropriate.

Scanners

Scanners capture information from paper or microfilmed documents using laser technology.

Scanners, also known as document or image digitizers, produce the electronic images from source documents, which could be paper of varying types and sizes, or microfilm. They capture information from paper or microfilmed documents using laser technology. Desktop scanners resembling photocopiers or fax machines are the most widely encountered type, although there are floor and handheld models. Desktop scanners are either flatbed models accommodating bound volumes or sheetfed models that are limited to unbound sheets. Sheetfed scanners can accommodate larger-sized pages than the flatbed models, and most digitize one side of a page at a time. It takes one to four seconds to scan an 8 1/2 × 11-inch page.

Disks and Disk Drives

An imaging system will have at least an optical disk drive, a magnetic-disk hard drive, and a floppy drive, which must be compatible with the disks being used. Magnetic disks are used for the indexing function and for storing the scanned images temporarily before they are transferred to the optical disk. The optical disk stores the images permanently.

Video Monitors and Keyboards

The high-resolution image processing monitor should be a larger size than a regular PC monitor and is available in 19-, 21-, and 24-inch (measured diagonally across the screen) sizes. A 19-inch screen allows the full document to be viewed at about a 25 percent reduction. Choice of monitor size depends on the size of documents that will be scanned. The **refresh rate**—the monitor redraws the screen—is also important to avoid an image flicker that will cause eye fatigue. Colour monitors are not desirable due to their lack of image clarity and slower refresh rates.

The keyboard is necessary for keying the data entry and retrieval instructions.

Laser Printers

Laser printers will produce high-quality hard copy from the stored images. They can usually produce four to six letter-sized pages per minute; high-speed laser printers are much more expensive and usually necessary only in large-scale installations.

Indexes

Imaging systems maintain a computer database on magnetic disks; this database serves as an index to the images stored on optical disks. A screen is presented on the monitor for an operator to fill in the indexing elements for each document. Indexing is usually carried out from the scanned image on the monitor screen before the document is transferred to the optical disk.

Jukeboxes (Autochangers)

Jukebox hardware stores and accesses optical disks similar to the way a jukebox stores and accesses phonograph records.

A jukebox, like its namesake of old, stores disks or cartridges and chooses the correct one on demand. In an imaging application, it is a mass storage device for multiple optical disk cartridges. In the most complex versions, a robotic arm or picker extracts the optical disk cartridge designated by the host computer and mounts it into an optical disk drive. The picker also removes previously mounted cartridges and returns them to their storage locations.

 Learning Check: Can you describe the components of a document imaging system?

The Imaging Process

Images must first be captured and indexed, then stored so that they can be found and retrieved, to be distributed, displayed, or printed. This process of inputting, storing, and retrieving imaged documents requires an understanding of certain terms associated with imaging.

Information Capture

Scanners use bit-mapping to capture images.

To understand how images are captured by a scanner, it is first necessary to know what bit-mapping means. **Bit-mapping** is one type of binary digital coded representations of information; the other type is ASCII coding. Whereas ASCII code assigns a unique 8-bit representation to each character of text, the bit-mapping process does not recognize characters at all. In bit-mapping the whole page of a document is divided into an imaginary grid of millions of black and white dots called pixels (picture elements). Black pixels are represented by ones and white pixels by zeros. The scanner reads a page from right to left, top to bottom and stores the ones as holes or pits on the optical disk and zeros as areas without holes called *land*. Shades of grey, photos, and coloured images can also be scanned by this process. Figure 9-7 shows how the black and white pixels make up a character.

Bit-mapping takes a great deal more memory than ASCII coding. As an example, a 400-word document takes 150 times more memory than the same document stored in ASCII code. For this reason, optical disks with their large storage capacities are excellent storage media for bit-mapping.[5]

Capturing the information involves three interrelated operations: scanning documents, inspecting the images, and assigning index values by data entry.

Scanning. Source documents are prepared by straightening folded papers, mending torn pages, and removing paper clips. In some applications documents are sorted first to keep related documents together.

Image Inspection. As documents are scanned, they are held in temporary memory until an operator makes sure their quality is acceptable. If the image is unsatisfactory, the document can be rescanned immediately.

Index Data Entry. Once the quality has been checked, index values for each document are keyed into the fields supplied by the database management software.

Figure 9-7
Bit-mapped Image

Source: Courtesy of ARMA International, Prairie Village, Kansas, 1-800-422-2762

---

[5] Don M. Avedon, "Electronic Imaging 101 Part I—What Is Electronic Imaging?" *Records Management Quarterly,* Vol. 28, No. 2 (April, 1994), p. 29.

Storage

After a quality check, documents are transferred to the appropriate optical disk for permanent storage. Until they are needed, these disks are stored off-line on shelves, in cabinets, or in jukeboxes.

Compression reduces the amount of memory required to store bit-mapped images.

To reduce the amount of memory required to store bit-mapped images, a process known as **compression** removes the bits representing unused white spaces or any large black areas on a page. The same software decompresses the images for retrieval. The degree of compression varies according to the amount of text and line work on a page, the way the information is organized, and the compression method used. Compression, of course, increases the number of documents that can be stored on a disk.

Retrieval

An operator requests a document using the database management software, which allows a number of different ways of searching. The requested document is located on the correct optical disk, which is inserted in the optical disk drive either manually or automatically, and the image is displayed on a monitor. It can also be routed through a network and printed with a laser printer.

Resolution refers to the sharpness of an image viewed on a monitor or printed with a laser printer.

Another factor relating to the retrieval process is **resolution**—the quality of an image displayed on a screen or printed by a laser printer. Resolution is measured in pixels per inch or dots per inch (dpi). Naturally, the higher number of dots per inch, the sharper the image as Figure 9-8 illustrates. Generally, a resolution of 200 dpi is considered satisfactory for most documents.

Figure 9-8
Effect of Resolution on Readability

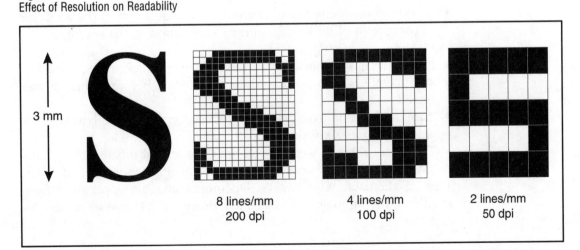

Source: *Courtesy of ARMA International, Prairie Village, Kansas, 1-800-422-2762*

COLD systems
record computer-
generated reports
on read/write
optical disks.

Some electronic document imaging systems offer a feature for storing and retrieving page-formatted computer output. **Computer output to laser disk (COLD)** technology records computer-generated reports on optical disks as character-coded text. This is not an image application, however, because the information is stored in character-coded form rather than by bit-mapping. By providing on-line access to the information in a network environment, physical distribution of the reports is eliminated.

✓ **Learning Check: Can you describe how information is captured, stored, and retrieved in the imaging process?**

An Example of Electronic Document Imaging: McGill University

The accounts payable section of the accounting department at McGill University in Montreal, illustrates the way an imaging system works. The description that follows is based on an article by Terry Monteiro that appeared in *Computing Canada*.[6]

McGill University has 30,000 students, an annual budget of $200 million, and puts an emphasis on research, much of which is dependent on grants. To obtain continuing support from grant providers, the accounting procedures must be carefully maintained, and control of the accounting process is extremely important. Analysis of the accounting procedures revealed the following factors:

- McGill's accounts payable section, the most paper-intensive part of its accounting department handles more than 300,000 invoices a year;
- All documents are maintained for five years;
- Workflow proceeds from (a) a purchase requisition to (b) an order to (c) receipt of an invoice and its verification to (d) issuing a cheque;
- Every purchase requisition and invoice went through six to eight staff members who processed the transaction before a cheque was issued;
- Turnaround time from purchase requisition to cheque issuance was as long as six weeks; and
- The paper records were stored both onsite and offsite.

McGill solved its problems with an imaging system called High-View, a Microsoft Windows PC Document Imaging application from Highland Technologies of Greenbelt, Maryland. The system components are:

---

[6] Terry Monteiro, "McGill Practising Paperless Payout," *Computing Canada*, August 16, 1993, p. 28.

- 25 IBM-compatible 80386 and 80486 PCs in a client/server environment,
- A Novell network,
- 3 Ricoh document scanners,
- Hewlett Packard and Ricoh laser printers,
- 4 Sony 12-inch optical disk drives, and
- A Sony optical jukebox.

In the new workflow arrangement, a paper-based purchase requisition goes to the accounts payable section where it is scanned and indexed by a reference number. When the invoice is received, it is scanned and routed to an accountant for verification. After the invoice is approved for payment, the information is uploaded to the IBM mainframe and a cheque is issued. All the documents are saved on a magnetic disk while they are active and transferred to optical disks for archiving.

The new system has resulted in a turnaround time of 48 hours, and now only two people are involved in the process. This example provides an excellent illustration of the way in which a relatively inexpensive installation of an imaging system can bring great benefits to an organization.

Keeping Up with Technology

New terms—re-engineering, workflow management, full-text retrieval, electronic data interchange—as well as new products and new uses of old products: How is the knowledge worker to keep up? We must educate ourselves if we hope to stay abreast of the latest techniques, methodologies, equipment, and software. After all, we can only assess what we know about, and that latest product may be just the solution we are looking for. Keeping abreast means reading periodicals, belonging to organizations, attending conferences and seminars, and talking to others in our field.

TERMINOLOGY REVIEW

Review the terms listed below in the Glossary on page 521.

American Standard Code for Information Interchange (ASCII)
bits
bit-mapping
compact disk read-only
    memory (CD-ROM)
compression
computer output to laser disk (COLD)

data files
diskettes
document imaging system
electronic records
electronic records management
    system
Extended Binary Coded Decimal
    Interchange Code (EBCDIC)

image files
jukebox
magnetic disks
magnetic media
magnetic tape
multifunctional media
operating system
optical disks
optical media
optical memory cards
optical tape

pixels
resolution
rewritable optical disks
root directory
scanner
text files
utility program
vertical refresh rate
workflow
WORM disks

REVIEW AND DISCUSSION

1. Describe what is meant by electronic records management.
2. Describe text, data, and image files.
3. Describe magnetic media disks, diskettes, and tape with their uses.
4. Describe the three most common optical storage media and their uses.
5. Describe the care and maintenance requirements for removable electronic media.
6. List and explain six elements in an electronic records management program.
7. Describe the procedures for organizing electronic media.
8. Explain the importance of filenames.
9. Define the term document imaging system.
10. Describe the basic components of a document imaging system.
11. Explain the purpose of a jukebox.
12. Describe the steps in the imaging process.
13. Explain how a scanner performs and the two main types.
14. What is bit-mapping?
15. Explain the benefits of compression.
16. Define resolution as it applies to the imaging process.
17. Explain the uses of COLD technology.

APPLICATIONS

1. Read three articles that describe imaging systems in different organizations. Summarize each article as your instructor directs and be prepared to describe the systems in class.

2. Prepare a table comparing the features of magnetic media and electronic media. Compare storage capacity, cost, legal admissibility, playback life (the period of time during which recorded information can be reliably retrieved), and security requirements. Check periodicals for articles that will help you with this information.

3. Find a brochure from an organization that is in the document imaging business. Study the specifications and prepare a short report describing the system.

CONCLUDING CASES

A. Goodley Automotive Sales and Service

Goodley Automotive Sales and Service has been in the business of selling cars for 25 years. Art Goodley, who started the company, has built it into a very successful dealership by selling at competitive prices and providing excellent service for the cars he sells. Some years ago the manufacturer began sending the parts lists to its dealers on microfiche, so Art bought a small microfilm reader. Recently, the manufacturer has notified Art that they are switching the parts lists to diskettes.

Art Goodley has decided this is the incentive he needs to computerize his operation. He knows that his old way of running the office is inefficient and outdated—information about customers is kept on index cards, paper correspondence is stored in vertical file cabinets, sales and service records are all in paper format, and an electric typewriter is the only office equipment.

What suggestions can you give Art Goodley about changing his office to a computerized system?

B. Maxi Manufacturing Company

Maxi Manufacturing Company (MMC) was founded in High Point, Manitoba, by two brothers, Joseph and Hal Mongansen, in the early 1970s. They began MMC by producing work shirts made of durable fabric and featuring superior workmanship. As the company grew, more products were added to the product line of the company. They expanded their manufacturing plant with three separate expansions of the facilities. Each expansion of the plant resulted in the addition of a new product division. Each division specialized in the manufacture of a product in the company's product line.

With each expansion, new sales personnel were added to sell the new product lines. As a result of the expansions and additional sales and office personnel, many problems have arisen in the last year. Customers are complaining that orders are not filled in a timely manner, many back orders are required, and incomplete and inaccurate orders are often delivered to the customers. It is such a serious problem that sales have declined slightly during each of the last two quarters, and some regular customers are threatening to go to other suppliers.

On a visit to the central office, you find the following situation. Many of the company's records are maintained in manual files, and the electronic files that are maintained are not compatible with each other. There is no standardization in the product inventory files of the different divisions, nor in the placement and processing of orders. Each division has simply devised its own means and dumped it on the records managers, who have been going out of their way to accommodate each of the division heads.

Although the networked PCs are all the same model and employ the same word processing software, each worker has complete control over the records he or she creates. The records managers have no way of knowing about the electronic records that have no physical counterpart.

What suggestions would you make to Joseph and Hal to help eliminate their records management problems?

SUGGESTED READINGS AND RESOURCES

"Automated Data Entry at Avon." *IMC Journal,* Vol. 2, No. 4 (July/August, 1992), p. 26.

Avedon, Don. "Electronic Imaging 101 Part I—What is Electronic Imaging?" *Records Management Quarterly,* Vol. 28, No. 2 (April, 1994), p. 28.

Avedon, Don. "Electronic Imaging 101 Part II—Disks and Backfile Conversions." *Records Management Quarterly,* Vol. 28, No. 3 (July, 1994), p. 34.

Avedon, Don. "Electronic Imaging 101 Part III—Analysis, Document Preparation and Digitizing." *Records Management Quarterly,* Vol. 28, No. 4 (October, 1994), p. 28.

Avedon, Don. "Electronic Imaging 101 Part IV—Indexing, Compression and Software." *Records Management Quarterly,* Vol. 29, No. 1 (January, 1995), p. 32.

"Canadian Patrol Frigate Program Installs Document & Image Management System." *IMC Journal,* Vol. 29, No. 2 (March/April, 1993), p. 7.

Cook, Terry. "It's 10 O'clock: Do You Know Where Your Data Are?" *Technology Review,* January, 1995.

"Document Image Processing at Eurotunnel." *IMC Journal,* Vol. 28, No. 3 (May/June, 1992), p. 30.

Kalstrom, David. "The CD-R vs. WORM debate." *Computing Canada,* November 9, 1994, p. 48.

Kerr, Monta. "Imaging: The possibilities are endless." *Computing Canada,* September 28, 1994, p. 21.

Kerr, Monta. "It's a matter of semantics." *Computing Canada,* August 16, 1993, p. 25.

Lougheed, Tim. "Images & Imaging." *Hum—The Government Computer Magazine,* November, 1994, p. 38.

Menkus, Belden. "Defining Electronic Records Management." *Records Management Quarterly,* Vol. 30, No. 1 (January, 1996), p. 38.

National Archives of Canada. *Managing Your Computer Directories and Files.* Ottawa, Ontario: Minister of Supply and Services Canada, 1993.

"Old World Meets New in Massive New Optical Storage Project." *IMC Journal,* Vol. 28, No. 3 (May/June, 1992), p. 32.

"Optical Disk System Speeds Response to British Airways Customer Queries." *IMC Journal,* Vol. 28, No. 6 (November/December, 1992), p. 11.

Phillips, John T. *Organizing and Archiving Files and Records on Microcomputers.* Prairie Village, Kansas: ARMA International, 1992.

Phillips, John T. "Preparing for Automation." *Records Management Quarterly,* Vol. 27, No. 3 (July, 1993), p. 48.

Saffady, William. *Electronic Document Imaging Systems Design, Evaluation, and Implementation.* Westport, Connecticut: Meckler Publishing, 1993.

Saffady, William. *Managing Electronic Records.* Prairie Village, Kansas: ARMA International, 1992.

Saffady, William. *Optical Disk Systems for Records Management.* Prairie Village, Kansas, ARMA International, 1988.

Skupsky, Donald S. "Establishing Retention Periods for Electronic Records." *Records Management Quarterly,* Vol. 27, No. 2 (April, 1993), p. 40.

Ward, Scott W., and Brian A. Cole. "Selecting Record Media." *Records Management Quarterly,* Vol. 29, No. 3 (July, 1995), p. 3.

White, Myles. "The Changing World of Magneto-optical." *Computing Canada,* June 7, 1995, p. 36.

Integrated Information Systems

Learning Goals

After completing this chapter, you should be able to:
1. Describe each of the steps in the implementation process.
2. Summarize the benefits of an integrated system.
3. Describe the four subsystems in an integrated information system.
4. Define the originating subsystem and describe how it is different in the integrated system than in a traditional office.
5. Describe input methods in the originating subsystem.
6. Define the processing subsystem.
7. Compare the functions of text processing and data processing in an integrated system.
8. List the devices for inputting information in a word processing application.
9. Describe two types of databases.
10. Define the communication subsystem.
11. Describe communication services available to an organization.
12. Explain the implications to the records manager of electronic mail services.
13. Describe the types of telecommunication services.
14. Define the storage subsystem.
15. Explain the capture and retrieval of information in electronic and on-line computer storage.
16. Describe three types of records management tracking systems.
17. Explain the use of bar coding in an integrated information system.
18. Explain the role of records management in the integrated information system.
19. Summarize the effect on records functions of each subsystem within the integrated information system.

There is nothing more difficult to take in hand, more perilous to conduct, or more uncertain in its success, than to take the lead in the introduction of a new order of things.... People do not truly believe in anything new until they have had actual experience of it.

—Machiavelli

Discussions of the "automated office," the "office of the future," and the "paperless office" continue. Most organizations are using the computer as a tool in information processing. But they do not know how to integrate the automated elements into their information system. Some of the decision makers involved find it hard to believe that an integrated information system is possible or that it can be very beneficial. However, although very few organizations have implemented a fully integrated system, most recognize the interdependence of all parts of the system and the benefits of integration.

OVERVIEW OF THE INTEGRATED INFORMATION SYSTEM

Four subsystems comprise the integrated information system.

A system is a group of separate but interrelated parts acting together to accomplish a goal. An **integrated information system** is a group of subsystems working together and communicating with each other to process information, distribute it to the appropriate persons in a timely manner, store information (records) for efficient retrieval, and dispose of stored information (records) when it is no longer needed. Before looking at the components of an integrated information system, it is important to recognize the benefits that an integrated system can achieve. Understanding what can be accomplished by an integrated information system will make the implementation process easier and will provide incentives for cooperation. To develop an appreciation of the potential value of an integrated system, this chapter will examine the network of subsystems in detail.

Benefits

Implementation of technology will enhance human resources productivity.

The extent to which an organization implements an integrated information system depends upon the organization's needs. These needs can usually be summarized as a desire to implement technological resources that will enhance the productivity of human resources—managerial and support personnel—in achieving the organization's overall goals.

Direct costs of office operations are rapidly increasing and have forced top-level management to focus on improving the productivity

Figure 10-1
The Network of
Subsystems
Comprising the
Integrated
Information
System

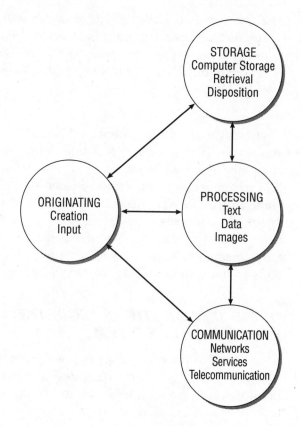

Office technology
improves
productivity by
decreasing
duplication of
effort.

of employees. One obvious technique for improving productivity of human resources is to provide better tools (equipment) to assist personnel in performing their duties.

Many organizations look to improved office technology to decrease the duplication of effort existing in many office tasks. Duplication may exist in repetitive keyboarding to achieve a final copy of an item of correspondence or a report, or duplication may be as simple as the time wasted in "telephone tag," as executives or support staff redial the same telephone number to obtain information or confirm meeting dates and times. Increased efficiency not only decreases overall costs of operations, but it also eliminates a great deal of worker frustration.

An integrated system provides control over all forms of information. The system allows access by multiple users, timely retrieval, and dissemination throughout the organization. The records management function is, therefore, central to achieving the benefits of integration.

Few organizations, however, are willing to devote time and resources to planning and implementing an integrated information system unless they determine that such a system will be a cost-effective method of achieving the organization's overall goal. Organizational goals are usually determined by top-level management. These individuals must be convinced that an integrated information system is potentially advantageous before any serious steps can be taken to implement such a system.

Learning Check: Why is it important to define the benefits of an integrated information system?

Implementation Process

To determine an organizations's technology requirements, a needs analysis should be carried out. After a needs analysis shows that a system will benefit the organization, the following steps should be taken: obtain approval of the system from top-level managers, design the system, install the system, and maintain the system.

Approval

An organization's top-level managers are not likely to approve any expenditure of time and financial resources that cannot be demonstrated to produce a significant and desirable return on investment. In preparing a presentation to these executives, one must consider how the new system will assist in achieving the organizational goals these individuals have established.

Presenting examples of effective integrated systems can help gain approval.

In seeking approval to design and implement an integrated information system, one must also be mindful that in the past the strategy for improving efficiency of information operations has been to centralize certain tasks. For example, data processing tasks went to the data processing centre; word processing tasks went to the word processing centre; and microfilming was done in the micrographics centre. In some instances these tasks were eliminated from the organization by outsourcing. However, the lines between specific tasks have blurred, and tools are now available to handle all forms of information—data, text, image, and sound. An integrated information system, in which a network is established to allow these tasks to be done in the office and communicated from one area of the office to another, results in significant efficiencies for an organization. To those who have never seen an integrated information system in action, tailoring each technology so that it works in tandem with others in the system while at the same time covering all of an organization's needs, may seem impossible. Because of this, one important presentation strategy is to show examples of similar organizations in which such systems are working effectively.

Presentation to top management of plans to integrate the information systems is a very important step. Be sure to discuss with these managers not only required technological changes, but also changes in work procedures and in roles for various staff members that must be a part of the new system. The character and the flow of work may change significantly. The approval and publicized support of the organization's top executives is important not only to the successful implementation of an integrated information system but to its continued effective functioning as well.

System Design

The first step in designing the integrated information system is to determine who has the responsibility for designing the system. A task force appointed for this purpose can provide a wide range of experience and knowledge. The task force should include members from all levels of the organization who will be affected by the implementation of the system and should actively seek input from other workers. Greater involvement of employees in the planning stages will decrease resistance to the new system when it is installed.

Employee input is important.

In determining where technology can enhance productivity and assist in achieving organizational goals, the task force may find it useful to survey employees about perceived bottlenecks and to ask for their suggestions for improving procedures. The task force must also make a comparative examination of available equipment and software. Equipment options should be evaluated based on how well they meet the organization's needs, compatibility with other types of equipment, ergonomics, and costs (including hardware, software, and maintenance). Many expanding organizations are especially interested in the modularity of equipment—the ability to expand the capabilities of the equipment as the organization's needs expand. Equipment is too expensive to replace when increased capabilities are needed. Participating in equipment demonstrations and observing other users permit a more realistic assessment of performance and an opportunity to question current users.

Installation

The revolutionary approach involves simultaneous installation of new equipment organization-wide.

Approaches to the installation of equipment for an integrated information system have been categorized as revolutionary or evolutionary. In general, the revolutionary approach of installing all the new equipment throughout the organization at one time has been found to create a great deal of user resistance and chaos in office operations. Employees feel their offices have been taken over by the new equipment, and everyone is learning new procedures and debugging software at the same time. An evolutionary approach allows some employees to become familiar with the equipment and to be able to help others adjust more quickly.

The evolutionary approach involves initial installation of new equipment at a test site.

The evolutionary installation approach uses a test site to evaluate software and user acceptance of the selected equipment. Software may need to be adjusted to meet the needs of a specific organization or may be determined to simply be a poor choice for one organization's applications. The appropriateness of the software should be determined before purchasing large quantities of equipment and software. If problems can be satisfactorily addressed, employee frustrations are minimized because they are experienced at only one location.

An additional benefit of using a test site is that those employees who use the system and see its benefits will help promote the installation of system equipment in other locations throughout the organization. Most organizations find it beneficial to select as a test site a department whose employees have demonstrated enthusiasm for the system, a department that will experience dramatic increases in efficiency, or a department with high visibility. The performance of the test site should be evaluated before additional installations are considered.

Maintenance

Once the installation is completed, the integrated information system task force may be disbanded, or it may continue to function as an advisory group for issues relating to the integrated information system. The integrated information system operation is assigned to one manager, usually the chief information officer or a person with a similar title, who is responsible for its maintenance and expansion.

Systems must adapt to changing organizational needs.

Successful maintenance of an integrated information system has four elements: (1) continuous review, (2) upgrading as needed, (3) employee feedback, and (4) education and training. Organizations are not static; their needs change. Consequently, the best technology for meeting their needs may also change. Workloads may shift; departments may expand their functions and need additional technological support; external pressures may require changes within the organization. Someone must be in a position to review and respond to these changing needs.

Upgrading the integrated information system may become necessary as a result of changing needs within the department, or it may be the result of technological innovations that better address existing needs. Proposed upgrading of equipment should be evaluated in much the same way that original equipment purchases were evaluated: How will the new technology better meet the organization's needs? Is it compatible with existing equipment in the integrated information system? What are the comparative costs of upgrading options versus continuing with the existing system?

Encourage employees to provide feedback on the system.

A feedback system is important in avoiding user resistance. Employees need a suggestion box or an open door to approach the manager with problems or suggestions for improving the system or procedures for using the system. Employee feedback is often the first indication that the system may need to be upgraded. The system was implemented to enhance the productivity of employees; these employees must have a means of communicating concerns in order for problems to be corrected and employee satisfaction to be maintained. When system problems are identified, the integrated information system task force may be called upon to develop solutions.

Education and training needs must be recognized.

When a new system is installed, employees must be given time for training and for learning the new system. During this learning period, productivity should not be an issue. This need will continue to exist as employees are moved to new positions in which they will use other equipment or new employees are hired. Several training options available to an organization were discussed in Chapter 2.

Learning Check: Can you name and describe the four steps used to implement an integrated information system?

Network of Subsystems

Four subsystems comprise the integrated information system.

The integrated information system is made up of four subsystems—the originating subsystem, the processing subsystem, the communication subsystem, and the storage subsystem (see Figure 10-1). In order for the whole system to function effectively, each interrelated subsystem must contribute its part in the processing, distribution, storage, retrieval, and disposition of information. The communication subsystem is a crucial element for the success of an integrated approach.

ORIGINATING SUBSYSTEM

The **originating subsystem**, the means of putting information into the integrated information system, is the first of four subsystems in the integrated information system (refer to Figure 10-1). The manner in which tasks are performed in each subsystem is significantly changed when the organization implements an integrated information system; however, many possible combinations of options can constitute an integrated information system.

Creation Phase

Much of the originating or creation phase of textual information such as correspondence, directives, reports, and agendas and the initiation of voice communications is performed at the executive and administrative levels of an organization, but similar tasks are performed throughout the organization. Often the top level of the organizational structure perceives the most dramatic changes in methodology when an organization implements an integrated information system. Data are captured with some of the same devices used to capture text.

Organizations are not likely to have a completely paperless office anytime in the foreseeable future. People will still make notes in longhand and want portable hard copy; they will receive some mail in the familiar format provided by postal services, and telephone message notes will continue to exist. The amount of paper appearing on the manager's desk will, however, undoubtedly decrease; and information will be created, distributed, stored, and disposed of without ever having been in paper format.

Text Input Methods

Input devices range from longhand notes to voice input.

In an integrated information system, input methods may range from longhand notes on a yellow legal pad to keyboarding or voice input into an executive workstation. Those individuals with no keyboarding skills usually prefer to write their notes and let their support personnel put the information into the system. However, keyboarding skills are increasingly required of everyone at all levels of an organization. Some executives still rely on dictation as a means of producing correspondence and reports. With fewer word processing centres and an increase in employees' responsibility for their own communication, this relatively costly input method has become less popular.

All word processors accept input from their keyboards, but there are other input devices such as disks, scanners, wands, optical character readers (OCRs), facsimile machines, and voice input. When finalized, information is usually stored on magnetic disks.

Disks can be reinserted into the word processor so that stored information can once again be manipulated. Manipulation of stored data and inputting new information may be necessary for minor changes in standard documents, such as incorporating policy changes in the employee manual and updating the organization's telephone directory.

Document scanners provide a third input device. Using them, one can scan documents and convert the images to digital data stored in the computer. Hard copy that does not have to be rekeyed eliminates the likelihood of keying errors during input and considerably reduces costs associated with inputting information.

A fourth input method is by using optical character readers. **Optical character readers** can read printed information and digitize it so that the computer can transform it to printed words on the screen. A document may also be typed using an element with an OCR-readable pattern. The document is fed into an optical character reader, where it is read by the scanner and stored on a removable disk or in the computer's memory. The information may then be manipulated and a final copy produced.

Facsimile machines provide a fifth method of input. Facsimile transmissions can be input directly to a computer without the necessity of rekeying.

Once thought to be far in the future, some professionals are dictating to a computer that transforms spoken words directly into text. An example of this input method is IBM's VoiceType Dictation product, which is based on speech recognition technology.

Although some communication initiates new actions, much is in response to previous correspondence, meetings, and personal encounters, or to summarize previously collected data. The executive workstation can significantly expedite the latter type of origination through the ability to recall previous documents to the viewing screen. In many instances the document can be annotated on the screen. If the individual is composing a report, the summary data can be recalled to the screen for review and manipulation before insertion into the report.

Retrieving information from paper files, microrecords, electronic files, or data storage banks is enhanced by a workstation's microprocessor and, of course, on these components of the integrated office being connected through a communication network that allows information exchange. (Networks will be discussed further in the communication subsystem section below.)

Data Input Methods

Optical character recognition equipment bypasses the keyboard.

Some input methods are used for both text and data. Before storage in an automated system, data must be captured through keystrokes, optical character recognition (OCR), bar code wands or laser scanners, touch-tone telephones, or computer input microfilm (CIM). Optical character recognition equipment, through optical readers or wands, bypasses the keyboard and feeds large volumes of pretyped data directly into the computer. OCRs are commonly used for identifying account numbers on cheques; however, computer printouts are prepared more and more frequently with machine-readable characters or patterns so that repetitive keying is eliminated. Related technologies are magnetic ink character recognition (MICR) and intelligent character recognition (ICR). Most often used for processing cheques, MICR relies on specially shaped numbers printed with magnetic ink. The numbers are magnetized and read into the computer as they are processed through a reader-sorter. ICR interprets handwritten numerical data and machine-printed characters as the information is scanned into a computer and converted to ASCII code. Table 10-1 illustrates some data entry alternatives.

Table 10-1

DATA ENTRY ALTERNATIVES

Entry Method	Operator Position	Need for Special Machine-readable Label	Entry Speed (10–12 digit ID)	Entry Errors (to total entries)
Keyboard/ monitor/LCD	Sit, 1 or 2 hands	No	10–20 sec.	1/30
Bar Code/ Wand	Sit/Stand 1 hand	Yes	2–3 sec.	1/300,000
Bar Code/ Laser Scanner	Sit/Stand 1 hand	Yes	1–2 sec.	1/300,000
OCR Wand	Sit/Stand 1 hand	Yes	3–5 sec.	1/1,000
Touch-Tone Telephone	Sit/Stand 1 hand	No	20–40 sec.	1/30

Source: Adapted from "Computer Speeds Records Retrieval," Office Systems Management, *Vol. 1, No. 4 (Spring, 1983), p. 12.*

After the information is captured, it can then be transferred to off-line electronic storage such as magnetic tapes or disks, or optical media. Storage choices are described in Chapter 9, "Electronic Records Management."

Image Input Methods

Images may be created with various types of software such as word processing, graphics, or presentation packages. Images such as photographs and illustrations may be scanned into a computer, or the originating source may be microfilm.

 Learning Check: Can you describe the role of the origination subsystem in the integrated information system?

PROCESSING SUBSYSTEM

The **processing subsystem** is the means of manipulating data within the information system to achieve desired results. This subsystem consists of three previously separate elements: word processing (usually referring to text), data processing (usually referring to manipulation of numbers), and image processing (graphics, drawings, and images). In an integrated system, these elements are brought together to achieve increased office productivity.

Text Processing

One of the most important developments to increase office productivity was word processing, the manipulation of ideas and data to produce a desired result (see Figure 10-2). Once input, this information can be moved, edited, and formatted; it can also be stored on a disk, printed, or sent to the recipient in electronic form. The most frequent desired results of word processing are error-free copies of correspondence, legal documents, and reports.

Figure 10-2
Text Processing
Equipment
Components

Source: Courtesy of International Business Machines Corporation. Unauthorized use not permitted.

Applications

Automating
repetitive tasks
improves office
productivity.

We tend to forget what an impact word processing has had on our productivity by automating repetitive tasks. Before the evolution of word processing, several draft copies of a report would usually be necessary before the originator was completely satisfied and would allow the final typing of the document. Each draft required the typist to rekey paragraphs that had no changes as well as those in which changes were made. Now, once the material has been input, the operator can scan the report for those paragraphs in which changes are to be made, make changes, and print an error-free copy containing both text and graphics on a high-quality laser or ink-jet printer in black and white, or in colour. Many word processing software packages now have the ability to send the document directly to a photocopier if several copies are to be made. Employing a photocopier for multiple copies is usually more efficient than using laser printers.

Desktop publishing software has further added to the complexity of the work that can be handled in an office. The software allows experienced users to plan layout, design, typesetting, and printing text and graphics with professional looking output. Many currently available word processors are able to interface with phototypesetters. This capability allows the copy for newsletters, brochures, manuals, and so forth both to be prepared by utilizing the text-editing feature of the word processor and to be typeset and printed without rekeying. A tremendous saving in time and in the amount of keying is achieved, and the need for a second proofreading is eliminated as well.

Additional time savings can be realized when forms, contracts, form letters, and form paragraphs are stored on disks to be recalled when needed. This eliminates any rekeying of standard documents or portions of documents while allowing the operator to personalize the document with names, addresses, account numbers, dates, and so forth. Another application that saves time is the ability of most word processors to merge lists of names and addresses with a form letter and print the necessary personalized copies of the letter while the operator is inputting a new document.

The document production process can be further integrated by adopting standards such as SGML. **Standard general markup language (SGML)** has been successfully applied within industries requiring stringent document control such as the pharmaceutical and defence engineering sectors. **Hypertext markup language (HTML)** has also become a widely used electronic publishing standard popularized by the Internet's World Wide Web. SGML and HTML are technologies that allow organizations to structure and manage their information by preserving text features such as font styles, underlining, and indenting separately from the content of a document.

Data Processing

Data are symbols that represent people, objects, events, or concepts; they are raw facts. **Data processing** is the use of a computer to manipulate data to achieve a desired result. When data is placed into a meaningful context for a user it becomes **information**.

Applications

While computer-directed printers can print items such as mailing labels, variable data on grade reports for students, and report titles, the use of data processing is most frequently associated with the manipulation of numbers. Typically, data processing has been used to perform accounting functions such as computing payroll and printing cheques; preparing comparative sales figures by products, sales division, or geographic area; and customer billing. New computers are sufficiently powerful to produce very sophisticated graphic representations of this data; some do this in colour. The colours range from vivid primary colours to pastels, depending on the software capabilities. A number of graphics and presentation software packages are available (see Figure 10-3). Many organizations moved to distributed data processing in the 1980s rather than having all their information and processing power in one location. Users are now able to retrieve and manipulate information within the office, bringing many organizations closer to an integrated information system. With the addition of other automated equipment and communications networks, the transformation will be complete. Other organizations are outsourcing their data processing functions as a means of increasing efficiency.

Figure 10-3
Personal Computer
with Colour
Graphics

*Source: Courtesy of International Business Machines Corporation.
Unauthorized use not permitted.*

Databases

It is obvious that computers have had a tremendous effect on businesses, but nowhere is that more evident than in the management of large volumes of information known as databases. A **database** is a collection of interrelated data files, organized so that the data can be used systematically. The data are stored in a way that makes the information easy to locate, retrieve, and manipulate by the user with a computer and a software program known as a database management system.

A database is a
collection of
interrelated data
files.

Most databases organize data in tables, called *relations,* and are known as **relational databases**, making it easy to link multiple data files. The database can be divided into four parts:

1. A **data character** is any symbol, digit, letter, or punctuation stored or processed by computers. Each character is represented by a group of binary digits called a byte.
2. A **data field** (data element) is a group of characters combined to create one unit of data.
3. A **data record** is a group of related fields describing one occurrence in the file.
4. A **data file** is a collection of records containing the same fields of data treated as a unit.

Relational databases are efficient at capturing the day-to-day activities of a business.

While today's relational databases are excellent at processing alphanumeric data, it is almost impossible for them to deal with complex data like blocks of text, images, and video. Digitized and graphical images are more common, especially through the World Wide Web, and an **object relational database** is needed to access these data types. **Objects** are small, reusable chunks of code in computer programs. Each object has a specific function and a standard interface, so it can be attached to other objects. Their great advantage is in reducing the massive amounts of programming required for complex applications. Object databases permit integration of different types of complex data.

Indexing

An index provides information to aid in locating a record. Numbers and/or text stored in computer memory are assigned addresses as the information is captured. When this index is recalled to the screen, these addresses (location codes or record identifiers) let the searcher determine where the information is stored. Classifying and indexing documents may occur at the time the documents are created so that the index may be called back to the screen to identify the location of the record. Many systems automatically index a document as it is created and may assign as many as 20 different identifiers—key words or descriptors—to each document. Accessing information stored in memory requires knowledge of the address(es) of the information and how to transfer the information from internal memory to an external form. The information may be called up on a monitor, printed, or transferred to external storage (magnetic or film media).

Indexing information on external magnetic media is accomplished in the same way as internal indexing—by using key words from the stored information. The index may be maintained on a disk or other magnetic form and can be viewed on a monitor. A printed index may be generated from the computer. The optical disk index may also be maintained on a disk or tape and viewed on a screen. The index may be generated from the optical disk system and printed if needed.

Key words and descriptors are used to locate documents.

 Learning Check: What is the purpose of the processing subsystem?

COMMUNICATION SUBSYSTEM

The **communication subsystem** is the means of getting information to users in a timely manner. This subsystem covers communication both within and outside the organization as well as developments in telecommunication.

Communication in the Organization

Communication networks join various technologies.

The sharing of information and processing ability that allows an office to become an integrated system is created by communication networks, which join various technologies and terminals (workstations) employing the same technology. Since the purpose of networking is to allow people to interact and communicate with one another, this subsystem is referred to as *interactive communication*.

Networks

A **network** consists of nodes such as workstations and printers plus the links between them. Nodes can be connected with twisted-pair cable, coaxial cable, fibre optics, or telephone lines. Depending on the area they cover, networks may be **local area networks (LANs)**, which serve an office building or an organization, Metropolitan Area Networks (MANs) serving a city, or Wide Area Networks (WANs) serving a country or the entire world. These communication lines and their nodes in a LAN form bus, ring, or star configurations, as illustrated in Figure 10-4. In the figure, the bus configuration shown in A has one communication line shared by all the nodes. Communication moves through the ring shown in B following the direction of the arrows. The star configuration in C represents a central node that controls all transmissions to and from the peripheral nodes.

Figure 10-4
Configurations in a Local Area Network

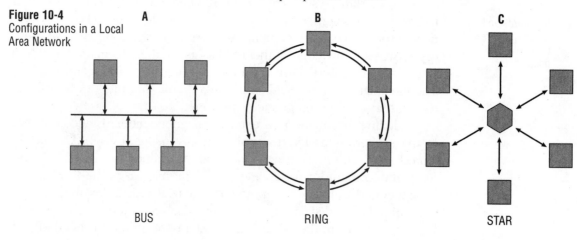

A   B   C

BUS   RING   STAR

Electronic Mail Services

An electronic message can be sent to a group of recipients simultaneously.

One application of the communication network is the ability to provide electronic mail service. Electronic mail uses the computer or a communicating word processor as a mailbox and allows each user to access mail through a terminal and to respond by using the terminal's keyboard. Messages can be composed, edited, distributed, and filed at the user terminal. The mailbox holds the message until the recipient calls for it; the sender does not need to wait until the recipient can be reached by telephone to relay a message. Additional time savings are realized for those applications in which the same message is to be distributed to several locations within the organization; these messages can be sent simultaneously. With prepared distribution lists the originator indicates that the message is to be sent to a designated category of people (such as department heads), and the message is delivered to each designated mailbox. The user may easily check the terminal to determine if messages are waiting, but no buzzing or ringing interrupts important conversations or composition. In addition, the service virtually eliminates telephone tag. Not only messages, but also files can be transmitted electronically by E-mail.

By subscribing to information utilities that provide E-mail services internationally, electronic mail can be transmitted anywhere in the world. With access to the Internet, for example, it is possible to exchange messages with millions of people far beyond a local area network. Electronic mail brings with it many complex considerations for records managers: Who owns it—the creator or the employer? Which messages are temporary records and which are active records? How should E-mail be scheduled?

Voice Mail

Voice mail eliminates telephone tag.

Voice mail is an alternative to the electronic mail networks that are tied to the typewritten word. Many people would prefer to deliver some messages orally, bypassing the time-consuming elements of keyboarding a message. This is particularly true when the message is to be delivered internally or to a branch of the organization. Voice mail should not be thought of as a replacement for telephone conversation. Telephone contact provides a two-way communication bridge, while voice mail allows only a one-way communication. Voice mail provides the ability to communicate a message to an individual or to groups of people and to pass along a message to others. The user dials an assigned number to enter the voice mail system, relays the message, and the system then attempts to deliver the message to the recipients immediately. If the recipient is not available to receive the message, it is filed in memory. Later, when the recipient dials the voice mailbox, the voice mail is received in its original form—the sender's voice. For priority messages, originators can instruct the system to keep trying to reach the recipient at specified intervals. Voice mail can also deliver messages at a specific time and on a future date.

Time Management Services

Within an organization, time management services are available that were not previously possible. One important time management application is scheduling meetings. Without an integrated information system, scheduling meetings may frequently require many hours of various support personnel time in checking the managers' schedules. The internal communication network allows access to personal calendars so that meetings can be scheduled and the date added to their calendars without talking to each attendee.

Calendars can be maintained at user terminals. Users can see on the screens at their desks appointments scheduled on a particular date. Appointments can be cancelled or rescheduled with a few simple motions, and the calendar is always up to date.

Telecommunication and Satellite Transmission

Time means money to today's business organizations. The speed with which communication can be transmitted to branch locations or to customers and associates outside the organization (in remote locations) continues to increase in importance.

Telecommunication is communication sent over telephone lines. A variety of telecommunication technologies makes it possible for all types of information to be sent electronically. Voice, data (words, symbols, and numbers), graphics, and video communication can be electronically distributed. The advancements in this technology have made it possible for communication between processors of almost every size. The only requirement is that the basic components be present in each workstation.

Facsimile Transmission

Facsimile transmission is the electronic transmission of hard-copy data over telephone lines. A similar hard copy is produced at the recipient's location. Facsimile equipment (see Figure 10-5) has vastly improved in speed and in the quality of the communication in the last several years. Much of this equipment can transmit unattended after regular business hours for savings in transaction costs or to reach recipients in other time zones. Some organizations are using microfacsimile transmission—the electronic transmission of microrecords—which reproduces microrecords at the recipient's location.

Terminals that have interactive communication may also be connected to communication (telephone) lines through the use of an external or built-in modem. The modem converts digital data from the sending machine into signals that can be transmitted over telephone lines or by satellite. These signals are reconverted to digital data at the receiving terminal. A call is placed to the receiving location, and when a connection is made, the transmission begins. Many terminals can be programmed to transmit unattended or store messages for transmission when costs are lower. Multipurpose equipment is available that combines a fax, printer, scanner, and copier in one machine.

Figure 10-5
Facsimile
Equipment

Source: Courtesy of Xerox Canada Limited

Conferencing

Several types of conferencing using telecommunication technology are also available. Computer conferencing is possible when interactive terminals are connected via telephone lines. Conference participants may be at their terminals simultaneously, or the information may be stored electronically and accessed at the recipient's convenience. If all participants are at their terminals simultaneously, information is received on their screens, and they may "talk" via their terminal keyboards.

Audio teleconferencing is the most familiar type of conference conducted by telephone connections. **Audio teleconferencing** is voice communication over telephone lines between two or more remote locations. Participants in several locations can talk with each other in a conference call, which may be arranged through an operator or established by the participants. If several people are to participate at each location, all parties are present in the same room and a speaker phone enables each to speak and projects the voice so that all may hear.

In addition to the advantages of teleconferencing in business settings, this interactive technology is employed in the delivery of courses through distance education. As an example, advanced communication methods of audio and audio-graphics teleconferencing combined with computer telephone linkages deliver university courses to sites remote from the originating campus. Students who may be far away from the university campus can communicate directly with faculty and with students in other communities. Figure 10-6 illustrates this method of course delivery.

Three forms of video teleconferencing are also possible. The first of these is *slow-scan video,* which requires separate phone lines for audio and video transmissions. The video transmission is sent from a camera, which scans the image from top to bottom in about 60 seconds. Receiving systems may store the image until the entire frame is received. This type of video teleconferencing is best suited to the transmission of blueprints and other documents.

Another form of video teleconferencing is *freeze-frame video.* This form allows one to freeze a single frame from the camera and transmit it. Although the transmission time remains the same as with slow scan, the potential problem of blurred images is eliminated. Freeze-frame systems with additional memory capacity can store multiple frames to allow forward or reverse image retrieval.

The most natural (and expensive) form of video teleconferencing is live, *full-motion video.* In this option the camera focuses on the speaker and transmits a visual image as well as the speaker's voice. These visual images are stored and transmitted as three-dimensional images.

Figure 10-6
Distance Learning
Via Audio and
Audio-Graphics
Teleconferencing

Source: Mount Saint Vincent University, Halifax, Nova Scotia (Dan Callis photo)

Satellite Communication

Satellite beams are used by large, geographically dispersed organizations to transmit videoconferences. A **videoconference** is similar to a live, full-motion video teleconference, except for the method of transmission. Both videoconferencing and video teleconferencing require heavy financial investments to equip the conference rooms; however, many organizations have found these applications to be cost effective because of the savings in time and travel expenses. For organizations unable or unwilling to make this investment, some telecommunication companies provide rental teleconferencing facilities.

Satellites are also used by independent telephone companies to transmit telephone conversations using microwaves. Some communication companies offer all-digital integrated voice, data, and image transmission through satellites.

Fibre Optics

Fibre optics are used to transmit analogue and digital signals.

Fibre optics are transparent glass fibres that conduct light (usually in the form of a laser) and transmit both analogue (tonal) and digital signals. The use of optical cables increased rapidly in the late 1980s and continues to increase because of the greater transmission speed provided. Transmission through fibre-optic cables also offers the advantage of immunity to electromagnetic and radio interference, which is particularly important in some industrial environments (such as steelworks) and for cars and aircraft. Other advantages include significantly less signal loss; better security as a result of the insulating quality glass provides; less weight and size; and the potential to carry 10,000 times as much information as copper wire of the same diameter.

✓ **Learning Check: Can you explain how the productivity of the communication subsystem is improved by an integrated information system?**

STORAGE SUBSYSTEM

The **storage subsystem** is the means of storing, retrieving, and disposing of information according to the organization's needs.

Storage

Traditionally, dealing with the stored information that becomes the records of the organization has been the job of records management staff. In an integrated information system, records management and information systems staff must work together closely to provide the best possible solutions. Information may be stored on-line and through several media such as magnetic, optical, and microrecords media, depending on the needs of the users and the characteristics of the information.

On-Line Computer Storage

On-line computer storage is the depositing of information in a computer database or in the memory of the computer. Information stored in an on-line computer database may be quickly accessed from any terminal connected with the computer. This information may then be further manipulated, printed for distribution, or distributed through an electronic mail service. If this information will be needed for future use, it should be transferred to a magnetic or optical storage medium.

Electronic Storage

Information that is to be stored on magnetic media is digitized and stored on computer hard disks, computer tapes, or removable disks. This information may also be readily viewed and manipulated once the appropriate tape or disk is located. Information may also be stored on optical disks. These storage media are described in Chapter 9, "Electronic Records Management."

Microrecords Storage

As described in Chapter 8, hard-copy documents may be reduced to microimages and stored on microfilm or microfiche. Microrecords may also be computer-generated (using computer output microfilm or COM). They can be duplicated very inexpensively and distributed through postal services (saving significantly over mailing hard copy) or through facsimile transmissions. Microrecords may be viewed on a reader-printer, which will also produce a hard copy of the information, if needed.

Information Retrieval

Retrieval is the process of locating stored information and getting it to users in an efficient manner. In an integrated information system, retrieval is usually accomplished with an automated system, making use of a computer to aid in retrieval. Basically, **computer-assisted retrieval (CAR)** uses various automation technologies to assist in timely location and retrieval of information. CAR can be used with manual, semiautomated, and fully automated systems.

When a specific document is requested, the operator calls up the address and supporting information on the monitor. Sometimes the information displayed will answer any questions the user may have without a need to go any further. High-speed printers attached to a computer provide the user with hard-copy output. The same information may be shown on a screen in those instances when hard copy is not required. Automated systems allow users to retrieve on-line or off-line documents by calling up a key word or words from the text. Users can also obtain a listing of all documents containing these words. Searching can be done by title, author, type of document, operator, department, user-defined words, or last date stored.

As mentioned, storage within the computer memory has a limited capacity and is primarily used to store information temporarily. For longer-term storage, the information is transferred from memory to an external form of storage such as magnetic media. Although the information itself is retrieved through automated systems, the disks and tapes on which the information is stored are often retrieved manually. For that reason, disks or tapes must be clearly labelled. Each should be labelled to indicate its contents, just as a file folder is labelled. And, in the same vein, the storage equipment for electronic media should be labelled to indicate the contents. Once the electronic media are retrieved and entered into or placed onto the equipment, the file number or key word(s) are entered on the keyboard, and the information may be printed or viewed on the screen. This is true for any electronic media whether they are optical disks or magnetic tapes and disks. Optical disks, however, use a high-speed laser printer that works more like a photocopier, storing information as complete pages rather than as individually encoded characters and retrieved as photographic facsimiles of entire pages, including illustrations.

In an integrated system, the user must be able to search and retrieve information based on the content of documents, not simply by title, author, number, or date. Content searching and retrieval relies on full-text indexes and structured query language (SQL), the industry standard for information retrieval. **Structured query language (SQL)** is a language by which a user can formulate requests for information and update, add, or delete information from the database. **Structured full-text query language (SFQL)** is a proposed standard for full-text databases.

The tools for searching and retrieval are becoming more powerful as more information is stored electronically. Basic systems use a keyword (a single word in a field), a phrase (two or more consecutive words in a field), and **Boolean logic** (more than one keyword or phrase plus a logic statement) to search a database. The **logic statement** (AND, OR, NOT, EXCEPT, IF, THEN) limits or expands the search. A **wild card**, a symbol representing one or more unknown characters, expands a search when only part of an identification is known. For example, the search command *Donald will retrieve all the McDonald and MacDonald surnames in a client database. Proximity searches can be performed for words that are located close to each other such as the words *colour* and *coding;* fuzzy matching relies on pattern recognition to retrieve misspelled words, plurals, and so on. Systems may use relevancy ranking (listing "hits" or matches by their context relevancy). Hierarchical concept trees create associations between terms to link related words or phrases, synonyms, preferred words, and broader or narrower words. Information retrieval technology empowers the end user who gains access to vast quantities of information. Technology is also replacing personnel such as reference librarians and file clerks who have traditionally retrieved information.

Disposition

Disposition is the final determination of whether to store or dispose of records (stored information) no longer needed by the organization. The timing of records disposition is determined by the retention schedule (discussed in Chapter 4). Methods of disposition vary from organization to organization and with the confidentiality of records. Interesting discussions are occurring about whether or not computer information can actually be erased. There are businesses engaged solely in retrieving information from discarded computers, for example.

 Learning Check: Can you explain the functions of the storage subsystem in an integrated information system?

MANAGING AN INTEGRATED SYSTEM

Managing an integrated system requires varied skills and a thorough knowledge of technology in order to choose the best tools with which to accomplish the organization's goals. There is a wide choice of software for managing databases and for tracking records. Bar code technology identifies storage media, files, and individual documents.

Database Management Systems Software

Database management system software (DBMS) is an integrated set of software programs that allows the user to create databases, maintain databases, and retrieve information from those databases in a predetermined report format. There are five advantages of the DBMS software.

- **The problem of data redundancy is reduced.** Because relationships can be established between and among files, the same data does not have to be repeated in every file. If a student file is maintained, the students' names and addresses may appear in that file, along with the student identification number. Other files related to the student file may contain only the student identification number, without repeating the students' names and addresses. This allows the user to make an address change only once instead of making the change in several files, as would be required with simple file management systems.

- **The integrity of the data is improved.** Because the problem of duplicate data has been eliminated, the integrity of the data results in better decision making for the users.
- **The data files are independent of the programs.** Because the data files are independent of the applications programs, the user can go in and change the database without concern that the applications programs used prior to the change will not work.
- **Files can be joined through established relationships.** A major advantage of database management system software is the joining of data from several files, for example, when preparing a report or simply retrieving information from the database.
- **The security of the data can be improved by establishing levels of security over the information in the database—"read only" for certain employees—making them restricted or not accessible to everyone.** Other databases may be open to all employees, allowing them to change data as well as retrieve the data. This is particularly useful when employees need access to certain databases, but management needs to restrict access to sensitive databases.

 Learning Check: Can you name five advantages of DBMS software?

Functions of a Database Management System

There are numerous database management system software packages on the market. These relational database management system software (DBMS) packages are capable of performing the following eight functions.

- **Creation of a Database.** Before the data can be entered in a database, the database must be planned and created. Planning the database involves deciding the data to be contained in the database, naming the fields needed, deciding the types of fields for each item of data, and selecting the size of each field.
- **Modification of a Database.** The original database can be altered easily. If all fields were not included when the database was created, additional fields can be added to the database structure. Fields originally included that really are not needed can simply be deleted from the database. The size and the type of field may also be changed.
- **Addition and Deletion of Data.** Once data are entered into the database, new records may be added, data may be edited or changed in existing records, and old records may be deleted from the database entirely.
- **Reorganizing the Data in the Database.** A DBMS software package allows the user to reorganize the data contained in the database through indexing and sorting procedures.

- **Searching and Retrieving Information.** Searching and retrieving information from a database file is an extremely useful function of a DBMS software package. Searching is the process of finding a particular record or piece of data. Information is retrieved from the database file by the use of search commands along with one or more conditions or specific criteria that a record must meet in order to be retrieved from the database.
- **Generating Reports and Labels.** Most DBMS software packages have report and label formats. These formats allow the user to generate reports and labels while pulling only the fields necessary for that specific report or label function. By combining the indexing, searching, and reporting features of the DBMS software packages, reports can be tailored to specific needs with very little effort on the user's part.
- **Formatting Customized Screens.** Screen formatting allows the user to customize the data entry screens. The screen formatting option allows the user to expand field names, add instructions, and position fields to correspond to the format of the source document. A customized screen makes it easier for users to enter data into the database file.
- **Establishing Security Measures.** Most DBMS software packages have the capability of establishing security measures to protect database files from unauthorized access. Once the security measures have been established, the database cannot be used without proper entry of the user name, group name, and password.

Learning Check: Can you name at least five functions performed by a DBMS software package?

Computer-Based Records Management Systems

Computer-based records management systems are used to maintain large databases of information. These databases may be the actual information on clients, patients, inventory, and so forth, or databases used to track the records of the organization. The records may be active or inactive, and maintained in paper form, as microforms, or magnetic media.

Computer-based records management systems can be used to track records.

Computer-based records management systems used for tracking records in an organization automatically track the in-and-out filing activity (usually with a bar code system for folders). By using bar codes and automated equipment, lost or misplaced records are reduced. Using computer-based records management tracking programs helps the organization maintain a complete inventory of records. It is also easy to prepare reports on the activity of the records by department, document, or specific user and to provide data for departmental chargebacks. Other applications include the management of inactive records, retention periods, and disposal of records.

Types of Computer-Based Records Management Systems

There are three types of computer-based records management systems that may be used for the tracking of records.

1. Database management software, such as dBASE IV, Paradox, and FoxPro can be tailored to the special needs of an organization.

2. Numerous computer-based records management tracking systems are commercially available. These software programs may index, track, monitor, set security levels of access to records, record charge outs, and perform a variety of other functions. They may be single-function programs that address only one aspect of the records management area such as active records management. On the other hand, they may be integrated packages that address the complete records management system of the organization. They may also be modular programs, with separate modules for each function of the records management area, such as active records (tracking file folders or individual documents), inactive records (tracking storage cartons), microrecords, vital records, disaster prevention and recovery, archives management, and so forth.

3. The third alternative is software developed in-house. If an organization is highly specialized and feels that its requirements cannot be readily met by available commercial software, the records management software can be developed in-house. However, programming and development usually take longer, and the software is much more expensive than off-the-shelf software.

 Learning Check: Can you describe three types of computer-based records management systems?

Bar Code Technology

Everyone is familiar with the identification symbols on packaged grocery products made up of a series of black lines and white spaces. This technology is an especially effective tool for locating records within a records management system, because each bar code label is unique and thus identifies the item to which it is affixed. Bar codes are used in records management anywhere that tracking is required and include:

- **File folder labels.** As a component of a file folder label, the bar code identifies each file folder in the system, no matter where it is located.

- **Single document identification.** Bar codes are affixed to each document and scanned as the document is processed, becoming a part of a document tracking system. For example, in an optical storage system, a bar code is placed on each document before it is scanned.
- **Computer tapes, disks, and cartridges.** Each item is identified by the bar code on its label.
- **Microfilm, microfiche, CAR systems.** A bar code is placed on each paper document before it is filmed and becomes the identifier of that document.
- **Inactive storage cartons.** Bar codes are a part of the label for each carton, so that the location and contents can be identified.

Advantages of Bar Coding

The big advantage of bar coding is that it eliminates the need for manual keying of data input and of rekeying identifying information. Once the bar code has been scanned into the records system, items can be located immediately. The labour of manual input is saved, service is improved, and misfiles are reduced. Table 10-1, presented earlier in this chapter, shows that human keyboarding input results in thousands of additional errors on average than bar code scanning.

Bar Coding Equipment

Special printers are needed to generate the bar code labels. Reading devices such as laser scanners, laser guns, light pens, and wands employ a light source to scan the bar codes. Decoding software called a symbol decoder manages the database (see Figure 10-7).

Figure 10-7
Bar Code Scanner

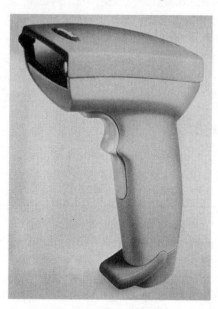

Source: Courtesy of Symbol Technologies Canada Inc.

Learning Check: Can you describe four ways in which bar coding is used?

Choosing a Computer-Based Records Management System

As with any other type of software, it is imperative that a thorough study be made before deciding on the type of records management software to purchase. Study the current procedures, concentrating on the volume of active and inactive records, workflow, and current activity. Decide which areas of the records management program will be automated (a single function or the complete records management area) and the benefits expected from the records management software.

Study the software packages on the market. Selecting records management software is just like selecting any other types of software. Will the system be easy to learn? How long is the learning curve? Will the employees be able to become proficient quickly? Does the vendor have a good reputation? Are there other installations in the area? Is the vendor experienced in records management applications? Are the manuals written in simple, easy-to-understand language? Is there a toll-free number for problem solution? Is there any training and, if so, how long and for how many employees? What about security of data? Is there a backup provided? How much does the software cost? How much does each add-on cost? Is installation included in the base price? Is there a maintenance contract available? What standard reports are available? Can reports be customized using the software? These and other questions should be answered. It helps to make up a chart of the areas of concern and evaluate each software application using the same criteria.

After narrowing down the selections, actually work with the software, if possible. It is best to work with a full copy of the software; however, if this is not possible, at least work with a demonstration or tutorial copy. Try making mistakes that would normally be made by users. By doing so, surprises after installation can be eliminated.

 Learning Check: Can you list at least five questions that should be answered when evaluating software?

RECORDS MANAGEMENT IN THE INTEGRATED INFORMATION SYSTEM

Records management is the systemic control of records from their creation to their final disposition. Within an integrated information system, the manner in which records are processed, communicated, stored, and retrieved may change significantly from procedures used in a more traditional office. These changes affect the role of the records manager in the office and the performance of many records functions.

Role of the Records Manager

Much has been written about who will be in charge of an integrated information system. Will it be the information systems manager? The data processing manager? A committee of managers from the various information processing areas? Each of these choices shares a limiting characteristic. These individuals, while competent in their own areas, are accustomed to managing equipment to produce results.

The records manager is familiar with the information needs of all divisions and departments of the organization.

Within the integrated information system, someone must manage information. The individual best prepared to perform this function is usually the records manager. This individual is familiar with the information needs of all divisions and departments of the organization. The records manager knows what records are kept in each office, what the distribution patterns are, what the retention requirements are, and when records may be destroyed. This is a background that no other manager within the organization has.

Records managers should, however, not assume that the integrated information system will be under their control. In order to be given this responsibility, records managers must demonstrate a thorough knowledge of each technology to be employed in the integrated information system and how each will affect overall office efficiency. Records managers must demonstrate leadership qualities that would let them lead in the implementation of new technology without alienating other employees and with minimal disruption of office routines.

Even if records managers are knowledgeable and well prepared to assume these responsibilities, they will not be expected to work in a vacuum. Effectively managing integrated information systems usually requires a team approach among the records manager, MIS staff, legal counsel, the internal auditor, and designated users.

Records Functions

Integrated information systems contribute to the speed and accuracy of input, processing, and output of information. The use of an integrated information system changes the manner in which many records functions are performed.

Origination

As previously discussed, the origination of records will frequently be done at an electronic terminal. This not only allows more rapid composition, but it also prevents misplacing incomplete documents. If the originator must leave the work before completion, the information is simply placed in storage to be recalled later. The availability of access to computer data banks and other automated retrieval systems speeds the accessing of previously stored information, which may be important to the composition of correspondence and reports.

Processing

Processing of data, text, and images is also completed at electronic terminals. This equipment continues to be upgraded to provide additional operations and to improve the speed of existing operations. Printer speeds are vastly improved over those of the best typists, and much keying is eliminated in the revision stage.

Communication

Communication used to be written or oral (face to face or by telephone). Now there are numerous other options. Electronic mail and facsimile services allow recipients at remote locations to receive hardcopy data without waiting for the postal services. Electronic mail has also eliminated a great deal of interoffice mail. Teleconferencing and videoconferencing via satellite allow some organizations to have participatory meetings of individuals in several locations and save time and travel costs.

Storage and Retrieval

The integrated information system is much less dependent on paper and paper files. Manually searching paper files to locate information is too slow and too costly. New storage media allow automated access, which reduces retrieval time from several minutes to a few seconds.

The integrated information system offers the opportunity for increased managerial and administrative support productivity within the organization and improved communication speeds, both internally and externally. The organization's needs should be carefully examined before beginning any implementation process. Employee involvement in each stage, from planning to installation, increases the probability of implementing the best combination of options for each subsystem and of minimizing employee resistance to the new equipment and procedures. A thorough knowledge of the organization's information needs makes the records manager an appropriate choice to manage this new system.

 Learning Check: Can you explain how the role of the records manager changes in an integrated information system?

TERMINOLOGY REVIEW

Review the terms listed below in the Glossary on page 521.

audio teleconferencing
Boolean logic
communication subsystem
computer-assisted retrieval (CAR)
data

logic statement
network
object relational database
objects
on-line computer storage

data character

data field

data file

database

database management
system software (DBMS)

data processing

facsimile transmission

fibre optics

hypertext markup language (HTML)

information

integrated information system

local area network (LAN)

optical character reader (OCR)

originating subsystem

processing subsystem

relational database

standard general markup
language (SGML)

storage subsystem

structured full-text query
language (SFQL)

structured query language (SQL)

telecommunication

videoconferencing

wild card

REVIEW AND DISCUSSION

1. What is an integrated information system, and what are its benefits?
2. Describe the steps in the implementation process.
3. What is the originating subsystem, and how is it different in the integrated information system than it is in a traditional office?
4. Describe input methods for creating textual information.
5. Compare data entry alternatives in an automated system.
6. What are the purposes of the processing subsystem?
7. Describe two general types of databases and how they contribute to the integrated information system.
8. Describe the functions of indexes.
9. Describe two types of organizational communication services and three types of telecommunication services that link remote locations.
10. What is the storage subsystem?
11. Describe three types of storage media.
12. How is information retrieved from
    a. Internal storage?
    b. Magnetic/optical storage?
13. Describe three types of records management tracking systems.
14. Explain the use of bar coding in an integrated information system.
15. List at least five questions that should be answered when evaluating software.
16. Explain the role of records management in the integrated information system.
17. Summarize the effect of each subsystem within the integrated information system on records functions.

APPLICATIONS

1. Trace the path through the integrated information system of (a) an incoming invoice and (b) an outgoing item of correspondence.
2. a. Which technique would be most desirable for inputting the following into the integrated information system?
     (1) Sales data
     (2) Internal reports
     (3) Legal documents from other offices
   b. Which storage technique would be most desirable for each of the following:
     (1) Reports
     (2) Weekly sales data
     (3) Correspondence

CONCLUDING CASES

A. Riverside Enterprises

Riverside Enterprises (RE) publishes trade journals in the fields of real estate sales and management. Each of its seven journals has a national readership, and getting them out on time from Riverside Enterprises' word processing centre to the printer is becoming more difficult. Someone is always late! In addition, RE's computer no longer has sufficient processing capability to handle advertisers' accounts, subscription notices and billings, reports of readership and industry surveys, and other business functions, such as payroll.

Michelle Williams, chair of the board of Riverside Enterprises, has asked that a consultant be hired to design and direct the implementation of an integrated information system for RE. Mrs. Williams emphasized to the board her concern that any system implemented should continue to provide the records needed for efficient, successful operations.

You have been hired as an information systems consultant to Riverside Enterprises.

1. What types of information would be required to prepare a cost justification for an integrated information system?
2. Outline the steps in the implementation process.

B. Court Records

The records in the provincial court in Marlow County are maintained in regular file folders in four-drawer file cabinets. There are approximately 9,000 records maintained concerning domestic matters. These files are continuously checked in and out by attorneys, guardians, judges, juvenile case workers, and other court personnel. The situation is desperate because a large percentage of the files are lost or missing when needed by a court officer. The clerk of court has been requested to suggest a system of tracking the files and maintaining records of who has what file. You have been called in as a consultant to make suggestions.

How would you solve this records management problem?

SUGGESTED READINGS AND RESOURCES

Avedon, Don M. "Electronic Imaging 101 Part V—Communications." *Records Management Quarterly,* Vol. 29, No. 2 (April, 1995), p. 36.

Connelly, Jim. "Designing Records and Document Retrieval Systems." *Records Management Quarterly,* Vol. 29, No. 2 (April, 1995), p. 30.

Davis, James V., Jr. "Choosing Records Management Software." *Records Management Quarterly,* Vol. 22, No. 3 (July, 1988), p. 3.

Du Rea, Mary V., and J. Michael Pemberton. "Electronic Mail and Electronic Data Interchange: Challenges to Records Management." *Records Management Quarterly,* Vol. 28, No. 4 (October, 1994), p. 3.

Mark, Teri J. "Decoding the Bar Code." *Records Management Quarterly,* Vol. 28, No. 1 (January, 1994), p. 22.

Mark, Teri J., and Jane M. Owens. "Comparing Apples to Oranges: Methods for Evaluating and Selecting Records Management Software." *Records Management Quarterly,* Vol. 30, No. 1 (January, 1996), p. 30.

Mennecke, Brian, and Sooun Lee. "Application of Expert Systems in Distributed Database Environments." *Records Management Quarterly,* Vol. 25, No. 1 (January, 1991), p. 10.

O'Connor, Dee Dee, "Automating a Records Index." *Records Management Quarterly,* Vol. 23, No. 1 (January, 1989), p. 10.

Phillips, John T. Jr., and Angela L. Beckwith. "Electronic Systems and Paper Forms." *Records Management Quarterly,* Vol. 25, No. 1 (January, 1991), p. 18.

Savić, Dobrica. "Designing an Expert System for Classifying Office Documents." *Records Management Quarterly,* Vol. 28, No. 3 (July, 1994), p. 20.

Stillman, Jaunita, and April Dmytrenko. "A Comparison of PC Based Records Management Software." *Records Management Quarterly,* Vol. 23, No. 2 (April, 1989), p. 21.

Volkema, Roger J. "Computer-Assisted Meeting Management and Recordkeeping." *Records Management Quarterly,* Vol. 22, No. 4 (October, 1988), p. 8.

Yen, David (Chi-Chung), and Hung-Lian Tang. "Future Trends of Computer-Based Information Systems." *Records Management Quarterly,* Vol. 22, No. 4 (October, 1988), p. 12.

Profile
Records Administration Supervisor

Pattie Smith is the supervisor in the Records Administration Department of the Dominion Life & Accident Insurance Company. The company processes its microfilm in-house, and Mrs. Smith started working in the micrographics area eight years ago. She has been in her current position for four years. The company has 359 full-time home office employees, and the Records Administration Department has nine employees. The positions in the Records Administration Department include records administration supervisor, CRT clerk, lead clerk, microfiche operator, camera operator, and file clerk.

The education and experience requirements for the records administration supervisor position include a high-school diploma, two years' postsecondary education and four years' prior experience in micrographics. The position requires technical expertise in the area of micrographics, particularly in the area of processing film. Personal computer and network knowledge and experience are important. Communication, supervisory, and scheduling skills are also desirable for this position.

Mrs. Smith is directly responsible and accountable for the planning, organizing, and controlling of all the personnel and functions of the Records Administration Department. The department functions include storage, retrieval, and maintenance of life application files (microfilm jacket system form), accident and health application files, and paid claim files. The department also produces paper copies of computer output microfilm and performs any special microfilming projects. Mrs. Smith is responsible for providing innovative ideas and research aimed at improving operations within the department or the company. She must also ensure that work standards and performance reporting systems are established to assist in maintaining productivity at the highest practical level.

Company growth and advances in technology have changed Mrs. Smith's duties and responsibilities as the company has implemented computer technology to help maintain records. The department implemented a computer-assisted retrieval system under Mrs. Smith's supervision. During the implementation of the CAR system, Mrs. Smith was required to help make decisions on hardware and software, specify program requirements on the mainframe, and teach employees keyboarding skills for information input.

Mrs. Smith is constantly researching new technology for possible implementation in the Records Administration Department. She forecasts that in three to five years the department will be completely automated with laser scanners. She is also studying the development of optical disks as a possibility for records storage.

Advancement opportunities for Mrs. Smith in the Records Administration Department are limited. She could have additional areas of responsibility added to her current supervisory responsibilities or she could be promoted to a position in another department. Mrs. Smith attends professional conferences sponsored by AIIM.

Part 5
Records Protection

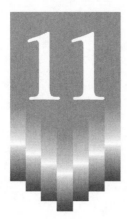

Vital Records, Disaster Prevention and Recovery

Learning Goals

After completing this chapter, you should be able to:

1. Identify vital records.
2. Identify primary methods of protecting vital records.
3. Identify procedures used to transfer and store vital records.
4. Identify the procedures used to protect electronic vital records.
5. Explain the use and importance of a vital records protection manual.
6. Explain the importance of having an up-to-date disaster prevention and recovery plan.
7. Describe the steps in planning for disaster prevention and recovery.
8. State the typical contents and format of a records disaster prevention and recovery manual.
9. Describe how a disaster prevention and recovery plan is tested.
10. Describe disaster prevention methods for paper records, microrecords, and magnetic media records.
11. State the factors that determine the appropriate recovery method to be used.
12. Explain various salvage methods.

_____ *Store loses all its merchandise and computer containing all company's vital records*

_____ *Hail storm in Calgary costs insurers $237.4 million*

_____ *1993 Floods in Winnipeg generate $160 million in claims*

_____ *Fire ruins books in Dalhousie University law school library*

_____ *Staff arrive to find 13 feet of water in basement of St. John's office building where most paper records are kept*

Newspaper accounts similar to the ones above are all too familiar to the public and to persons responsible for the protection of business records. However, many people have the attitude that it cannot happen to them and therefore do not take the precautions needed to protect their records. Security is a responsibility that cannot be regarded lightly, and records managers must plan to safeguard records from damage and destruction. The consequences of a disaster are enormous. For example, 60 percent of organizations that experience a business closure of more than two days go out of business within one year.

Business records must be protected.

The importance of records was addressed in Chapter 1. Because records and information are becoming increasingly critical to the continuing successful operation of an organization, more and more attention is being directed toward protecting the physical properties and content integrity of records. Original records that are destroyed cannot be replaced. While attaching a monetary value to a record is difficult, imagining the impossibility of a business continuing to operate without records is not difficult. There would be no sales contracts, no accounts receivable records, no strategic or tactical plans, no correspondence documenting action, no payroll records, no customer lists, no shareholders' reports—no basis for continuing operation. The paper itself or other storage medium may have little intrinsic monetary value, but the value of the information contained in the record is incalculable. Records are not generally appraised or insured, and even those that have been appraised are often undervalued. When inventory records have been destroyed, collecting insurance is difficult. Organizations exist and prosper based on action taken as a result of the information to which they have access. If records are destroyed, the database is eliminated.

The first part of this chapter focuses on a description and analysis of what constitutes a vital record (the most important of any organization's records) how the determination is made, and appropriate storage and protection methods for vital records. The chapter will then present a detailed discussion of disaster prevention and recovery.

IDENTIFICATION AND ANALYSIS OF VITAL RECORDS

Vital records are
Class 1 records.

Although it is important to safeguard all records in a business organization, it is particularly important that a program be established to protect its vital records, often also known as *essential records*. **Vital records** are those records essential to the continued life of a business, also called Class 1 records. Vital records may take any form: hard copy, magnetic tape, microform, optical disk, and so forth. Vital records may be active or inactive records. Some vital records, such as the company charter, may be stored in the archives of the organization. In whatever medium or stage of life, the information contained in the vital records is needed for the continuation of the business.

The vital records protection program identifies vital records and outlines procedures to store those records, or duplicate copies of them, in a secure location. According to Gerard J. Kane,

A Vital Records Program is a systematic method of selecting, protecting, and having available at time of emergency:

1. Records considered absolutely essential to the continued operation of any agency or business, commensurate with its emergency responsibilities,

2. Records required to protect rights of individuals and the government, and

3. Records that are absolutely essential to reconstruction.[1]

The identification of vital records and the implementation of the protection program for those records evolves from the records inventory. As discussed in Chapter 3, part of the records inventory and appraisal process is to identify the vital records. During this process, it is important that only the records absolutely necessary for the continuation or resumption of the business be selected and protected as vital records. Normally, vital records represent approximately 1 to 5 percent of the records maintained by the organization. In order to select vital records, the management must have a thorough knowledge of the functions of the records and an overview of the life cycles of the records.

Organization Analysis

Before a comprehensive safety program can be implemented, management must conduct a thorough study of the organization itself to determine its vital functions. A functional organization chart is helpful. The vital functions may be administration, finance, research, human resources, marketing, sales, manufacturing, and so forth. Determining the organization's operational, legal and governmental requirements

[1]Gerald J. Kane, "A Vital Records Program to Insure Survival," *Records Management Quarterly*, Vol. 15 (April, 1981), p. 54.

will also help identify the vital records. Basically, this question must be answered: What information and/or records are needed to resume business immediately following a disaster?

Classification of Vital Records

Records are classified as vital, important, useful, or nonessential.

The National Fire Protection Association in the United States suggests one method of records divisions, or classifications, which is shown in Table 11-1. The NFPA classifies all the records of an organization as either vital, important, useful, or nonessential. The association defines vital records as those needed by the organization for the continuation of business and necessary to re-establish the organization's legal and financial position. Destruction or loss of records in this classification would usually require the organization to cease business. Examples of records that fall into the vital records category will vary from one type of business to the other. However, common examples might be accounts receivable, copyrights, patents, stocks, bonds, tax records, list of shareholders, contracts, minutes of board meetings, and leases. Vital records exist in all areas of a business organization.

Table 11-1

RECORDS CLASSIFICATION

Class	Definition	Example	Recommended Protection
Class 1—Vital	Records *essential* to the continued life of the business. These records are irreplaceable because they give evidence of legal status, ownership, and financial status. Vital records are generally housed in inactive records storage.	Accounts receivable Inventory Contracts Creative materials Research documentation	Fireproof safes Fire-resistant vaults Dispersal
Class 2—Important	Records *necessary* to the continued life of the business. While these records can be replaced or reproduced, this can be done only at considerable cost in time and money. Important records may be housed in either active or inactive storage.	Accounts payable Directives Payroll records	Safes Vaults
Class 3—Useful	Records *needed* for the uninterrupted operation of the business. These records are replaceable although their loss could cause temporary inconvenience.	Bank statements Correspondence	File cabinets
Class 4—Nonessential	Records having no present value; should be destroyed.	Requests answered Advertisements Announcements	Use, then destroy

Source: Gordon P. McKinnon, ed., Fire Protection Handbook, 15th ed. (Boston: National Fire Protection Association, 1981).

Important records are those records necessary to the continued life of a business; they are also called Class 2 records. Important records are replaceable, but at considerable expense of time and labour. Important records include such records as accounts payable, inventory records, customer records, manufacturing records, purchase orders, and payroll records. Many of these records relate to the day-to-day activities of the organization.

Useful records are those records needed for the uninterrupted operation of the business; they are also called Class 3 records. Useful records are replaceable although their loss could cause temporary inconvenience. Examples of these records might include bank statements and reconciliations, employment applications, and general correspondence. Useful records are usually reference materials with a limited value to the organization. Vital and important records may be reduced to useful records after the information contained has been outdated or superseded by more current information.

Nonessential records are those records having no present value to the organization; they are also called Class 4 records. Examples of nonessential records include requests answered, advertisements, and announcements. Nonessential records either never had a retention value or have served their usefulness to the organization and are no longer of value.

Much of this classification information may be determined by reference to a previous records inventory or by an actual survey of the records. By using the retention and disposition schedule and considering the vital functions of each department, a preliminary list of vital records can be made. Each type of vital record should be assigned an identification code, which will be used to make a master list of vital records and help to keep track of the records. Operating managers in each department should be involved with the selection of the vital records.

✓ **Learning Check: Can you name the four classifications used to determine the value of records?**

Determining the Physical Volume of the Records by Class

The next step after classifying the records also relies on information collected during the records inventory or survey. The storage media should be identified and the physical volume of records by class should be measured. For paper records, how many square feet of shelf space do the records occupy? How many file drawers house records, and what is the square footage of these file drawers? Of the total space required, how much is required for Class 1 records? How much of the total space required is needed for Class 2 and Class 3 records? What should be done with Class 4 records?

To develop a master list of vital records in electronic form, the following information should be gathered for each record series: the series title, storage media and other physical characteristics, location, method of protection and security requirements, and a brief rationale for categorizing the series as vital.

Determining Space Needed to House Inventoried Records

Based on the physical volume of the records by class, how much space should be allocated for each class of records? What is the estimated rate of accession at which records are added to each class? What is the rate of transfer or disposal for each class? How much space would be needed if the total allocation for each class included accessions and transfers?

Determining Protection Necessary for Safe Records Storage

The amount of protection necessary should be based on the information obtained in the survey. Naturally, vital records require the most protection. Fire is the main hazard, and types of protective storage are rated by tests conducted under standard fire conditions.

Protection for paper records and magnetic media records must be considered.

Any sizable collection of records not contained in vaults, safes, or insulated cabinets creates a fire hazard regardless of the storage method, the storage location, or the record medium. The trend toward making maximum use of available space through open-shelf housing presents a particular fire hazard. The close proximity of the opposing sides of the aisles could result in rapid fire expansion and increased heat feedback. The higher the stacks and the narrower the aisles, the more severe and rapid is the fire development.

Magnetic media and their containers do not represent a hazard more severe than that of paper. Polystyrene cases and reels, however, present a severe fire hazard because they burn fiercely. The storage systems designed to safeguard materials of cardboard or paper composition do not provide adequate protection for polystyrene materials; special storage systems are required.

Analysis of Risk

To determine the degree of protection needed for each class of records, the risk of loss must be evaluated. The greatest cost to the organization concerns the loss of all records classified as vital. To put this cost in dollar terms, questions such as the following should be considered: If all vital records were destroyed tomorrow, how long would it take to reconstruct the information, and how much would it cost? How much time would be unproductive, and what would the dollar cost be? How many contracts would be lost, and what is their monetary value? How many accounts receivable would not be collected, and what is that total cost?

All costs incurred by the loss of *vital* records should be totalled, and the process should be repeated for the other classes of records. All costs incurred by the loss of *all* records should be totalled; the total will be much higher than anticipated. Of those organizations whose records are destroyed, 35 percent go out of business; this fact provides clear evidence of the importance of a records protection program. Not only does the dollar figure provide an appraisal of the value of the records, but it is also a valuable tool for convincing management of the importance of records, and it more than justifies any costs involved in their protection.

Fire Risks

The primary risk to records safety is fire.

There are a number of potential hazards to records safety; however, the primary risk is destruction by fire or by the water or chemicals used in fire containment. Every organization encounters some degree of risk from fire. The cost of fire losses is rising each year; therefore, protection against fire losses is critical.

When new buildings are constructed, the proper authorities inspect and approve both the architectural drawings and the buildings as they progress through the construction stages to completion. New buildings, therefore, are more likely to have greater fire resistance and modern detection systems than older structures. The existing older buildings should be upgraded in terms of fire deterrents, detection systems, and safety alarms. Scheduled inspections should be a part of the total safety protection program in both new and older structures.

Other Natural and Human Hazards

In addition to damage by fire, the risk of damage to vital records by other types of natural or human hazards must be assessed. Possible damage or destruction could occur from earthquakes, wind and rainstorms, broken water mains, mould and mildew, insects and rodents, dust, theft, and vandalism.

METHODS OF PROTECTING VITAL RECORDS

A vital records protection program is more important than insurance.

Vital records must be protected. A program of safety and security, often time consuming and costly because of its labour-intensive operation, involves the entire corporate structure. Vital records are found in every organization and in every department that plays a legal, financial, or operational role. Because the protection program affects so many people and is so critical to the continuation of "business as usual," the program must be an integral part of the total records system. "Why is a vital records protection program more important than insurance?" is a frequently asked question. The answer is that protection of the organization's vital records ensures the continued life of the business, while insurance pays the organization after its death following a disaster.

Protection of the records from loss may be accomplished by several methods. Documents may be duplicated in various forms, or documents may be stored in minimal-risk containers at either onsite or offsite locations. For maximum safety, duplicate records should be made, and these records should be stored in minimal-risk areas. Since only vital records are affected, the volume of records to be duplicated should not exceed 10 percent of the total records of the organization.

Duplication

Duplication is a method of vital records protection.

Duplication is a method of providing a copy of an original document. If duplication is selected as the preferred safety measure, other considerations must be addressed. The following questions highlight some of these considerations.

- *What form should duplicates take?* Duplicates can take the form of paper copies, roll microfilm, microfiche, magnetic tapes, or other media used by the organization. The selection should be made on the basis of the needs of the organization and the equipment and facilities available. This analysis should include questions such as the following:
  1. Will users have ready access to readers for microfilm or fiche?
  2. Will printers be available if hard copy is required by the users of tape, film, or fiche?
  3. Will equipment be available for accessing information stored on computer disks or tapes?
  4. Is there adequate file space for paper copies?
  5. Is equipment available to make multiple paper copies?
  6. What facilities and equipment are needed for housing any duplicates?
- *Do duplicates now exist?* Are duplicates available for records that are already generated? If so, what form are they in, and where are they located?
- *When should duplicates be made?* Consideration must be given to whether duplication should occur at the time the record is created or at a scheduled time. This decision, of course, affects

where the duplicate should be made. If duplication occurs at the time of creation, controls are needed to ensure that the duplicates are made. Duplication at the time the record is generated would normally be in paper form.

- ***Where should duplicates be made?*** If offsite storage is provided and duplication occurs at that location, equipment must be provided at the offsite location. Consideration must also be given to providing access to the duplicates, if necessary. In some instances having a limited quantity of reproduction equipment onsite may be necessary.

- ***How often should updates be made?*** A schedule for updating the information must be maintained. The amount of time between updates would greatly affect records reconstruction following a disaster; this should be taken into consideration when decisions concerning intervals are made. For example, if records updates are scheduled on an annual basis, data would have to be gathered for an entire 12-month period in order to reconstruct that record to a current basis.

- ***Should the original or a duplicate be used?*** A frequently discussed issue is when to use the original record and when to use a duplicate. If the vital records are active records, the user normally works with the source documents (original records); the duplicates, in whatever form, are stored in another location where they can be safeguarded. Examples of active vital records for which originals are used are accounts receivable, current contracts, and creative works in progress. Original inactive vital records, in contrast to active vital records, are stored for protection; and the duplicates are used when the need occurs. Examples of inactive vital records are corporate charters, minutes of stockholders' meetings, and completed creative works.

It is virtually impossible to provide protection that is 100 percent risk-free.

Many organizations recognize the need for and value of the dual protection afforded by the provision of duplicate copies and minimum-risk storage. The term "minimum risk" is used because it is virtually impossible to provide protection that is 100 percent risk-free. For example, provincial governments require that duplicates of records be kept at provincial records centres. Figure 11-1 shows how records in various media can be efficiently stored underground.

Special requirements for storage must be considered.

When decisions are being made concerning the storage facilities necessary to house either the originals or the duplicates (depending on whether the vital record is considered active or inactive), attention should be given to the total volume to be stored and to any special requirements, such as temperature or humidity or record size or shape.

Figure 11-1
Underground
Storage

Source: Courtesy of Perpetual Storage Inc.

Dispersal

Dispersal can be
either internal or
external.

Dispersal is one method of providing a copy of an original document
for records reconstruction by having copies distributed externally or
internally. Dispersal is normally used with paper copies only. Internally, copies may be sent to other persons who have interest in the
particular document. This method, however, does not provide a consistent procedure for ensuring that every document will have a duplicate. A method of routine dispersal is followed when information is
sent to external sources. For example, if an organization's federal
income tax forms were destroyed, duplicates could be obtained from
the government; if bank records were destroyed, the bank could provide duplicates; if insurance policies were destroyed, the insurance
companies could provide duplicates. In some instances, this form of
records safety is all that is needed.

 Learning Check: Can you name two methods of vital records protection?

VITAL RECORDS TRANSFER AND STORAGE PROCEDURES

Successful implementation of a vital records protection plan requires adherence to established transfer and storage procedures. These procedures include a vital records master list and the transfer of vital records.

Vital Records Master List

A vital records master list identifies all vital records in each department.

After vital records are identified, a vital records master list should be prepared for each department. In large organizations, this list identifies the vital records for each department and gives the department information concerning the procedures to protect the records. For small organizations, a single vital records master list is adequate. Figures 11-2a and 11-2b show a vital records master list. The information contained on that master list includes (1) department name, (2) storage location (3) page number, (4) vital records identification code, (5) vital records name, (6) retention periods, (7) office of record—the office responsible for maintaining the "official record copy" of a given record, (8) vital records protection, and (9) protection instructions. A complete set of the master lists should be maintained in a designated minimum-risk location.

Figure 11-2a
Vital Records
Master List,
Front Side

VITAL RECORDS MASTER LIST (See reverse side.)								
Department *accounting*				Storage Location *Sims, 2nd Floor*				Page *1 of 4*
Vital Records Code No.	Vital Records Name	Retention Periods			Office of Record	Vital Records Protection		Protection Instructions
		Office	Records Centre	Total		Method	Frequency	
AC	*Income Tax Records*	3	3	6	*accounting*	AD	A	*Copy of Income Tax records to be duplicated and stored in Administration Building*
Approval—Records Management Committee		Date		Approval—Records Management Committee			Date	
Approval—Records Management Committee		Date		Other Approval			Date	

Figure 11-2b Vital Records Master List, Reverse Side

RETENTION AND VITAL RECORDS PROTECTION CODES

CODE	DEFINITION	EXPLANATION
AC	Completion of Audit	Retain records subject to audit until auditing authority either completes its audit or waives its right to audit plus the number of years stated. Audits may be performed by internal, external, or governmental organizations or by combinations of these organizations. This code is most often used for financial records.
C + N	Current + N (number) of years/months (M)	Retain records for the current year or month plus the number of years or months stated. For example, CY + 3 means current year plus 3 additional years, and CM + 3M means current month plus 3 additional months.
LA	Life of Asset or Disposal of Property	Retain records for life of asset (land, facility, or equipment) plus the number of years stated. This code is used for records of company ownership of land, equipment, or facilities and other physical assets.
LC	Life of Corporation	Retain records as long as the organization responsible for the record or the legitimate successor to that organization is in existence. This code is used for company records having permanent value for operational, legal, historical or other business purposes.
LE	Last Entry	Retain these records until the last entry is made plus the number of years stated. This code is used for registers, bound journals, scientific logs, etc.
SO	Until Superseded or Obsolete	Retain only until an updated copy of the same record is received or until records have no further value for operational or reference purposes. This code is often used for records with cumulative information and for records whose retention cannot be expressed in terms of a specific time period.
T + N	Termination + N (number) of years/months (M) Or whichever is later	Retain the record until the termination, settlement, cancellation or expiration of the action, event, or period plus the number of years or months stated. This code is often used for contracts, financial instruments, project records, claims, personnel records, etc./ when inserted between two codes means "or ... whichever is later."

VITAL RECORDS CODES—METHODS OF PROTECTION

AD	Automatic Dispersal	Refers to the protection of vital records by dispersal of copies to offsite locations in the normal course of business.
FC	Fire-Resistant File Cabinet	Self-explanatory.
FS	Fireproof Safe	Usually a two- or four-drawer safe: indicate rated hours of protection.
FV	Fireproof Vault	Usually a walk-in: indicate rated hours of protection.
MF	Microfilm	Refers to the protection of vital records by microfilming.
OS	Offsite	A location that is not in the same office building in which the vital records are maintained.

VITAL RECORDS CODES—FREQUENCY OF PROTECTION

D	Daily	
W	Weekly	
M	Monthly	} indicates frequency of protective action.
Q	Quarterly	
A	Annually	

GENERAL INSTRUCTIONS AND DEFINITIONS

Record	For purposes of this master list, a record is defined as being any paper, book, catalogue, drawing, microfilm, microfiche, photograph, magnetic tape or disk or information in any other documented form that is of legal consequence, that has historical or operational value, or that is essential to the conduct of company business and is therefore subject to controlled management and protection for a prescribed length of time.
Record Type No.	Numbers assigned for unique identification of each record type.
Record Type	A clear, concise name or description given to a record series for purposes of fixed identification and referral.
Method	Refers to the means by which the vital record is maintained and protected.
Vital	A record is considered vital if it safeguards the legal rights and assets of the company, the employees, or the customer, of if the record will ensure the survival of the company during or immediately after a major disaster.
Remarks	May include special instructions and any other information that may be helpful in determining retention requirements or special handling and release restrictions.
Office of Record	Office responsible for maintenance of "official record copy" of a given record.

Transfer of Vital Records

Vital records can be transferred on a daily, weekly, or monthly basis.

Procedures for transferring and protecting vital records must be established and disseminated to each department. Vital records may be transferred to the vital records location on a daily, weekly, or monthly basis. It is imperative that the procedures established for each vital record be carried out without fail. A responsible person in each department should be given the responsibility to make sure that vital records are transferred to the vital records centre according to the established procedures. To maintain an accurate record of vital records transferred, a vital records deposit slip should be prepared for all transfers of vital records. This slip identifies the transaction by including the name of the organizational unit, a description of the record, media of deposit, control numbers, and disposition instructions.[2]

 Learning Check: Can you explain why a vital records master list is important to a business organization?

Procedures for Handling Vital Records

Most companies choose to protect only their vital records, but some companies will also include their important records. Procedures should be established for handling records under all conditions. What are the responsibilities of the people who handle the records? Do they have, in writing, what they are expected to do in the event of fire or other natural disasters? Have they had opportunities to practise the established procedures with follow-up and evaluation of the process? If the answer to any of the questions is no, management should take immediate action to correct the situation. Some procedural considerations in the protection of records under both ordinary and extraordinary conditions include the following:

1. In case of a disaster during working hours, records in use should be returned to their proper places within the files if at all possible. Responsibility for this process should be designated, and one person should oversee the operation and have authority to direct everyone to exit the building for personal safety.

2. Records in use but belonging in vaults should be returned to the safe or vault at the end of each working day. Under no circumstances should the records be left out overnight.

3. Employees should not allow important records to accumulate on desks or in in-baskets. These records should be returned promptly to a protected area.

4. Records normally protected may be unprotected when temporarily in other hands. For example, important documents may be at an attorney's office; engineering drawings may be at the construction site, and records may be in the process stage at another branch office. Whenever possible, originals should be retained for their protection, and copies should be distributed for use.

ELECTRONIC VITAL RECORDS PROTECTION

Electronic records present special problems.

A disruption in the electronic data processing in an organization must be a consideration when establishing a vital records or disaster preparedness program. Many organizations could not survive for more than a few hours if the data processing function of their organization

---

[2]Ibid., p. 59.

were involved in a fire or other disaster. A disaster plan for electronic records differs from a disaster plan for paper records because of the storage medium, the medium's storage requirements, and the equipment needed to retrieve, analyze, and duplicate the information.

Analysis of Computer Applications

Analysis of each computer application must be done.

An analysis must be made of all computer applications in all areas of the organization. Some of these applications are vital for the continuation of business, and others are not. Each application should be taken separately and analyzed as to its importance in the case of a disaster. What are the requirements for each application, including hardware, software, documentation, staff, and storage medium? What would happen if this system were not backed up and procedures were not established for a quick restoration of the application? Each computer application must be evaluated. A determination must then be made as to the effect a fire or other disaster affecting this application would have on business operations. The classifications can be a minor, moderate, or major damage to the business operations.

Establishment of Procedures

Procedures must be established to protect the information contained in the electronic records. These procedures include the specifics on how to back up the system, who backs up the system, how often it is done, and where the backup is stored. Once the procedures for backup have been established, the procedures must be followed explicitly. If the records are to be backed up daily, that means daily. A specific employee is given the responsibility to make sure the backup is done on a regular basis according to the procedures. As new applications are added to the systems, they should be incorporated into the protection plan.

An alternative site location for the processing of data must be considered.

The backups may be stored in a fireproof safe onsite or they may be stored in an offsite storage area. Either site should be secure from fire and other disasters, such as flood, theft, vandalism, earthquake, or storm. Backup copies of information are very important to an organization after a disaster; the organization *must* be able to continue business immediately. Because of this, businesses have a contingency plan for computer hardware and software after a disaster. During a disaster not only is the information stored in the computers lost, but also the hardware and software used by the organization. The plan should include provisions for an alternative site location for the continued operation of data processing after a disaster. Eight methods are used to set up an alternative site location so that the organization can begin its electronic data processing operations immediately.[3]

---

[3]Brett Balon, "Disaster Planning for Electronic Records" (Proceedings of the ARMA International 34th Annual Conference, New Orleans, Louisiana, October, 1989).

Alternative Site Location

The dependence of the organization on its computer applications will determine the way an alternative site is set up. The eight methods of setting up an alternative site are reciprocal agreement, cold site, warm site, vendor agreement, commercial service bureau, hot site, redundant site, and electronic vaulting. Table 11-2 illustrates the characteristics of each method and the advantages and disadvantages of each.

Table 11-2   **Alternative Site Location Methods**

Method	Characteristics	Advantages	Disadvantages
Reciprocal Agreement	An agreement between two or more compatible organizations to provide computer time for each other in case of a disaster.	Inexpensive, little cash outlay.	Hardware and software configurations may change; both organizations may experience same disaster; not to be used on a long-term basis.
Cold Site	An alternative site without environmental controls or hardware.	Inexpensive, may be shared by two or more organizations, long-term use.	If sharing, two organizations may need at the same time.
Warm Site	An alternative site with environmental controls and some or all computer peripherals.	More expensive, may be shared by two or more organizations, long-term use.	If sharing, two organizations may need at the same time.
Vendor Agreement	Contracting organization uses vendor's corporate facilities.	Availability, lower cost than other options.	May not be available for long-term use, lack of configuration compatibility; other organizations may have similar arrangements.
Commercial Service Bureau	This company provides data processing facilities.	Pay only for the time used, immediate availability.	Variable service, possible security problems, expensive for long-term use, may not have the time and capacity for processing needed.
Hot Site	Fully equipped facility on continuous standby, on a first-come, first-served basis.	Security, availability, ease of plan testing, costs may be covered through business-interruption insurance.	Very high costs, possible distance from data centre.
Redundant Site	Duplicate of the current data centre at an alternative site run by your organization.	Assured compatibility, availability, security, ease of use.	Most expensive option; trying to keep both sites compatible through reconfigurations and software updates.
Electronic Vaulting	Backup is done on a real-time basis. Data are duplicated in real-time and transferred to an offsite but connected system.	Direct access, tape vaults with communication facilities.	Very expensive, new technology for disaster recovery.

Source: Adapted from Brett Balon, "Disaster Planning for Electronic Records" (Proceedings of the Association of Records Managers and Administrators International 34th Annual Conference, New Orleans, Louisiana, October 2–5, 1989).

 Learning Check: Can you define alternative site location?

Action Plan

The action plan contains procedures to protect electronic records.

A plan must be devised to protect all the computer records. The plan should include whose responsibility it is to make sure records are backed up, who reviews the procedures periodically, and who takes over when a disaster occurs or has been declared. The action plan will also contain the procedures to be followed in case of a disaster, including what needs to be done and the logical order of the activities? The plan should also address when, where, why, and how the records are to be protected and the recovery process to be implemented after a disaster. In larger organizations, personnel should be divided into teams and take on specific responsibilities during and after a disaster. When the business depends on computer applications, it is imperative that the processing of data begin as soon as possible.

Testing and Maintenance

The action plan must be tested.

After the plans have been devised and implemented, they should be tested in a way similar to that in which fire drills are carried out in schools. The plan should be tested before a disaster occurs so it can be perfected. A written report should be prepared to include the strengths and weaknesses of the plan as well as when the test was carried out and any problems encountered. Testing should be carried out on a regular basis and the procedures updated.

VITAL RECORDS PROTECTION MANUAL

Instructions are contained in the vital records protection manual.

Once all decisions have been made regarding identification of vital records, the procedures to be followed for implementation, and the most appropriate method of protection, the next step is to develop a vital records protection manual. This **vital records protection manual** should list all vital records according to department and contain both the vital record code number and the retention date. The manual may be a separate document, part of the records management manual, part of the records retention and disposition manual, or included in the records disaster prevention and recovery manual described later in this chapter; its form depends on the needs of the organization. Instructions on how to fill out any forms associated with the vital records protection plan and procedures for transferring vital records should be included.

RECORDS DISASTER PREVENTION AND RECOVERY PLANNING

While identifying and protecting vital records are crucial to an organization's continued success, another of the responsibilities of a records manager is to safeguard records from damage and destruction and to recover, to the extent possible, those records that sustain damage. The key is to have a plan—a plan that clearly defines the actions to take to prevent or minimize the effects of potential disasters, actions to take in the event of a disaster, and actions to take to recover records after a disaster occurs.

Develop Plan

The plan should include objectives.

The records disaster prevention and recovery (RDP&R) plan should have defined objectives and procedures for achieving the objectives. General objectives may include:

1. Facilitating effective and efficient methods of preventing records destruction or damage.
2. Facilitating effective and efficient coordination of recovery tasks.
3. Minimizing interruptions to normal operations.
4. Limiting extent of damage and preventing escalation of disaster.
5. Establishing alternative means of operation.
6. Providing rapid and smooth restoration of services and operations.
7. Preventing injury to personnel and public.
8. Preventing damage to company property.
9. Minimizing economic impact.
10. Ensuring continuation of the organization.[4]

There are five steps in developing a disaster plan.

Developing a disaster prevention and recovery plan involves five steps: obtaining approval and commitment for the plan; identifying records to be protected; establishing a disaster team; gathering the information required to carry out the plan in the event of a disaster; and setting up a safety education program.

 Learning Check: Can you explain the importance of having an up-to-date records disaster prevention and recovery plan?

Obtain Approval and Commitment

As with any project requiring additional resources, approval of and commitment to the project by top-level management are critical. To obtain the approval, the records manager will be prepared to convince others that there is a need for disaster prevention and recovery planning. Chances for approval can be enhanced by conducting a risk

---

[4]Annie Hoffman and Bryan Baumann, "Disaster Recovery—A Prevention Plan for NWNL," *Records Management Quarterly,* Vol. 20, No. 2 (April, 1986), p. 40.

assessment and a cost benefit analysis and by graphically and dramatically presenting the results to management.

A **risk assessment** is an evaluation of the probabilities of a disaster occurring and the possible extent of the damage. The risk varies from one geographic location to another and the extent of potential damage from one company to another. For example, the risk of a hurricane destroying a building is greater in the coastal areas than inland; the risk of an older building not withstanding the effects of a disaster may be greater than that of a new building.

Following the risk assessment, a cost benefit analysis is conducted. This compares the cost of making and implementing a disaster plan (including business interruption insurance, where appropriate) with the cost to the organization associated with the total loss of the records. Examples and illustrations of those companies who had a disaster plan and those who did not and what happened to the latter following a disaster may be included.

Management commitment should accompany approval. Commitment can be formalized by having an agreement detailing authority and fiscal responsibility and by describing a formal company policy of disaster prevention and recovery planning.

Risk assessment and cost benefit analysis provide necessary information.

Identify Records to Be Protected

As discussed in the first part of this chapter, most companies choose to protect only their vital or essential records. Some companies will also include their important records.

Establish Disaster Teams and Responsibilities

One person must be in charge and have the responsibility for being the disaster recovery coordinator. An administrative committee may work under the direction of the coordinator.

Brett J. Balon and H. Wayne Gardner have suggested that an electronic data processing disaster contingency action plan include specific teams.[5] However, the teams suggested are also appropriate as a general contingency plan. A small organization would not require all of these separate teams; many of the duties could be combined, depending on the size of the organization. Each team needs checklists and progress logs to ensure compliance with systems procedures.

The extent of the plan depends on the size of the organization.

Administrative Team. Duties of the administrative team include providing insurance liaison for onsite damage assessment; initiating salvage; procuring hardware, software, and supplies; estimating the time to repair or replace and to resume operations (this should be reported within four to six hours after the disaster, if possible); establishing

---

[5]Brett J. Balon and H. Wayne Gardner, "Disaster Planning for Electronic Records," *Records Management Quarterly,* Vol. 22, No. 3 (July, 1988), p. 20.

a command post for the disaster recovery coordinator and team; providing administrative and clerical support to the coordinator and recovery teams. This team also deals with expenses, personnel, and administration of family-related problems resulting from the disaster, such as extensive time spent by employees at the disaster site and any emotional problems experienced by the families because of loved ones being exposed to the dangers associated with the disaster.

Support Services Team. Duties of the support services team include securing housing and office space for personnel and arranging transport for supplies, equipment, and personnel to alternative site.

Backup/Offsite Storage Team. Duties of the backup/offsite storage team include establishing control and organizing offsite records; providing operators, an application programmer, systems staff, and systems librarians to pull data for specific applications from the offsite storage vault and to move records to the backup site; and checking procedures for what has to be done differently at the backup site for each application.

Other Teams. In addition, staff should be assigned security duties at the damaged facility; financial duties such as arranging for emergency funds and lines of credit; public relations; facilities restoration at the damage site; user liaison such as coordinating applications restoration with users; input/output for data entry and production; software installation and backup; voice and data communications; acquiring and installing hardware; and establishing operations at the alternative site.

Gather Required Information

Time is critical when a disaster occurs.

To put a records disaster recovery plan into action, certain information must be immediately available. There is no time to waste trying to locate telephone numbers, names, or supplies. The following information is the minimum required; additional information necessary for quick action may be specific to each organization.

- Insurance agent contacts, with telephone numbers (both office and emergency numbers) for immediate use following the disaster.
- Roster of the coordinator and disaster teams, including telephone numbers of each.
- List of telephone numbers of key officials, including appropriate maintenance, building systems, and security personnel.
- Telephone numbers of the local fire, police, and utilities companies.
- Detailed building layout, including the location of plumbing and gas shutoffs; electrical boxes; heating, ventilating, and air-conditioning system controls; and fire extinguishers and alarms.
- List of emergency equipment and supplies, indicating either where they are kept or where they may be acquired on short notice. The equipment, supplies, and quantities needed depend on each

company's unique situation. Commonly needed items include fans, electrical extension cords, a portable generator, battery-operated lanterns or flashlights, carts, plastic milk crates, records boxes, plastic sheeting, heavy-duty plastic bags of several colours, crowbars, mallets, cotton ribbon, safety helmets, coveralls, gloves, notebooks, pencils, and markers. The equipment and supplies should be kept in a designated place and reserved exclusively for immediate disaster recovery use.

- Designation of an area to be used for records processing, along with contact person and day and night telephone numbers.
- Information regarding the availability of local commercial freezing and cold-storage facilities for storing water-damaged records until restoration arrangements can be made.

Quick action depends on the availability of information. All of the above information should be a part of the records disaster prevention and recovery manual and *must* be kept up to date.

Begin a Safety Education Program

A safety education program is an important planning element.

Disasters occur in all locales, in all environments, and at all hours. Employees should be prepared to deal with the emergency in a planned and careful manner. Procedures for ensuring personal safety, of course, are of highest priority. All employees should know where the fire extinguishers are, how and when to use them, where the alarms are located and how to use them, and how to deal with panic and confusion. Practice should be provided via simulated disaster conditions; assignments should be made for exiting, and responsibilities should be designated for those who may need assistance. In theory and in practice, disaster plans are the ultimate safety education program for any business.

 Learning Check: Can you describe the steps in planning for disaster prevention and recovery?

Develop and Distribute Manual

The records disaster prevention and recovery manual provides the vehicle for communicating the RDP&R plan.

The **records disaster prevention and recovery manual** is a document that details the course of action required to prevent or minimize the effects of a disaster and to recover, to the extent possible, those records that sustain damage. The manual is the most effective tool for communicating the disaster prevention and recovery plan. The plan will be only as effective as the manual is in communicating to everyone the actions that must be taken. A manual, written in layman's terms, is logically organized so that information can be located easily. The manual is updated as required to keep it current.

Determine Content

The manual
provides
information
to prevent
disasters and
recover records.

This manual should include all types of information that will aid in preventing a disaster or will expedite the work of recovering from a disaster. The manual may be more or less detailed, depending on the size of the organization and the complexity of the records held. However, it must be complete enough to provide all necessary information to its potential users. A suggested manual content outline is shown in Figure 11-3.

Figure 11-3
Records Disaster
Prevention and
Recovery Manual
Outline

Records disaster prevention and recovery manual outline

Part I. Introductory Material

Includes title page, preface and authority statement, and table of contents. States the overall policy and management support for the disaster avoidance, preparation, and recovery plan. Contains an overview of the project and addresses the benefits of the plan in cost, image, and business enhancement. Also includes recognition of those who participated in the development of the program and the preparation of the manual.

Part II. Prevention

Includes methods of preventing or minimizing the effects of a disaster on various records formats used within the organization.

Part III. Initial Response

Includes a description of initial responses, and documents emergency activities such as activation of the plan, notification of key personnel, setting up a command centre to coordinate information and activities, insurance activation, and all other necessary details that must be attended to during the first hours after a disruption occurs.

Part IV. Assessment

Documents, through narrative and photographs, the disaster site for purposes of insurance coverage and physical safety of disaster recovery workers. Security, staffing requirements, and recovery supply needs are based upon the assessment.

Part V. Stabilization

Guides employees through technical procedures necessary to prevent further deterioration of business assets and services. Describes how to "packout"—remove records from a disaster site to a recovery site.

Part VI. Interim Processing

Describes alternative procedures implemented during the period between disruption and return to normal operations.

Part VII. Recovery and Restoration

Explains how to recover and restore the various forms of the organization's records. Also includes specific steps to alter the input method, where required.

Part VIII. Relocation

Discusses relocation of any of the operations within the organization, including the data operations centre. Includes special environmental needs as well as new housing.

Part IX. Summary of Responsibilities

Provides a recap of responsibilities by job title for all sections of the records disaster prevention and recovery plan. Serves as an orientation aid for new personnel and provides a compliance checklist.

Source: Adapted from a plan developed by Janet C. Whitehead and Diann Conyers as reported in "Survival in a Computer Environment—The Synergistic Approach," Records Management Quarterly, *Vol. 22, No. 1 (January, 1988), p. 8.*

Select Format

An updatable
format is preferred.

Techniques and methods for preventing damage to records and for recovery and restoration are constantly being evaluated. As new techniques and methods become available, the manual should provide for these updates. The best way to incorporate changes is to have the manual in loose-leaf format if paper copies are distributed. There are many software products available to develop comprehensive disaster recovery plans that make it easy for users to maintain and update their own plan.

Learning Check: Can you outline the typical contents and format of a records prevention and recovery manual?

Determine Distribution

Manual distribution
is determined by
staff needs.

Managers, disaster team leaders and members of the team, emergency management, fire departments, police departments, security and facility personnel should all receive complete copies of the manual. Within the organization, each individual, section, or department should receive only the material that applies directly to them. For example, the personnel department should receive the part of the manual that deals with their types of records and the actions appropriate for their activities.

Learning Check: Can you explain how distribution of the manual is determined?

Test the Plan

A testing program
is critical to the
plan's success.

Any disaster plan is only as good as its testing program. Testing the plan helps to identify weak areas that might not otherwise be known until a disaster occurs, which is too late.

A good testing program will determine if the plan is workable, check for any details that may have been overlooked, ensure that the alternative site is compatible, and confirm that the backup routines are adequate. A "dry" run is the best way to test the plan.

One example of a "wet" test run occurred in the city of Regina before the scheduled test run could be performed. Three students were working on the 16th floor of City Hall, where a large number of city records were stored. The students noticed that water was leaking under a storage room door into the records area. A broken water pipe in the boiler room was flooding the hallway. The students immediately contacted the building superintendent and the records section. The water on the 16th floor was turned off; and water vacuums, mops, and pails were brought in. Fans were used to reduce humidity levels. Several of the records staff started removing records from the water and built a dam with a piece of an old rug and some computer printouts that were slated for destruction.

Within four hours, all of the water had been mopped up, fans were in place, records from wet boxes had been transferred to dry ones, damp records were set out to dry, and damaged records that had been slated for destruction were ready to be moved out. One of the benefits from this "wet" run was identifying problems that could occur during a major disaster, but without the tragic results of a disaster. Specific problems identified were:

- Certain key personnel could not be contacted;
- No procedures were in place to handle the purchase of services after hours; and
- Procedures relating to insurance were not followed because they were not known.

Another benefit was identifying those actions and procedures that went according to plan. Fast action by the building and records personnel saved valuable records and minimized the damage that might otherwise have occurred.[6]

A "wet" test is not as desirable as a "dry" run.

A simulation of a disaster can provide data for the tests. A variety of tests can be run including whether the right people were notified in the right sequence and the amount of time it took; how the plan was activated; whether the various members of the disaster teams were able to simulate their tasks and how long it took; and whether the communication between members of the disaster team was effective.

After testing the plan, the results should be reported. The report would include those things that went according to plan as well as those parts of the plan that need to be adjusted. This testing, or evaluation part of the plan, is critical, for here is where the plan is determined to be viable or not.

Learning Check: Can you describe how a records disaster prevention and recovery plan is tested?

DISASTER PREVENTION METHODS

Methods of prevention differ according to the type of hazard and the records media.

Records disaster prevention plans should include procedures for preventing records damage and for reconstructing records damaged in a disaster. Methods for preventing damage differ according to the type of hazard and the records medium—paper, microrecords, and magnetic media. All records are vulnerable to both natural and human hazards. Among the hazards that pose particular threats to records are fire, earthquakes, wind and rainstorms, water, mould and mildew, insects and rodents, and dust.

---

[6]Brett J. Balon and H. Wayne Gardner, "Disaster Contingency Planning: The Basic Elements," *Records Management Quarterly,* Vol. 21, No. 1 (January, 1987), p. 17.

Paper Records

Often paper records are ignored during planning for disaster prevention because the majority of the company's records have been transferred to the computer and stored on tapes, disks, or hard drives. Computer centres usually have elaborate safeguards, including offsite backups and sophisticated protection systems. However, the originals (usually paper) of signed contracts, leases, creative works, original charters, and so forth, are the official record copies, not the computer-stored copies of these documents. Record copies were described in Chapter 1 as the official copies retained for legal, operational, or historical purposes. Therefore, to ensure timely and effective continuation of a business, paper records must be protected.

Fire

Of all the hazards, fire has the potential to do the greatest amount of damage to records. Protection from fire is provided by storing records in vaults, safes, cabinets, rooms, and boxes. Fire resistance of records containers is measured in terms of the time it takes for the interior of the storage facility to reach 177°C. Paper requires a higher temperature to ignite, but the 177°C standard provides a safety cushion.

The trend toward making the maximum use of space has often meant using open-shelf storage, with the records held in file folders or various kinds of open or closed cartons. Typically, rows of records face each other across long service aisles about 30 inches wide. The aisle presents a wall of paper with the loose ends of the paper sticking out of the file folders. These loose ends can be ignited almost instantly by any source ranging from a match to a faulty fluorescent ballast or by direct contact with an exposed incandescent lightbulb.

Attempts have been made to develop methods for increasing flame resistance of cardboard boxes. The most frequently attempted method is coating the box with a type of fire-retardant paint. Tests of records boxes protected by such paint, properly applied, show that the coating will substantially delay actual ignition of the boxed material. However, since this type of paint does not effectively react to heat under about 230°C, the temperature of any modest exposure fire (such as might occur on a file cart) will weaken the paper of the box to the point where the box will break open under the weight of the paper it contains and expose the ordinary combustible contents of the box to ignition.

All records containers do not have the same fire resistance.

Fire resistance of records containers varies a great deal—from five minutes for uninsulated steel files or cabinets to up to six hours for insulated vault doors. Insulated modern safes are rated fire resistant for up to four hours. Steel storage cabinets are not fire resistant. Although it is true that the cabinets will not burn, the fire resistance of the contents is rated at about five minutes. A study of the case records of 2,597 fires, compiled by the Safe Manufacturers' Association, revealed that when four-hour safes were used, 94.6 percent of the contents were saved compared with 34.7 percent for inspected insulated cabinets with a 45-minute rating.

When using vaults or file rooms to house records, the doors and walls of the vault or file room should have the same fire resistance rating. For example, a six-hour vault should have a six-hour door. Spending the money for a storage area that is rated at six-hour fire resistance and then installing a one-hour fire resistance door is a foolish waste of money.

Other fire risks in records storage areas can be reduced by applying some common sense precautions, such as:

- Using manual instead of power-operated equipment when possible.
- Using electric instead of gas-fuelled forklifts.
- Prohibiting the use of portable space heaters, lights on extension cords, hot plates, coffee makers, battery chargers, welding or cutting torches, and other such ignition sources.
- Prohibiting the storage of chemicals (such as those used in maintenance), oils, paints, and other flammables in or near the records areas.[7]
- Restricting smoking to other areas, providing ash trays or cans outside the entrance(s) to the storage areas, and enforcing the smoking rule. Many organizations now provide smoke-free working environments.
- Limiting records storage to at least 12 inches from the nearest light source.

Sprinkler systems are a must. The systems should be installed by experts, be appropriate for the building, and be maintained regularly. Smoke detectors, heat detectors, handheld fire extinguishers, and alert staff members help to control a fire before it gets out of hand. Smoke and heat detectors should be checked often to be sure that the batteries are still strong. Workers should know where the handheld fire extinguishers are located and how to use them. Halon gas is a particularly effective fire fighting agent but is now considered an ozone depleter and unsafe for human beings; its use is no longer recommended.

Water and Other Liquids

Water can be as devastating to records as fire; therefore, precautionary measures against water should be just as carefully planned as those against fire. Any signs of leaks from the roof or upper floors must be

Use common-sense precautions.

Sprinkler systems provide a safeguard.

---

[7]Gail L. Bautsch, "What You Don't Know Can Hurt You," *Records Management Quarterly,* Vol. 20, No. 4 (October, 1986), p. 20.

reported immediately and repaired. Personnel who know the procedures for coping with either major or minor emergencies can minimize the amount of damage. As one National Fire Protection Association (NFPA) manual says: "It is important for the archivist or records manager to realize that wet records can be recovered, but burned records can't."[8]

Records may be damaged through human-caused minidisasters such as may occur when liquids are accidentally spilled on the records. Care must be exercised so that records are not damaged by coffee or other drink spills. A good policy is not to consume liquids in areas where records are kept.

Earthquakes, Wind, and Rainstorms

If the building housing the records is substantial and watertight, little else can be done in a preventative way to protect the safety of the records. If the location is one where there is a history of earthquakes or where earthquakes are probable, shelving should be adequately, though not severely, braced to allow for the sway factor.

Potential damage from water should be considered.

The damage from storms is directly related to either flooding or leakage. When the building location is being considered, careful evaluation should be given to ground absorption and susceptibility to flooding. When there is any doubt, records should be raised at least four inches above the floor and stored in watertight containers at the lower shelf levels. The installation of a pump that operates automatically when moisture is present is an additional precaution. Figure 11-4 shows what floods can do to records.

Mould and Mildew

Mould and mildew damage can occur on any type of record and is usually caused by poor control of humidity and temperature levels. The temperature should be kept between 18°C and 24°C, and the relative humidity should be maintained at 50 percent for best preservation of paper records.

Humidity levels must be controlled.

Ventilation retards the growth of mould spores. In warm, humid atmospheres, mould growth on damp materials will appear within 48 hours. The air should be kept circulating. Because records should be kept from heat, in cold weather the heat should be turned down; in hot weather the air conditioning should be turned on.

Periodic inspections and an awareness of mould or mildew and the places that would tend to stimulate the development of those substances are important preventative measures. If records are relatively

---

[8]*NFPA 232 Protection of Records* (Quincy, Massachusetts: National Fire Protection Association, 1986).

inactive and housed in an area that has little traffic, one of the assigned duties of a records clerk should be to take a quick walk through the area and specifically look for signs of mould or mildew. As with other types of damage, one must know how to care for the problem without causing further damage to the records.

Figure 11-4
Flood Damage

Insects and Rodents

Insects and rodents can destroy records or make them unusable in a relatively short period of time. Periodic inspections are helpful in preventing damage. Signs of the presence of insects and rodents are usually observable if one is specifically looking for their existence. If insects and rodents are found, an exterminator should be called for an appraisal. Damage to the records should be ascertained. Where portions of the records have actually been destroyed, replacement is not possible. The remaining portions, however, should be repaired or reproduced.

Dust

Air conditioning with filtered air helps reduce dust levels.

Excessive dust also has an effect on the legibility and the rapidity of deterioration of the records. The type of record influences the extent of the damage that can be caused by dust. Proper control of air conditioning with recirculated filtered air reduces the amount of dust in the air.

Learning Check: Can you describe disaster prevention methods for paper records?

Microrecords

Many of the precautions used for paper records are also appropriate for both microrecords and magnetic media. There are, however, some exceptions as described in the following sections.

Fire

Microforms are more vulnerable to heat than is paper.

Microforms and other photographic records cannot withstand the same level of heat as can paper. Film should not be allowed to exceed 66°C or it can be useless. Therefore, microrecords should be stored in a data safe with an Underwriters Laboratories (UL) rating of 150; the interior temperature limit is 66°C (or 150°F), and the relative humidity limit is 85 percent.

Mould and Mildew

Microfilm is even more susceptible to growth of mould and mildew than paper and is quite sensitive to temperature changes. A preferred relative humidity level of 40 percent discourages the growth of mould and mildew in film. Prolonged exposure to humidity levels at about 60 percent causes emulsion surfaces to become unstable. High humidity promotes fungal growth and chemical reactive processes.

Dust

Sustained very low humidity can cause edge peeling, flaking, cracking, and an increase in static electricity, which attracts dust particles. Humidity levels below 15 percent can cause brittleness. For short-term storage, air purity is not a major issue; however, dust particles can react with the film surface.

Other Hazards

Silver microfilm is susceptible to damage from scratches, abrasions, acids, impurities found in paper, fingerprints, smoke, and food. To help protect images from any of these potential dangers, white lint-free gloves should be worn when handling master silver film. Master silver film should not be used as the working copy and should be protected from direct sunlight, heat, excessive humidity, food, and drink. Rubber bands and paper clips should never be used on silver film.[9]

The trays or containers used to store microforms should be smooth and free of sharp edges, dust, dirt, or other contaminants that will

---

[9]*Filing Procedures* (Prairie Village, Kansas: Association of Records Managers and Administrators, 1989), pp. 11–12.

scratch or mar the film. Paint fumes can cause damage to the film base and the image quality. Therefore, masters should be removed for at least two weeks when a room is painted.

Some ink, crayons, felt marking pens, and adhesive labels may be reactive with the silver film surface. Any envelopes or boxes used for storing silver microforms should meet the standards for storage containers. Buffered acid-free slip sheets should be placed between microfiche to prevent sticking when more than one microfiche is stored in a single envelope.

 Learning Check: Can you describe disaster prevention methods for microrecords?

Magnetic Media Records

Specific requirements for magnetic media may be somewhat different than for microrecords or paper. However, the general precautions discussed above are appropriate for all records. Exceptions are described in the following sections.

Fire

Magnetic media have special requirements.

Nine out of ten data processing disasters are caused by fire. All disks and tapes not being used in the day's run should be kept in protective containers. Magnetic tape, like microforms, is far less tolerant of heat than is paper and should not be allowed to exceed 66°C and 85 percent humidity. Disks are even less tolerant; they should not be allowed to exceed 52°C and 80 percent relative humidity.

Magnetic media should be stored at temperatures between 10°C and 52°C and between 8 and 80 percent humidity. Temperatures really should not vary more than a few degrees. These conditions will keep them from becoming warped or brittle, which would inhibit free movement in the disk drive.

Underwriters Laboratories has established standards for fire safes that are typical of those found in other countries. Note in Table 11-3 how much more protection is required for computer-related magnetic media.

Table 11-3

FIRE SAFE STANDARDS

Inside Temperature			Relative Humidity
	Fahrenheit	Celsius	
Paper documents	350°	177°	No limit
Magnetic tape, Microfilm, photos	150°	66°	85%
Flexible diskettes	125°	52°	80%

Mould and Mildew

Magnetic media have somewhat different requirements for relative humidity levels. When these levels exceed 80 percent for a sustained period of more than four hours, fungus growth is accelerated.

Dust

Static electricity can cause damage to disks or tapes.

Dust accumulated on computer tapes, on disks, or on microfilm can be highly damaging and in some cases can affect the output. For magnetic tape, relative humidity levels below 45 percent cause static electricity, which attracts dust to the tape. The signal density of the tape also makes it especially susceptible to dust collection.

The loss of information on magnetic media generally occurs when there is impeded contact between the medium and the read/write head, making cleanliness vital. Fingerprints and cigarette smoke, in particular, attract dust and other contaminants.

Power Interruption

Protection from power interruption must be planned.

Power can be interrupted during thunderstorms; indeed, lightning is the predominant cause of power interruption. There are other causes, however, of power discrepancies. Power overloads, blown fuses, and motors switching on and off are examples of other causes of changes in power. To avoid losing data, power protection should be installed. Power protection can range from surge suppressors to uninterruptible power systems to battery packs.

Other Hazards

No magnetized material should be placed near any magnetic medium such as hard disks or floppy disks. Building passkeys, credit cards, message holders with magnetic strips or magnetized tools such as a screwdriver, should not be placed or used closer than three inches from the hard disk.[10]

Hard disk crashes usually occur after many hours of use. Crashes can also be caused by physical shock or contamination, such as hair, cigarette smoke, or even a fingerprint. Because hard disk failure is unpredictable, frequent backup of information is critical.

 Learning Check: Can you describe disaster prevention methods for magnetic media?

DISASTER RECOVERY METHODS

There are many methods for recovering damaged records. The method selected depends on a number of factors and must be applicable to each organization's needs.

---

[10]Ibid., p. 8.

Selecting the Method

Factors that need to be considered when selecting a recovery method include extent and type of damage incurred, type of records media, availability of immediate technical assistance and resources, and the knowledge of the records staff.

Extent and Type of Damage Incurred

Whether the damage is confined to a small area or encompasses an entire building will affect the recovery procedures. Large volumes of extensively damaged records often require outside assistance; whereas fewer, less-damaged records may be recovered in house.

Records Media

Different media forms require different recovery methods. For example, documents require different techniques than do film and magnetic media. Knowledge of the various methods and how to apply them as appropriate for the different media types helps prevent additional damage.

Availability of Immediate Technical Assistance and Resources

If the equipment to begin records recovery is not immediately available, the records staff may need to take intermediate steps to stabilize the materials and to gain time either to get the damaged records to a facility for recovery or to bring the equipment to the records centre to begin recovery.

Knowledge of Records Management Staff

The knowledge of the records management staff in recovering damaged records will vary from organization to organization, depending on the priority given to a records disaster prevention and recovery program. The length of service of the records staff and their involvement in the program will also affect the extent of their knowledge. Recovery methods are only as effective as the ability of the staff to effectively implement them.

A Costly Fire

Dalhousie University's law library is housed in the five-storey Weldon Building on University Avenue in Halifax. In the early morning hours of August 16, 1985, lightning struck the top floor of the library; fire smouldered in the ceiling until the cleaning staff switched on the lights at 7:10 a.m. Although the fire spread quickly through the fifth floor, the fire department was able to contain it to the one floor and extinguish it by 9 a.m. However, there was smoke and water damage on every floor, and the contents of the building had to be removed quickly to prevent further damage.

Without a disaster manual to assist them, senior university administrators met immediately that morning to put together a contingency plan. They found space for the 90,000 books, arranged to use a local commercial freezer facility, and called for volunteers to help remove the books. By early afternoon the volunteers were able to enter the building and start removing the soggy, sooty books.

The building housed almost the entire collection of law books, bound and current issues of law journals, audiovisual software and hardware, some primary-source legal materials, and a rare book collection containing books once owned or used by prominent Nova Scotians. The rare books were removed first; some went to the university gymnasium for air drying and others temporarily went to the commercial freezer.

Within several days, all the books had been removed and relocated, and the process of drying, cleaning, and sorting began. To prevent mould and mildew from forming, books were placed either in freezers or on tables where they were fanned. One week after the fire, a specialist was engaged to dry many of the books with a mobile vacuum drying system and to clean them. A 50-foot-long tanker truck held pumps, heaters, and room for up to 10,000 books per drying cycle of 10 to 20 days each. After a moisture recovery period of about 10 additional days, 40 cleaners used raw rubber sponges to remove the soot, completing their job in six days.

A computer-assisted system was developed for sorting the books so that they could be packed in boxes and labelled with the proper shelf location. The library was at that point contained in 2,500 numbered boxes accompanied by a computerized listing. Five months after the fire, the new shelving arrived, and the law library was back in business.

 Learning Check: Can you state the factors that affect selection of a recovery method?

Salvage Methods

Water-damaged materials result from 95 percent of all disasters. Not only is the water damage itself a problem that must be dealt with, but the often-resulting mould that begins to develop quickly must also be minimized.

Vacuum Freeze Drying

Vacuum freeze
drying is a safe,
successful, but
expensive recovery
method.

Vacuum freeze drying is a process in which paper materials are frozen and then dried in a high-heat chamber. It is the safest and most successful recovery method; it is also the most expensive. Materials must be frozen when they are placed in a sublimation chamber. A sublimation chamber operates under high vacuum and high heat and turns the ice crystals in and on the frozen materials to water vapour. The vapour is then collected on a cold panel that has been chilled to at least −130°C.

When materials are removed from the vacuum freeze chamber, they will be *very* dry and should acclimate for at least one month before they are opened. They may be placed in a high-humidity room to accelerate the acclimation process, but must be monitored closely for signs of mould.[11]

Vacuum Drying

Vacuum drying is a process by which wet paper materials are placed into a chamber that pulls the moisture out by means of a vacuum. This method is *not* recommended, as the heat involved is damaging to paper and photographic materials. Microwave ovens are not recommended for the same reason.[12]

Freezing

Freezing buys time while provisions are made for recovery.

Freezing reduces wet paper materials to below freezing temperatures, stabilizes them, and provides time to determine the appropriate course of action. Mould will not grow, and further deterioration from water will not occur while materials are frozen. Rapid freezing is recommended to minimize damage from ice crystals. Temperatures below −10°C will freeze and dry out wet materials.[13]

Freezing is an intermediate stage. After materials have been removed from the freezer, they must be placed in a vacuum freeze dryer or air dried.

Air Drying

Air drying should be performed only in a stable environment to inhibit the growth of mould. The ideal environment for air drying is 10 to 16°C and 25 to 35 percent relative humidity.[14]

Recovery Priorities and Methods

Some types of media require different recovery priorities. Table 11-4 provides information about recovery priorities by type of records media as they apply to magnetic media, photographic materials (including microfilm), and paper.

---

[11]Toby Murray, "Don't Get Caught with Your Plans Down," *Records Management Quarterly,* Vol. 21, No. 2 (April, 1987), p. 12.

[12]Ibid., p. 12.

[13]Ibid.

[14]Dixon, p. 15.

Table 11-4 RECOVERY PRIORITY BY TYPE OF RECORDS MEDIA

Media	Recovery Priority	Salvage Techniques				Comments
		Initial		**Follow-up**		
		Action	Purpose	Action	Purpose	
<u>Magnetic Media</u> Mag tapes Disk packs Floppy disks Audio and video tape cassettes	Immediately.	Contact vendor.	To obtain professional advice.	May include freeze or vacuum drying, special cleaning techniques, or professional assistance in retrieving data.	To remove all moisture and other contaminants from the media; to access data in case of damaged media.	Such advice should be sought well in advance of a disaster. Contingency plans for data and word processing groups may be advisable. Heat and water damage to media may result in subsequent damage to hardware or in irretrievability of data. Proper backup and salvage procedures are essential. It is worth noting that such records are among the easiest to duplicate and store offsite.
<u>Photographic Materials</u> Colour films and photographs	Immediately.	Once wet, keep wet.	To avoid further damage and image loss.	Freeze if professional help must be delayed longer than 48 hrs.	To stabilize colour dyes.	Colour dyes are inherently unstable and should be handled immediately to prevent loss of colour and other damage.
	Within 48 hrs.	Obtain professional advice and/or assistance with cleaning, drying, and restoring.				
Silver or emulsion films and photographs (includes microfilm)	Immediately.	Immerse totally in water.	To avoid further damage	Seek professional advice and help with cleaning and drying. Freeze only if necessary.	To restore film to original state. Freezing may lead to image damage, but less damage is likely to be caused by freezing than by delayed treatments.	
	Within 48 hrs.	Formaldehyde, to a 1% solution, may be added to cool, clean water. One teaspoon of salt may be added to hard water.	To avoid softening or frilling of gelatin or emulsion layer. If allowed to dry out, materials tend to stick to adjacent surfaces, with image loss and other damage.			

Table 11-4   RECOVERY PRIORITY BY TYPE OF RECORDS MEDIA, *CONTINUED*

Media	Recovery Priority	Salvage Techniques				Comments
		Initial		Follow-up		
		Action	Purpose	Action	Purpose	
Diazo or vesicular (duplicate) films	Last	If time and staff are available, rinse off and lay out flat to dry; otherwise, leave until last.	To prevent water spotting and curling of films or fiche.	Wash with liquid detergent and rinse and lay out on absorbent paper to dry.	To remove water spots and other contaminants and to restore film.	Diazo and vesicular films are nearly impervious to water damage and should clean up easily. Diazo films sometimes fade with age. Fading or other damage discovered after the disaster can be related to poor quality control rather than to the disaster.
Paper Bond, rag, duplicating, other	Within 48 hrs. (depending on temperature and humidity levels at disaster site and on extent of damage) In fires, paper is least vulnerable medium.	Air dry in well-ventilated area. If volume of wet records is large, consider freeze or vacuum drying.	To prevent further deterioration of paper materials and eruption of mould or fungus.	May include freeze or vacuum drying. If mould erupts, treat with fungicides.	To remove moisture from materials and to reduce humidity levels in damaged materials, to eradicate mould.	In high humidity levels, deterioration of wet paper records can begin within 2-3 hours.
Coated or clay papers	Immediately	Freeze	To hold damaged materials until freeze or vacuum drying can be arranged.	Freeze or vacuum drying.	To remove all moisture from paper, without damaging or removing coated surface.	Freeze or vacuum drying is the only successful technique for this medium.

Source: *Taking Control of Your Office Records, edited by Katherine Aschner. © 1983 by Knowledge Industry Publications, Inc.*

Specific, detailed methods for recovering different types of records media are beyond the scope of this book. A number of sources are available that detail recovery methods for all types of media. Many of these sources are provided in the Suggested Readings section at the end of this chapter. Vendors are also a source of valuable information about the appropriate methods of recovery for their products.

Learning Check: Can you describe the various types of salvage methods and generally explain the recovery priorities?

Restoring the Facility

The facility or area must be thoroughly cleaned.

After the damaged materials have been removed and the environment has been stabilized, the damaged area must be thoroughly cleaned. Walls, floors and ceilings, furniture, and equipment must be scrubbed with soap and water and a fungicide. Carpeting, and the padding underneath, should be checked to see if mould is developing or if the carpeting or padding is still damp. Any removal of smoke odour or fogging with fungicides or insecticides should be done only by professionals.

TERMINOLOGY REVIEW

Review the terms listed below in the Glossary on page 521.

dispersal	useful records
duplication	vacuum drying
important records	vacuum freeze drying
nonessential records	vital records
records disaster prevention and	recovery manual
risk assessment	vital records protection manual

REVIEW AND DISCUSSION

1. Define vital records.
2. Name the four records classifications and describe the types of records that would fall into each classification.
3. Why is a vital records protection program essential to the survival of an organization?
4. With regard to the natural hazards to records,
   a. Which present the most danger?
   b. What responsibility does the records manager have for building safety?
   c. What steps can be taken for minimizing the danger of records destruction?

5. Categorize the methods that may be used to protect vital records and evaluate the protection provided by each method.

6. When evaluating possible methods of protecting vital records, what considerations should be reviewed?

7. Briefly describe procedures for transferring and storing vital records.

8. What special procedures should be used to protect electronic records?

9. What importance does the vital records protection manual have? What information should be contained in that manual? How is the vital records protection manual used?

10. Explain the importance of having an up-to-date disaster prevention and recovery plan.

11. Describe the steps in planning for disaster prevention and recovery.

12. State the typical contents and format of a records disaster prevention and recovery manual.

13. Explain how distribution of a manual is determined.

14. Describe how a disaster prevention and recovery plan is tested.

15. Describe disaster prevention methods for paper records, microrecords, and magnetic media records.

16. State the factors that determine the appropriate recovery method to be used.

17. Explain various salvage methods.

APPLICATIONS

1. Classify your personal records as Class 1, Vital; Class 2, Important; Class 3, Useful; or Class 4, Nonessential. Provide a rationale for your classification of each item, examples, and recommended protection. Your records may include cancelled cheques, insurance policies, income tax returns, purchase records, bills to be paid, birth certificates, and so on. Prepare a table similar to Table 11-1.

2. Visit the registrar's office at your college and prepare a report on the vital records protection plan for the educational institution.

3. Records disaster prevention and recovery programs are relatively new. Contact at least five organizations, either local or out of your area, to determine the extent to which these programs exist. In addition to asking for specific information, request a copy of their manual, if available. Write a report based on your findings.

4. Visit your local library and review the periodicals to find some additional examples of a records disaster. Prepare to give an oral report on the disaster and recovery from the disaster.

CONCLUDING CASES

A. Hampton Office Supply, Ltd.

Thomas Kimble, the records manager of Hampton Office Supply, Ltd., has been attempting to establish a vital records protection and disaster preparedness program to protect the organization in case of a disaster. Despite many informal discussions with several of the vice presidents, Thomas has not been able to convince top management that a vital records protection and disaster preparedness program is necessary for the continuing success of the organization. Typical responses included "We have insurance to cover disasters"; "Thomas said that only 4 to 10 percent of our records are essential anyway"; and "It won't happen to us."

1. What is the first step Thomas should take to establish a vital records protection and disaster preparedness program for Hampton's records?
2. What steps should be taken next?

B. Oxford Square Children's Zoo

Oxford Square Children's Zoo (The Zoo) is a manufacturer of stuffed toys. The Zoo was started in Mary Oxford's home 10 years ago when she began making toys for her children. Soon friends were asking her to make toys for their children, grandchildren, and even themselves; so Mary expanded her business. The Zoo has outgrown Mary's home, the garage, and the small outbuilding.

Mary just heard that Stuffed Toys, Inc., is for sale. She is particularly interested because the building in which they make their toys has recently been renovated and new equipment installed. Mary and her company vice president, Bruce Canning, have an appointment with the real estate agent at noon to inspect the facilities.

The Stuffed Toys, Inc., manufacturing plant appears to be in good order. Mary has asked to see the office space and the area in which the records are kept. The real estate agent reluctantly takes Mary and Bruce downstairs to the basement. Mary has to step over a bucket, which is placed to catch water from a tiny leak in the wall. The office space is small, but adequate. Paper records are kept in open-shelf files; disks seem to be either on each person's desk in plastic containers or on the top of the conference table. The basement is damp, and Bruce notices that there are two portable space heaters in use. One of the clerks offers Mary and Bruce coffee from the coffee maker located on the sorting table.

Just beyond the office is warehousing for completed products. Gas-fuelled forklifts move the boxes from the warehouse area to the freight area. The custodial staff comes in to pick up supplies and have a cigarette. Ashtrays are provided throughout the area. Mary sees no signs of smoke detectors, sprinkler systems, or fire extinguishers in the area.

"Did you notice that they make good use of their space? The open shelves go all the way from the floor to the ceiling," remarked the real estate agent.

Mary didn't notice for she was much too busy stepping over some type of insect.

When Mary and Bruce returned to The Zoo, Mary said, "Bruce, did you notice all of those potential hazards in the office area?"

List the potential hazards Mary saw in the basement.

SUGGESTED READINGS AND RESOURCES

Bautsch, Gail L. Blount. "What You Don't Know CAN Hurt You." *Records Management Quarterly,* Vol. 20, No. 4 (October, 1986) p. 40.

Brett J. Balon, and H. Wayne Gardner, "Disaster Planning for Electronic Records," *Records Management Quarterly,* Vol. 22, No. 3 (July, 1988), p. 20.

Bulgawicz, Susan L., and Charles E. Nolan. *Disaster Prevention and Recovery: A Planned Approach.* Association of Records Managers and Administrators: Prairie Village, Kansas, 1988.

Ciura, Jean M. "Vital Records Protection: Part I, Identifying Essential Information." *Information Management,* Vol. 19, No. 2 (February, 1985), p. 11.

Ciura, Jean M. "Vital Records Protection: Part II, Systems Design and Implementation." *Information Management,* Vol. 19, No. 4 (April, 1985), p. 16.

Cook, T. "It's 10 O'clock: Do you know where your data are?" *Technology Review,* Vol. 98, January, 1995, p. 48.

Cote, Arthur E., ed. Fire *Protection Handbook,* 16th ed. Boston: National Fire Protection Association, 1986.

Eulenberg, J.N. "Plan for Records Recovery Before a Disaster Strikes." *Office,* Vol. 107, January, 1988, pp. 76-77.

Filing Procedures (Prairie Village, Kansas: Association of Records Managers and Administrators, 1989), pp. 11-12.

Gast, Bruce M. "Data Safes Secure Computer Records Against Fire and Other Risks." *Administrative Management,* Vol. 47, No. 6 (June, 1986), p. 56.

Guide to the Preservation of Essential Records. Emergency Preparedness Canada and National Archives of Canada: Ottawa, Ontario, 1987.

"Is Getting In Getting Out of Control?" *Today's Office,* Vol. 20, No. 4 (September, 1985).

Joseph, Anthony J. "Safety Considerations in Designing Accommodations for Information Systems." *Records Management Quarterly,* Vol. 27, No. 4 (October, 1993), p. 28.

King, Susan L. "What If: A Case Study of A Hurricane." *Records Management Quarterly,* Vol. 28, No. 3 (July, 1994) p. 30.

Manual for Fire Protection for Archives and Records Centres. National Fire Protection Association, 1986.

McKinnon, Gordon P., ed. *Fire Protection Handbook,* 16th ed. Boston: National Fire Protection Association, 1986.

"Microfilm Disaster Recovery Pays Off After Plane Crash." *IMC Journal,* Vol. 25, No. 1 (January/February, 1989), p. 20.

Phillips, John T., Jr. "Electronic Vaulting and Records Centres." *Records Management Quarterly,* Vol. 27, No. 1 (January, 1993), p. 38.

"Preventing Disaster with Power Protection." *Modern Office Technology,* Vol. 33, No. 6 (June, 1988), p. 76.

Romei, Lura K., Patricia M. Fernberg, and Mary S. Malik. "Disaster Recovery: Are You Ready?" *Managing Office Technology,* Vol. 40, January, 1995, p. 26.

Romei, Lura K., et al. "Disaster Recovery: Our *Real* Story." *Managing Office Technology,* Vol. 40, June 1995, p. 24.

Vossler, Janet L. "The Human Element of Disaster Recovery." *Records Management Quarterly,* Vol. 21, No. 1 (January, 1987), p. 10.

Whitehead, Janet C., and Diann Conyers. "Survival in a Computer Environment—The Synergistic Approach." *Records Management Quarterly,* Vol. 22, No. 1 (January, 1988) p. 8.

Profile
Disaster Planning, Preparedness, and Recovery Coordinator

John C. Whitehead, CRM, has been the county clerk in Chester County for 16 years. The county clerk is charged with keeping many of the county's vital records, such as real estate deeds, liens, property assessments, sales, and taxes. Also under the clerk's jurisdiction are auto titles, marriage records, County Council election records, and budgetary/personnel records. There are 220 employees in Chester County, with 23 in the clerk's office.

Although Mr. Whitehead's responsibilities are broad ones, as cited above, he is additionally responsible for the records disaster planning, prevention, and recovery program for the county. When Mr. Whitehead assumed his position, there were no records management practices in effect; in fact, stacks of miscellaneous files cluttered the floor of his office. Now all information and recordkeeping processes have been totally automated.

On the evening of Thursday, August 1, 1992, the importance of disaster planning and preparedness became painfully evident. On that evening a freak storm settled over the area, and in less than three hours, more than 160 mm of rain was dumped on an area that normally receives that amount over the whole summer. The lower floor of the County Courthouse was inundated with a tide of water that swept through the halls with enough force to rip away public seating that was bolted to the floor. Some of the records soaked by the flood were more than 100 years old—irreplaceable for their historic value alone. The fiscal and court records were also soaked. With lots of help from volunteers and staff, the historic paper records were dried successfully and put in a safe place. But the disaster had a silver lining, as Mr. Whitehead explained:

"The things we learned are innumerable and invaluable: A viable disaster plan including vital records identification and analysis is indispensable! Backup, offsite copies of diskettes, microfilm, mag tapes, and disks are a must! And don't forget offsite copies of software, operating systems, and documentation. An alternative hot site for automated recovery operations is recommended. The little things count too: always use an indelible black pen for signatures, labels, and so forth. Coloured file folders look nice, but in a water disaster, they bleed and add to recovery problems. Paper clips and staples cause rust spots on documents and encourage one more type of contamination. The most important lesson of the disaster was 'Yes, it can happen to us!' Never again will we be unprepared!"

Mr. Whitehead has been very active in professional organizations including the Association of Records Managers and Administrators, where he was actively involved in developing guidelines for records disaster prevention and recovery.

12

Records Security and Information Privacy

Learning Goals

After completing this chapter, you should be able to:

1. Describe the federal government's Privacy Act and Access to Information Act.
2. Explain the reasons for organizational attention to records security.
3. Explain the impact of increased security controls on recordkeeping.
4. Identify the major responsibilities of the records manager for protecting the security and confidentiality of records.
5. Describe the steps in a records security management program.
6. Describe methods for controlling access to areas and facilities.
7. Describe the information provided by audit trails.
8. Describe methods for controlling access to equipment.
9. Describe procedures for controlling access to paper documents.
10. Describe procedures for controlling access to electronic files.

NEED FOR CONTENT SECURITY

One of the key issues in managing information is the need to keep that information secure from unauthorized users. **Content security** provides protection against intentional destruction, disclosure, modification, or breach of confidentiality of information. The need for content security is based on the fundamental principle that people have the right to decide what personal information they wish to divulge, to whom, and for what purpose. They also have the right to expect that that information will be kept private and that it will be used only for the purpose for which it was obtained.

Governments are planning to deliver more services electronically, as are many businesses in the private sector. All levels of government collect information to build databases around their citizens; businesses collect information to build databases around their customers. Income tax forms, for example, require taxpayers to state their age and marital status. As another example, supermarkets have their own customer cards that do more than allow payment by cheque; these cards also provide a customer profile including credit history and buying habits. With the potential of the information highway to link thousands of different databases around the world, the need to protect the content of records is the most important issue of the 1990s. The **information highway** is the term given to integrated computer, communication, and cable TV networks: a global network. All these trends mean that both governments and private industry must be vigilant in preventing information from being obtained by unauthorized users while at the same time giving people access to as much information as possible.

Legislated Protection

The Privacy and Access to Information Acts protect personal information, while furnishing Canadians with access to information held by the federal government.

Part IV of the Canadian Human Rights Act, in place since 1978, gave limited protection of privacy and limited access to personal information. The Privacy Act of 1983 expanded on that act by giving Canadian citizens and people present in Canada the right to have access to information held about them by the federal government; it does not cover information held by provincial governments or the private sector. Our government collects and uses personal information from almost all Canadians for such operations as income tax at Revenue Canada, pension and family allowance payments at Health Canada, and the employment and insurance program at Human Resources Canada. Five key objectives of the act are to:

- Restrict the right of the federal institutions to collect personal information;
- Establish rules concerning the use and disclosure of personal information;

- Set out rules concerning the retention period of personal information;
- Give the individuals concerned the right of access to their personal information kept by federal institutions; and
- Offer an independent review mechanism to individuals who feel they have been denied their rights under the act by
  - Establishment of the Privacy Commissioner's office and
  - Right of review in the Federal Court (in certain cases).

There is some personal information the federal government may not release under the act, much of which relates to other people, national security, or law enforcement. In addition, the act excludes certain information such as public material already available in museums, libraries, and at the National Archives; published material or material available for purchase by the public; and confidences of the federal Cabinet. There is no charge for applying to see personal information or for complaining to the Privacy Commissioner. An information kit from the federal government answers questions an individual may have about the scope of the act and the way to use it.[1]

A companion act, the **Access to Information Act** of 1983, gives any Canadian citizen as well as people and corporations present in Canada the right to examine or obtain copies of records of a federal government institution that are not of a personal nature. With limited exceptions, the information is available by making a formal request. Much government information is already available through libraries, public affairs offices, and regional information centres. But the act places the responsibility on a government institution to provide the information requested as long as it is not exempted or excluded. Exemptions afford protection to certain kinds of information when its release could cause identifiable harm or would be contrary to the law, such as information on national security, law enforcement, or trade secrets. Exclusions cover material already available to the public in government publications and libraries or museums, and material directly connected with the operation of Cabinet, such as cabinet documents and minutes or records of decisions. As with the Privacy Act, the Access to Information Act cannot give people access to records outside the control of the federal government—provincial or municipal records or those in private institutions like banks and credit bureaus. The Info Source book, published annually, is widely available to make it fast and easy to find out about the government of Canada, its organization, and its information holdings. Access Request Forms contain instructions on how to apply for access to information. If a

---

[1] *InfoSource Privacy Act Brochure,* Government of Canada and information kit material from Privacy Commissioner of Canada.

person has complaints about the operation of the act, the Office of the Information Commissioner deals with them. An application fee applies to requests for access to information.[2]

All provinces but Prince Edward Island have enacted similar laws to cover information held by the provincial governments, and in some instances the legislation is extended to cover local governments and institutions like hospitals and universities that may not be wholly controlled by provincial governments. The province of Quebec has extended its access rights and privacy legislation to the private sector as well. In the future, other provinces may also cover the private sector in their legislation. As an example of provincial legislation, the province of Nova Scotia's Freedom of Information and Protection of Privacy Act, which came into effect on July 1, 1994, provides Nova Scotians with access to most records under the control of the provincial government and protects the privacy of individuals who do not want their personal information made public.[3]

The consequences of personal information falling into the wrong hands can be far reaching, even devastating. Both the public and the private sectors have a responsibility to their employees and to their customers and clients. The employer's responsibility to employees is to make them aware of the provisions of privacy and access to information laws and of the organizational commitment to strict enforcement both in content and intent of the laws. The responsibility to the public is to keep employees informed and to monitor activities so that the public can be assured that everything possible is being done to safeguard personal information.

A major task at present of federal and provincial government departments and agencies is to identify all records affected by privacy and access to information legislation. In order to be effective, the results must be incorporated into the department's records retention and disposition schedule.

Voluntary Organizational Protection

Voluntary programs by businesses are emerging in the private sector.

In addition to the need for legislated records protection, organizations in the private sector are also recognizing the need to establish their own programs of internal records integrity and security. Voluntary programs are beginning to emerge as businesses accept their responsibilities in this area of records management. Certainly part of the motivation

---

[2]*Access to Information Act Brochure*, Communications and Coordination Directorate, Treasury Board of Canada Secretariat, Ottawa, Ontario.

[3]*Freedom of Information and Protection of Privacy Act User Guide*, Department of Justice, Province of Nova Scotia, Halifax, Nova Scotia.

is a genuine concern for records integrity; however, some motivation can be attributed to the desire for voluntary compliance before there is a need for legislated compliance. In this manner, the private sector can adopt protective measures appropriate for its own needs without government intervention.

A major factor to be considered is the increasing number of lawsuits for breach of confidentiality and invasion of privacy, with settlements often in favour of the plaintiffs. If information is released without permission, an organization could be liable for damages. Thus, organizations have a proprietary interest in protecting themselves from any action that could be construed as a breach of confidentiality or of privacy.

✓ **Learning Check: Can you describe the effect of legislative and organizational attention to records security?**

Effects of Security Controls

Organizations are increasingly affected by the impact of both mandatory and voluntary controls of information security. A new law may very well be added to Murphy's Law, Parkinson's Law, and others. The new law is Ricks' Law of Increasing Paperwork: "As controls on paperwork increase arithmetically, the paperwork necessary to accomplish the controls increases geometrically."

Increased paperwork has resulted from increased controls.

One result of the emphasis on content security is the potential for increased recordkeeping both to establish strategies of implementation and to assure accountability. Most legislation requires records to be maintained with such accuracy, timeliness, completeness, and relevance as is reasonably necessary for fairness. In order to accomplish the required documentation, a major overhaul of current recordkeeping procedures may be necessary. New procedures need to conform to the objectives of the individual organization with regard to security as well as with regard to the laws and their intent.

Principles of personal information management have been established.

In the United States, the Federal Privacy Protection Study Commission, authorized by that country's privacy legislation, issued a report in July 1977. This report, entitled "Personal Privacy in an Information Society," identified eight principles of personal information management practices. Any organization considering the development of a program of records confidentiality should study these principles and incorporate them into its own system.

1. **Openness.** There should be a policy of openness about an organization's personal recordkeeping policies, practices, and systems; there should be no secret systems.
2. **Individual access.** An individual about whom information is maintained by a recordkeeping organization in individually identifiable form should have a right to see and copy that information.

3. **Individual participation.** An individual should have the right to correct or amend the substance of personal information maintained by a recordkeeping organization.
4. **Collection limitation.** Internal collection of personal information within a recordkeeping organization should be limited to necessary information.
5. **Use limitation.** Internal uses of personal information within a recordkeeping organization should be limited to those who have a need to know.
6. **Disclosure limitation.** External disclosures of personal information by a recordkeeping organization should be limited.
7. **Information management.** A recordkeeping organization should bear affirmative responsibility for establishing reasonable and proper information management policies and practices to assure that its collection, maintenance, use, and dissemination of information about an individual are necessary and lawful and that the information itself is current and accurate.
8. **Accountability.** A recordkeeping organization should be accountable for its personal recordkeeping policies, practices, and systems.

 Learning Check: Can you identify the responsibilities of the records manager for records security?

SECURITY MANAGEMENT

Security management has become important to protect records.

A program of security management should be established. This would include (1) establishing objectives; (2) defining responsibilities; (3) assessing risk; (4) establishing information security policies and procedures; and (5) establishing procedures for auditing, monitoring, and evaluating the system.

Establish Objectives

Before any management system is installed, objectives should be established. A security management system has the objectives of providing:
- Confidentiality of personal, proprietary, or sensitive information and data.
- Records content integrity and accuracy of data.
- Safeguards against unauthorized access of systems and data.
- Quick access by legitimate users to information and data.

Define Responsibilities

Security management responsibilities belong to both management and individual users.

Management and individual users share responsibilities for security management. Each entity has a particular focus in managing the security of the records.

Management Responsibility

Management's responsibility begins with providing the lead in promoting and assuring the security of the records. The focus should be on protecting the information contained within the records and the means for accomplishing this. Management develops the policies and procedures for the security management program and assigns responsibility and necessary authority for security management for the entire organization. Without some formal security management structure and associated guidance, users cannot be expected to apply consistent and effective controls. Management is also responsible for communicating the policies and procedures to those who will be originating or using the records.

Records security is not limited to paper documents.

The management of records security applies to information and data stored on a personal computer, a minicomputer, a mainframe, or available through a network. The information may be in any form: paper, microrecords, or electronic media. Although the technology and economics of security have changed, the basic objectives have not—the confidentiality, integrity, and availability of information must be protected.

Management is also responsible for assessing the threat of security breaches from within the organization and for taking action to reduce that risk. Fellow employees present the greatest risk to security of information, and the cost can be significant. Respondents reported in a 1994 North American study by Ernst and Young and *Information Week* on security trends, concerns, and practices that the cost of security breaches often exceeds $100,000 and is occasionally more than $1 million for a single incident.

Individual User Responsibility

The basic operational responsibility should be placed with those who "own" the information and those who use the information. Owners and users are responsible for knowing, understanding, and following the established policies and procedures for records security management.

Assess Risk

Valuable information as well as some confidential, sensitive records are housed in every organization. In planning a security management program, special attention must be paid to protecting these types of records. A formal risk assessment approach need not be taken unless the majority of records housed contain valuable and sensitive information. Rather, the value and the risk can be assessed when the records are inventoried and the retention schedule is established. The vital records (Class 1 records, Chapter 11) would receive special consideration and protection when the disaster prevention program is established.

Establish Information Security Policies and Procedures

Policies and procedures to protect information should be established and communicated to all who generate or use the information. A formal information security policy is a prerequisite to a workable program. This requires identifying the types of information that require protection and specifying the types of control measures that apply to each type of information. Procedures must be in written form and distributed to members of the organization. The procedures should be specific in terms of the physical protection that will be offered to the various types of information and the equipment used to generate the information, the specific administrative procedures that will be used to legitimately access the records, and the procedures used to access facilities and equipment. Each of these will be addressed in the sections on accessing information below. In addition, training of staff should be an ongoing process, and staff should be reminded periodically of the proper procedures.

Audit, Monitor, and Evaluate Security Management

As with any other control system, auditing, monitoring, and evaluating the security management program is critical to its effectiveness. Systems, organizations, and environments change quickly in the 1990s, often resulting in different risks facing an information system. There should be a program of regular audits and evaluations to ensure the continued adequacy, effectiveness, and appropriateness of current security measures. The process of monitoring and keeping up to date is ongoing as records users and managers provide feedback about the effectiveness and efficiency of the procedures. The periodic audits provide information to be used for subsequent evaluations of the security management program.

 Learning Check: Can you describe the steps in the security management program?

AREA AND FACILITY ACCESS

Procedures must be established for access to areas and facilities, to equipment, and to information contained in the records. The extent to which security measures are required will depend on the organization's needs.

A system of controlled access to an area or a facility must be established to maintain safeguards against unauthorized invasion of equipment and records. The primary criterion for entrance should be that only those whose work requires access should be admitted.

Types of Access Controls

Multiple options are available for security control of areas and facilities, ranging from old-fashioned key locks to computer-controlled biometrics. The primary access controls that minimize checking by guards or security personnel are keys; electric, electronic, or mechanical entry; coded plastic cards; biometric and physical attributes; and combination systems.

According to Larry Grady, marketing vice president of Microcard Technologies, Inc., there are three classifications of security. They are:

1. What you have—key, card, photopass.
2. What you know—password, code, personal identification number (PIN).
3. What you are—unique characteristics that only you possess.

In the first two categories—what you have and what you know—you are issued a method of access. You are given a key, a card, a password, a PIN, or a code. In the last category—what you are—you are enrolled in an access system biometrically or through physical attributes.

Keys

Keys may not offer needed security.

Keys are used to unlock doors, cabinets, or equipment. Keys are easily duplicated and lost; anyone can use them. The lock itself is vulnerable to entry and cannot distinguish between persons authorized to enter and those who are not.

Electric, Electronic, or Mechanical Entry

Electric, electronic, or mechanical push-button entry controls require memorizing a series of numbers, letters, or both in correct sequence. These combinations are then keyed in by depressing a set of push buttons or by keying in a password on a keyboard. Figure 12-1 shows one keypad entry system.

There are numerous options available on these keypad systems. These include:

- Combination time, in which a fixed time is allowed for entry of the correct combination under the assumption that any authorized person could enter the code quickly.
- Error alarm, which activates when there is successive entry of incorrect numbers. This prevents unauthorized persons from trying a large number of combinations in the hope that they may hit the right one.
- Time penalty, in which the system is automatically deactivated for an interval after entry of an incorrect sequence of numbers. This prevents an unauthorized person from rapidly trying a series of combinations.
- Door delay, which controls the amount of time the door will remain unlocked without triggering an alarm. This limits the number of people who can enter at any one opening.
- Remote indication, which provides a signal at a guard station or at a central log-in station indicating that the door was opened.

Figure 12-1
Keypad Entry

Source: Simplex Access Controls Corp.

Electric, electronic, and mechanical devices have security options.

Some problems with this entry system are that people often forget the code or record the code where others may find and use it. Push-button systems should not be used where there is a risk of employee collusion, since the combinations can be easily shared. This form of access is also vulnerable to electronic lock picking.

Plastic Cards with Coded Strips

Plastic cards are equivalent to a key and lock.

Plastic cards with coded strips can control a single door or multiple entry points. The card may be inserted into the reader, which controls the lock; or the reader may act as a remote terminal controlled by a central microcomputer. The cards may be coded to distinguish authorized doors from unauthorized doors.

The plastic card system is equivalent to a conventional lock and key. A card can be lost and, as with keys, should carry no identification that would allow its finder to know what the card unlocks. Although like the traditional key in many ways, a plastic coded card is more difficult to duplicate or master-key. The card, unlike the key, can have additional safety features, including some of those described above relating to the push-button entry controls. Figure 12-2 shows a plastic coded card entry device.

Figure 12-2
Plastic Coded Entry
Card

Source: Photo courtesy of Rusco Electronic Systems, Glendale California

Biometric and Physical Attributes

Biometric devices
match individual
characteristics
electronically.

With a biometric or physical attributes system, some unique characteristic of the person to be admitted is recognized. This, traditionally, has been the human face; and the access control system consisted of a guard comparing the person's face with the picture shown on a picture card or badge. Although this system still has wide use, more sophisticated systems are now available.

Biometric devices measure and record unique personal characteristics, such as fingerprints, voice, chromosomes in a strand of hair, or retinal eye patterns. These characteristics are matched electronically as one attempts access to an area or to a facility.

Voice access systems require that users record voice templates, which are stored on the computer. To gain access, a designated phrase is spoken into a microphone. The computer then matches the voice with the recorded voice template to allow access. The computer actually compares a number of voice characteristics, from pitch and inflection to resonance and timbre. Studies have shown that even skilled impressionists or identical twins cannot fool the system.

Three-dimensional
fingerprint access
is foolproof.

Fingerprint access systems are virtually tamperproof. The security of keys and codes can be compromised; the security of a fingerprint is unique. Three-dimensional fingerprint templates are entered into the computer. The person seeking access places the finger into the reader, where the computer compares the template with the fingerprint. The three-dimensional feature prevents the machine from being fooled by the placement of a photograph of a fingerprint on the lens; an actual fingerprint with ridges and valleys is necessary for verification (see Figure 12-3).

Figure 12-3
Biometric Device

Source: Identix, Inc.

Combination Systems

Combination
systems enhance
security.

A combination of the key, push button, plastic coded cards, and bio-metric and physical attributes may be used. Some systems require one either to use a plastic coded card or to enter a correct sequence of numbers in the keypad or a combination of both. These systems can also require use of a PIN number in combination with the card.

Another combination system is shown in Figure 12-4. This system enhances user authentication by requiring that the users not only enter the correct password but also have the correct access key. The access key is inserted into the keypad. When the user enters the proper pass-word, the system returns a unique alphanumeric sequence to be entered on the keypad, which transmits the sequence to the access key. The access key then returns a unique, random password, which the user then enters on the computer keyboard to gain access.

There are, of course, numerous combinations of the basic systems that can be used, depending upon the needs and resources of the organization.

Where access controls to areas and facilities are in place and enforced, there should be a central place for visitors to apply for entrance. Once inside the facility, the visitors are subject to all of the other access controls; unlimited access is not granted.

Figure 12-4
Combination Keypad and Coded Card Entry System

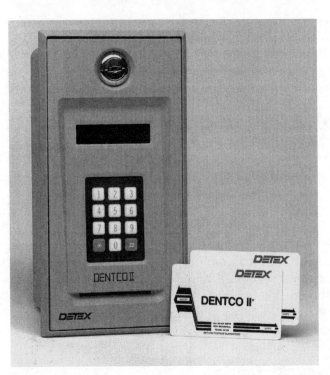

Source: Detex Corp.

 Learning Check: Can you describe methods for controlling access to areas and facilities?

Audit Trails

Printouts showing who has had access are available.

The ability to record an audit trail of all access attempts, both successful and unsuccessful, can be built into many of the area and facility access systems. A reader electronically records authorized entry and unauthorized attempts at entry. The date and time of entry, as well as the door(s) entered, are recorded; and at the end of the day (or other specified period), a printout is made of who entered the area, at what time, and through which entry. This information is particularly useful in monitoring the access system.

EQUIPMENT ACCESS

Equipment security refers to many kinds of equipment.

The need to safeguard the equipment is recognized as an important component of the security management system. As more and more organizations turn to a totally integrated system of records management that combines the equipment and technologies of word processing, data processing, telecommunications, micrographics, and reprographics, procedures for controlling theft and unauthorized access must be provided.

Procedures

To prevent hardware theft, procedures must be established, implemented, enforced, and monitored. The following procedures are suggested:

- Keep a current inventory, including date of purchase, serial numbers, and cost of each piece of equipment.
- Tag equipment and all components with ID numbers, on both the inside and the outside of the equipment.
- If taking home a piece of equipment is permitted by the organization, require employees to sign out any such equipment. Have a specified return date.
- Supervise and monitor equipment use during break times, lunchtimes, and while employees may be working late.
- Train building guards to check for computer equipment.[4]

Be sure to communicate the procedures to all employees in a positive way. Although the procedures are necessary, employees should not be made to feel that they are potential thieves and are being treated in a punitive way. It may be difficult to balance employees' rights to privacy with the need for security.

Security Devices

Security devices range from locks to computer alarms.

A number of security devices are available for hardware, ranging from locks to computer alarms. An organization concerned about hardware security should consider using any of the following security devices:

- Cables attached to the equipment and controlled by a strong lock.
- Locking cabinets, which can be secured during breaks and at lunchtime when there are usually few people around. Using locks during this time as well as at the end of the workday reduces the chances of unauthorized access to records. See Figure 12-5.
- Computer alarms that sound if the unit is moved or a sensor is removed.
- Anchoring pads, consisting of a steel plate attached to the equipment and another attached to the desk. The two plates are locked together either by bolts or a strong adhesive.[5] See Figure 12-6.

When a key is used in any of the security devices, precautions should be taken to safeguard the key by keeping it in a safe place, one not obvious to others.

 Learning Check: Can you describe methods of controlling access to equipment?

---

[4]Susan N. Kesim, "Computer Security, An Open-&-Shut Case," *Office Systems '88,* Vol. 33, No. 7 (July, 1988), pp. 22-23.

[5]Ibid.

Figure 12-5
Magnetic Media
Safe

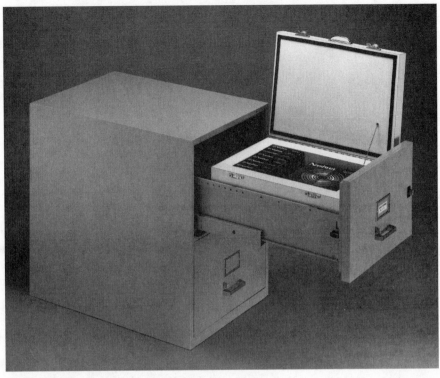

Source: *Melink Safe Company, Whitehouse, Ohio*

Figure 12-6
Equipment
Lockdown Device

Source: *Anchor Pad International, Incorporated*

INFORMATION AND RECORDS ACCESS

Information may be obtained in many ways, including manual retrieval of paper documents, visual display on the CRT, computer printout from stored data, hard copy from stored word processor documents, or facsimile. Because the possibilities for storing and retrieving information are greater than ever, precautions against misuse must be consistently and constantly exercised.

Paper Document Access

Requesting paper documents should follow established guidelines.

A central source for records access, with one person responsible for compliance with company guidelines, is desirable for ease of control and delegation of responsibility. These guidelines should be written, disseminated, and enforced. All employees at all management levels should be informed regarding the procedures to be followed when requesting paper documents or when providing requested information to another.

When access to a record is requested, the person processing the request should follow established procedures. These procedures might include the following:

1. If review of a personal record is requested by the individual, two forms of identification should be required if the person is unknown; completion of an authorization form should be required.
2. If a copy of a personal record is requested by the individual, two forms of identification should be required if the person is unknown; completion of authorization form and a signature for receipt of copy should also be required.
3. If the requester is a company employee with a need to review, copy, or log out a record, a signature on a receipt for the copy or a signature on a log identifying the record reviewed or logged out should be required.
4. If the request is made by mail, its legitimacy should be verified; and when necessary, written permission for the release of the information should be obtained.
5. If records are highly confidential, only authorized persons may be allowed to review the records. When this situation exists, an "authorized to see" list should be available, and the requester's name must appear on that list for access to be permitted.
6. In all other instances, the records manager or designee must grant authorization on a case-by-case basis. Documentation may be provided by signature on a log or request form.

Request forms may range in complexity from a very detailed form to a simple notation of the name of the person requesting the record, the date, the record requested, and request for a copy, if applicable.

The federal government's Personal Information Request Form for Canadians to request personal information about themselves is shown in Figure 12-7.

Figure 12-7
Privacy Information Act and Request Form

Info Source — Personal Information Request Form

TBC 350-58 (Rev. 1990/11)

Privacy Act

Step 1
Determine which federal government institution is most likely to hold personal information about you. Decide whether you wish to submit an informal request for the information or a formal request under the *Privacy Act*. If you wish to make an informal request, contact the appropriate institution. The address can likely be found in *Info Source* publications which are available across Canada, generally in major public and academic libraries, federal government offices, such as Employment Immigration Centres, and the constituency offices of federal Members of Parliament.

Step 2
To apply for personal information about you under the *Privacy Act*, complete this form. Describe the information being sought and provide any relevant details necessary to help the institution find it. If you require assistance, refer to *Info Source (Sources of Federal Government Information)* for a description of personal information banks held by the institution or contact its Privacy Coordinator.

Step 3
Forward the personal information request form to the Privacy Coordinator of the institution holding the information. The address is listed in the "Introduction" to *Info Source*.

Step 4
When you receive an answer to your request, review the information to determine whether you wish to make a further request under the Act. You also have the right to complain to the Privacy Commissioner should you beleive that you have been denied any of your rights under the Act.

Federal Government Institution

I wish to examine the information   ☐ As it is   ☐ All in English   ☐ All in French

Provide details regarding the information being sought

Method of access preferred   ☐ Receive copies of originals   ☐ Examine originals in government offices

Name of applicant

Street, address, apartment   City or town

Province   Postal Code   Telephone number

I request access to personal information about myself under the *Privacy Act* as I am a Canadian citizen, permanent resident or another individual, including an inmate, present in Canada.

Signature   Date

Government   Gouvernement
of Canada   du Canada   Français au verso   Canadä

Learning Check: Can you describe procedures for controlling access to paper documents?

Electronic Files Access

Control of the electronic files system is especially important because of the proliferation of networks and the volume of information that may be accessed. Entry into the system may require a code, a password, a key, or a smart card. A **smart card** is a credit-card-sized device incorporating a tiny computer chip that limits access to individual computers to legitimate users. A more recent development is "firewall" security software that creates an electronic barrier preventing unauthorized access to an organization's information.

Nonremovable Media Security

When data are stored on nonremovable media (hard disk), preventing access to the data requires controlling access to the equipment. This is true whether a personal computer or the mainframe is used. The person desiring information stored on a hard disk or mainframe must key in an assigned numeric code, a password, or a combination of the two to gain entry into the system and retrieve the desired information.

Use of two types of identification is preferable.

A more secure system requires two identifiers when logging on the system. The first is usually a nonsecret identifier, such as an account number. The second identifier is a secret password, which is then keyed in to authenticate the user's right to have access. Many organizations require this procedure every time the system is powered up. For additional safety, some systems may require a key to unlock the keyboard.

Since passwords may give access to a good deal of information, some guidelines should be kept in mind. Passwords should be at least six characters long, made up of nonsense syllables, preferably a combination of letters and numbers, frequently changed, and *not* meaningful. They should never be written down and left around a work area.

Removable Media Security

If the data are stored on removable media, such as floppy disks, a simple key-and-lock approach will probably be the most cost-effective. There are, however, other precautions that should be taken when using removable media to store information. These include:

- Locking up the disks when they are not in use.
- Scanning directories to review work, rather than scanning the actual document.
- Denying access to employees who resign, and then immediately changing the access codes.
- Making frequent backup copies and supervising crucial information backup.
- Encrypting (scrambling) sensitive and confidential files. A number of special encryption device products are available to secure sensitive information.

- Mutilating or erasing disks before they are thrown away. Discarded disks should never be given to anyone outside the organization. Utilities that can reconstruct erased files are readily available, but reformatting a disk will make it very difficult to reconstruct erased files.
- Turning off modems when they are not in use.
- Installing automatic dial-backs where the computer calls back an employee before permitting access to information.
- Turning off computers when not in use so unauthorized persons cannot access the files.[6]

Optical disks are another type of removable media. Because few pieces of equipment allow use of an optical disk cartridge, security is enhanced. The security measures taken for optical disks are the same as for a personal computer environment. As with personal computers, the levels of security depend on the requirements of the organization.

External labels may be used on disks.

External labels used to identify confidential or sensitive records make it easier for personnel to identify those files that require special protection. The disadvantage is that these labels may also make the files obvious to a would-be thief. When external labels are used as identifiers, it is critical that users provide appropriate protection of the records.

Protection Against Viruses

With the rise in corporate networks, E-mail usage, and the Internet, the risk of acquiring a virus is significant. A **computer virus** is a bug deliberately inserted into a computer system. Most viruses do little or no damage; others are capable of wiping out everything. There are over 3,000 known computer viruses, and two or three new ones are added every day. One of the most famous is Michelangelo, which infected 64,000 personal computers in the United States when it first hit in 1992. Michelangelo wipes out data on March 6, Michelangelo's birthday. Antivirus software is readily available for both detection and removal; it should be used regularly to check for and remove viruses.

 Learning Check: Can you describe procedures for controlling access to electronic files?

TERMINOLOGY REVIEW

Review the terms listed below in the Glossary on page 521.

Access to Information Act
biometric devices
computer virus

---

[6]Ibid.

content security
information highway
Privacy Act
smart card

REVIEW AND DISCUSSION

1. Describe the protection provided by the Access to Information Act and the Privacy Act.
2. Explain the reasons for organizational attention to records security.
3. Explain the impact of increasing security controls on recordkeeping.
4. Identify the major responsibilities of the records manager for protecting the security and confidentiality of records.
5. Describe the steps in a records security management program.
6. Describe methods for controlling access to areas and facilities.
7. Describe the information provided by audit trails.
8. Describe methods for controlling access to equipment.
9. Describe procedures for controlling access to paper documents.
10. Describe procedures for controlling access to electronic files.

APPLICATIONS

1. Do you agree or disagree that records management practices have only been minimally affected by recent legislation? Support your answer.
2. Review another student's response to Review and Discussion Questions 6, 8, 9, and 10. Write a report pointing out the deficiencies and strengths in the procedures described and making recommendations for improved security.

CONCLUDING CASES

A. Anderson and Best, International Personnel Consultants

Michelle Greene is the records manager at Anderson and Best, a large international firm specializing in locating and matching high-level managers with the needs of clients. The firm has a high volume of clients whose records contain confidential information. For some time, Michelle has been concerned about the safety and security of the client records. The records centre is "bulging at the seams"; it is understaffed; records are everywhere. Boxes of accessions are stacked in the receiving area. Neat piles of refiles are stacked on the counters. The desks in the reference area seem to have papers and microfiche scattered all over. Personnel records stored in the computer require no passwords or other access codes.

Anderson and Best has always had a practice of open access. All consultants have free access to the records. In fact, everyone seems to have access!

Michelle's predecessor, Max Slack, did not believe in a lot of red tape. He always said, "Just go get what you need to do your work. If you sign for something every time you need one little item, we'll be flooded with paper."

1. What are some specific concerns Michelle should address immediately?
2. How can Michelle solve the problems identified in Question 1?
3. What kinds of long-term planning must Michelle do?

B. The Apple Tree Learning System

The Apple Tree Learning System began as a small organization dedicated to producing books and software for kindergartens and elementary schools. After establishing themselves in this area, Apple Tree expanded and began building learning centres for children aged 4 to 10 who were experiencing learning difficulties in traditional schools. Apple Tree Learning Centres are now operating in four provinces, have plans to expand into three more, and have residence learning centres in several provinces.

The five teachers who had the idea for Apple Tree continue to be actively involved in the operational aspects; however, their primary interest at this time is in the Apple Tree Learning Centres. When Apple Tree began, the records were kept in paper form; but as the tremendous expansion occurred, a consultant was brought in. He recommended (1) that a corporate records manager be employed to oversee the management of all company records; (2) that records clerks, who would be responsible to the corporate records manager, be employed in each of the learning centres; and (3) that the records of each child enrolled in the centres be stored according to their origination (i.e., records incoming from physicians, psychologists, psychiatrists, or other referrals be stored in lateral file cabinets while the records originating in house—teacher evaluations of student progress and other internal communications regarding a child—be maintained on computer hard disks).

1. What recommendations should the new corporate records manager make regarding access to the records areas?
2. What recommendations should the new corporate records manager make regarding access to the incoming student information?

3. What recommendations should the corporate records manager make regarding access to the student information generated internally?

SUGGESTED READINGS AND RESOURCES

Anderson, John C. "Brave New World: The Impact of Access Legislation on Retention in Alberta Municipalities." *Records Management Quarterly,* Vol. 29, No. 4 (October, 1995), p. 19.

ARMA International Filing Systems Subcommittee of the Standards Advisory and Development Committee, Association of Records Managers and Administrators. *Filing Procedures Guideline.* Prairie Village, Kansas, 1989.

Balon, Brett. "Secrecy and Authenticity." *Records Management Quarterly,* Vol. 29, No. 4 (October, 1995), p. 24.

Bolton, John. "Freedom of Information and Protection of Privacy Information." *Records Management Quarterly,* Vol. 30, No. 1 (January, 1996), p. 20.

Fernberg, Patricia M. "Risky Business: How Safe is Your Office?" *Modern Office Technology,* Vol. 34, No. 5 (May, 1989), p. 110.

Gooderham, Mary. "Living in the Data Shadow." *The Globe and Mail,* August 14 to August 20, 1993 (six parts).

Hill, Lisa B., and J. Michael Pemberton. "Information Security: An Overview and Resource Guide for Information Managers." *Records Management Quarterly,* Vol. 29, No. 1 (January, 1995), p. 14.

Lemieux, Victoria. "Selling Information: What Records Managers Should Know." *Records Management Quarterly,* Vol. 30, No. 1 (January, 1996), p. 3.

Leyzorek, Michael. "A Missing Feature in Some Records Management Systems." *Records Management Quarterly,* Vol. 25, No. 1 (January, 1991), p. 24.

Morgan, Owen J., and Miranda Welch. "Protecting Confidential Computer Records Against Careless Loss." *Records Management Quarterly,* Vol. 29, No. 3 (July, 1995), p. 16.

"Principles of Access Control." *Modern Office Technology,* Vol. 34, No. 11 (November, 1989), p. 44.

Roy, Patricia Graham, W.J. Kenny Jih, and Ashok Roy. "Computer Viruses: An Overview for Records Managers." *Records Management Quarterly,* Vol. 25, No. 2 (April, 1991), p. 18.

"Selecting an Access Control System." *Modern Office Technology,* Vol. 34, No. 11 (November, 1989), p. 53.

Tapscott, Don. "Going Public with the Issue of Privacy." *The Globe and Mail,* June 8, 1994.

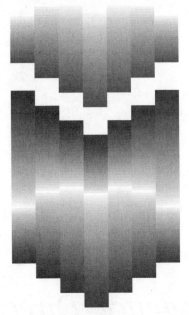

Part 6
Records Creation and Control

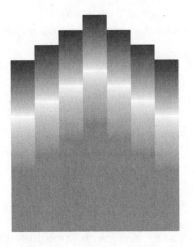

Correspondence, Directives, and Copy Management

Learning Goals

After completing this chapter, you should be able to:

1. Identify the goals of a correspondence management program.
2. Describe the procedures for determining the current status of a correspondence management program.
3. State the cost factors associated with correspondence.
4. Describe strategies for accomplishing the goals of a correspondence management program.
5. Explain methods for evaluating correspondence management.
6. Define directive.
7. Describe the steps in developing a directives management program.
8. Relate the importance of a classification system to directives management.
9. Describe the format of a directive.
10. Explain the rationale for a directives distribution system.
11. Describe copyright and methods to avoid copyright infringement.
12. Distinguish among copy practices, procedures, and devices.
13. Describe considerations in the selection of copy methods and printing methods.
14. Identify cost factors associated with copy functions.

In order to contain costs, every office should examine its practices relating to correspondence, directives, and copy management. Correspondence includes hard-copy letters and memorandums and electronic mail. As hard copy or electronic communications, directives are instructions from management that address policies or procedures. Making copies, usually by a photocopying process, has resulted in a dramatic increase in the volume of paper produced. Significant savings can result by controlling correspondence, directives, and copying practices.

CORRESPONDENCE MANAGEMENT

Correspondence management can reduce costs.

Correspondence management tends to be very loosely structured; therefore, written communication and the resulting records have grown at unprecedented rates. As the cost of management time has increased, the cost of other office personnel time has also increased. When these costs are combined with the expenses of paper, materials, storage and retrieval equipment, and all of the other peripheral costs of correspondence, correspondence management is essential. Hundreds of millions of dollars a year are spent to generate millions of documents, most of them paper—the paperless office is far from realization.

Program Goals

Program goals for the organization need to be determined. Goals of a program of correspondence management typically include improving correspondence quality, improving correspondence productivity, reducing correspondence costs, and facilitating correspondence storage and retrieval.

Organizations have differing emphasis on correspondence management goals.

Depending on specific needs, the emphasis placed on each goal will vary from organization to organization. One organization may need to place more attention on improving the quality of its correspondence and facilitating correspondence storage and retrieval; another may have to concentrate on improving productivity and reducing correspondence costs. Other organizations may find it necessary to focus on developing a program of correspondence management that encompasses all of these goals. This determination of emphasis on goals has to be made within each organization.

Improve Correspondence Quality

Correspondence quality is improved by clarity.

Letters, memorandums, and other written communications must be constructed in a way that clearly communicates the information and action desired. Correspondence should be written in such a way that the person receiving it should not have to decipher, draw inferences, or make assumptions about the intent of the writer. Nor should the correspondence present the recipient with additional questions to be answered before the requested action can be taken.

Improve Correspondence Productivity

Typically, there has been little improvement in the time required to produce correspondence. Also, the emphasis on productivity improvement has been in the administrative support area, with little attention given to the need for managers to increase correspondence productivity. Since managers earn 74 cents of each white-collar dollar, focus on management productivity would result in greater productivity returns.

Reduce Correspondence Costs

The costs of producing letters have increased dramatically—from 29.6 cents (U.S.) in 1930 to anywhere from $13.02 to $19.87 (U.S.) in 1995, according to the Dartnell Corporation's Institute of Business Research. The acceleration of correspondence costs, along with the increased volume of correspondence, makes reduction of costs essential.

Facilitate Correspondence Storage and Retrieval

Clearly written and coded correspondence facilitates retrieval.

A link exists between the creation of quality correspondence and the ability to properly store and efficiently retrieve correspondence. Clearly written, concise letters facilitate easier and faster identification both in the storage process and in retrieval.

 Learning Check: Can you describe the goals of a correspondence management program?

Determine Current Status

Prior to making any change in the correspondence program, the present procedures should be examined and evaluated. This examination and evaluation may lead to the determination that no formal procedures are in place; that the present procedures are effective; that the present procedures, with modifications, will be effective; or that new procedures need to be developed and implemented.

Survey Present Correspondence Procedures

Conduct a survey to identify current practices.

One of the ways to determine the present procedures is to conduct a survey to identify current correspondence practices, and the strengths and weaknesses within the present system. Some of the questions that provide data for the identification of strengths and weaknesses include the following:

- What percentage of the originator's time is spent in composing correspondence?
- What percentage of correspondence is dictated to a secretary or to a machine?
- What percentage of correspondence is composed in longhand?
- What percentage of correspondence is keyboarded by the manager on a computer and given to another worker for processing?
- How is the correspondence produced (word processing software, electronic mail)?

- How many hours a day is the dictation and word processing equipment in use?
- Are paper copies made of outgoing correspondence, and if so, how many copies are normally made?
- What is the average number of pages for letters? memorandums?
- What is the usual turnaround time? Is current turnaround time adequate?
- What percentage of correspondence does the originator require in rough-draft form?
- What percentage of correspondence is returned to the word processor for revision?
- To what extent are form letters, guide letters or guide paragraphs used?

In addition to conducting a survey, the records manager and the records staff may review a large sample of the organization's correspondence to determine the quality of the correspondence. This review allows identification of organization-wide problems in correspondence quality as well as individual weaknesses in correspondence creation.

Collect copies of all correspondence.

Another approach to reviewing organizational correspondence is to require an extra copy of all correspondence to be forwarded to the records manager; this should be done for a short period of time—perhaps two weeks. The copies should be forwarded on a daily basis to allow the records manager and the records staff time to review the correspondence in small quantities. Either approach allows the records manager to obtain the kind of information needed to begin the evaluation of the present correspondence program.

Evaluate Current Correspondence Procedures

An analysis of the survey responses and the correspondence sampling provides information from which judgments may be made regarding correspondence quality and the efficiency of the correspondence management program. The results of this evaluation should be used as the basis for recommendations regarding the program.

 Learning Check: Can you describe procedures for determining the current status of a correspondence management program?

Analyze Cost Factors

Each organization needs to be aware of cost-effective correspondence.

Communication costs associated with correspondence are an important consideration for any organization as it attempts to meet the information needs of its managers in a cost-effective manner. Correspondence costs can be categorized as origination, processing, maintenance, distribution, and user time costs.

Correspondence origination costs are those costs directly related to the writing and research time necessary to draft correspondence. Origination costs are difficult to determine accurately as most originators make little effort to clearly define actual time spent in document creation.

Correspondence processing costs are the costs involved in actual preparation of the document; these costs include equipment, materials, supplies, and administrative support.

Correspondence maintenance costs are the costs associated with storing and retrieving correspondence.

Correspondence distribution costs are the costs related to distributing correspondence to appropriate recipients.

Correspondence user costs are those costs that represent user time—the time necessary for the recipient to efficiently interpret and use the information. User costs are directly related to the quality and timeliness of the information. For example, a poorly written letter will require more of the user's time to interpret and follow through on requested action than a clearly written letter that leads the user directly to the action required.

An analysis of each of the correspondence factor costs identifies areas in which the records manager and staff should focus their attention in their efforts to improve the organization's correspondence management program. The chart in Figure 13-1, from Dartnell Corporation, illustrates one method of determining letter costs.

The records management staff can help correspondence improvement efforts.

 Learning Check: Can you state the cost factors associated with correspondence creation?

Develop Plan for Accomplishing Goals

After the correspondence program goals have been clearly identified, a plan for accomplishing these goals must be developed. Specific strategies that lead to reaching the established goals should be included in the plan. These recommendations become a part of the working plan and are incorporated into the total package when it is presented to top management for endorsement.

Improve Correspondence Quality

Managers have to regard any changes as beneficial.

The development of guidelines for effective writing and a program of assistance for developing writing skills are used to improve the quality of an organization's correspondence. The records manager and staff provide the originator with guidelines that allow for more efficient achievement of correspondence responsibilities. For these guidelines to be accepted, managers must regard them as beneficial rather than as additional red tape or rules that must be followed. Standard procedures can be more efficiently presented in a correspondence manual or guide.

Figure 13-1
Letter Costs

Determining The Cost Of One Letter

Cost Factor	Average Cost	Your Cost	Determining Cost
Dictator's Time . . . For the cost, it was established that the executive received an average weekly salary of $920 and takes approximately 8 minutes to dictate a single business letter.	$3.07		Based on a 40-hour week, this cost is determined by calculating an executive's salary for 8 minutes.
Secretarial Time . . . Based on a salary of $396 for the secretary, this figure includes all the time involved from dictation through filing of the letter.	$2.97		This cost is obtained in the same manner as the dictator's cost, using 18 minutes for all time involved.
Nonproductive Labour . . . This is the time consumed by both dictator and secretary that is not directly productive when a letter is being prepared. It has been set at 15% of labour costs for both.	$0.91		This cost is arrived at from the use of previous studies. It is especially aimed at interruptions during dictation or transcription and time lost when participants are involved in producing a letter.
Fixed Charges . . . A catchall charge that wraps up the share of overhead, depreciation, taxes, heating, etc. given to the letter. It also includes the fringe benefits share for the time consumed by letter preparers. Set at 52% of total labour costs.	$3.14		This is that necessary cost of doing business that is allocated to one letter handled by all of the people involved using all of the equipment, etc. involved.
Materials Costs . . . Stationery, envelopes, carbon paper, copy machine paper, typewriter ribbons and cartridges and other supplies needed to get out a letter.	$0.29		This cost is easily arrived at if you maintain records covering your supplies and basic equipment expenses. Multiple copies cost extra money.
Mailing Costs . . . First class postage (25¢) added to cost of labour for gathering, sealing, stamping, sorting done by personnel other than the secretary.	$0.47		If you are using more express mail for your correspondence, this cost could go much higher. Otherwise it is easy to determine.
	TOTAL COST $10.85	**YOUR COST**	

It should be pointed out that the figures presented here are based on a formula to determine the cost of a single, traditional boss-secretary type of letter dictated face-to-face with the secretary completing the transcribing and connected filing. Communications with repetitive copy, lengthy reports and/or bids are not represented in this survey.

Copyright © 1990, The Dartnell Corporation

Source: *Adapted from Dartnell's Target Survey, Dartnell Institute of Business Research, 1990.*

Improve Correspondence Productivity

There are a number of practical ways in which the production of letters, memorandums, and other forms of correspondence can be improved and the quality of the output enhanced. Some of these methods include the use of

- **Preprinted form letters.** Preprinted form letters save time in preparation, especially for mass mailings. In organizations where similar requests and inquiries are frequent and where similar responses are used, a file of form letters is a cost-saving device.

- **Guide letters and paragraphs.** Guide letters provide a suggested pattern of responses for routine letters and project a more personalized appearance. Guide letters and paragraphs can be stored in the word processing system and merged automatically with a list of names and addresses.

- **Alternatives to hard-copy correspondence.** Hard copy (paper) has been the primary mode of correspondence for most organizations. Only in the past few years have other alternatives become feasible. As technological advances become more economical and integrated systems more prevalent, dependence on hard copy may be minimized. Alternative methods of correspondence fall into three major categories: electronic mail networks; telecommunications, including telephone, wire and satellite services, teleconferencing, facsimile transmission, voice mail, and communicating computers and word processors; and microforms.

- **Use of word processing equipment and word processing software.** As personnel costs have increased, technology costs have decreased correspondingly. One of the alternatives to hiring more people is to use word processing and to take advantage of the benefits of the decreased cost of technology while improving productivity.

- **Standardized format.** A standard format for letters, memos, and other written correspondence provides for more efficient production of the correspondence. A standard format saves time. The processor is familiar with the format; therefore, decisions about placement of letter parts, margins, tabs, and other variables do not have to be made.

- **Productivity standards.** To schedule and control routine work effectively, a manager should know how much work the employees are capable of performing (work standards), the status of work in progress and scheduled (work load), how much work is received (volume), and how much employees are doing in relation to work scheduled (work performance). The first step is to establish the unit of work against which performance will be judged. An ongoing program can aid in determining how many

Hard-copy correspondence is not the only method to use.

people are needed to perform certain functions, how to cope with peak work loads, and how to evaluate the performance of individual workers.

Reduce Correspondence Costs

Training improves correspondence quality at creation.

There is a reverse correlation between correspondence costs and correspondence productivity. Therefore, as the productivity increases through use of a combination of the previously discussed methods, correspondence costs decrease.

Additional reductions in costs may be obtained by providing training and making information available to managers so that they are more skilled in correspondence creation. Training and information should also be made available to those who process the correspondence so that they spend less time in producing, revising, distributing, storing, and retrieving correspondence.

Facilitate Correspondence Storage and Retrieval

A clear writing style makes it easier to index and code records, and they are then easier to store and retrieve. The person coding the record should be able to quickly identify where the record should be stored. The record can be quickly retrieved if it has been properly coded and stored.

 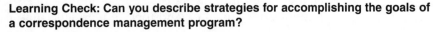 **Learning Check: Can you describe strategies for accomplishing the goals of a correspondence management program?**

Disseminate New Procedures

One way to disseminate information is through a correspondence manual.

Written policies, procedures, and guidelines are essential for establishing and maintaining uniform procedures for correspondence management. The correspondence manual is one tool for providing information regarding standardization in preparation and distribution of letters, memorandums, and other written communications. The correspondence manual may be a part of a comprehensive records management manual, be integrated in a communications manual, or be a separate publication.

The manual should be distributed to all persons who originate and process correspondence. To be effective on a continuing basis, the distribution list should be updated as a part of routine management procedures. Manual preparation and use are discussed in Chapter 16.

Establish Correspondence Evaluation Program

Any new or established program should be monitored for evaluative purposes.

Procedures should be established for monitoring the total correspondence control program so that this very important function is done in an efficient, orderly manner. Decisions should be made regarding how often a program review should be made, how extensive the review should be, who should conduct the review, and what methods should be utilized to gather data.

An in-depth review should be conducted at least every three years for an ongoing, effective program. A new program would require more frequent monitoring, perhaps annually. It is not desirable, however, to allow a new program to operate through the entire year without frequent progress checks. The progress checks could be made quarterly.

Scheduled reviews should be used to evaluate the program.

Several methods may be used to evaluate the correspondence control program. These methods include monitoring the standards, using program checklists, and obtaining feedback.

Monitor Standards

Established standards of performance should be monitored on a regular basis. This procedure will help to determine whether the standards are reasonable, whether the standards are being adhered to, and whether the standards need to be revised to reflect more realistic performance expectations.

Use Checklists

Checklists may be developed to assist the records manager and staff in determining the strengths and weaknesses of the correspondence management program. Checklists allow a number of issues to be addressed in a consistent manner, and they require little time for completion.

Obtain Feedback

Feedback, in many forms, is valuable.

Feedback should be requested from employees, and they should feel free to express their opinions. The feedback may be obtained through both formal and informal, and structured and unstructured methods. On a formal, structured basis, scheduled observations and interviews, formal surveys, and correspondence sampling may be conducted with conclusions drawn from the information obtained. On an informal, unstructured basis, feedback may be obtained from interviews with users and from informal observation of the effectiveness of the program. Information gained from both types of feedback is valuable, and the methods are usually complementary.

Learning Check: Can you explain methods of evaluating correspondence management?

DIRECTIVES MANAGEMENT

A directive communicates information.

A **directive** is an instruction from management—a form of downward communication—usually addressing policy or procedure. It communicates information from managers to individuals who have a need to know or are required to act. Directives may include policies, procedures, notices, orders, guidelines, rules, and regulations—any of the many formal communications that provide direction from upper management about what, why, how, when, and by whom action is to be taken. The purpose of directives management is to provide clear instructions for action and to minimize duplicative or conflicting instructions.

 Learning Check: Can you define "directive"?

Records Management Responsibilities

Responsibility for operating the directives program should be placed in a single, specific unit of the organization. The responsibility for directives management may be assigned to the records management staff, although frequently no one unit has responsibility for directives.

The contact person coordinates the program.

For consistency, a contact person should be selected from within each office or department. This contact person is responsible for coordinating directives activities with the records management department. The contact person also sets the tone of cooperation within the department and establishes good working relationships with the records management staff.

Develop Directives Management Program

To plan an effective directives management program, the volume, content, currentness, and distribution of directives in place should be determined. This is accomplished by inventorying and analyzing existing directives, determining the content, establishing the format, and developing a conversion schedule.

Inventory and Analyze Directives

An inventory of each directive is the first step in the development program.

An inventory of all directives should be conducted. The inventory should include a copy of each directive issued by a department, office, or unit. The contact person can be very helpful in the inventory process by securing copies of the directives and forwarding the copies along with an inventory to the records management department, where the directives will be grouped into broad subject categories and obsolete directives separated from current ones.

The directives are then returned to the contact person in the **originating unit**—the department creating the directive or office responsible for the function or subject described in the directive. The originating office reviews the directives for possible revisions, deletions, or discarding. Directives may also be condensed, consolidated, rearranged, or rewritten. The directives, including revised and deleted materials, are returned to the records management department.

Determine Directive Content

Directives may be classified as long-term or temporary. Long-term directives remain in effect until cancelled or revised. Temporary directives have a short life, designated by the specific time of effectiveness on the directive. Immediately upon the date of expiration, the temporary directive is destroyed. By carefully following this procedure, obsolete directives are not confused with permanent ones.

Directives usually address policy, procedure, or both. **Policy** statements provide guidelines for making decisions; **procedure** statements tell how to implement the policies. A policy might state that "each user should have access to appropriate records in a timely manner to promote efficient and effective decision making at the lowest cost." The procedures statements would define the steps for accomplishing this policy.

The subject of a directive is determined by the originating unit. The originating unit also assures that content is complete, accurate, and appropriate; does not duplicate or conflict with existing directives; and complies with program controls. For example, if a directive requires completing a form, the originating office should review the form with a forms analyst to ensure that the form is properly designed and economically printed and that adequate supplies of the form are available.

Actual writing of the directive is also the responsibility of the originating office. A printed, illustrated directive coordination sheet should be used where feasible. Hundreds of words can be replaced with an illustration of a properly completed form with annotated instructions for its preparation.

Where multiple departments are involved, primary responsibility for approval lies with the originator. However, all the departments involved can review the directive concurrently to save time.

Establish Directive Format

A standard format should be used for all directives. If originators are required to put their thoughts in an organized, logical format, the directive is better organized. Users receive a directive that contains all the necessary information, and they know that vital information is always found in the same place on all directives.

All directives should include the following information, though they are not limited to the format shown in Figure 13-2.

1. The **name of the issuing or originating unit** appears at the top of the directive and at the top of each succeeding page.
2. The **directive number** appears in the upper right-hand corner of the first page and on all succeeding pages. If back and front pages are used, the directive number appears in the upper left-hand corner of even-numbered pages and in the upper right-hand corner of odd-numbered pages.

Figure 13-2
Directives Format

1 HUMAN RESOURCES DEPARTMENT

2 Directive No. 844

3 January 14, 199-

To: All Employees

Subject: Absence Without Leave

A. Policy Statement. The employee shall receive no pay for the time period he or she is absent without leave.

B. Purpose. The purpose of this policy is to establish a city-wide disciplinary guideline for unauthorized absences and to accomplish maximum utilization of available personnel resources.

   1. Definition. Absence without leave shall be defined as an absence from the job during a scheduled work period without approval of the employee's supervisor or department head.

   2. Applicability. All merit employees (as defined by Chapter 2—76.4 of the Code of the City of Marshall) are covered under this policy.

C. Disciplinary Process. The following disciplinary process shall be followed.

   1. The first occurrence of two consecutive workdays or less of absence without leave shall result in at least a reprimand with a copy to the *official* personnel file.

     (a) The severity of the reprimand shall be at the discretion of the supervisor.

     (b) The reprimand shall be made immediately upon the return of the employee to the workplace.

   2. The second occurrence of two consecutive workdays or less of absence without leave within a 12-consecutive-calendar-month period shall result in at least a suspension without pay.

D. Appeals Process. The following appeals process shall be followed.

   1. Within 10 days of the reprimand, the employee may appeal, in writing, to the supervisor. The appeal shall contain all relevant information.

   2. The supervisor's response shall be made within four working days from the date of receipt of the appeal.

   3. If the supervisor's original decision stands, the employee has the right to appeal to the Grievance Committee.

     (a)   The appeal must be made within five working days of the receipt of the supervisor's response.

     (b)   The appeal must contain a copy of the original appeal as well as a copy of the supervisor's response.

       (1) The Grievance Committee must respond within five working days.

       (2) The Grievance Committee must include a rationale for its decision.

       (3) The decision of the Grievance Committee is final.

     (c)   Copies of the decision of the Grievance Committee shall be sent to the employee, the supervisor, and to the employee's personnel file.

Distribution: 1C

3. The **date the directive takes effect** is shown just below the directive number. Usually the effective date is the same as the issue date. However, the directive may be retroactive or future-dated, if appropriate.

4. The **addressees** are indicated just below the issuing organization. Addressee identification must correspond with that used in the distribution list.

5. The **subject** appears just below the addressee. For filing purposes this wording should agree with the approved subject classification list.

6. The **content** follows an established pattern that allows for subdivisions. A suggested pattern is A. 1. (a) (i); each of the four symbols represents a finer subdivision of the paragraphs. All major paragraphs carry a heading; subparagraphs may carry headings to assist the reader. Generally, a directive follows this pattern: purpose; forms, reports, records required by the directive; narrative or text; and list of attachments or exhibits, as shown in Figure 13-2.

7. The **distribution code** appears as the last item on the first page. Some organizations prefer to use a distribution list. A code, however, is more efficient in large organizations.

Learning Check: Can you describe the format for a directive?

White paper is more practical than coloured paper for policy and procedure directives.

Some organizations use different colours of paper to distinguish between policy directives and procedures directives. However, white paper is more practical to use for all types because a less expensive printing and binding process is required and only one colour of paper is stocked. Also, the policy statement and the implementation procedures can be placed on the same page of the directive.

Develop Conversion Schedule

After the directives and their revisions and deletions are returned to the records management department, a decision about which directives are to be immediately incorporated into the program is made. The directives requiring substantial revision would not be included in the program at this point. A conversion schedule is then developed to show at what point additional directives will be integrated into the program.

Learning Check: Can you describe steps in developing a directives management program?

Develop Classification System

A subject classification system for directives allows all directives relating to one subject to be filed together. This eliminates the necessity for looking in more than one place for related information.

The subject of the directive is the basis for classification.

The classification system should be based on the subject of the directive—*not* on whom the directive affects, whom it is from, or to whom it is addressed. The preliminary basis for establishing the classification system is from the directives inventory conducted during the planning phase. When the central clearing staff originally categorizes the directives, the directives are divided into broad subject areas. Subject classification for each directive is assigned by the originating office so the central clearing point staff can verify the subject and the classification number.

Subjects may be primary, secondary, or tertiary.

The classification system uses a primary subject and secondary or tertiary subject designators if appropriate. The words chosen for the subjects must be short, simple, and commonly understood by the users. For example, a section of a subject classification system for directives about the broad human resources category might have a secondary subject, such as compensation.

Once subjects have been determined, a numbering system is selected that permits expansion and distinguishes between consecutive directives on the same subject. Chapter 6 describes the subject-numeric classification system, which suits directives very well.

 Learning Check: Can you relate the importance of a classification system to directives management?

Implement Directives Management Program

The manual and distribution system are key to program implementation.

Implementation of the directives management program includes preparing the directives manual and determining a distribution system for directives. Both of these activities are important to successful implementation of the program.

Prepare Directives Manual

The **directives manual** consolidates all the organizational directives, including the primary document—the directive on directives—in one place. The directives manual may be a separate publication or may be a part of the records management manual. Employees may reference any current directive without having to refer to a number of sources. All directives referring to any one subject are placed together in the directives manual.

Content. The directives manual contains a title page, a table of contents, an alphabetic subject index, a numeric index, the directive on directives, and a copy of each current directive.

The index is an important part of the directives manual.

Indexes are numeric and alphabetic subject listings. Each entry includes the directive number and subject title. Revisions must also be listed. A portion of a directives numeric index is shown in Table 13-1.

Table 13-1   **Portion of a Numeric Index**

Directive Number	Subject
320	Administrators and supervisors new to system, salary schedule guidelines
440	Hazardous work
514	Gifts to employees
611	Employee health examinations
630	Firearms, carrying of
640	Grievance procedures
644	Hospitalization plans
650	Employee leave—general
652	Jury duty
653	Employee leave for illness/death in family
654	Employee disability benefits, long-term
656	Employee annual leave
657	Employee educational leave
680	Employment of relatives

A separate alphabetic subject index is useful.

Before the quantity of directives makes finding directives and using the manual a time-consuming task, create an alphabetic subject index. The alphabetic subject index is an alphabetic listing of words and terms by which an employee may reference the directives. Each index entry includes the index word or term selected and the subject classification number. A separate index entry should be made for each key word when the classification contains two or more key words. This index is similar to the index in the back of a book. A copy of the index must be maintained in all manuals. A portion of an alphabetic subject index is shown below in Table 13-2.

Table 13-2   **Portion of an Alphabetic Subject Index**

Subject	Directive Number
EMPLOYEES	
Administrators and supervisors new to system, salary schedule guidelines	320
Disability benefits, long term	654
Employment of relatives	680
Firearms, carrying of	630
Gifts to employees	514
Grievance procedures	640
Health examinations	611
Hospitalization plans	644
Hazardous work	440
Leave	
annual	656
educational	657
general	650
holiday	655
illness/death in family	653
jury duty	652

The directive on directives is the first directive in the manual.

The first directive in the directives manual is the one that provides authorization for the program—the **directive on directives.** This directive also provides originators with information regarding when directives should be written, how they should be written, how to obtain approval, and the procedures for distribution. The remaining portion of the directives manual contains all of the current organizational directives.

Changes and Revisions. An essential part of directives management is maintaining current contents. When a minor portion of a directive is changed, only the new pages are reissued. Users insert revised pages into their directives manuals and remove superseded pages. Each revision date is noted on the appropriate page. If major changes must be made in a directive, the entire directive is rewritten and reissued as a revised directive. Major revisions affect 40 percent or more of the directive.

One person in each unit or department has the responsibility for maintaining directives.

One person in each office should be assigned the responsibility for maintaining directives. This employee inserts any new directives in binders, removes and destroys cancelled material, circulates notices and transmittal sheets and then destroys them, checks the directives in the binder whenever a new numeric index is issued, posts changes to the numeric index when required, and obtains necessary copies of directives for replacement. Revised tables of contents and indexes for directives should be issued periodically or at least once a year.

Format. Most directives manuals are housed in some type of loose-leaf binding. This allows additions and deletions to be made with minimal effort and maintains grouping of directives according to subject. Use of tabbed divider sheets to indicate the primary subject classification number and key word(s) allows quicker reference.

Determine Distribution

Distribution is usually made according to a pattern established along organization lines. Distribution codes are assigned for each category of recipients. A control number is assigned to each directives manual as it is charged out to a particular individual.

Directives manuals are assigned to a title or function, not a specific person.

Distribution lists, like directives, must be kept up to date. Although people within the organization may change, the directives manual is assigned to a particular title or function. Individual offices are responsible for seeing that the manual is placed in the hands of the right person(s).

Transmittal sheets sometimes accompany directives. The transmittal sheet gives a summary of the contents of the directive, outlines changes that have occurred in a revision, or cancels a directive.

 Learning Check: Can you explain the rationale for a directives distribution system?

Evaluate Directives Management Program

An essential component of the directives management program is evaluation. Feedback provides the information necessary to determine how effective the directives are in supporting and contributing to management decision making and employee productivity. In addition, information gathered in the evaluation identifies needed improvements in the directives management program. Records managers should remember, however, that compliance with directives requirements does not guarantee program effectiveness. For example, an audit of originators and users might reveal that directives are being created, approved, and distributed but are either not received, not properly understood, or simply not implemented by the user groups.

COPY MANAGEMENT

Copy management is necessary to control copy proliferation.

The concept of copy management is relatively new. In the past several years, a rather remarkable phenomenon has occurred. While the cost per copy has decreased, total expenditures for copying have increased. Copying volume is rising at a much greater rate than copying costs.

A **copy** is a duplicate record—a reproduction of the original. The growth of relatively inexpensive, easy-to-operate, multifunction copying equipment to the office environment has resulted in a dramatic increase in the number of copies produced.

Here are some interesting statistics from the *Factmatcher Bulletin:*
- The average office keeps five copies of the same document in as many different places. There are an average of 26 other copies of that same document in other locations.
- The knowledge that a file copy even exists for a document is unknown 65 percent of the time.[1]

Copy management may be defined as the management of copying practices, procedures, and control devices to ensure the effective and economical creation of copies. Consideration is given to how people use the equipment (practices), to the requirements for duplicate records (procedures), and to the management and control of the copiers and duplicators (devices).

Practices, Procedures, and Devices

Copy practices, procedures, and devices are all important.

Economical creation refers not only to the cost per copy but also to the need to limit creation (or re-creation) to necessary business copies.

---

[1]*Factmatcher Bulletin #2*, Hawthorne, New York: International Technology Group Inc. (January, 1986).

A system must be designed to provide a comprehensive copying service that coordinates the three elements of the program—practices, procedures, and devices.

Copy Practices

Good copy practices require instruction in equipment use and application of common sense. New employees often are given no instruction in machine operation; this results in improper and sometimes damaging use of the equipment, wasted supplies, and poor copies. Employees familiar with efficient machine operation may be guilty of making "one more copy just in case" or rounding off the requested number. Good copy practices include checking for the following:

- **Acceptable copy.** When multiple copies are to be made of a document, a test copy should be made to see if it is acceptable.
- **Copy destination.** If the copy is for internal use and quality is not critical, legible copy should be accepted instead of discarding legible copy to attempt perfect copy.
- **Quantity indicator.** After copies are made, the quantity indicator should be returned to *1* so that the copier is ready for the next user. Some equipment automatically performs this function.
- **Type of paper in the feeder.** As in the case of the quantity indicator, failure to check the type of paper in the feeder will result in a legal-sized document being copied on standard-sized paper or vice versa. Many copiers now automatically choose the paper size.
- **Staples, paper clips, and so forth.** Foreign objects cause the equipment to malfunction. The operator needs a work surface other than the copier for taking apart or assembling documents to avoid the possibility of objects falling into the mechanism.
- **Machine malfunction.** If the machine is not functioning properly, a note should be left on the copier so that the next user will not waste time and supplies.

As copiers become more sophisticated, appointing a "key operator" to train others in the efficient use of the machine and to maintain its performance level on a daily basis prevents inefficiencies. The key operator is not the copier operator, but rather the support person for the copier and its users.

Copy Procedures

A copying activity profile provides needed information.

Copy procedures for controlling duplicate copies must be developed based on the unique needs of each office or department, focusing on copy creation rather than copy production. In order to determine basic copy requirements, attention is given to developing a current copying activity profile. The profile should include the following:

- Kinds of documents routinely copied (including personal and unauthorized copies);
- Purpose served by copies (information copy; copies of forms, directives, and other documents that should be obtained through supply channels; and so forth);
- Urgency of copying requirements;
- Copying requiring special handling for either copy quality, confidentiality of documents, or other unique requirements;
- Volume of copying;
- Composition of copying (one copy of 75 documents or 75 copies of one document); and
- Procedure for validating need prior to copying.

Based on the profile, each office or department can have an analysis prepared of its unique requirements. Then, ways of improving information distribution and eliminating copying costs resulting from inefficient practices and procedures can be recommended.

Copyright

All types of media are covered under the copyright law.

Creators of original works have a right in most countries to control the use of their original work through copyright. Basically the right to copy, **copyright** is the sole right to produce or reproduce a work or any substantial part of it in any form and resides in most cases with the creator. In Canada, the Copyright Act and Copyright Rules prohibit others from copying a work without the creator's permission, which is why copyright is addressed here. Copyright applies to all original literary (including computer programs), musical, dramatic, and artistic works; it also applies to all kinds of recordings. Through international agreements, copyright is recognized and respected in most countries. The Universal Copyright Convention symbol of a copyrighted work is ©; it is often accompanied by a warning such as:

All rights reserved. No part of this publication may be reproduced, stored in a database or a retrieval system, or transmitted, in any form or by any means, electronic, mechanical, photocopying, recording, or otherwise, without prior written permission of the publisher.

The advent of photocopiers, tape recorders, the VCR, and the Internet has made the task of protecting original works even harder because copying materials is so easy to do yet so difficult to monitor. However, the penalties can be severe when anyone, knowingly or not, engages in **copyright infringement**—which occurs when anyone produces or reproduces a copyrighted work without permission. One area of great concern is the copying of computer software, depriving the creator of rightful sales or rentals. Software companies estimate they lose $316 million a year in Canada ($17.3 billion worldwide) in computer software theft. To a certain extent, this theft can be prevented by encryption—embedding a code in the software that scrambles its output, prevents its duplication, or tracks its use.

In addition, **copyright collectives**, licensing bodies that offer blanket licences to copy without seeking individual permission, are providing a way to prevent copyright infringement while at the same time allowing users to copy materials for legitimate reasons. On behalf of its members, the Canadian Reprography Collective (CANCOPY) negotiates with users such as schools and organizations the conditions and fees for photocopying copyrighted materials.

To avoid copyright infringement and its consequences, all users should check that their activities are covered under an agreement with a licensing collective or make an individual agreement with the creator of the work.

 Learning Check: Can you describe Canada's Copyright Act and methods of avoiding infringement of copyright?

Copy Control Devices

Copy control devices help limit copier use to authorized personnel.

Copy control devices are usually attached to copy machines to limit access to authorized users. More sophisticated versions of the mechanisms are available that not only control access but also provide an accountability system. With this system a transaction recorder unit controls, records, and accounts for use of copiers. Users identify themselves with access cards, or PIN (personal identification numbers) to unlock the machine.

Recorded data include the copier station, number of copies, the user, department code, and job category. The copies are then run, and the data are recorded on a digital tape cassette. Cassettes are processed by computer to produce usage reports that are given to the person responsible for copy control. The reports are also available in summary form to be distributed to department heads for their analysis. An additional function allows for charge-back to the user. Information provided through this report allows for a more objective evaluation of the current copying activity than a simple recording of the number of copies produced by each department in the aggregate. This information, combined with the procedural analysis previously discussed, provides the basic data for the development of a comprehensive copy management system that is designed to meet the needs of individual users. Figure 13-3 shows one type of copy control device.

Learning Check: Can you distinguish among copy practices, procedures, and control devices?

Figure 13-3
Copy Control
Device

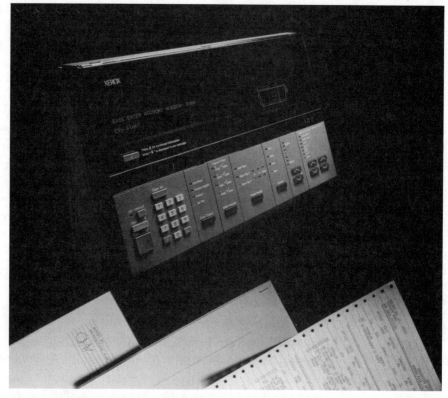

Source: Courtesy of Xerox Corporation

Selection of Method

Copies may be produced using convenience copiers, contracted services, quick copy centres, and in-house printing plants. The choice should be matched to the copying needs of the organization—the number of copies required of a single document, the complexity of the job, the quality required, and the cost related to each alternative method.

In-House Facilities

In-house copy
facilities are
located within the
company.

Copy services can be categorized as in-house or contracted. **In-house copy facilities** are located within an organization as either a centralized or decentralized operation. A centralized operation is one in which all copying is produced in one place—a copy centre or a printing plant. A decentralized operation provides copying capabilities in locations throughout the organization; access is usually controlled by an access key or code.

Decentralized operations are usually more convenient and provide quicker turnaround time than centralized systems. Turnaround time is controlled by the availability of personnel to make the copies and the availability and accessibility of the equipment. Centralized operations generally require a greater turnaround time, and the paperwork involved in requesting any form of centralized copying is greater than that required in a decentralized operation. Decentralized operations, however, can be more difficult to control as more people have free access to the equipment, and the operation itself is far less formal than in a centralized operation.

Self-Service Copiers

Unattended, self-service copiers are often referred to as **convenience copiers** because they are located throughout the facility to provide for convenient copies. Each office makes its own copies by using an access key or code to operate the machine. Convenience copiers range from desktop machines to floor models that perform multiple tasks. Small desktop models are often restricted to one copy at a time and may be limited to single sheets of paper; there may be no capacity for copying bound pages. At the other end of the range is the large floor model that copies in black and white, and in colour, makes transparencies, collates, duplexes (produces doubled-sided copies), adjusts for dark or light originals, reduces, enlarges, accommodates several paper sizes, and feeds automatically. Many companies offer leasing arrangements rather than outright purchase since multifunction machines and new copiers with added features are constantly being introduced. Figure 13-4 shows a typical photocopier.

Figure 13-4
Photocopier

Source: Courtesy of Xerox Canada Limited

Match copiers to
their intended use.

The copier should be matched to the use. The cost of making one copy of a document may vary widely from machine to machine because high-capacity, multiple-task machines are used to make too few copies. Self-service unattended copiers are usually recommended for runs of fewer than 50 copies; some organizations recommend 25 copies as the upper limit for convenience copiers. Many of the copiers are limited to 25 copies per run if sorting is required.

Attended Multifunction Copiers

The more sophisticated attended floor model copiers that are centrally located perform more functions than self-service copiers. In addition to the various functions possible with self-service copiers, the attended copiers may pad, staple, fold, cut, bind, slipsheet, and add covers. They may also offer more than one size reduction or enlargement and accept continuous unburst computer printouts. For some organizations attended copiers fill quick copy needs for 50 to 250 copies.

Control of equipment purchase should be centralized, and criteria for selection of machines should be based on the proposed use of the copiers. Figure 13-5 shows some of the considerations in selecting the right copier for an organization.

Figure 13-5
Copier Selection
Considerations

How To Determine Your Copier Specs

Address these questions to determine if you need a certain specification on your copier:

- **Copying process.** Does the copier use dry or liquid toner or ink?
- **Configuration.** Is the copier small enough for a desktop or large enough to stand alone on the floor? Can it be moved around on a cart?
- **Original.** Can we make copies of books, magazines and large sheets?
- **Copy size.** How large and small in inches can copies be made?
- **Reproduction ratio.** How many sizes of copies can be made from the same original?
- **Warm-up time.** How long does it take for the machine to function each time it is turned on?
- **First-copy speed.** How many seconds does it take for one copy or for the first copy to be made?
- **Copying speed.** After the first copy, how many copies does the machine produce in a minute?
- **Quantity indicator.** How many copies can be made before accessing the start key again?
- **Paper feed.** How many sheets can be put into the paper feed bin for any given run?
- **Copy-paper weight.** What are the heaviest and lightest weights of paper that can be fed for legible copies?
- **Copy-run interrupt.** How is the copying process stopped without losing count of how many pages were produced and how many still have to be done?
- **Power consumption.** How much will running a copier 8 hours a day, 20 days a month cost?
  In general, refuse to accept an answer you don't understand. Always respond to such an answer with, "What will that do to increase or decrease my expenses if I purchase your copier?"

Source: "A Look at the Future in Copier Technology," Office Systems '90, Vol. 7, No. 3 (March, 1990), p. 42.

Centralized copy control not only allows for uniformity in selection, but also minimizes the proliferation of printing and copying centres. Responsibility for monitoring facilities and equipment selection to assure that capacities are matched to requirements should be vested in the office of the records manager. High-volume use of convenience copiers reduces the cost per copy but results in higher total copying costs. As discussed earlier, this is a major trend and one that must be managed.

Centralized copy control allows for uniformity in selection.

Quick Copy

Quick copy is a centralized system representing one of the forms of in-house copying. A paper master is produced on equipment that resembles a copier. To produce the copies, the paper master is placed on a printing press—an offset printing operation. Copies made via quick copy are of high quality—usually higher than copies made on convenience copiers. Economically, it is not feasible to run fewer than 50 copies by using the quick copy method. Because of the breakdown of the image on the master, quick copying is generally not recommended for more than 700 copies.

Turnaround time varies according to the capacity of the in-house printing facility, the schedule, and the demand on the system. Most organizations aim for 24-hour turnaround. Because this is a centralized operation, completed paperwork must accompany the material to be copied.

Printing

Printing is for large, complex copying jobs.

When more than 700 copies are needed or when the job is a complex one that uses a number of photographs, illustrations, or colours, printing is the appropriate method. The decision should be based on size, content, complexity, and cost of the material to be copied. Phototypesetting equipment, compatible with copiers and word processing equipment, is available so that direct transfer from the copier or word processor may be made to the phototypesetting equipment.

Desktop Publishing

Some organizations have software programs that allow them to develop complex documents in-house and, depending on the quality and quantity needed, may print the output themselves or send it outside for printing.

Contracted Services

Organizations with minimal copying needs that will not justify equipping, staffing, and operating an in-house printing system use the services of outside printing contractors. Some organizations, while maintaining their own in-house printing facility, may still find it necessary to contract some jobs that their own operation cannot accommodate because of the size, complexity, or urgency of the printing job. Many firms, however, have found that operating their own print facility has produced very positive results.

A combination of printing services may be appropriate.

Many organizations use a combination of services. Convenience copiers may be strategically located for making a minimal number of copies; a quick copy centre may be operated to accommodate multiple copies when quality copy is important; a print shop may be located within the facility; and outside printing services may be contracted. Any combination of these services may meet the needs of the organization.

 Learning Check: Can you describe considerations in the selection of copy methods and printing methods?

Cost Factors

Costs of copying are important to the company.

The cost factors associated with copies are important to any organization as it attempts to provide information to users within imposed budget constraints. Costs of copying can be categorized as processing, maintenance, distribution, and user time costs.

Copy processing costs are the costs involved in making necessary copies; these costs include equipment and equipment maintenance, materials, supplies, and administrative support time.

Copy maintenance costs are the costs related to storing and retrieving the copies.

Copy distribution costs are the costs associated with distributing the copies to the appropriate recipients.

Copy user costs are those costs that represent user time—the time necessary for the recipient to efficiently interpret and use the information. User costs are directly related to the quality and timeliness of the information. A poorly reproduced copy will require more of the user's time to interpret and to follow through on a requested action than a copy that is clear and easy to read.

 Learning Check: Can you identify cost factors associated with copy functions?

Evaluation

Success of the program depends on the degree to which the program objectives are met.

In the final analysis, success will be based on the degree to which the objectives of the program are met. If the objectives are to ensure effective and economical creation of necessary copies, then the success of the control program must be measured by the degree to which these objectives are achieved.

TERMINOLOGY REVIEW

Review the terms listed below in the Glossary on page 521.

convenience copier   directive on directives
copy   directives manual
copy control device   in-house copy facilities
copy management   originating unit
copyright   policy
copyright collective   procedure
copyright infringement   quick copy
directive

REVIEW AND DISCUSSION

1. Identify the four major goals of a correspondence management program.
2. Describe the procedures for determining the current status of a correspondence management program.
3. State the cost factors associated with correspondence creation.
4. Describe two strategies for accomplishing each of the goals of a correspondence management program.
5. Explain three methods for evaluating correspondence management.
6. Define directive.
7. Describe the steps in planning a directives management program.
8. Relate the importance of an appropriate classification system to directives management.
9. Describe the format of a directive.
10. Explain the rationale for a directives distribution system.
11. Explain what copyright means and how to avoid copyright infringement.
12. Distinguish among copy practices, procedures, and control devices.
13. Describe considerations in the selection of copy methods and printing methods.
14. Identify cost factors associated with copy functions.

APPLICATIONS

1. As director of printing and publications, you have been asked to recommend the most appropriate method for copying the following materials:
   a. 150 copies of a memo
   b. 22 copies of a letter for intracompany distribution
   c. 800 copies of a questionnaire
   d. 350 copies of a colour brochure

    e. 15 copies of an advertisement including several photographs

    f. 10 very high-quality copies of a proposal to be submitted for funding a $2.4 million contract

2. Outline the format for a directive.

3. Using the format shown in this chapter, write a directive to establish a policy, procedure, or regulation regarding an issue that your instructor assigns. Suggested issues might include establishing a dress code, tardiness policy, class attendance policy, procedure for applying to a sorority or fraternity, or a regulation regarding smoking or alcohol use on campus.

CONCLUDING CASES

A. Merchandise Mart Wholesalers

Meg Richards is manager of the administrative services division of Merchandise Mart Wholesalers. One of Meg's responsibilities is to approve all expenditures for office equipment and supplies.

    Meg has just received purchase requisitions for 45 new five-drawer cabinets. These requests represent an increase of 50 percent over the previous year. Meg is surprised by the increase and concerned about the cause(s) for the increase.

1. What steps might Meg take to determine the cause(s) of this increase in requisitions for storage equipment?

2. What steps can be taken to contain future requests for storage equipment?

B. McKinney, McNamara, and Associates

Rita McKinney, after serving for a number of years as records manager in a major utilities company, has opened her own very successful consulting business—McKinney, McNamara, and Associates. Jim McNamara was brought in after the first year of operation as a partner because of his management expertise and experience as owner of a family-operated clothing business. Rita now employs 15 consultants, who have expertise in areas ranging from technical writing to management information systems. She has been more than satisfied with their performances until recently; there appear to be major misunderstandings among the staff. Rita, believing in the importance of employee participation in decision making, has allowed a high level of decentralization. In an effort to determine the source(s) of the staff misunderstandings, Rita has the following conversation with Roberto Dietz, one of the consultants.

    Rita: There appears to be some communication problem within the company, and I'd like your thoughts on what the problem is.

    Roberto: Well, Rita, to be honest with you, I simply do not know what the policies of this company are. It seems that when I make a decision, someone says, "That's not company policy." I find that I've violated something I didn't even realize existed!

Rita: Are there other problems?

Roberto: Yes, often when I am working on a consulting job, the client tells me he simply doesn't understand our company's procedures. As I'm not sure of the company's policies or procedures, it's difficult to offer an explanation.

How can I explain something that I don't know about?

1. Identify two major problems that Rita must recognize.
2. What would you suggest as Rita's first action?
3. What other actions must she take?
4. With whom does the responsibility for poor communications reside?

SUGGESTED READINGS AND RESOURCES

Cady, Peg. "A Look at the Future in Office Technology." *Office Systems '90,* Vol. 7, No. 3 (March, 1990), p. 42.

Cannata, Frank G. "Copying Machines are Cost Effective." *Office Systems '88,* Vol. 5, No. 3 (March, 1988), p. 28.

Dykeman, John B. "The Paperwork You Save May Be Your Own." Editorial. *Modern Office Technology* (December, 1989), p. 10.

Fernberg, Patricia M. "High-Volume Copying Doesn't Tax Their Machines." *Modern Office Technology,* Vol. 33, No. 10 (October, 1988), p. 66.

Fernberg, Patricia M. "Mastering the Basics." *Modern Office Technology,* Vol. 34, No. 7 (July, 1989), p. 64.

"High Volume Copying: In-House or Outsource." *Managing Office Technology,* June, 1995, p. 49.

Kaplan, James S. "Match Copier Selections to What the User Wants." *Office Systems '87,* Vol. 4, No. 11 (November, 1987), p. 38.

LeGallee, Julie. "Copier Technology Improves with New Features and Uses." *The Office,* Vol. 117, No. 4 (April, 1993), p. 38.

Long, G. Gordon. "Copier Technology and What You Require." *Office Systems '89,* Vol. 6, No. 7 (July, 1989), p. 56.

Marco, Joe. "Acquiring a Copier to Fit Your Needs." *Office Systems '90,* Vol. 7, No. 3 (March, 1990), p. 35.

Morgan, Cindra. "Uncontrolled Use of Photocopiers Breeds Inefficiency." *The Office,* Vol. 117, No. 3 (March, 1993), p. 20.

"The Office Buyer's Guide to Copier Control Systems." *The Office,* Vol. 117, No. 2 (February, 1993), p. 24.

Thompson, Jim. "A Strategic Approach to Copier Selection." *Office Systems '88,* Vol. 5, No. 11 (November, 1988), p. 38.

Forms and Reports Management

Learning Goals

After completing this chapter, you should be able to:

1. Define the function of forms within an organization.
2. List and explain the benefits of a forms management program.
3. Explain the importance of top management support for forms management.
4. Describe the steps to be taken in completing a forms analysis.
5. Differentiate among the types of forms files.
6. List and explain the guidelines for forms design.
7. List and describe the categories of software available for forms design and management.
8. Define the function of reports within an organization.
9. Differentiate between the responsibilities of the records manager and those of other managers for reports management.
10. Outline the procedures to be followed in establishing a reports management program.
11. Explain the importance of a report review request form (or similar form) in the reports management program.
12. List and explain the criteria that should be applied when establishing or reviewing report requirements.
13. Differentiate between the types of reports files.
14. Explain the need for periodic report evaluation.
15. Describe how the use of computer technology can result in more efficient distribution of reports within an organization.

Gathering and processing information is a critical task in every organization. The quality, completeness, and usability of the information gathered affect the productivity of administrative support personnel; the accuracy of many business operations, such as accounting and personnel functions; and the quality of most business decisions.

Forms and reports are the two types of business documents used in gathering, processing, and distributing information. Forms are primarily used for information gathering and processing. Reports present data to management for use in decision making. Because each is very important to information processing within every organization, forms and reports management functions are essential in records management.

PROCESSING INFORMATION WITH FORMS

Forms are carefully designed documents used to gather and transmit information necessary for operational functions and for historical records. For example, an invoice received by an organization is a record of a purchase, which is used to make a payment. Once paid, the invoice becomes part of the organization's historical records and provides documentation of items purchased, total amount of purchases by category for a month or year, or total purchases from a particular vendor. Traditionally, forms have been preprinted on paper media. Today many organizations with computerized electronic information systems are using electronic forms. These forms, called **templates**, are blank forms stored electronically in an information processing system. They are displayed on a terminal, such as a microcomputer, for fill-in.

Forms Management

A **forms management program** is a records management function designed to achieve the efficient collection and distribution of information through the use of forms. The forms management program should ensure that all necessary information (and only necessary information) is collected in the most efficient manner and distributed to those who need the information. It is estimated that for every dollar spent to print a form, $20 to $80 is spent to process, copy, distribute, store, and destroy the forms. Therefore, it is imperative that only essential forms be used and that unnecessary forms be eliminated.

Objectives

An efficient forms management program should produce time and cost savings in information processing for the organization. These benefits are achieved through the accomplishment of four objectives: (1) forms creation control, (2) elimination of obsolete forms, (3) standardized format, and (4) standardized and streamlined information distribution.

Control Creation of Forms

A great temptation exists within organizations to create a new form to collect information for each task as a need is perceived. Often the required information is already being collected for another purpose in the same department or in another department. The organization must pay not only for the cost to design and print new forms but also for additional personnel costs for processing the forms. To control this problem, many organizations assign control of forms creation to one individual. The forms supervisor receives and reviews all requests for new forms to determine the need for the form and the most economical method of producing it.

Eliminate Obsolete Forms

Organizations without forms management programs often retain old forms that have not been used in years. Perhaps a new form has taken the place of the obsolete one, or there is no longer a need for the form. The old or unusable forms should be destroyed to make room for forms that are in use. The space occupied by obsolete forms is very costly. In addition, someone may use the obsolete forms still retained, wasting time and effort.

Standardize Formats

Most organizations have several forms that require some of the same information. Standardizing the order in which that information is requested increases the efficiency with which those forms can be completed and processed. Also, standardizing the manner in which fixed data, such as the organization name and address, appear on a printed form may result in printing economies.

Standardize and Streamline Distribution

A final benefit of a forms management program is that careful review of forms allows the distribution of information to be standardized and streamlined. The number of copies of each form must be justified so that those persons or departments who were receiving nonessential information merely because it is "nice to know" will no longer receive that information. Those persons or departments who receive essentially the same information from two or more forms will no longer have to deal with this duplication.

 Learning Check: Can you name four objectives of a forms management program?

ESTABLISHING A FORMS MANAGEMENT PROGRAM

If an organization has no forms management program, the records manager must carefully assess the benefits of such a program to the organization and present these to top management. This presentation is a critical task, as the support of top management is essential to the success of the program.

Top Management Support

Since fewer forms are used in executive offices than in most other offices of the organization, the records manager must collect data to support the need for the program and present the data to top management in a logical, businesslike manner. The goals of the presentation to top management on the need for a forms management program are to gain approval and to have top management communicate this approval to all departments of the organization. This communication will usually take the form of a directive that firmly establishes which individual has responsibility and authority for forms management. Top management support should be communicated in writing to ensure the recognition of the new forms management program and the individual responsible for it.

Forms Analysis

A new forms management program can be undertaken only with a thorough knowledge of the current status of forms within the organization. **Forms analysis** is the process of determining whether a form is necessary and, if so, how it should be designed to assure maximum efficiency. The first step in completing this analysis is to conduct a forms survey. Information obtained from the survey should include what forms are being used, what the purposes of these forms are, how effectively the forms are designed, who is using the forms, and what forms are no longer being used.

Survey Current Forms

A **forms survey** is an inventory, by department, of the forms currently in use or in stock. A survey form such as the one in Figure 14-1 is distributed to each department head. In addition to requesting copies of forms originated in that department, the survey form should request information that identifies the form, its purpose and type, the number of copies distributed, the persons or departments receiving copies, its frequency of use, the date it was last used, the date it was last revised, and its retention period.

This inventory provides the forms supervisor with a good overview of the current status of forms within the organization. Missing, duplicate, or inconsistent form numbers should identify unauthorized forms within each department. After being identified, unauthorized forms can be eliminated or replaced with legitimate forms. The forms survey also identifies the distribution path of each form. Analysis of these paths often reveals that copies are being distributed unnecessarily. Controlling distribution assists in controlling printing costs of the form and, more important, minimizes the indirect costs of time to complete, process, and store the forms.

Figure 14-1
Forms Survey
Form

FORMS SURVEY*									
DEPARTMENT _Accounting_　　　DIVISION _Payroll_　　　　　　DATE OF SURVEY _1/13/--_									
PREPARED BY _Pamela Mayes_　　APPROVED BY _Linda McLeod_									
Form No.	Title	Purpose	Type**	Frequency of Use	No. of Copies Distributed	Persons/ Departments Receiving Copies	Date of Last Use	Date of Last Revision	Retention Period
T101	Time sheet	compute pay	S	W	O	purchasing	weekly	1/91	2 yrs.

*Please attach three copies of each form listed.

**Identify the type of form as follows:　　C – carbon interleaved unit sets　　　S – single sheet
　　　　　　　　　　　　　　　　　　　　D – duplexed　　　　　　　　　　　　U – carbonless unit sets
F100-1　　　　　　　　　　　　　　　　　F – continuous feed
Rev. 9/90

Evaluate Flow of Forms

A minimum amount of time should be spent in transferring a form from one location to another. At least 75 percent of the time required to process a form should be working time. Consultation with users of forms will reveal if forms reach their destinations in a timely manner; for example, at off-peak work periods when the forms can be quickly processed.

Eliminate Inactive Forms

If the forms survey indicates that a particular form has not been used for a year or more, consideration should be given to eliminating that form or to combining the form with another one. Of course, further consultation with the department head should be undertaken before this decision is reached.

Establish Forms Files

At the time of the forms survey, three copies of each form inventoried should be collected to establish three necessary forms files—numeric, functional, and specifications.

A numeric forms file is a historical record.

A **numeric forms file** is established for each form in use. The numeric forms file becomes a historical record of that form and should contain such information as the original request for the form, a sample of the original form and each subsequent revision, a reorder record, and any correspondence related to that form.

A functional forms file helps locate duplicate forms.

The **functional forms file** groups forms according to their function or use. This grouping allows ready recognition of duplicate forms. So that there can be no misinterpretation of the contents, each classification title must be carefully selected to denote clearly the purpose of the forms contained in that file. Any lack of clarity may result in lost forms and may contribute to the design of new forms when forms are already available for a particular function.

A specifications forms file may help save money on printing costs.

A **specifications forms file** groups forms according to the manner in which they are printed. Consequently, all carbon-interleaved forms are filed together as are all single-sheet forms, continuous-feed forms, and so forth. Having these forms grouped together may contribute to printing economies if several forms of the same type can be reordered at the same time.

Consolidate Forms

Organizing all forms into functional files allows the forms analyst to easily identify those forms that serve the same function. If very small differences occur on two or more forms in terms of the information requested, it should be determined whether one of the duplicative forms could serve both purposes or whether one form could be designed to serve two or more similar purposes. Such consolidations of forms may be numerous in large organizations that have had no previous forms control, as each department may have designed its own form for its own purpose.

Evaluate Forms Design

A final step in forms analysis is the evaluation of forms design. Specific guidelines for designing new forms are discussed later in this chapter. At this point, the forms analyst will want to evaluate how well each existing form works from the standpoint of the originator and the user. If electronic equipment is available, determine if the form should be in an electronic format or in a paper format. The following questions may assist in this evaluation:

- Does the form request the required information in a concise, unambiguous manner?
- Is the information requested in a logical sequence?
- Is sufficient space provided to record the requested information?
- Would an electronic form be more efficient?

 Learning Check: Can you list the types of information obtained from a forms survey?

Establish Staff Responsibilities

Organization size affects scope of responsibilities.

Assignment of staff responsibilities varies greatly with the size of the organization. In a very small organization, the forms management program, along with the management of all other written communications and documents, may be the responsibility of the office manager. The office manager may find it advantageous to have the forms vendor assume some responsibilities, such as design and inventory maintenance. A somewhat larger organization may have a records manager directly responsible for forms management. Many medium- to large-sized organizations, however, have a designated forms supervisor and perhaps several persons who are directly responsible to this person. Outsourcing of the forms management program is now commonplace as more vendors are specializing in this function.

Publicize Forms Management Procedures

After the forms analysis has been completed and staff responsibilities have been assigned, departments in the organization should be informed of the operating procedures that have been established. Specific procedures differ from organization to organization; however, policies must cover at least three areas—originating forms, ordering forms, and evaluating forms.

Originate Forms

Each new form must be created based on need.

Department heads need to be informed that they must discuss any perceived need for a new form with the forms analyst to review their forms needs with them. Department heads must submit a form request (see Figure 14-2) that describes the purpose and justification for a new form. Comparison of the proposed form with forms already in the functional forms file is essential to ensure that no form that could meet this need is presently available. Once it has been determined that there is no existing form for this purpose, the forms analyst can work with the department head in designing the required form.

Order Forms

Printing, inventory, and ordering procedures must be established.

Several procedures for ordering forms need to be clearly defined. The first of these procedures is to establish printing specifications and quantities for initial orders. These decisions are usually made by the forms analyst and form originator during the design phase. Type and size of the form are determined by cost considerations as well as by the originator's needs. At this time, a decision is also made as to whether this form will be printed in-house (if in-house printing facilities are available) or contracted out. Printing specifications are indicated on a form such as the one shown in Figure 14-3 and sent with a sample copy to the printer or print shop.

Inventory procedures must also be established. Forms may be stored in the department from which they will originate or in a central location. Once reorder points have been established for each form, it must be clearly established whether the department is to reorder or to notify the forms department (usually the forms clerk) that the form should be reprinted. Without clearly defined inventory procedures, user departments may be tempted to order new unauthorized forms as well as to reorder authorized forms.

Figure 14-2
Form Request

REQUEST FOR A NEW OR REVISED FORM		1. Date of request July 1, 19--	2. Form No. BC-487
		3. Date required Aug. 4, 19--	4. Cost Project No. BC 68-007
Complete all applicable items. Facts not known at time of request should be submitted as soon as available.		5. Department Programs Management	

6. TITLE OR DESCRIPTION
Monthly Programs Schedule

7. Forms superseded
BC-228

8. EDITION
☐ New   ☐ Other
☒ Revised

9. TYPE OF FORM

a. Category
☒ Administrative
☐ Processing
☐ Letter or memo
☐ Other
_____

b. Number and/or title of prescribing directive
OR ☒ None

d. Budget number and expiration date
N/A

c. Related forms
none

(Attach correct confidential statement when required.)

10. USAGE

a. Frequency of use
☐ One time
☐ When required
☐ Daily
☒ Monthly
☐ Quarterly
☐ Annually

b. Point of usage
☐ Single department
☒ Multiple departments
☐ Regional office
☐ Other

c. How data will be filled in (all or part)
☒ Computer
☐ Hand
☐ High-speed printer
☐ Other
_____

d. Number of copies prepared at one writing

e. Estimated monthly usage
125 copies

f. Total number required
1,000

11. REPORTING, ADDRESSING AND MAILING METHODS

a. ☐ Personal interview ⟶   Starting date

(1) Description of portfolios, binders, etc., to be used

N/A

b. ☒ Mail ⟶   Mailing date
Aug. 30, 19--

(2) How forms are to be addressed
☒ Computer
☐ High-speed printer
☐ Other _____

(3) Description of envelopes to be used
Enter form numbers or attach sample(s)
plain white
☐ Self-mailer

12. DESIGN SPECIFI-CATIONS

a. Size of form
10 1/2" X 8"

b. Paper stock
24 lb.
Hammermill

c. Other specifications

N/A

13. STOCKING AND DISPOSITION

a. Where forms will be stocked
☐ Department
☒ Central
☐ Mail service
☐ Other _____

b. Disposition of revised or superseded forms
☐ Use
☐ Dispose of when revision received
☒ Dispose of immediately

14. Purpose of form

to furnish progress information
on scheduled programs

c. Number of forms on hand ⟶   200

15. Person to contact regarding this form
Mary Way

Building No. Annex Q	Room No. 480	Telephone Ext. 6547

16. APPROVALS

Form B13
12/93

a. Department Manager *Harry Smith*	Date July 2	b. Records and Information Administrator *E. J. Stokes*	Date copy released July 5

SUBMIT TWO (2) COPIES TO: Records Management Division

Figure 14-3
Forms
Specification Form

Forms Specifications

(TO BE COMPLETELY FILLED OUT and SUBMITTED WITH EACH FORM ORDERED FROM THE PRINT SHOP)

Department		Account Number	Date Ordered
Marketing		*93-425*	*10/15/--*

Person Requesting Material	Signature of Supervising Authority	Telephone Number
Heather Brunson	*James Woods*	*7621*

Brief Description of Form or Form No.	No. of Copies Per Page	Size of Form
17-E	*100*	*4¼ × 14*

Number of Pages	Check Appropriate Box:		
1	☐ New Form (Make metal plate & store)	☐ Quick copy	☒ Rerun of Form Previously Printed

Color of Paper	Color of Ink	Miscellaneous Information
white	*black*	

CHECK APPROPRIATE BOXES

☐ FORM PRINTS ON ONE SIDE ONLY   ☒ PUNCH HOLES: ☐ 2 Across top

☐ FORM PRINTS ON BOTH SIDES   ☒ 3 Down side

☐ RESET TYPE   ☐ COLLATE IN SETS   ☐ STAPLE

☒ PAD IN TABLETS   ☐ PERFORATE

☐ WRAP IN PACKAGES   ☐ NUMBER: Red Ink   ☐ Start ....

   Black Ink   ☐ End ....

(DO NOT WRITE BELOW THIS LINE)

For Reproduction Services Use Only

Job Number	Date Completed	Date Promised	Date Received	Initials

STOCK	$	CLEANUP	$	Miscellaneous Information:
PLATEMAKING		COLLATE		....
PRESSWORK		PERFORATING		....
WRAP		PUNCHING		....
PADDING		NUMBERING		....
FINISHING CUTS		STAPLING		....
CUTTING DOWN LARGE STOCK		FOLDING		....
TYPESETTING		TOTAL CHARGES	$	Impressions

NUMBER of SHEETS	SIZE and DESCRIPTION

#827
5-1-90

WHITE COPY — Reproduction Services   ●   CANARY COPY — Retain for Your Records

---

Evaluate Forms

Procedures for forms management should clearly establish the intervals at which each form is to be evaluated for continued use. Any form that has not been used in over a year may not be needed. Periodic evaluation also offers an opportunity to revise forms if the need for the data they collect should change. Revisions could mean additions, deletions, or new arrangements of sections of the form to accommodate changing needs.

Learning Check: Can you explain why it is important to publicize forms management procedures?

FORMS DESIGN

Efficient and cost-effective information collection and processing can only be achieved with well-designed forms. Forms design affects the accuracy and efficiency with which forms can be completed and processed. Because the design of the form affects its success in collecting information, careful attention must be given to this element of a forms management program.

Goals of Forms Design

The basic goal of forms design is to facilitate the collection and use of data. In addition, forms design should seek to achieve printing economies.

Facilitate Collection and Use of Data

If a form meets the goal of facilitating the collection and use of data, the forms user should find it easy to determine what information is being requested and to complete the form. The form's originator (individual or department requesting information) should also be able to rapidly extract the needed data from the form.

Proper design contributes to better collection and use of data.

Specific design guidelines are discussed in the paragraphs that follow; however, four general principles contribute to meeting the goal of facilitating data collection and use. First, each form should present a good visual effect. A form that has a jumbled or crowded appearance contributes to a poor attitude and a haphazard response on the part of the individual(s) who must complete it. An attractive, professional appearance is more conducive to care in the completion of the form.

Second, the writing required should be minimized. This not only contributes to the ease of completion, but it also provides more uniform responses, subject to minimal misinterpretation. Uniformity of responses allows for more efficient processing of the information on the forms.

Third, items should be placed on the form in logical sequence. This aids the user in completing the form and, again, aids in the processing function. If the same information is requested on more than one form, it should be requested in the same order on each form to assist in processing and in transferring the information from one form to another. The principle of consistent sequencing is particularly important if information from several forms is to be summarized on another form. The information should be placed on the summary form in the same order in which it appears on the forms being summarized.

Fourth, consider the capabilities of the equipment used with the form. Typewriters are disappearing from offices, making it necessary to redesign forms in which information was previously filled in using typewriters. For electronic forms, the computer must be available to all users. Pen or pencil fill-ins must be clear on all copies of the form.

Achieve Printing Economies

At least three areas should be examined in order to meet the goal of printing economies. The first area is the size of the form. Forms should be designed on standard paper sizes whenever possible. These sizes are shown in Table 14-1. Using standard paper sizes saves in printing costs because of better use of paper and fewer paper cuts. An added benefit of standard paper sizes is ease of filing and finding forms.

Table 14-1

Standard Forms Sizes

Size of Form (in Inches*)	Standard Sheet That Permits Form in Column 1 to be Cut Without Waste (in Inches)	Number of Forms Obtained from Single Standard Sheet	Number of Single Forms Obtained from One Ream of Paper
$2\frac{3}{4} \times 4\frac{1}{4}$	$8\frac{1}{2} \times 11$	8	4,000
$2\frac{3}{4} \times 8\frac{1}{2}$	17 x 22	16	8,000
$5\frac{1}{2} \times 8\frac{1}{2}$	$8\frac{1}{2} \times 11$	2	1,000
$5\frac{1}{2} \times 8\frac{1}{2}$	17 x 22	8	4,000
$8\frac{1}{2} \times 11$	17 x 22	4	2,000
$8\frac{1}{2} \times 14$	17 x 28	4	2,000
11 x 17	17 x 22	2	1,000

*The equivalent metric sizes are available from the American Paper Institute and from forms manufacturers.

Source: Norman F. Kallaus and B. Lewis Keeling, Administrative Office Management, 10th ed. (Cincinnati: South-Western Publishing Co., 1991), p. 581.

A second area that should be carefully considered is the number of copies ordered. Before printing decisions are made, consideration must be given to the number of copies of the form that will be used and to the quantities at which printing costs decrease. A final consideration is the colour, quality, and weight of the paper to be used. These characteristics should be determined after considering the life and use of the form and, in the case of unit sets, the number of copies in the set. Forms that are routed through several departments and are, therefore, subject to much handling must be on better-quality paper than those that are used once and are not retained more than a few weeks. Colour is an especially important consideration if documents are to be microfilmed. For example, blue paper will not reproduce well on microfilm.

Learning Check: Can you name four general principles that help in the collection and use of data on forms?

Guidelines for Forms Design

Large organizations may develop a very specific set of guidelines for use in forms design. The guidelines contained in the following paragraphs should be helpful to organizations of all sizes.

Divide Form into Parts

Every form can be divided into two parts: the facilitative area and the working area (see Figure 14-4). The **facilitative area** is usually at the top of the form and provides information that, although necessary, is peripheral to the main purpose of the form. Examples of information that may be contained in this area are the organization name and address, form title, form number, form revision date, instructions for completing the form, and routing instructions. Some of this information may be indicated in the bottom margin (either corner), thus splitting the facilitative area of the form. The location of form numbers and revision dates should be consistent within the organization. The **working area** of the form is the portion that requests information necessary to achieve the purpose for which the form was designed.

Figure 14-4
Parts of Forms

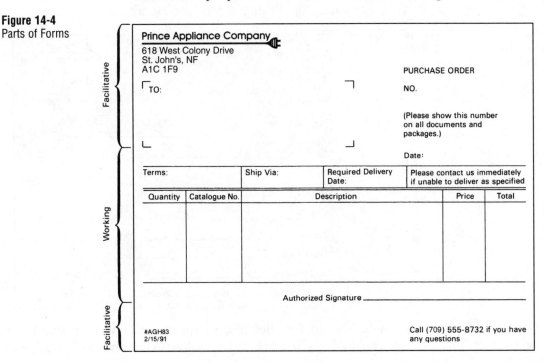

Allow Adequate Spacing

The spacing of items and lines on a form contributes to the good visual effect, ease of completion, and efficient processing of the information collected. Spacing must accommodate the characteristics of the method of completion. Forms are generally completed in one of three ways: handwritten, typewritten, or completed by computer. The spacing of the form should accommodate the most likely completion tool. Many forms are completed in handwriting or by machine fill-in; therefore, the form design must accommodate both methods of completion. The spacing used most frequently to accommodate both is 3-by-5 spacing, which allows three writing lines to a vertical inch (double spacing in word processing) and five characters to a horizontal inch to provide sufficient space for handwritten responses. The arrangement of space for each item can then be determined by the length of the expected response.

Use Clear Captions

When forms are filled in by machine, either typewriter or computer, responses must be distinguishable from the captions to allow the efficient extraction of information. Captions could be in bold type, for example. Upper-left captions (ULC) achieve more efficient use of space by not taking up writing space (see Figure 14-5).

Figure 14-5
Upper-Left
Captions

USE UPPER-LEFT
CAPTIONS

REQUEST FOR COMPANY PARKING STICKER			
Name		Social Insurance Number	
Department		Office Phone	
Home Address	City, Province		Postal Code
Make of Auto	Year	Colour	Licence Number
T-3 12/1/90			

AVOID THIS

REQUEST FOR COMPANY PARKING STICKER

Name _____ Social Insurance Number _____

Department _____ Office Phone _____

Home Address _____

City, Province _____ Postal Code _____

Make of Auto _____ Year _____ Colour _____ Licence No. _____

Captions should be brief but, more importantly, they should be very specific in the information they request. The form user should not have to question the intent of the form designer when responding. Captions should be carefully chosen and used consistently with all forms when the same or similar information is requested.

Place Ballot Boxes in Front of Responses

This guideline applies whenever it is possible to predetermine all responses and to have the respondent select the appropriate response. Ballot boxes should be used whenever possible to improve the accuracy and efficiency of form completion and processing. Boxes for *yes* or *no* choices, to be indicated by *X*s or check marks, should appear at the end of the question.

Make Forms Self-Instructing

Instructions for completing forms should be clear and concise and placed near where they are needed. Unless instructions are very lengthy, they should not be printed on the back of the form or on a separate sheet, as this increases the probability that they will not be read.

Identify Organization on All External Forms

On forms that have interoffice functions, the organization's name, address, and logo are likely superfluous. However, when forms such as purchase orders, invoices, and customer surveys are sent to persons outside the organization, organization name and address are essential. This identification provides information critical to the processing of the form by the recipient and its proper return to the organization. In addition, this identification becomes an advertising tool for the organization.

Display Form Number and Identifying Title

This guideline may seem obvious, but it should not be overlooked. Having the form number and title printed in the same location on each form provides immediate identification of the form and alerts the recipient to its purpose. In addition, it is necessary to the maintenance of inventory and the forms files and for user identification.

Display Date

Each form should display its original date of printing or most recent revision date. This information usually appears with the form number. It may appear in any location; however, placement on the form should be consistent within the organization. Printing the date on the forms ensures the use of current forms and identifies obsolete forms, which should be purged from inventory and users' files.

Show Distribution and Routing on Forms

The individual who completes a form should know where the form is to be sent and who will have access to the information contained on that form. Including distribution information at the top or bottom of the form is recommended.

Computer Forms Design

Computer software packages may be used to design business forms, and the expense associated with paper forms can be greatly reduced by automating the processing steps. The head office of a large Toronto-based company estimated that the company saved $30,000 in the first month alone by instituting an electronic forms system. Forms software packages are used to create forms such as invoices, purchase orders, and many other types of forms. **Forms software packages** fall into three major categories. Category one includes forms software packages that allow the user to create an on-screen template that corresponds to a preprinted form. After the template has been created, the user enters the data in the template on the screen; and when the form is printed, the data will be positioned precisely on the form.

Category two includes forms software packages with a collection of basic business forms ready for use. In most of these packages, the user fills in the company name, address, and so forth, as the information is to appear on the forms. Once the user completes the customization, a form is selected, the data entered, and the form printed. This software does not require the user to design a form or template. The forms contained in these software packages are usually stock forms that can be used in most businesses.

Category three includes forms software packages that allow the user to create forms. These software packages include commands for use in drawing lines, specifying fonts and formatting type, defining text blocks, changing horizontal and vertical spacing, and storing and retrieving forms.

Using Electronic Forms

A company with electronic equipment should consider using electronic forms. With a LAN (local area network) or WAN (wide area network), all users have access to the electronic forms without having to print them. The electronic mail capability of LANs allows forms to be routed as needed. All currently used forms should be evaluated to determine if the forms are candidates for the electronic format. Users of forms that require frequent updating will certainly benefit from the use of a forms software package, since the forms can be updated without the worry of wasting any old forms on hand.

Templates, or blank forms that include lines, type, artwork, and logos, can be created and stored. These forms may be produced in colour if appropriate printers are available. A user may enter the variable information into the template directly from a terminal and have the completed electronic form transmitted to another workstation or printed onto paper. Or blank forms created electronically may be printed and then filled in. Savings are achieved because no inventory of forms needs to be kept on hand. The same principles of form design apply to forms created by hand or electronically.

Many forms software packages allow the user to import data from databases and spreadsheets created with other software packages to be used in the creation of forms. In addition, the information collected from a form can be stored in a database, and sorted, queried, and retrieved from the database.

Forms software packages may have a feature called an **edit check**, based on the mapping process forms designers use to create electronic forms. **Mapping** programs each fill-in space or data field to restrict the type of information that can be entered in that field, thus preventing certain errors from occurring when the data is being keyed into the form. For example, an edit check feature could prevent an alphabetic character from being entered into a data field in which a number should be entered.

Computer Management of Forms

The computer can also save a company money in the area of inventory management of forms. **Forms management software** is a software package specifically designed for forms management. By using these software packages, companies can gain control over forms and have a more efficient and productive forms management program. The number of forms used, the frequency of orders, the number of forms on hand, and printing and pricing information are only a few of the information items included. Specialized reports can be created to detail any information in the system.

Forms Design Checklist

Forms design is a multistep process. At the completion of the design process and before the form is released for printing, reviewing the form by using a forms design checklist is helpful. The checklist shown below and on the following page demonstrates the types of items that should be checked and provides a beginning checklist for those organizations that do not already have one.

FORMS DESIGN CHECKLIST

	Yes	No

Arrangement

1. Considering the source of the information, its use, and the way users normally write or read it, are all items and groups of items arranged in the right sequence?

2. Considering the type of storage equipment used, is the key information (data used to retrieve the form from a file) in the most visible location?

Spacing

3. Considering the preparation method, has the proper amount of space been provided for each piece of requested information?

4. Does the horizontal spacing visually direct the user from one section to the next?

5. Is the vertical spacing set so that data can be entered on the form using a typewriter or computer without vertical adjustments?

6. Is all extra space used properly for emphasis, separation, and balance instead of looking left over?

Captions

7. Will all captions be understood by everyone who might use the form?

8. Are captions placed in the upper-left corner of each fill-in area?

9. Will abbreviations be readily understood?

10. Are group captions or headings used to identify major areas?

Multiple-Choice Answers

11. Are possible answers given (including check boxes) whenever they would help the users provide better answers in less time?

12. Are the answers and check boxes arranged properly for the most productive and accurate fill-in?

Instructions and Distribution

13. Can someone unfamiliar with the form complete it without referring to any other source for help?

14. Have all unnecessary instructions and explanations been left off the form so that the user's intelligence will not be insulted?

15. Are the distribution instructions shown on the form in the most effective way for its usage pattern and construction?

16. If an interior copy is to be removed from the set before the others, is that copy slightly longer so that it can be easily identified and removed?

17. Is the self-mailer format used whenever applicable?

18. Is the form designed to fit a window envelope whenever appropriate?

Margins

19. Does the form have adequate margins for the required lock-up (gripper) space on the press?

20. Are the margins adequate for any binding technique to be used, such as hole punches for notebooks and post binders?

21. Are the margins adequate for other handling characteristics, such as filing, copying, stapling, and so on?

FORMS DESIGN CHECKLIST, *CONTINUED*

Type, Lines, and Screens	Yes	No
22. Do all of the lines on the form do what they are supposed to do? (Some guide, some separate, some stop.)	____	____
23. Is screening (shading) used where helpful to separate, highlight, or identify fields or zones and not just to decorate the form?	____	____
24. Within the same typeface, is there variation in the size of type, its boldness, and use of capital and small letters and italics to enhance the appearance and legibility of the form?	____	____

Construction

	Yes	No
25. Is the size appropriate for the printer, all users, and storage equipment?	____	____
26. Is the construction right for the way the form will be handled?	____	____
27. Is the paper right for the use and retention needs of the form?	____	____
28. Is the colour of ink appropriate?	____	____
29. Are all appropriate holes, perforations, scores, and so forth, shown on the layout and not interfered with by the copy?	____	____

Identification

	Yes	No
30. Is the title meaningful?	____	____
31. Is the form properly identified with a number and date for ease in referencing, ordering, inventorying, and so on?	____	____
32. Is the organization properly identified?	____	____

General

	Yes	No
33. Will this form accomplish its purpose with the minimum amount of effort by all users?	____	____
34. Is this the best possible tool to do this job?	____	____

Learning Check: Can you describe the three types of forms software?

PROCESSING INFORMATION WITH REPORTS

Reports are upward communication to management used for decision making.

Reports are generally upward communications to management. Reports management is necessary to control reports proliferation, while providing managers with the information resources necessary for responsible decision making.

A **report** is a written presentation of information useful in the decision-making process. A report may be narrative, tabular, or graphic; it may be on paper, microfilm, or on a computer screen. A report should be presented in the format that is most appropriate for the information presented and the audience to which it is presented.

Types of Reports

Reports may be manually prepared or machine-generated; they may be onetime occurrences, or they may be provided on a recurring basis. A variety of report types may be used in defining policy and in planning, controlling, and evaluating organizational operations. Among the most frequently occurring types of reports that should be included in the reports management program are:

1. Activity reports, which reflect participation of personnel in special activities;
2. Feeder reports, which reflect contribution (as in a production report);
3. Forecasts, which provide projections;
4. Status reports, which reflect existing conditions;
5. Summary reports, which provide a recapitulation of activities;
6. Consolidated reports, which provide a compilation of existing data;
7. Onetime reports, which provide information required for one time only or by one or more departments; and
8. Special studies reports, which show results of research, development, and operational testing concerning a particular program or problem.

Many routine documents should be excluded from the reports management program. Minutes of meetings, administrative procedures, and technical manuals are examples of reports to be excluded.

Objectives

Special needs of an organization must be incorporated into the objectives of its reports management program. Among those objectives common to most programs are the following:

1. Identify reports production and the need for these reports.
2. Provide visibility of report volume and its costs.
3. Control creation of new reports.
4. Establish a method for purging unnecessary reports from the system.
5. Determine the number of hours expended in report preparation.
6. Control distribution and provide audit controls.
7. Improve the quality and true effectiveness of reports.
8. Promote exception reporting where appropriate.
9. Reduce the number of items in reports through content analysis.
10. Consolidate, simplify, and standardize reports.

 Learning Check: Can you list five objectives of a reports management program?

ESTABLISHING REPORTS MANAGEMENT

As with other aspects of managing information in an organization, obtaining top management support for reports management is vital to its success. If the program is to succeed, responsibilities, procedures, distribution, and evaluation must be clearly defined.

Responsibilities

The first step in establishing a reports management program is to define responsibilities for implementing and maintaining the program. Reports management should be a responsibility of the records manager and staff. However, certain segments of reports management rest with other management levels. Management at all levels is responsible for generating reports. Therefore, management is also obligated to ensure that reports are limited to those essential to efficient operations, are produced in the most economical manner, and are distributed only to those with a need to know. Managers may also play a significant role in the initial and periodic inventories of recurring reports as requested by the records manager.

The reports originators and recipients have a responsibility beyond the generation and use of reports. They coordinate the completion of an inventory and report questionnaire as required by the records manager. As a result of the questionnaire findings, the report originator and recipient also initiate action to cancel a report or to reduce the number of copies distributed.

One of the purposes of reports management is to provide a continuous advisory control over the ever-growing reports proliferation. However, since reports are operational tools, the final control remains with the individual or department requiring the report. The reports management system provides overall surveillance of reports. It initiates actions for conducting inventory and audit functions; it provides planning, implementation, and audit of machine-generated reports, in cooperation with word processing and data processing personnel. Finally, the reports management program staff prepares annual summaries, which identify cost savings and reduction in, or containment of, reporting for management's review.

Procedures

After the decision to initiate a reports management program has been made and before implementation begins, policy is established for the program. This policy is communicated by outlining the scope of the reports information program and clearly enumerating procedures, including approval procedures for all report requests and reviews, output formats and layout, final report approval, and evaluation and follow-up.

Reports Inventory

The first step in the implementation of the program is to conduct an inventory of existing reports. A reports inventory form, along with a letter of instruction and a listing of reports to be included or excluded from the inventory, is routed to all department heads. Data requested on the reports inventory form includes department, location, account number, report title, number of pages, originator, and method of preparation. The completed inventory form is returned to the reports management staff.

Reports Questionnaire

The reports inventory is followed by a report questionnaire distributed first to each report's originator. A questionnaire is completed for each report. One copy of each form is then reproduced for each name on the distribution list and then forwarded to these recipients, who complete another set of questions dealing with the need for the report, suggestions for improvement, and so forth.

The records manager reviews the completed questionnaires to:
- Delete from the distribution list the names of individuals no longer requiring the report,
- Eliminate the report if distribution is reduced to zero,
- Take follow-up actions to update distribution lists and improve reports based on comments made by recipients, and
- Prepare a report inventory log.

Report Inventory Log

The last step is to prepare a report inventory log that provides a summary of the report questionnaire data presenting a before-and-after picture of the results of the report questionnaire.

 Learning Check: Can you outline the steps of a reports inventory?

New Reports

Each new report request must be evaluated in order for control to be maintained over new reports. A report review request is completed for each new report in order to ensure uniformity of review. This report review form serves several purposes. It provides authorization, forms a nucleus for a functional file, and provides for review at regular intervals.

Reports Criteria

Some of the criteria that should be applied when establishing or evaluating report requirements are:
1. **Use.** The use of the report should justify the cost of preparing, submitting, and distributing the report.
2. **Essentiality.** Reports should be instituted or continued only as a means to maintain essential data. A report is not directed merely as a device to verify the accuracy of another report.

3. **Economical procedures.** Data should be collected, processed, and transmitted by the most economical means; the means should be consistent with any established priorities. Economical means include collecting information by sampling methods and reporting only when changes or exceptions occur.

4. **Utilization of data.** Data submitted to an office should be used to the maximum extent by other offices within that group. Data collection and storage must be limited to users for which a valid need exists.

5. **Coordination.** Requests for reports should be fully coordinated with preparation and processing activities.

6. **Combined reports.** The redesign of reporting requirements should be a continual process to provide efficient compilation of essential data. Duplication of data collection and transmission should be held to the minimum and be consistent with the need to identify information in separate reports.

7. **Summarization.** Reports should be briefly summarized. Only information that is essential should be incorporated.

8. **Deadlines.** Deadlines should be realistic. Attempting to meet impossible or impractical deadlines can result in additional costs, inaccuracies, and the need to resubmit.

9. **Levels of organizations.** In order to be monitored for accuracy, reports should flow through established levels of organizations.

10. **Frequency.** Frequency of the report should be dictated by the rate of data change.

11. **Simplicity.** Data should be prepared and processed by the most direct method.

12. **Applicability.** Reports should include only that information deemed essential to a specific activity.

Reports Files

Reports files are helpful in maintaining a sound reports management program. A file that includes the written procedures for use of the report, a copy of the report, and a report control form should be established for each report. The report control form includes a description of the report, the initiator, frequency of report, distribution, analysis of cost, and a date for annual review. Some organizations prefer to maintain two files—a functional reports file and a historical reports file. The **functional reports file** maintains information about reports with a like function. This file helps to minimize duplication, as each new request for a report would be checked against the functional reports file. In instances where an existing report contains much of the information that is requested on the new report, an examination of the functional reports file makes that comparison relatively easy. It may be that information not included could be incorporated into an existing report; this would eliminate the need for an additional report. The **historical reports file** maintains a history of each report. When questions arise regarding the origination or purpose of a report, reference should be made to the historical reports file.

Reports Catalogue

Large organizations often issue a reports catalogue. This is helpful in making organization members aware of information available to them in report form. A reports catalogue often curtails the need to print large numbers of copies of reports; employees receive reports catalogues and know that these reports are available to them in a central location.

Distribution

The method of distribution for reports can be the same procedure as that for directives distribution (see Chapter 13). This system provides control, verification, and an audit trail.

Evaluation

Report evaluation is provided via feedback from originators, users, and recipients. All recipients of a report should be users. Several methods are available for establishing usage. One method is to request feedback by using a questionnaire such as the one shown in Figure 14-6. The problem with this approach is that many managers think they must have copies of all reports whether the reports are used or merely filed. Answers to this type of questionnaire are often less than accurate. A different approach, which is usually highly effective (though less forthright), is to bury the same questionnaire deep within the report. You will notice the notation: "If you wish to continue to receive this report, you must respond within 10 days."

A more comprehensive analysis of each report should be made on its anniversary date. This analysis is an in-depth review of all aspects of the report from the viewpoints of the users and of the preparers. A sample reports review guide is shown in Figure 14-7.

Figure 14-6
Report Evaluation
Form

REPORT EVALUATION FORM

TO: Report Recipient   DATE:

To assist in reducing the volume of paperwork, your evaluation of this report is needed. Please check the item below that, for you, best describes the attached report copy—

☐ 1. I don't really need this report; please discontinue it.

☐ 2. I need the information in the report but could obtain it from a reference copy if one were made available in my general area.

☐ 3. I need the information, but on a less frequent basis.
I would like a copy (circle one): weekly, monthly, quarterly, annually.

☐ 4. I need this report, but it would be much more useful if the report could be modified in format or content.

☐ 5. I need the report as is; please continue it. (I keep it on hand for ___ months.)

Additional comments on Item No.:

1._____

2._____

3._____

4._____

5._____

Date	Your Name	Department

Note: If you wish to continue to receive this report, you must respond within 10 days.
F80
1/89

USING COMPUTER TECHNOLOGY

Computer technology has a significant impact on preparing, transmitting, and controlling reports. Report writers and users can employ word processing, graphics, and database software to improve efficiency and to expedite the reporting process.

Document Preparation

Word processing software assists the report writer in writing and editing reports quickly and efficiently. Software is available that checks for grammatical, punctuation, and spelling errors as well as correct word choice. When reports are stored electronically, they are easily corrected or revised and ready for reuse.

Figure 14-7
Reports
Review
Guide

REPORTS REVIEW GUIDE	DATE	FILE NUMBER

TITLE OF REPORT

Note to Reviewing Officers—Check appropriate column. If "Questionable" is checked, use separate sheet for recording changes or observations.

PART I: To be completed by the using office.

	Questionable	Satisfactory

1. USEFULNESS

1. THE REPORT AS A WHOLE. Who uses it? How is it used? What is its purpose? Should it be continued?
2. USE OF EACH ITEM. Is every item used? Are there any items missing?
3. USE OF EACH COPY. Are all distributed copies used to good purpose?
4. USE OF NEGATIVE REPORTS. Are negative reports required? What use is made of them?
5. FREQUENCY. Is frequency adequate? Is a lower or diminishing frequency feasible?
6. VALUE VERSUS COST. Is the value of the report worth its cost?
7. EFFECTIVENESS. How effective a management tool has this been?
8. CONTENT. Do the contents develop trends by properly mixing historical, current, and projected conditions?

2. QUALITY

1. ADEQUACY AND SUITABILITY. Are scope and content of the report tailored to needs?
2. COMPARISONS. Are comparisons provided against goals, standards of past performance, or some other known factor?
3. REPORTING UNITS. Are units proper for meaningful interpretation?
4. SIGNATURE AUTHENTICATION. Are signatures of verifying and approving officials included when necessary?
5. ACCURACY. Is source data accurate? What is its record of dependability?

3. TECHNIQUES

1. INTEGRATED REPORTING. Are data needs of other levels and offices tied in?
2. EXCEPTION REPORTING. Would it be appropriate to report conditions only when other than normal?
3. SAMPLING. Would sampling of a few offices provide representative and reliable data?
4. STANDARDIZATION. If forms are used, do all offices use the same form? If narrative is used, is there a standard of acceptability?

4. EASE OF USE

1. STYLE OF PRESENTATION. Does the style of presentation
   provide clarity and finding ease? Is it condensed?
   Are graphics used well?   _____   _____
2. SUMMARY INFORMATION.
   Would just a summary be better?   _____   _____

PART II: To be completed by the preparing office.

	Questionable	Satisfactory

1. POLICY

1. PREPARATION. Has a procedure been written for the
   preparation of the report.   _____   _____
2. REVIEW. Are the report and the preparation procedures
   regularly reviewed?   _____   _____

2. SHORT CUTS

1. ANOTHER AVAILABLE SOURCE. Is the data in some
   other report? Is the data more accessible from another office?   _____   _____
2. COMBINATION. Could this report be combined
   with another report?   _____   _____
3. BY-PRODUCT. Is it possible to get the report as a
   by-product of some other process (i.e., multicopy form set)?   _____   _____
4. DISTRIBUTION. Are all copies distributed essential?   _____   _____

3. TIMING

1. ADEQUATE TIME. Do due dates give enough time
   for preparation and review?   _____   _____
2. OFFICE WORKLOAD. Has preparing office workload
   been considered? Could end-of-month or end-of-year
   reports be avoided?   _____   _____
3. REPORTING PERIODS. Are there periodic conflicts among
   respondents or between feeder and summary reports?   _____   _____
4. SUBMISSION. Has complete and/or timely submission
   of this report been a problem?   _____   _____

4. FORMAT

1. PRESENTATION. Does the type of presentation—narrative,
   graphic, or tabular—best portray information?   _____   _____
2. STRIP REPORTING. Is it possible to match feeder
   reports from several sources and compile by stripping?   _____   _____
3. ARRANGEMENTS AND SIZE. Are items grouped and
   sequenced to work flow? Is spacing adequate for responses?   _____   _____
4. LAYOUT. Does the layout lead the reader to prompt
   and accurate conclusions?   _____   _____
5. ARRANGEMENT OF RECORDS. Should records be
   arranged differently to simplify reporting?   _____   _____

5. SOURCES

1. FEEDER REPORTS. Are procedures for feeder reports
   provided to ensure uniformity and simplicity?   _____   _____
2. DIRECT USE OF RECORDS. Could actual records
   or copies be sent instead of the prepared report?   _____   _____
3. CUMULATIVE DATA. Can fiscal or statistical data
   be kept on a cumulative basis in order to eliminate
   last-minute workloads?   _____   _____

In many information processing systems, the user can access data from a company database and incorporate it into a report. Graphics software makes possible the conversion of tabular and numeric information into graphic displays, such as charts and graphs. Most database management systems have their own report-generating capability.

Document Transmission

Reports stored electronically may be transmitted over communication lines from one terminal to another rather than being sent manually in paper form. Also, they may be stored in a database until accessed by a user. In electronic storage systems, reports are available in a more timely manner, yet time and money are not wasted in distributing reports unnecessarily.

Document Control

Databases may be used to store indexes of reports prepared within the organization. In addition, catalogues describing available reports may be stored. Such a system may also record who accesses reports and should restrict access to authorized users. Also, functional and historical report files may be stored electronically for improved access.

 Learning Check: Can you name and explain the two types of report files?

TERMINOLOGY REVIEW

Review each of the terms listed below in the Glossary on page 521.

edit check	functional reports file
facilitative area	historical reports file
forms	mapping
forms analysis	numeric forms file
forms management program	report
forms management software	specifications forms file
forms software package	templates
forms survey	working area
functional forms file	

REVIEW AND DISCUSSION

1. Define the function of forms within an organization.
2. Define a forms management program. What benefits does it offer an organization? What is the importance of top management support?

3. What is forms analysis? Describe the steps to be undertaken in completing a forms analysis.
4. Many organizations maintain three types of forms files. Define each in a manner that clearly differentiates its function.
5. Which two types of files are also maintained for reports? What is the purpose of each?
6. List at least five guidelines for forms design and state the importance of each.
7. List and describe three types of forms software.
8. What are reports? What is their function within an organization?
9. Differentiate between the responsibilities of the records manager and those of other managers for reports management.
10. How can the use of computer technology result in more efficient distribution of reports within an organization?

APPLICATIONS

1. Prepare a one-page application for employment form. Include the following categories of information:

   a. name
   b. address
   c. form number/revision date
   d. date of birth
   e. education and training
   f. work experience
   g. form title
   h. current date
   i. social insurance number
   j. references
   k. company name and address
   l. title of job applied for

2. Using current periodicals, find two articles on forms management. One article should be on the subject of forms management principles and one on forms design software. Prepare a one-page critique of each article and be prepared to discuss the articles in class.
3. Obtain a poorly designed business form and redesign the form using proper design techniques. (Your instructor may provide the form.)
4. Simon Enterprises has never had a reports management program. Selman Parker, the new records manager, has obtained top management approval for such a program.
   a. Outline the procedures to be followed in establishing this program.
   b. Explain the importance of establishing a functional reports file and a historical reports file.
   c. List and explain at least five criteria that should be applied when report requirements are established.
   d. Explain the importance of periodic report evaluation to the success of the reports management program.

CONCLUDING CASES

A. Frequent Travel

Leslie Hawkins has just been hired as the reports supervisor of Frequent Travel, a large travel agency. Leslie was hired to develop and implement a reports management program for the organization. In accordance with current procedures, each department now gets an information copy of every report generated by the staff. Since the organization now has a staff of 500 and generates an average of 20 reports each month, this distribution is presenting processing cost and storage problems.

Leslie decides to finalize her plans for controlling reports. List the steps to be completed in developing and implementing the reports management program.

B. Southland Corporation

Robert Ellis has just been hired as the forms manager for Southland Corporation, a philanthropic organization the primary goal of which is the support and encouragement of community theatres. The Southland Corporation employs 300 workers at its headquarters in Toronto.

Robert's first step in designing a forms management program is to conduct a forms survey.
1. How should Robert conduct the forms survey?
2. How does the forms survey relate to forms analysis?
3. When the forms survey is completed, how can the information be used?

SUGGESTED READINGS AND RESOURCES

Forms Management

Brown, Andrew. "Get Organized—Implement a Forms Management Program to Improve Efficiency." *Forms and Label Purchasing,* Vol. 3, No. 2 (June, 1990), p. 10.

Creating User-Friendly Forms. Department of Public Works, Supply and Services, Province of Alberta, March, 1993.

Kallaus, Norman F., and B. Lewis Keeling. *Administrative Office Management,* 10th ed. Cincinnati: South-Western Publishing Co., 1991.

Langemo, Mark. "Shaping Up Your Forms." *Office Systems '90,* Vol. 7, No. 4 (April, 1990), p. 60.

Phillips, John T., and Angela L. Beckwith. "Electronic Systems and Paper Forms." *Records Management Quarterly,* Vol. 25, No. 1 (January, 1991), p. 18.

"Selling Forms Management to Top Management." *Forms and Systems Professional,* Vol. 2, No. 3 (Winter, 1989), p. 14.

Smith, Ken. "How-to: The Basics of Good Forms Design." *Forms and Label Purchasing,* Vol. 3, No. 2 (June, 1990), p. 14.

Taylor, Allen G. "Product Comparison: Windows Forms Processing." *Info Canada,* January, 1993, p. 22.

Theofanos, M.F., and John T. Phillips. "Digital Signatures: Signing and Notarizing Electronic Forms." *Records Management Quarterly,* Vol. 28, No. 2 (April, 1994), p. 18.

Reports Management

"Developing a Standard Practice or Procedure on a Reports Program." *Records Management Quarterly,* Vol. 18, No. 2 (April, 1984), p. 44.

"Documenting the Results from a Reports Improvement Program." *Records Management Quarterly,* Vol. 18, No. 1 (January, 1984), p. 38.

Hayes, Kenneth V. "Creating a Reports Catalog or Inventory." *Records Management Quarterly,* Vol. 17, No. 1 (January, 1983), p. 21.

Records Control—Audits and Reports

Learning Goals

After completing this chapter, you should be able to:

1. Describe the role of control and its relationship to the records management system.
2. Identify types of control and apply these controls to specific examples.
3. Describe links in the scope of control and explain the relationships among the links.
4. Assign control responsibilities to appropriate records personnel and users.
5. Describe an administrative audit and problems an administrative audit may reveal.
6. Describe an operational audit and problems that may be revealed in an operational audit.
7. Identify process-specific operational audits and describe the information gained from each.
8. Describe procedures for conducting an audit.
9. Identify various reports resulting from records management audits and their contents.

Control is the function that compares achieved results with planned goals. It is the process of getting feedback, comparing what was planned with what actually happened, evaluating the results, and taking corrective action when there is deviation from the expected. Control is a subsystem of the overall records management system and should be viewed as a part of the process function of that system. As with all systems, the control subsystem is composed of interdependent parts operating as a whole to accomplish a given purpose.

THE CONTROLLING PROCESS

The control function provides essential information for records management. Through the process of control, the records management staff can determine the effectiveness and efficiency of its operations. The process can be especially useful if controls are in place throughout the records management system.

Types of Control

Three types of control, with differing emphases, provide records managers with three opportunities to detect and correct any problems in the records management system. These controls are precontrol, concurrent control, and feedback control.

Precontrol

Precontrol takes place before work is performed. Precontrol attempts to eliminate potential problems before they occur by focusing on inputs into the system—the resources that are used—information, equipment and supplies, money, and people. For example, a precontrol would be to carefully screen and select employees (people) who have the right skills for the job, to provide the type of equipment that meets a particular need, or to have the right kind of supplies on hand when they are needed (equipment and supplies). Management creates information, through its policies, procedures, and rules, that reduces the possibility of problems occurring. For example, a policy may be established that allows only key management personnel to issue directives. This is a type of precontrol that addresses the potential problems of too many directives or directives that are conflicting.

Concurrent Control

Concurrent control takes place as work is being performed. Concurrent control affects personnel, equipment, procedures, and performance. One form of concurrent control is demonstrated by the requirement that all retrieved records must be charged out and followed up for prompt return. Security measures used on a daily basis are another form of concurrent control. Reports, correspondence, and forms management programs exercise both precontrol and concurrent control. As policies are established for creating and distributing the various forms of communication, precontrol is being exercised; concurrent control is exercised in the use, maintenance, and updating of the communications.

Feedback Control

Feedback control focuses on results.

Feedback control, sometimes called *postcontrol,* focuses on results or output and takes place after the work is completed. In the case of records management, feedback control examines the results of the control subsystem as it relates to the effectiveness of the records control—the output of the system. The basis of feedback control is a comparison of historical data with current performance data. For example, data may be compiled regarding the number of misfiles in an organization. These misfile statistics may then be compared to previous years' records to determine the need for corrective action. Cost analysis of forms design and production is another type of feedback control, as is the provision for receiving comments from users of any of the established procedures.

All aspects of the control subsystem should be used to establish (precontrol), maintain (concurrent control), and evaluate (feedback control) the effectiveness of the records management system. There are many other examples of control in a records management system. Control applications range from simple to complex and from short- to long-term; each application contributes to establishing and maintaining order in the system. Many of the procedures discussed in previous chapters are types of control. For example, records retention and disposition procedures combine precontrol, concurrent control, and feedback control. Precontrol is applied by the establishment of a timetable for retaining records and policies for records disposition; concurrent control is applied by adhering to the established schedule and by preparing records for disposition; feedback control is applied by monitoring the system and taking corrective action when appropriate.

 Learning Check: Can you describe the three types of control and tell when they occur? Can you also give examples of each?

Scope

The control function monitors three major areas of records management: employee performance, information quality and quantity, and supplies and equipment use. The result of an effective system of control will be an information network that provides the manager with the information necessary to make management decisions. The three elements that comprise the scope of the records management control system are employee performance, information quality and quantity, and supplies and equipment use. The linkage of these three elements is shown in Figure 15-1.

Figure 15-1
Linkage of
Elements of the
Control
Subsystem's Scope

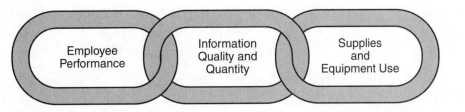

Employee Performance

The first link in the chain is the effectiveness of employee performance. Performance evaluation includes all levels of employees who are involved in the creation, distribution, use, maintenance, and disposition of records. Employee performance is reflected in administrative costs and in productivity. Under no circumstances should one believe that only clerical workers make up this link; that perception is far too narrow. While individual performance is very important, one must not lose sight of the importance of the performance of the records management unit as a whole. This would include effective sequencing and scheduling of their services to provide managers with the required information in a timely manner.

Information Quality and Quantity

Quality information is necessary for good decision making.

The second link in the chain is information quality and quantity. The goal of records management is to provide the "right record to the right person at the right time and at the lowest possible cost." Implicit in this statement is the assumption that information will be provided to the manager in a quantity and quality that will increase the probability that managerial decisions will be substantially correct for the situation. Information, however, cannot compensate for poor decision-making skills, replace common sense, or guarantee correct decisions. Appropriate information can, however, enhance the skills of the manager and provide the quality and quantity of data necessary to make objective evaluations and reach a decision from the available alternatives. Information quality and quantity is the central and primary link in the scope of the control subsystem.

Supplies and Equipment Use

Efficient use of supplies and equipment is important.

The scope of the control subsystem must include an evaluation of the efficient use of supplies and equipment, the third link in the chain. Misuse of materials and supplies may occur routinely unless this aspect of control is monitored carefully. Selecting the wrong equipment for the job, making too many copies, carelessly handling records, and purchasing excessive quantities of materials with a limited shelf life are all examples of ways in which waste can occur. A program should be established for materials control that includes a regular review of all office supplies and inventory needs. Random checks on individual use rates are advisable. Feedback should be provided to those persons who are responsible for and concerned with supplies control.

Idle equipment is a costly waste, as is equipment whose use is poorly scheduled. Equipment selected without regard to its compatibility with current office equipment is a waste of the organization's funds and results in inefficient use of both equipment and personnel. The control system should provide for appropriate selection, effective use, and reduced downtime of equipment.

The links in the scope of the control system are interdependent.

An interdependency exists among the elements of the control subsystem. The central link—information quality and quantity—is dependent upon the other two elements: effective employee performance and use of supplies and equipment. With the primary objective of providing the "right record to the right person at the right time and at the lowest possible cost," the end links of this chain are crucial ones.

✓ **Learning Check: Can you describe the links in the control system and their relationship to each other?**

RESPONSIBILITIES FOR RECORDS CONTROL

Responsibilities for records control are shared by two groups: those involved in the creation and use of records and those involved in processing records. Both groups have important contributions to make to the successful implementation of records control.

Records Creation and Use

Those persons responsible for the creation and use of records are the originator, the recipient, and the administrative support staff. The originator of the record has the primary role in controlling. Seventy-five percent of the cost of a record is incurred at the creation phase. Therefore, special restraint should be exercised at this time.

Originator

The use of good judgment by the originator is essential. Written requests or replies are often unnecessary. A phone call may not only meet the need but also provide a quicker response. Therefore, the first rule of good judgment is to write only those messages that require documentation. Second, the request or response should be concise, complete, and correct. If paper is used for interoffice correspondence, replies written or typed on the original letter are appropriate.

The originator should designate the number of copies to be made, which should be limited to essential copies. In the case of routine replies or inquiry letters, no copy need be made.

Depending on the system used, the originator may be the appropriate person to indicate the filing preference and cross-reference notations. This is particularly appropriate where there are no centralized records, where there is high staff turnover, or when the manager is the sole person using the office file. Whether this is the case or whether there is a coding clerk, all persons should abide by an established, uniform procedure for coding documents for filing.

In a centralized records system, it is efficient to have one person responsible for designating and marking (coding) each document or record. Uniformity that may not be present when each originator is responsible for coding can be achieved when one person is assigned this responsibility.

Control of electronic mail is an important part of a records management program.

The mushrooming use of electronic mail for both internal and external communication makes E-mail control a necessity. Procedures should be established to identify E-mail records in the retention and disposition schedule. Records important to the organization could be lost if they are not identified by the originator and incorporated into the system.

Recipient

The recipient, too, has an opportunity to share in the control of records. Once the particular record has been acted upon, the recipient follows the same procedure as the record originator. Incoming junk mail should be thrown away after its use; routine response letters and requests should be thrown away after action has been taken. Only those documents that may be required later should be stored. If the recipient is aware that the original record or a copy is retained elsewhere and is available on request, the record can be discarded on completion of all related work. Guidelines about including electronic mail in the system should be followed by the recipient of external E-mail so that all information of value to the organization is retained.

Administrative Support Staff

A major role in records control is played by the administrative support staff.

The administrative support staff plays a major role in records control. The primary responsibility for the preparation of records lies with staff personnel. Efficient use of supplies and equipment is essential during the preparation phase.

Many support staff assume the responsibility for deciding the disposition of the records, as well as for preparing and distributing any copies. In fact, and in practice, it is at this level that the system either succeeds or fails. Therefore, the administrative support staff must understand the importance of records control, know the applicable policies and procedures, and take the actions that support the control system.

Records Processing

A number of people share the responsibility for processing records. These people include the records manager, department heads and supervisors, the active records staff, and the administrative support staff.

Records Manager

The records manager is the person ultimately responsible for the development, implementation, and evaluation of the total records control system. Under the direction of the records manager, persons involved in records preparation and use, as well as in records processing, perform their responsibilities relating to records control. The records manager must have the authority to establish and require a system of records control, set the standards, and establish the procedures for implementation and follow-up on compliance by others within the organization.

Requests for records flow through the office of the records manager. Decisions that affect all levels of management are made by the records manager regarding correspondence, directives, reports, forms, printing, electronic records, and micrographics.

To control the creation and retention of records, the records manager can:

1. Approve requests for new reports. These requests must be channelled through the records manager, and new or revised reports will not be prepared until and unless they have been approved.
2. Approve requests for new or revised forms. As with reports, no new or revised forms will be prepared until approval has been obtained.
3. Establish guidelines for use by all originators for an efficient flow of correspondence and directives, in whatever form they are communicated.
4. Evaluate all requests for printing. In order for this procedure to be effective, the in-house printing operation must be under the direction of the records manager. When contract printing is used, requests for each contract must be channelled through the office of the records manager.

The records manager provides guidance, assistance, and advice regarding all aspects of the creation, distribution, use, maintenance, and disposition of all records.

A survey of records professionals conducted by the authors revealed that many organizations recognize the need for records control in the form of documented policies and procedures provided in records management manuals. Table 15-1 shows the percentage of use of certain control programs.

The records manager is ultimately responsible for the effectiveness of the records control system.

Table 15-1   **Records Management Programs Survey Results**

Type of Program	Percent of Organizations Using
Records management manual	92.86%
Microrecords management program	57.14
Vital records protection program	50.00
Forms management program	42.86
Correspondence management program	28.57
Copy management program	28.57
Reports management program	21.43
Directives management program	10.71

The percentage of use of correspondence, copy, reports, and directives management programs is especially low. However, the need for controls in these areas is critical to an efficient records management system. The methods for managing correspondence, directives, copy, forms, and reports are discussed in detail in Chapters 13 and 14.

Department Heads and Supervisors

Follow-through and follow-up are responsibilities of departmental personnel.

The responsibilities of heads of departments and supervisory personnel are largely in the area of follow-through and follow-up—follow-through with procedures established by the records manager and follow-up on adherence to procedures by personnel within their departments. They must ensure that employees know and follow the control procedures. For example, department heads and supervisors must adhere to the records retention schedule in order to have an effective system of records retention and disposition. At the same time, the persons they supervise must use the established procedures for maintaining records to be kept and for disposing of records in the manner and at the time prescribed.

Records Staff

Records personnel are responsible for the major portion of records processing procedures. In a centralized system, this staff receives the records, prepares the records for storage, checks out records to users, and prepares the records for disposition. The total records system is really tested in an active records centre. It is important, even critical, that the records centre staff fully understands its responsibilities for control, understand and implement the control procedures, and provide feedback to the records manager if procedures are inappropriate or difficult to maintain.

Administrative Support Staff

In many small and medium-sized offices where there are no records centres and where all records are decentralized, the administrative support staff has the same responsibility for records as the records centre staff has in a centralized system. The administrative support staff receives records, prepares records for storage, finds records upon request, and prepares records for disposition. The quantity of records may differ, specialization of individual employees may differ, and the system may differ because of the level of sophistication employed; but the responsibilities remain the same.

 Learning Check: Can you assign control responsibilities to appropriate records personnel and users?

AUDITING THE RECORDS MANAGEMENT SYSTEM

Audits provide information for action.

Evaluating the effectiveness of established controls is accomplished by scheduled audits of the system. **Audit** is defined as a regularly scheduled examination and verification of a specific activity. An **audit trail**, then, is a procedure that provides a paper trail (documentation) that may be used when conducting an audit. For example, when a record is requested and is provided to the requester, an audit trail begins. This trail continues as the record is returned or as follow-up requests for the record to be returned are made. Audits should determine if the system provides for the information needs of managers in their decision making and if the operation of the information system itself is effective.

Why Audit?

Audits provide information that can be used as a basis for evaluating the records management system. Information from audits can be used to answer questions such as: How efficiently is our total system in meeting its goals? How efficiently are individual functions being carried out and how do they contribute to meeting our goals? Audits also help to identify strengths and weaknesses within a system. And, finally, audits help enforce compliance with established policies by making individuals and departments accountable.

Types of Audits

Audits may be either administrative or operational. An **administrative audit** is a review of the effectiveness of the system in terms of the functional quality and quantity of the records available. An **operational audit** examines the system's effectiveness as a process of ensuring that specific tasks are performed effectively and efficiently.

Administrative Audit

Administrative audits examine the overall system.

The administrative audit may begin with an analysis that attempts to answer the question, Does the system accomplish the function efficiently at the lowest possible cost? The analysis is typically conducted by using a questionnaire. This analysis can be made only if all users actively participate in the audit. If a large number of responses to the analysis are negative, an administrative audit is needed. Questions such as the following should be asked regarding the use of information and the quality and quantity necessary to make business decisions (providing a list would help respondents identify specific information):

- What specific information or reports do you currently receive?
- What information do you require in more detail than is presently available?
- What information would be helpful in summary form?
- What information do you receive but seldom or never use?
- What information is not currently needed but is available for decision making?
- How long does it take you to receive requested information?

Questions should also be asked addressing the role of the manager in the creation and distribution of information. Such questions might include:

- What records or documents are created?
- What records or documents are distributed and to whom?

A final set of questions should be asked regarding how well the system functions. Because these elements have an impact on the decision-making process, they are included in the administrative audit. Information derived from these types of questions, however, would be used in the operational audit. These questions might include:

- What records are stored?
- What records are maintained?
- How often are records referenced?
- How long does it take to receive requested records?
- How many misfiles are encountered on a monthly basis?

This audit data would then be correlated with the use data and appropriate changes made. The administrative audit looks closely at the entire records management system in relation to its effectiveness as a tool for management decision making. This audit should include regular monitoring and review processes and should identify the areas where there are administrative breakdowns or bottlenecks in the records control system.

 Learning Check: Can you describe an administrative audit and identify the specific problems it may reveal?

Operational Audit

Operational audits
examine specific
processes within
the system.

Operational audits, unlike administrative audits, which are system-wide, examine specific processes to provide feedback on their effectiveness. If an audit of the control programs has never been conducted or if it has been a long time since one was done, the records manager may wish to find out which control programs are still in place. A simple way to find the information is to distribute a questionnaire such as the one shown in Figure 15-2.

Figure 15-2
Records
Management
Interview
Instrument

Records Management Questionnaire

Name of Person Interviewed_____

Title_____   Department_____

Office Location (No.)_____   Telephone No._____

		Yes	No

1. Is there at least one person responsible for managing the records in this department?   ____   ____

2. If so, what are the responsibilities of that person(s)?

   _____

3. Do you have a retention and disposition schedule?   ____   ____
   Is the schedule regularly used?   ____   ____

4. Is your storage area adequate for current needs?   ____   ____
   Is your storage area adequate for projected 5-year needs
   (including paper, microforms, optical data disks, magnetic media)?   ____   ____

5. Do government regulations affect your departmental records?   ____   ____
   If so, which regulations specifically?

   _____

6. Do you have a records management manual?   ____   ____
   Is the manual regularly used?   ____   ____

7. Do you have a directives management program?   ____   ____
   Is the program regularly used?   ____   ____

8. Do you have a correspondence management program?   ____   ____
   Is the program regularly used?   ____   ____

9. Do you have a forms management program?   ____   ____
   Is the program regularly used?   ____   ____

10. Do you have a reports management program?   ____   ____
    Is the program regularly used?   ____   ____

11. Do you have a copy management program?   ____   ____
    Is the program regularly used?   ____   ____

Use the back of this page for the following items.

12. Explain your perception of records management.

13. What problems do you encounter in your daily records use?

14. What kinds of records security are exercised?

15. Diagram the flow of records in your office.

If a process is not as effective as it should be, it may be necessary to diagram the flow of information and list specific persons and routing procedures. The purpose of this diagram is to identify all of the persons involved in the flow of information and to isolate problem areas. After the persons involved have been identified, the operational audit then examines who performs the task, when it is performed, why it is performed, where it is performed, and what method is used to accomplish the task. Figure 15-3 shows the types of questions to be asked in an operational audit.

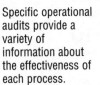 **Learning Check: Can you describe an operational audit and identify the problems it may reveal?**

Specific Operational Audits

Specific processes can be selected for operational audits. Included in these processes are storage and retrieval; reference, accuracy, and personnel ratios; records time/activity; and records retention and compliance.

Specific operational audits provide a variety of information about the effectiveness of each process.

Storage and Retrieval. Measuring storage and retrieval activity provides information from which managers can determine the effectiveness and the productivity of the storage and retrieval system. The following are questions that should be asked:

- How many times was requested information not located?
- How long does it take, on average, to locate a record?
- What is the ratio of unlocated records to total record requests?
- Are standards in place for measuring storage and retrieval effectiveness?
- Are procedures in place for reporting the number of items filed and the number of requests received?

Documentation provides this baseline data for auditing. The best measurement of storage and retrieval processes is how quickly requested information can be retrieved and provided to the person requiring the information. Several factors affect the speed with which information may be retrieved—the number of records that are misfiled, the number of records that cannot be located, and the number of places that must be searched before locating the requested information. This assumes, of course, that adequate, trained personnel are available for the task.

Cooperation among users is essential for audits to be accurate.

To establish a database for records storage and retrieval efficiency, the records manager must have the total cooperation of the records clerks and records supervisor(s). Accurate information must be obtained regarding the number of records filed, number of misfiles and unlocated records, record preparation time, number of requests for retrieval, and retrieval time.

Figure 15-3
Guide for Task Analysis for Operational Audit

Initiating Records	Why	Re-evaluating Records
NEED		**NEED**
What do the records in this procedure accomplish that justifies their existence?		Does the cost exceed the worth?
		Is the information needed?
What other records are related or duplicate in whole or in part the same information?	Why this need?	Is there a better source or a better way to keep this information?
		Can the record be combined?
		Can the record be eliminated?
What inadequacies are there in the records in the procedure?		Can the record be simplified or resequenced?
		Can the record be added to another procedure?
PEOPLE		**PEOPLE**
Who requires the data?	Why by	Can the work be assigned to other units or clerks to simplify the work or combine its handling?
Who enters the information?	these	
Who extracts the information?	people?	
		Can the records in the procedure be resequenced to simplify the entering or extracting of the information?
PLACE		**PLACE**
Where are the records in this procedure written and processed?		Can the writing and processing be combined with similar work done by another unit?
Where are the records sent?	Why here?	
Where are the records stored?		Does the design of the record aid in storage, retrieval, and disposition?
TIME		**TIME**
When are the records in the procedure written?		Are the various processing steps in their proper order?
When are these records processed?	Why at this	Can the peak load be leveled off by better scheduling of the flow?
When are the records stored?	time?	
		Can information be requested so it can be processed during a slack period?
METHOD		**METHOD**
How are the records in this procedure written?		Can the writing method be improved?
How is the information processed?	Why this	Can the routing or mailing method be charged?
How is the information transmitted?	method?	
How is the information stored?		Have the records been geared to the most efficient use of office equipment and systems?

Information necessary to determine storage efficiency and retrieval effectiveness may be obtained by having persons responsible for those activities keep records similar to those shown in Figure 15-4. A **records time/activity chart** provides information regarding the volume of records, types of records activities within each department or file station, and time spent in records activities. Individual time/activity charts may be used to identify the specific activities of records clerks and the amount of time that is spent on various types of records. For small file volume, such as might be kept by a department secretary, recording several weeks' retrieval data three or four times a year would be sufficient to establish a database. Other organizations might desire detailed information to include storage and retrieval efficiency on a periodic basis. Large organizations using central file facilities may wish to keep a daily record of storage and retrieval efficiency. Companies that have records management software can use their retrieval system to record lost files, count the number of searches, and print a report each month.

Figure 15-4
Records
Time/Activity
Chart

RECORDS TIME/ACTIVITY CHART

Division*_____ Department_____ Chart maintained by_____

Directions: Beginning on _____ and continuing for ten working days, maintain this chart for all records activity in your department. Place "tick marks" (卌) each time you file, refile, or charge out a record. Follow the same procedure for identifying the record as correspondence form, or other type of record.

Date	File	Refile	Charge-out	Correspondence	Form	Other

*Only for large divisions where there are several departments using the same file station. In this case, please use separate Activity Charts for each department within the division.

To measure storage and retrieval efficiency, records should be maintained for each request for either information or records retrieval. Figure 15-5 illustrates information required to evaluate the effectiveness in filing records and the efficiency in finding records. In this figure, "No. Pieces Received" refers to the number of separate papers (memos, letters, forms, and so forth). If a letter is multipage, it still represents one piece; a memo stapled to several documents to be stored together also counts as one piece. The number of pieces per inch can be estimated if a physical count has previously established the average number of sheets per piece; that is, on the average, how many sheets of paper are filed together as one piece. A one-inch stack of material normally contains 200 sheets, though not necessarily 200 pieces. Divide 200 by the average number of sheets per piece as previously established to determine the average number of pieces per inch. An estimate can easily be made of the number of pieces received by measuring in inches the stack of incoming material. In Figure 15-5 the number of pieces received for storage, not the number of sheets received, is provided on the form.

Figure 15-5
Storage and Retrieval Efficiency

EFFECTIVENESS IN FILING RECORDS			Type of File *Case*			EFFECTIVENESS IN FINDING RECORDS			Type of File *Subject*
Date (a)	No. Hours Filing (b)	No. Pieces Received (c)	No. Cross-References			Date (a)	No. Requests Rec'd. (b)	No. Not Found (c)	No. Requiring a Search in Three or More Folders (d)
			Forms (d)	Extra Copies (e)					
7/3	3	145	10	15		7/3	23	4	9

If file activity needs to be determined by department, this information can be obtained at the same time as the previous information. Some computer programs using a database will automatically count, store, and print an annual report of all searches by department, type of record, and age of material requested.

Filing time spent per item may be obtained by dividing the total time in minutes used to file (shown in hours in Figure 15-5) by the number of items filed. **Retrieval time** may be obtained by dividing the time in minutes used to retrieve items (shown in hours in Figure 15-5) by the total number of requests received.

Reference Ratio. **Reference ratio**, which measures file activity, can be determined by dividing the number of retrieval requests by the number of pieces stored. The following formula is applied to data collected through an operational audit:

$$\text{reference ratio} = \frac{\text{number of retrieval requests}}{\text{number of pieces stored}}$$

A ratio of less than 5 percent is considered low and indicates that the records are inactive and should be transferred to inactive storage or destroyed.

Accuracy Ratio. **Accuracy ratio**, which measures the effectiveness of the records system and records personnel, can be determined by dividing the number of records located by the number of records requested. This provides an overall accuracy ratio. Many organizations operate with a 99 percent ratio. The following formula is applied to the data supplied through reporting.

$$\text{accuracy ratio} = \frac{\text{number of records located}}{\text{number of records requested}}$$

Even 1 percent of records not located is unacceptable in most instances. More specific breakdowns may also be made by determining the ratio of misfiles to total requests as well as determining the ratio of records unlocated to total requests. Typically, misfiles represent 3 percent of files. Although this figure is typical, it is high and causes a decline in productivity.

Further accuracy measures may be obtained by determining the ratio of records requiring a search in more than one location before retrieval to total records located. This ratio may indicate poor indexing or inadequate cross-referencing.

Staff requirements for specific records tasks vary with the tasks.

Personnel Ratio. **Personnel ratio**, which measures the adequacy of the records staff to perform specific functions, may be determined by analyzing the standard staff requirements for particular tasks. One employee is required for each 5,200 cubic feet of records received; one employee is required to handle reference activity for each 7,000 cubic feet of records stored annually; and one employee is required for each 4,700 cubic feet of records destroyed. The results of personnel ratios will suggest overstaffing or understaffing and provide information regarding the specific area(s) requiring staff adjustment.

Records Retention and Compliance. A major factor in a sound records retention program is compliance with the schedule. Motivating department members to remember to follow the schedule established through a careful records inventory and appraisal requires reminders and enforcement. Determination of whether the records retention schedule is followed may be made through a compliance audit and review.

Compliance may be encouraged through the records retention audit and subsequent reporting that informs upper-level managers which departments are following the procedures and which departments are either lax or ignoring the schedule. This also encourages and reinforces those departments that are developing good records management habits. The audit also provides an opportunity for the records management department to demonstrate its commitment to company policy as well as to continue a working relationship that developed during the records inventory and retention process.

Other Measures. Audits may also include data regarding the file activity of particular departments or users. This information provides a basis for analyzing overutilization or underutilization of records by departments.

Because the information obtained is already identified by classification system in use (subject, numeric, and so forth), statistics may be generated that reflect the efficiency of the particular classification system. For example, if most of the misfiles or unlocated records are identified in the subject classification system, this information could suggest that a careful evaluation be made of the procedures within that system or of the appropriateness of that classification system to the filed material.

Learning Check: Can you identify and describe process specific audits?

HOW TO AUDIT

Auditing is necessary to evaluate the records system.

Auditing various records management functions is a time consuming, but necessary task. Therefore, establishing auditing procedures and following them is important.

Audit Schedule

The auditing workload should be distributed evenly to effectively use resources.

The first decision to be made is when the audit will be conducted. Audits should be scheduled so the work load is evenly distributed with regard to both time and staff. Once the schedule has been developed, those who are undergoing audits for the first or second time need to be notified in writing that an audit is pending. The letter will also state that the department representative will be contacted to arrange a mutually convenient time. Notice of the pending audit has these advantages:

1. It allows a grace period between the time the department contact receives the letter and the date of the meeting, so that if there has been no opportunity to work on the records during the year, time can be scheduled.
2. It provides department contacts with sufficient time to think about their schedules (retention periods, wording, and so forth) in the event that changes need to be made.
3. It provides recognition that the audit is an imposition on their time. Regardless of the fact that department contacts are told that they will be subject to audits, they are still faced with having to find time in already busy schedules to go through a records audit.[1]

Audit Procedures

To provide consistency in treatment and to have consistency in results, audit procedures must be established, distributed, and implemented as stated. Established procedures lend authority to the process, making it easier for auditors and for those who are being audited.

One organization has established procedures for scheduling audits,[2] and although this time frame is specifically for records retention compliance audits, the timing and procedures may be appropriate for other types of audits.

---

[1]Jean K. Crary, "The Teeth of the Program—the Records Audit," *Records Management Quarterly,* Vol. 19, No. 3 (July, 1985), p. 16.

[2]Ibid., pp. 19–20.

Audits in years one and two are intensive and detailed reviews. These reviews provide the auditor with an opportunity to evaluate the system being audited as well as the auditing process. They also permit people within the department to ask questions, to suggest solutions to problems, and to interact with the records management staff.

Third-year audits are conducted by questionnaire, which the departmental contacts are asked to complete (see Figure 15-6). This questionnaire involves each department and makes each accountable for supplying the audit information to the records management unit. Departments are informed that departmental compliance results are reported annually to the appropriate persons, such as the vice president for operations or the chief information officer. If the questionnaire is not returned after a few reminder phone calls, a zero percent compliance is reported for that department.

In the fourth and following years, the percentage of total compliance is based on a random sample. During the audit, five records series are chosen at random and physically audited. The random audit offers the advantage of saving time for the auditor, while still providing an audit that yields reliable results. If a department is in compliance for the five series selected at random for audit, the probability is that the department is in compliance for the entire schedule. Figure 15-7 shows a worksheet used as a checklist to ensure consistent questions about each series selected for audit.

To accommodate changes in the records series that were not selected for audit, a general worksheet (Figure 15-8) is used. This worksheet allows the departments to suggest additions, deletions, changes in retention periods, and any other comments that are relevant to the audit.

REPORTING THE FINDINGS

The overall purpose of a records management audit is to provide information about the efficiency and effectiveness of the records management system as a whole and of the individual functions that make up the system. Providing this information to the appropriate people is the purpose of audit reports.

Figure 15-6

Records Retention Audit Questionnaire

Department_____

Contact_____   Schedule #_____

	Yes	**No**

1. Have any of your department's records been
   transferred to the Records Centre since last
   year's records retention schedule audit?   ____   ____

   If no, state reason._____

2. Have your department's records been purged for
   destruction in-house since last year's records
   retention schedule audit?   ____   ____

   If no, state reason._____

3. Does your records retention schedule need revision?   ____   ____

   If yes, which of the following apply:

   Additions_____

   Deletions_____

   Rewording of existing series_____

   Total revision_____

4. Does your department currently have records
   stored in the Records Centre?   ____   ____

   If yes, do the records need to be reviewed for
   destruction or permanent retention in the Archives?   ____   ____

5. Is your department's filing scheme effective?   ____   ____

6. Does your records retention schedule reflect the
   filing scheme?   ____   ____

   If no, would you like to schedule a consultation to
   discuss a revision to either the filing scheme or the
   records retention schedule?   ____   ____

7. After reviewing your records and your schedule, please indicate on the attached page(s) what
   action has taken place during the past year.

Questionnaire completed by _____

Date_____

Figure 15-7

Records Retention Schedule Compliance Audit Worksheet

SERIES #_____

1. Is it necessary at this time to make any changes in the retention procedure?

   Yes_____   No_____

   If yes, what changes need to be made?
   Retention period   Yes_____   No_____   N/A_____
   Change in wording   Yes_____   No_____   N/A_____
   Deletion of series   Yes_____   No_____   N/A_____
   What is the justification for the change?_____

   _____

2. Has the retention procedure for this series been followed as currently specified on
   the records retention schedule?
   In-house review   Yes_____   No_____   N/A_____
   In-house destruction   Yes_____   No_____   N/A_____
   Transfer to Records Centre Yes_____   No_____   N/A_____
   Review of records in R/C for permanent retention/destruction
                             Yes_____   No_____   N/A_____

3. If records have been destroyed in-house, has a "Notification of Destruction
   of Records" form been filed?
                             Yes_____   No_____

   For records eligible for destruction in the Records Centre, has the
   Unit Head signed the "Intent to Destroy Records" form?
                             Yes_____   No_____

4. Is this series vital?   Yes_____   No_____
   If yes, is there a vital records protection
   for these records?   Yes_____   No_____
      Has the plan been implemented?
                             Yes_____   No_____

      If not, why not?_____

   _____

5. Department is in compliance with the schedule for this series.
                             Yes_____   No_____

6. Audited by_____

Figure 15-8

Records Retention Schedule Compliance Audit Entire Schedule Review Worksheet

_____ (total) series have been selected at random and physically audited. In addition, the following general information is required to complete the audit.

1. Are there any *problems* with any of the other series on the schedule?

   | | | Yes_____ | No_____ |

   If so, what?   Change in retention   Yes_____   No_____
   Rewording of series   Yes_____   No_____
   Which series are affected?
   Series   Change

   _____

   _____

   _____

   _____

2. Is it necessary to make *additions* to the schedule?

                                                   Yes_____   No_____

3. Is it necessary to make *deletions* from the schedule?

                                                   Yes_____   No_____

   If so, which series?_____

4. What is the justification for the deletion?_____

   _____

   _____

   _____

5. Have other series on the schedule been reviewed for any of the following?
   In-house destruction   Yes_____   No_____
   Transfer to Records Centre   Yes_____   No_____
   If not, why not?_____

6. Which series have not been reviewed this year?_____

   _____

   _____

7. Remarks?

   _____

   _____

   _____

   _____

8. Audited by_____   Date_____
   Title_____

Information Presentation

Audit reports may be presented in different formats.

Audit reports may be manually prepared and processed, or they may be computer generated (Figure 15-9 shows the manually prepared type). But each reports the same information. Different types of reports may use different types of presentations. Percentages of changes in filing and retrieval efficiency could be shown in tabular form; dramatic changes in any status might be best presented in a bar graph; trends might be graphically shown in a line drawing.

Figure 15-9
Manually Prepared Records Search Analysis

77-09 (12-79)

RECORDS ANALYSIS

DEPARTMENT: *Finance and Administration*   SCHEDULE NO. *RS16-D*

ACTIVITY

DATE OF SEARCH: *12/31/89*

| RECORD TITLE | ITEM NO. | CURR. YEAR | YEARS SEARCHED | | | | | | | TOTAL SEARCHES |
			1	2	3	4	5 - 9	10 - 14	15+	
Accounts Receivable	2410							1		1
Cash Vouchers	2413	265	3,630	3,566	115	72	417	53		8,118
Closing Reports	2414						1			1
Consolidated Earnings Preparation	2415									0
Expense Accounts Detail	2416									0
Expense Subsidiary Ledgers	2417		1				1			2
General Ledger Accounts	2420									0
General Ledgers (Dec.)	2421						2	1		3
General Ledgers (Jan-Nov)	2422						1	2		3
General Ledger Identification	2425					1				1

PERIOD COVERED: TO   TOTAL

SUMMARY:

Some reports lend themselves more readily to narrative presentations, while other results are better shown in a form. Figure 15-10 shows a records retention compliance report in this format.

Figure 15-10
Records Retention
Schedule
Compliance Report

RECORDS RETENTION SCHEDULE COMPLIANCE AUDIT

SCHEDULE NUMBER *36-11* DATE NOTIFIED *1/27* DATE OF AUDIT *2/9*

DEPARTMENT _*Accounting*_ EXTENSION *3564*

LOCATION _*Bldg 2-B*_

DEPARTMENT MANAGER _*Jane McGrath*_

DEPARTMENT CONTACT _*Mike Glass*_

OTHERS CONTACTED _*None*_

NUMBER OF RECORDS SERIES ON THE SCHEDULE *15* NUMBER SAMPLED *5*

RECORD SERIES SAMPLED:

SERIES #	NAME OF SERIES	COMPLIANCE (IN/OUT)
21-10	Travel Vouchers	In
21-11	Receipts for Airline Tickets	In
21-12	Reimbursement	Out
21-13	Advances-Cash	In
21-14	Company Car Loan-Travel	In

TOTAL PERCENTAGE OF COMPLIANCE WITH RETENTION SCHEDULE *80%*

DEPARTMENTAL RECORDS STORED IN THE RECORDS CENTRE HAVE BEEN REVIEWED FOR DESTRUCTION OR PERMANENT RETENTION *✓* YES ___ NO

COMMENTS:

AUDITOR _*Marvin Slattery*_

TITLE _*Auditor, Administration*_

Reports Distribution

Distribute audit
reports to those
who require the
information.

Reports, like all other records, should be distributed only to those people who have a need for the information. The reports should provide a basis for users to improve their methods, increase their efficiency, and improve their effectiveness. The reports also provide managers with information that allows them to evaluate the effectiveness of the functions for which they are responsible. Reports are discussed in detail in Chapter 14, "Forms and Reports Management."

 Learning Check: Can you identify various reports resulting from a records management audit and their contents?

TERMINOLOGY REVIEW

Review each of the terms listed below in the Glossary on page 521.

accuracy ratio	filing time
administrative audit	operational audit
audit	personnel ratio
audit trail	precontrol
concurrent control	records time/activity chart
control	reference ratio
feedback control	retrieval time

REVIEW AND DISCUSSION

1. Describe the role of the control subsystem and its relationship to the records management system.
2. Define the three types of control, giving an example not cited in the text of each type of control.
3. Describe the three links in the scope of control and the relationships among the links.
4. How would you determine whether an administrative or operational audit is more appropriate?
5. Discuss three problems that might be discovered during (a) an administrative audit and (b) an operational audit.
6. Describe three specific operational audits. What information can be gained from each?
7. Describe the procedures for conducting an audit.
8. Identify three reports resulting from a records management audit and their contents.

APPLICATIONS

1. Select one record that is processed either through your workplace (if employed) or through your educational system (if not employed). Then take this record through the task analysis for an operational audit as shown in Figure 15-3.
2. Identify the type(s) of control represented by each of the following:
   a. personnel selection
   b. performance appraisal

     c. retention schedule

     d. records activity report

     e. records centre design

     f. records management manual

     g. central files supervisor

     h. forms design

     i. reports, in general

     j. vital records protection program

3. Justify your selection of the type(s) of control for each of the items in Application 2.

4. Assign two control responsibilities to each of the following categories of users or processors: originator, recipient, administrative support staff, department heads, and supervisors. Where there may be dual responsibility, specify.

CONCLUDING CASES

A. Madison Lumber and Supply Company

Madison Lumber and Supply Company, located on the outskirts of a large metropolitan area, is the major supplier of lumber and supplies to large construction projects such as shopping malls, housing developments, and recreational complexes. The company has been in operation since 1918 and has maintained a reputation for high-quality products, excellent service, and efficient operations.

Over the last few years, the company has moved to computerized billing and plans to expand the computerization to include some of the records management functions. The records manager, Ron Owens, has been eager to modernize the entire records management system.

Before Ron begins to make recommendations for the changes in the records management department, what actions would you suggest he take now? Why these specific actions?

B. B & T Company

During lunch in the B & T company cafeteria, a number of the employees were discussing their pet peeves. Their conversation was overheard by Meg Turner, the records manager.

Marsha (records centre clerk): Records don't come to us on any systematic basis. For several months we will receive no records; the next month we are swamped with records. We just can't handle them.

Joey (secretary): The letters I type are so long; I rarely type a letter that is less than two pages with at least one p.s. Even though I use word processing, it is still a waste of time, and I wouldn't want to have to read those letters.

Ramon (clerk): It seems that we send copies to everyone, even the custodian!

Violet (central files clerk): Letters we get for filing from one department are always coded—wrong. The coding never matches the ones we are supposed to use.

Tom (secretary): My department files everything—including memos that are no longer of interest—like the one about the Christmas party.

Sumio (management trainee): We seem to generate reports for everything. We must have a report on reports!

Joey: Marsha, I don't mean to be personal about this, but the last three times we requested records from the records centre, we had to wait a long time to get them. By the time we got the records, they were not as useful as they should have been.

What control responsibilities should Meg examine, based on the comments she overheard?

SUGGESTED READINGS AND RESOURCES

Boyd, F. "The Measurement of Work." *Records Management Quarterly,* Vol. 26, No. 2 (April, 1992), p. 20.

Kaufhold, Penny. "Rough Edges of the Learning Curve." *Records Management Quarterly,* Vol. 21, No. 2 (April, 1987), p. 33.

Pennix, Gail B. "Try a Little TQC." *Records Management Quarterly,* Vol. 21, No. 4 (October, 1987), p. 4.

Wolchak, William H. "Conducting a Systems Analysis." *Records Management Quarterly,* Vol. 20, No. 3 (July, 1986), p. 16.

Profile
Project Administrator

The project administrator of the Provincial Children's Foster Care Review Board is Denise Ruff, who has been with the board for 11 years. The board has 18 employees. The position titles include the director, the project administrator, review board coordinators, administrative specialist, and administrative assistant.

Education and experience requirements for the project administrator position include a baccalaureate degree, management experience, and computer expertise. Ms. Ruff has a B.A. in counselling/psychology. The position requires that she be thoroughly familiar with provincial regulations governing child welfare and have an ability to work well with other people. She works closely with the Department of Social Services, lawmakers, judges, review board members, and the volunteers.

The project administrator's position did not originally have the responsibility of maintaining an automated database of over 5,000 records. However, as the need for additional and better information grew,

Ms. Ruff realized that only an electronic database would meet the needs of the board. She did not have formal training in records management or computers, but knew the types of information needed. So, in 1993 she decided what she wanted and hired a consultant to help her design a special software system. As a result of this system, the staff and review board members have access to the most up-to-date information on all the foster children in the province.

Ms. Ruff continues to refine the system to improve the care of foster children in the province. Currently she is working on refining the database to focus on problems such as drug abuse, teenaged mothers, and other areas that need special attention today.

Advancement opportunities are from the present position as project administrator to director of the department. Ms. Ruff is active in several organizations concerned with foster care and has taken part in a national study on child abuse and neglect.

Records Management Manual

Learning Goals

After completing this chapter, you should be able to:

1. Define a records management manual.
2. List the purposes of a records management manual.
3. Explain the five types of records management manuals.
4. List and describe the steps in preparing a records management manual.
5. Describe the procedures for distribution and maintenance of a records management manual.

A records management manual is an essential tool, serving a variety of purposes in both large and small organizations. If the manual is to be an effective tool, its preparation, distribution, and maintenance must be carefully planned.

NEED FOR A RECORDS MANAGEMENT MANUAL

The records management manual increases efficiency.

Most functional units within large organizations use the services of the records management unit. To aid users in getting the most benefit from records management services, many organizations use a records management manual to increase efficiency and expedite requests for records unit services.

Definition

A **records management manual** is a guide to the functioning of the records management system. Information on the who, what, when, where, and how of the records management system (for employees of the records unit and for others in the organization who may need to use the services of the records unit) is provided in the manual.

Large organizations find comprehensive records management manuals indispensable to the functioning of their records units. The comprehensiveness and formality of the manual generally increase as the size of the organization increases. Small organizations may need a less extensive manual to achieve the desired results; however, every organization needs a records management manual in some form.

Purposes

Four specific purposes are served by the records management manual.

The development and use of a records management manual serves four specific purposes: (1) standardizing procedures, (2) establishing responsibility, (3) assisting in employee training, and (4) providing for updates of policies and procedures.

Standardizes Procedures

Whether an organization has a centralized or decentralized records system, certain procedures need to be performed consistently by each unit. Examples of these procedures include establishing records retention periods, selecting equipment and supplies, and transferring records to the records centre. An organization with a centralized records system has an even greater need for standardized procedures: records sent to the active files area need to be properly coded. Records centre clerks can then respond to requests for information or retrieve files more efficiently.

Oral instructions are frequently forgotten or misinterpreted. Written instructions are more likely to elicit consistent, correct performance. In addition, establishing written procedures minimizes questions concerning how to perform a task. Questions of this kind are very costly to the organization since they cause the inefficient use of two employees' time—the one who must ask what to do and the one who must provide an answer.

Written instructions provide clarity.

Establishes Responsibility

Records management manuals help define tasks and responsibilities.

When the organization establishes responsibility for the performance of certain records-related tasks, it determines who—which individual, group of individuals, or department—is responsible for completing the tasks. Specific instructions for responsibility prevent employees or departments from "passing the buck" when a job is not done properly or on time. Establishing the "who" also allows users of records unit services to determine with whom to discuss a records problem or whom to ask to perform a certain service.

Assists in Employee Training

Records management manuals usually contain detailed job descriptions for members of the records unit staff. Complete procedures for performing the duties of each position are included in these job descriptions. Flowcharts illustrating the flow of work within the records unit and into the records unit from other units within the organization may also be included in the manual.

New employees can easily obtain information.

A list of procedures to follow in completing each assigned task, illustrations of the source of each task, and locations of documents to be filed or forms or reports to be delivered are valuable tools for newcomers to the records unit, those promoted to new positions within the unit, or other employees of the organization. These procedures do not replace experience in the performance of assigned duties or on-the-job training. However, they provide a ready reference until procedures become familiar; this will prevent additional time from being lost in asking and answering the same questions.

Provides for Updates of Policies and Procedures

New directives provide current information.

Records policies may be updated through the issuance of new directives. Sometimes, however, not everyone is notified or someone fails to dispose of the old directive when the new one is issued. Many times, procedures are not examined at regular intervals to determine if more efficient methods or tools are available. A records management manual can alleviate these difficulties by providing a complete set of written procedures, a format that can be easily updated, and a procedure for regular review and revision of records policies.

> ✓ **Learning Check: Can you describe the purposes a records management manual serves?**

PREPARATION

Effective manuals require careful preparation.

Preparing a records management manual is an extensive task, which demands a thorough knowledge of the organization, its goals, and the manner in which the records unit is organized to help achieve these goals. Manual preparation demands careful planning and consistent attention to detail. The preparation process involves completing the following eight steps:

1. Obtain the approval and support of upper-level management.
2. Determine the type of manual needed.
3. Assign authorship responsibility.
4. Identify sources of information for the manual.
5. Determine the content of the manual.
6. Collect and analyze data.
7. Write the manual.
8. Publish the manual.

Obtain Approval and Support

Approval and support from upper-level management are essential.

As has been stated many times in previous chapters, tasks affecting the operation of the entire organization should be undertaken only with the approval and support of upper-level management. In most organizations, the records manager does not have the final authority on records policy decisions. Even though the records manager may create the policy wording and intent, approval from a higher level of management is still necessary. Requests for approval and support for a records management manual from upper levels of management would include the definition and purposes of the manual (as discussed earlier in this chapter) and the benefits resulting from increased efficiency in the records unit.

Once approval has been obtained for the development of a records management manual, the approval should be communicated to everyone involved in this project. Department heads, division heads, records liaison persons, and records unit staff members will be asked to perform extra tasks to assist in the preparation of this manual. Cooperation may come more readily if all participants are aware that the upper-level managers consider this project important to the overall functioning and success of the organization.

Determine Manual Type

The manuals found in a company may be classified as one of five types. These types are (1) policy, (2) organizational, (3) administrative, (4) operational, and (5) combination.

Policy Manual

A policy manual provides guidelines for daily decision making.

A **policy manual** establishes general guidelines for consistent decision making. Establishing written policies requires managers to anticipate needed actions. A manual based on these guidelines provides a framework for day-to-day procedures and operations. Employees are responsible for working and making decisions within the established framework. The major disadvantage of this type of manual is the possibility of multiple interpretations of some guidelines because of the general framework described. Some records management policies that might be contained in a company policy manual include when and how to transfer records to inactive storage, which records are considered vital records, and how to use the subject classification system.

Organizational Manual

An organizational manual details working relationships among units.

An **organizational manual** describes the structure, duties, and responsibilities of each unit and explains the relationships between other units and the records unit. Each section of the organizational manual contains an organization chart and a description of the duties and responsibilities of each position within that section of the records unit. A separate listing is often made of managers of those units of the organization using records unit services.

An organizational manual provides the opportunity to place proper emphasis on line and staff relationships within the unit and within the organization. Careful thought in preparing such a manual may eliminate overlapping responsibilities or gaps in responsibilities. The major disadvantage of this type of manual is that it is not possible to illustrate the informal relationships within the records unit and the organization that contribute to the smooth functioning of the records unit. In addition, once the relationships are established and published, the organization may find the published structure to be inflexible in dealing with changing needs.

Administrative Procedures Manual

Standard operating procedures are included in an administrative procedures manual.

An **administrative procedures manual** includes standard operating procedures that facilitate the completion of tasks requiring the work of more than one unit of the organization. Procedures are prescribed courses of action for stated conditions, and their publication clearly establishes authority and responsibility. Administrative manuals for a records management system would include guidelines for preparation and distribution of correspondence and directives; approval, printing, and use of forms; and transfer of records to the records centre.

Operational Manual

An operational
manual provides
information about
one unit and is
used in that unit
only

An **operational manual** contains detailed information on the structure, policies, and procedures of one unit of an organization. An operational manual is used only in the unit for which it was prepared. Examples of frequently used operational manuals include a records retention and disposition manual, a records disaster prevention and recovery manual, a filing manual, and a vital records manual.

A **records retention and disposition manual** includes the records retention schedule, procedures for establishing retention periods, procedures for transferring inactive records to the records centre, and procedures for the destruction of records, as discussed in Chapter 4.

A **records disaster prevention and recovery manual** details the course of action required to prevent or minimize the effects of a disaster and to recover, to the extent possible, the records that are damaged. The benefits of this manual are described in Chapter 11.

A **filing manual** contains rules and regulations for filing that standardize procedures, assist in training personnel, and make storage and retrieval more efficient. The content of this manual should include indexing rules and classification guidelines, which were discussed in Chapter 6.

A **vital records protection manual**, which was discussed in Chapter 11, contains policies on how to determine whether a record is vital, what to do to protect a vital record, and how to access and retrieve a vital record.

Combination Manual

A combination
manual includes all
of the information
in one manual.

A **combination manual** includes information on records policies, the structure and responsibilities of the records unit in relation to other units, administrative procedures, and operating procedures. Many organizations have found that a manual that brings together all four elements of administering and operating the records management system can be more effectively utilized by all organization employees. Having all the information in one manual eliminates time lost in determining which manual contains the needed information.

Distribution of a combination manual may include supplying the complete manual or separate sections to different levels of personnel—managers and administrative support personnel. When a combination manual is distributed by sections, a complete copy of the manual should be available to each unit and to each user who has a need for a complete manual.

 Learning Check: Can you describe the types of records management manuals?

Assign Authorship Responsibility

Preparing a records management manual is seldom considered to be a one-person task. A committee of employees from the records unit and other units in the organization as shown in Figure 16-1 can provide a broader input source. Through delegation of information gathering and writing responsibilities, the preparation time can be reduced. All employees should be notified that a manual is being prepared and encouraged to make suggestions to the manual committee.

Figure 16-1
Manual Authorship
by Committee

Authorship is usually under the direction of the records manager.

Successful completion of the preparation process requires a thorough knowledge of all aspects of the records management system as well as familiarity with the organization and the special records requirements of various units. Because of these requirements, the records manager will usually chair the committee and direct the completion of this project. Consideration should be given to appointing to the committee those managers and supervisors who will be involved in the implementation and use of the manual.

Identify Sources

Records management manuals may be seldom used because of poor selection or presentation of material. Knowing this, the manual committee should identify all possible sources of information before beginning to write.

Information from
records
management
manuals of other
organizations is
helpful when
preparing a
manual.

One of the most readily identified sources of information is the records management manuals of other organizations. An examination of these manuals will suggest topics to be included, methods for presenting information, and printing formats. Often this examination process will reveal as much about what to avoid as about what to include. Committee members may identify ambiguous or wordy instructions, improper sequencing of instructions, difficulty in locating information, and irrelevant content. Observing these faults in other manuals may make committee members more aware of and likely to avoid these errors when preparing their own manual.

Additional sources of information for the manual include:

- Organizational directives that include items about records.
- Surveys of employees within each unit that will be using the manual.
- Vendors of records management equipment and supplies.
- Records management and other professional organizations and publications.
- Grievance records concerning past problems with records management policies and procedures.

The organization's legal counsel and auditor should also be consulted for input on meeting legal and fiscal requirements. In addition, the committee may wish to consider hiring a technical writer as a consultant to make suggestions or to direct the committee in its manual preparation efforts.

Determine Content

A records
management
manual should
include all
information
necessary for
efficient use.

The records management manual will be only as effective as the information it contains. The manual should contain all information necessary to the efficient functioning of the records unit itself and for the efficient use of the records unit by other units within the organization. Contents of the manual can be divided into these sections: (1) introduction, (2) records policies, (3) records services, and (4) appendices.

Introductory Material

Introductory material should include title page, preface, authority statement, and table of contents. The title of the manual, organization name, authorship of the manual, and publication date should appear on the title page. Authorship should give recognition to all personnel who assisted in the preparation of the manual. The preface explains the reason for the manual, defines records management, and describes the scope of material included in the manual. The authority statement advises users that the procedures and policies established by the records manager and upper management are legitimate and binding. An organization chart of the structure of the records unit and of other units that depend on its services may also be included here. The table of contents lists the subjects covered in the manual and their locations by page number.

Records Policies

Records policies offer guidelines for decision making to both the records management staff and users about the work of the records management unit.

This section includes policies and procedures for each task performed within the records unit. Other policies and procedures that affect the creation, distribution, use, maintenance, storage, or destruction of records in all other units are also included. These statements will reflect the basic position of the organization relating to its recorded information. Typically policies and procedures are included for the following topics: correspondence creation and distribution; directives creation and distribution; forms and reports creation, distribution, and use; records storage and retrieval; confidential information policy and freedom of information; records retention; records destruction; storage equipment and supplies selection; disaster prevention and recovery; electronic records; microrecords applications; and telecommunications use.

An example of a procedure on records retrieval that is included in a records management manual is shown in Figure 16-2. A policy on records destruction might inform the users of the approved methods of records destruction, and of who has the authority for records destruction, and emphasize the necessity for all scheduled records to be destroyed according to the approved retention periods. Forms for records transfer and destruction, along with instructions about how to complete the forms, would also be included. A flowchart showing the path for the records to be destroyed might also be helpful.

Records Services

Records services provides information about how the records management staff can aid users within the organization.

This section outlines the kinds of records services the records management unit can offer to users. Records handling services that are available in-house and those available outside the organization are also included. For example, the users need to know that the records manual is administered by the records manager and that if there are questions regarding any policies or procedures included in the manual, the contact person is the records manager.

If the organization provides records storage and destruction facilities, users need to know whom to contact to use these facilities. This section also contains information about obtaining specialized services, such as micrographics assistance, any specialized filing requirements, space planning, reprographics, forms and reports management, and any other services that the records management unit makes available to its users.

Figure 16-2
Information
Retrieval
Procedures

Records Management Manual
Part 1

Mountain Bell

I.M. 140

Form 5076
(Rev. 10/91)

REQUEST FOR INFORMATION, WITHDRAWAL, OR EXAMINATION OF RECORDS

TO: Records Centre Supervisor
1585 Allison Street
Lakewood, Alberta

DATE _July 16, 19--_

REQUESTED DATA
(TO BE COMPLETED BY RECORDS CENTRE)

REQUESTED BY:
NAME _J. A. Barton_ _____ DEPARTMENT _Accounting_
ADDRESS _601 East 8th Ave._ CITY _Calgary_ STATE _Alberta_
ROOM NO. _____ TEL. NO. _555-1617_

REQUEST TAKEN BY:
V. A. Clark

REQUESTED BY:
TELEPHONE ☒ TWX ☐ FORM 5075 ☐

	INFORMATION OR RECORDS REQUESTED			
ROOM NO.	**DESCRIPTION**	**PERIOD**		
		Beginning	Ending	
SN 865	Routine Estimates - Alberta	1-1-90	12-1-90	

TRANSMIT DATA BY: DATE

TELEPHONE ☐ _____
CO. MAIL ☒ _July 26, 19--_
CDN. MAIL ☐ _____
PREPAID EXP. ☐ _____
DUPL. COPY ☐ _____

QUANTITY:

BOXES _____
PACKAGES _/_
ITEMS _____

RECORDS RECEIVED BY _____ DATE _____

RECORDS RETURNED TO RECORDS CENTRE
BY _____ VIA _____ DATE _____

RECORDS RECEIVED AT RECORDS CENTRE
BY _____ DATE _____

LOCATED IN RECORDS CENTRE

SECTION NUMBER _3_
SHELF NUMBER _4_

ESTIMATED DATE RECORDS WILL BE RETURNED:
July 30, 19--

INSTRUCTIONS FOR PREPARING FORM 5076

1. In general the data required to prepare the form are self-explanatory. The Records Centre will enter the data in the blocked area.

2. If the request is made by Form 5076, the "estimated date records will be returned" should be entered by the person preparing the form.

3. Requests may be made by telephone or TWX. In these instances the Form 5076 will be prepared by the Records Centre. An alternative method is to originate Form 5076 in triplicate and send all copies to the Records Centre.

4. Upon receipt of the request, the Records Centre will secure and forward the records to the requester, returning the original and duplicate copies of Form 5076 by separate mail.

5. Upon receipt of the records, the original copy of Form 5076 should be signed and returned to the Records Centre.

6. When the records are returned, the manner and date of the return should be shown on the duplicate copy of Form 5076 and returned to the Records Centre by separate mail.

7. Upon receipt of the records in the Records Centre, the manner and date of the return should be shown on the original copy of Form 5076.

Source: Adapted from Mountain Bell Telephone Co.

Appendices, Glossary, and Alphabetic Index

Appendices provide information to make using the manual easier.

Appendices are meant to make using the manual easier. Some materials to be included to enhance the use of the manual are sample forms, records volume conversion tables, and any specialized information (such as a vital records protection manual or government regulations) that may have value to specific groups or individuals within the organization.

The glossary should include definitions of all technical and records-related terms, such as *record, nonrecord, long-term record, temporary record, active temporary record, inactive record, vital record,* and *microrecord,* as well as abbreviations used in the manual.

An alphabetic index to the contents of the manuals is essential for efficient access to the information within the manual. When the writing is completed, a thorough search should be made of each page of the manual for key words to include in the index. To minimize the omission of key words or page numbers, two people should independently prepare indexes. Some word processing software assists in the preparation of indexes.

Collect and Analyze Data

Existing policies and procedures are reviewed for currentness.

Once the content has been determined, the manual committee must begin the task of collecting information. The committee may wish to have the records manager meet with unit heads to "sell the program" and encourage their cooperation and that of their staffs. A brief explanation of the benefits to be derived in terms of more efficient operations will emphasize the importance of having a records management manual. Unit heads or members of their staffs may be asked to write or review existing procedures for inclusion in the manual. Involvement in this stage of the development process will increase the likelihood of widespread use of the completed manual.

The task of collecting information is then divided among the manual committee members. Deadlines are established for the collection process so that the work of the manual committee can proceed in a timely manner.

All of the data gathered are categorized according to function within the records unit, such as micrographics, forms and reports, active records, and so forth. The number and types of categories will vary with the size of the organization (particularly the size of the records unit).

The information, which has been sorted into categories, is then analyzed to determine appropriateness and importance in the manual. Because it is a time-consuming task, this analysis is usually done by subcommittees determining the different elements to be included. Then each subcommittee presents its suggestions to the manual committee, which may accept, reject, or make changes in these recommendations before the material is accepted for inclusion and presented to the manual writers.

Write the Manual

Individuals knowledgeable about the functioning of the organization and records management are chosen to write the manual.

After content decisions have been made, the actual writing of the manual may begin. The writing is usually done by the records manager and supervisors of the sections of the records unit. These individuals are more qualified to write the manual because of their knowledge of the organization and their experience in the records management program.

Style

Several writing formats may be used, depending on what is to be communicated.

The major objective of the writing phase is to write in a manner that will be easily understood. The manual may not be used unless this objective is achieved for all potential users. For this to be accomplished, the level of writing should be such that it will be understood by those employees possessing the lowest level of reading comprehension.

Understanding will be more easily achieved if the writers remember three essential elements—simplicity, strength, and conciseness. Simplicity is achieved by using simple terms and short sentences and paragraphs to convey information or procedures. Build on basic concepts.

Strength comes from a positive style of writing. Use specific, active verbs to state actions to be taken. Instructions should be given in positive rather than negative terms; use *dos* rather than *don'ts*. Put instructions in list rather than paragraph form. This makes them easier to find and to follow.

Conciseness is achieved by avoiding unnecessary information or repetition of information. If users need the same information in two or more types of circumstances, state the procedures once and refer users to the appropriate page(s). Completed forms are helpful and reduce repetitive instructions.

In addition to these three elements, correct grammar, spelling, and punctuation are also essential. A careless presentation of information will make the manual appear less important to users. Readability is enhanced by the use of major and minor headings to organize the material. Headings make it easier for the eye to locate information, and they break up large blocks of narrative writing. Sections and pages should be identified clearly and in a consistent manner.

Manuals may be written in narrative style, contain lists or flowcharts of step-by-step procedures, or be written in playscript format. The narrative style is the most commonly used style, although it requires the most reading to determine the action to be taken. Some organizations compile lists of step-by-step procedures from existing directives on records management and republish them in a manual.

Many organizations have found the playscript format effective in presenting procedures (see Figure 16-3). The playscript style of writing uses two columns. The left column designates the position title of the person responsible for completing a certain task or making a certain decision; the right column describes the task to be performed or the decision to be made.

Figure 16-3
Procedures Written
in Playscript Form

SUBJECT: Storing Active Records

Position	Action
Record Recipient	1. Places a release mark on record indicating that the record may be stored.
Active Records Clerk	2. Prepares records for storage by checking for filing condition.
	3. Indexes and codes the records.
	4. Makes cross-reference notations.
	5. Arranges records in filing order, according to the classification system.
	6. Files records in appropriate locations.

Using charts, cartoons, and photographs wherever these might contribute to the clarity of the material in the manual is helpful. Sometimes people remember illustrations when narrative material is forgotten. When presenting correspondence styles or forms design, appropriate examples assist the reader.

A limited number of copies of the first draft of the records management manual are distributed to key managers and supervisors for review. This process usually results in several suggestions for clarity or presentation improvement and may result in the addition of overlooked information. Suggestions are reviewed by the manual committee. Those suggestions that will improve the manual will be incorporated into a second draft and be presented to the executive committee or upper-level managers for approval before the manual proceeds to final-draft stage.

Format

An easy-to-use
format encourages
manual use.

A manual is a tool. It will guide and advise, allocate authority, and provide information on a variety of topics. Like most tools, the easier it is to use, the more it will be used. The format of the manual contributes to ease of use.

In small organizations a simple paper-covered booklet will suffice. However, in large organizations, especially those with multiple geographic locations, a more complete manual of more durable material will be required.

For the larger organization, there are several formats from which to choose:

- **Looseleaf ring binders** usually have a rather high initial cost for the purchase, but the binders can be reused, and the manual can be updated easily by just inserting pages. With any type of binder, left margins of $1\frac{1}{2}$ inches are necessary so that the holes are not punched into the paper where information is printed.
- **Plastic-comb binders** are frequently used for binding small manuals. This format is not updatable, but new copies are fairly inexpensive if updates are infrequent.
- **Electronic formats** are relatively new and practically eliminate the need for hard copy circulation. Small and large organizations with compatible systems can access, search, and sort to meet their individual needs. Electronic formats have many advantages including access by many users and ease of updating. This is becoming a common method of formatting and distributing a manual.
- **Microfilm and microfiche formats** are alternatives to both hard copy and electronic manuals. Depending on available viewing equipment, this format is ideal for distribution in large organizations with offices in various geographic locations.

Publish the Manual

Quantity, cost, and appearance will affect the "how to publish" decision.

The approved records management manual may be published in several ways. Photocopy and offset printing are the two most commonly used procedures for hard copy. Selection of the printing method will be affected by the needed quantity, unit cost, and desired appearance.

The quantity of required copies is frequently determined at the beginning of the preparation process by identifying all employees who will be using the manual. Unit costs of the manual are affected by quantity, size, paper weight, number of ink colours used, and type of binding selected. These factors determine the appearance of the manual and will reflect the importance the organization places on this manual.

Standard-sized paper is more convenient for users and more cost-efficient.

The $8\frac{1}{2}$-by-11-inch size is most convenient for use as a reference book and is preferable if the manual is prepared in typed form. Other page sizes may be considered if the manual is to be printed. However, standard-sized paper is less expensive to buy, copy, and store. Binders for the manual are also less expensive to purchase in standard size.

If reproduction is in paper form, the lightest weight that provides sufficient strength to prevent tearing with repeated use of the manual should be chosen. If the manual is very thick, printing on both sides of the paper will make it easier to handle. To print on both sides, however, requires that the paper have sufficient opacity to prevent "bleeding through" (having copy show through on the reverse side of the paper). Tabs (along the open side of the manual), which indicate the beginning of each section, allow more efficient use. Covers or binders reflect the importance of this manual to the organization. If the organization has other published manuals, using a different colour cover or binder on this manual will make it easily distinguishable. The title, printed or imprinted in a manner indicative of importance, adds to the credibility. Too much cost cutting in the printing process will increase costs later through decreased manual use.

 Learning Check: Can you list and describe the steps in preparing a records management manual?

DISTRIBUTION AND MAINTENANCE

A primary consideration throughout the preparation process is that the manual will be widely used. Wide use can be assured by careful preparation, distribution to the most likely users after publication, and continuous maintenance.

Distribution

Manuals should be readily accessible to those who require their use.

Determination of which employees are to receive copies of the records management manual is made early in the preparation process. The number of manuals needed also includes copies for designated executives. The records manager maintains a list of manual recipients by position title for control purposes. Manuals may be numbered and assigned to specific recipients. So that frequent updating is not necessary, positions rather than specific position holders should be listed as recipients of the manuals.

Many organizations find it helpful to distribute manuals at a training session. Such a session is designed to familiarize users with the manual. Instruction in the use of the records management manual is also included in subsequent orientation sessions for new employees.

 Learning Check: Can you explain the procedures for distribution of the records management manual?

Maintenance

 Continued usefulness of manuals depends on their being kept current.

Maintaining the records management manual includes determining the amount of use and usefulness of the information in the manual; it also includes updating the contents to enhance the manual's value to users. During the early preparation phase, provisions are made for the maintenance process to include regular audits, quick updates, periodic revisions, and prompt revision distribution.

Regular Audits

The audits in the maintenance process are surveys of manual use conducted at planned intervals. Such audits should be conducted at least annually, preferably more frequently. The survey results will reveal how frequently the manual is referred to; who refers to it; and what, if any, material is out of date.

Quick Updates

Because procedures are not static, procedures manuals are soon unusable if no provision is made for updating information. Some procedures will change in response to new equipment, government regulations, or organizational needs. An updatable format allows these changes to be made quickly on an as-needed basis. This need to alter procedures is the reason many organizations select the looseleaf format for their manuals. When the looseleaf format is used, only the affected pages need to be revised, reprinted, and replaced within the manual. Revisions are usually marked in some way to indicate that this is a revision. Options include following the page number with the letter *R* or a revision number. Otherwise, changes must be written around current printed information or new manuals prepared. If an employee must consult another source—such as a new directive—for procedural information, the manual soon loses its usefulness.

Periodic Revisions

To keep the manual properly maintained, a schedule for reviewing the entire manual at regular intervals should be established. Such a comprehensive review is conducted every two years. This review cycle will help maintain continuity within the manual through updates of particular procedures and will ensure that interdepartmental relationships affected by changes are reflected in the manual.

Prompt Revision Distribution

Prompt distribution of revised pages is critical to continued usefulness.

Little is accomplished by revisions if employees are not aware of the changes. Some organizations assign one individual the task of inserting revised pages in all manuals throughout the company. If revised pages are distributed to each manual holder for insertion into his or her manual, a checklist of procedures that have been added or deleted accompanies the revised pages. Confusion about which update is most recent can be eliminated by dating each revised page. Completely revised manuals are more easily identified if the cover colour is changed in the revised copy.

Some organizations require users to initial a memo that accompanies the revised pages and return it with the outdated manual pages to a central location. The user's name is checked off the distribution list as the pages are returned. Users who fail to return outdated pages by the deadline are contacted again and reminded to follow through.

 Learning Check: Can you explain the procedures for records manual maintenance?

TERMINOLOGY REVIEW

Review each of the terms listed below in the Glossary on page 521.

administrative procedures manual
combination manual
filing manual
operational manual
organizational manual
policy manual

records disaster prevention
   and recovery manual
records management manual
records retention and
   disposition manual
vital records protection manual

REVIEW AND DISCUSSION

1. What is a records management manual?
2. What purposes does a records management manual serve?
3. List and explain each of the five types of records management manuals.
4. List and describe the steps in preparing a records management manual.
5. Describe the distribution procedures that are essential for a records management manual.
6. Describe the maintenance procedures that are essential for a records management manual.

APPLICATIONS

1. You have been hired as a consultant for Quality Shoe Stores (QSS) to direct a revision of QSS's records management manual while its records manager is recovering from surgery. Administrative approval has been obtained for this project. List and explain the other steps that will be necessary to revise the records management manual.
2. Procedures may be written in many styles. The playscript format is illustrated in Figure 16-3. The following procedure is written in narrative style. Convert the procedure to playscript format. Compare the advantages and limitations of each format.

Procedures for Transferring Inactive Records to the Records Centre

The active records clerk determines which records have achieved inactive status according to the retention schedule and should be transferred to the Records Centre. The active records clerk then prepares a transfer list to accompany records sent to the Records Centre, packages records to be transferred in storage cartons, notifies the Records Centre of the planned shipment of records, and arranges the physical movement of records (whether within the building or offsite).

When records are transferred to the Records Centre, the Records Centre clerk receives records cartons and checks contents against the transfer list, stores the records cartons in the appropriate area of the Records Centre and notes the locations on the transfer list, and returns a copy of the transfer list with locations of the records noted to the originating office, department, or division.

---

3. Bring to class a records management manual. With other students compare the types of manuals in use.

CONCLUDING CASES

A. Micropoint Computer Systems

Asa Hoffman has been the records manager for Micropoint Computer Systems in Gloucester Point for just over three years. Until that time, Micropoint's records program had operated in accordance with a few administrative directives throughout its 25-year existence.

Eighteen months ago a large office equipment manufacturer opened a plant in Gloucester Point. Since then, the town's population has nearly tripled, and Micropoint's computer business has boomed. The company has expanded to include not only hardware and software, but consulting services as well. In the capacity of consultants, Micropoint furnishes advice on maintaining records on computers as well as recommendations for computer records security.

Asa Hoffman received administrative support for the development of a records management manual; the manual was written and has been in use for over a year. The response from users has been very positive. The records management manual is the only manual in use at Micropoint. After seeing the success of that manual, Ted Hopkins, assistant to the chief information officer (CIO), decided to write a policy manual for the organization.

Ted wrote the manual, which consists of all of the policies still on the books in the company, and distributed the manual to those who were interested enough to come to the office of the CIO to obtain them. Ted's rationale was "If they don't care enough to come get one, they'll never use it." After the manual had been typed and stapled together and made available for six months, Ted came to Asa's office and said, "I just don't understand what is wrong. No one is using the policy manual. There have been changes in policies, but since no one uses the manual, I really don't see any point in spending the time and effort to make the changes. What do you think? Can you tell me where I went wrong?"

If you were Asa, what would you tell Ted? What specific mistakes do you think he made?

B. Toys for Kids, Inc.

Toys for Kids, Inc., is a national distributor of children's toys. Fariah Dodd, Toys for Kids records manager, has just completed a use audit of the company's records management manual. This was the first audit of the manual since it was published two years ago. Much to Fariah's surprise and disappointment, the audit showed that the manual was seldom referred to, in part because many of the procedures were out of date. In addition, the feedback revealed that users had difficulty locating material in the manual and that all potential users did not have copies of the manual.

1. What steps should Fariah take to make the records management manual more useful?
2. What steps can Fariah take to ensure that the records management manual does not become unusable in the future?

SUGGESTED READINGS AND RESOURCES

Chippie, Wendy L. "A Procedure for Procedures." *Records Management Quarterly,* Vol. 20, No. 1 (January, 1986), p. 36.

Mims, Julian L. III. "Writing for Results." *Records Management Quarterly,* Vol. 29, No. 1 (January, 1995), p. 27.

Posner, Bruce G. "The Best Little Handbook in Texas." *Inc.,* (February, 1989), p. 84.

Robinson, Rita. "It's Easy to Develop an Employee Handbook." *Office Systems* '87, Vol. 4, No. 5 (May, 1987), p. 96.

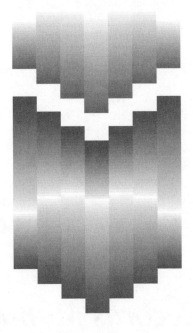

Part 7
Inactive Records

Inactive Records Management

Learning Goals

After completing this chapter, you should be able to:

1. Describe the major uses of records centres.
2. Discuss the factors to be considered when deciding whether to use a commercial or a company-owned records centre.
3. Explain the advantages and disadvantages of onsite and offsite company-owned records centres.
4. State factors to be considered when selecting the site for a records centre.
5. Describe the physical layout required for an inactive records centre.
6. Explain the necessity for special-purpose storage in a records facility and describe what these special purpose storage facilities might house.
7. Illustrate and explain the row/space numbering system.
8. Describe the process of receiving records in the records centre.
9. Discuss charge-out and follow-up for inactive records.
10. Compare methods of records destruction.
11. List criteria that affect an organization's selection of a destruction method.

PURPOSES OF RECORDS CENTRES

Chapter 5, "Manual Systems of Active Records Management, Equipment and Supplies," pointed out that, as a general rule, 40 percent of an organization's records are classified as inactive—30 percent inactive and 10 percent long-term, which are usually inactive. The two questions one then has to ask are: where should the inactive records be housed so that they are available when needed, but where cost is less than expensive office space? How can we get the best use of the space?

Uses

Records centres are facilities designed to house inactive records. The centres are used to fulfil two major needs: to serve as low-cost storage centres for inactive records and to serve as reference service centres. Records centres have moved from basic warehousing of records to become sophisticated centres for guaranteeing the protection, security, and retrievability of corporate records. Managers and records personnel alike now recognize the important and continuing role of inactive records in the corporate information network.

Although the focus of this book is on private industry, the significant contributions of the federal and provincial governments should be recognized. For example, seven regional inactive records centres across Canada store all inactive records from federal government departments and agencies. The provinces maintain their own inactive records centres for provincial departments and agencies. Government records management departments are willing to share information with other institutions and often set the standards adopted by private industry.

Storage Centre

Inactive records centres must provide records safety and security.

When serving in the role of storage centre for inactive records, records centres must provide housing that is safe in terms of the physical protection of the records themselves and safe in terms of protecting the contents of the records from theft, alteration, or observation by unauthorized parties. Safety and security are the responsibilities of the records manager and the records centre staff.

Inactive records centres provide cost savings.

The amount of savings realized by using records centres to house inactive records has been documented by a number of organizations. For example, a major auto manufacturer consolidated 16,770 square feet of storage spread over three areas into a single room of only 5,000 square feet: a 70 percent reduction. This was accomplished through more efficient storage and through microfilming many of the inactive records. As a result, the company is realizing savings of as much as

$500,000 per year while boosting safety, reducing fire hazards, speeding retrieval, and improving file integrity.[1]

Reference Service Centre

Records centres also serve as reference service centres, where people may refer to any inactive record. Requests for semiactive, long-term, or historical records (or copies) are made to the records centre staff, who then provide the appropriate records or requested information obtained from the records.

Many reference service areas provide a comfortable space with tables, chairs, and any necessary equipment (terminals, microfiche readers, etc.) so that all of the use of the records may be made in that area.

Objectives

The overall goal of a records centre is to provide safe storage and access to records at a reduced cost. Specifically, records centres have as their objectives to:

- Reduce the total volume of records held in office and storage areas, thereby reducing the cost of housing an organization's records,
- Establish controls to ensure a continuous flow of records from offices to low-cost storage, to see that records are transferred to less expensive space when their status becomes inactive,
- Free space and reduce the need for storage equipment, which also contributes to reducing the cost of housing records,
- Establish an efficient retrieval system, making access to the records available when required for decision making,
- Develop a cost-justified microfilm program (if appropriate), and
- Maintain total security over the organization's records.

All records centres should strive to meet these objectives in order to provide a more efficient records management program.

Learning Check: Can you describe the uses of a records centre?

RECORDS CENTRES FACILITIES

Commercial records centres provide a wide range of services.

Records centres may be company-owned or commercially provided. Organizational circumstances and company preferences will determine which type is the more desirable choice. Each organization must make that decision based on its own needs and available resources. Rather than providing their own inactive records facilities, many organizations are now choosing to outsource this activity.

---

[1]"Compact Filing's Loaded with Economies," *Modern Office Technology,* Vol. 33, No. 2 (February, 1988), p. 51.

Commercial Centres

Commercial records centres may offer a variety of services, ranging from self-service to full service. Full-service facilities offer a wide range of services.

Self-Service

A self-service facility, an outgrowth of household storage, is sometimes referred to as a **landlord/tenant agreement**. Under a landlord/tenant agreement, the landlord provides the space and the shelving to house records. Storage charges are based on the amount of space or number of cartons used by the tenant. The tenant has the responsibility for maintaining records inventories and for controlling retrievals. This type of offsite storage allows the depositor (tenant) to place any type of records in the space and to remove or add records as needed. The storage and retrieval responsibilities reside with the tenant. The records centre (landlord) is obligated to provide "reasonable" care in the maintenance of the storage areas.

Under a landlord/tenant arrangement, the landlord may provide additional services at additional costs. These additional services may include copying, packing records, transferring records, pickup and delivery, facsimile services, and mailing services. A landlord/tenant arrangement provides relatively inexpensive storage due to site location and to fewer services being offered.

Full Service

Full-service offsite commercial records centres can generally provide any of the following services:
- Original records transfer to facility (including transfer boxes and transfer forms)
- Records inventory
- Records security
  - fireproof vaults
  - sprinkler systems
  - burglar and fire alarms
  - authorized signature systems
  - confidentiality
  - backup water and power systems
  - blanket insurance policies covering liability and damage
  - bonded employees
- Temperature and humidity controls
- Storage facilities for a variety of media
- Pickup and delivery service, scheduled and random basis
- Computerized tracking systems from records receipt to destruction
- Retrieval of box, folder, or document

- Copying services
- Facsimile services
- Destruction services
- Computerized client activity reports providing information concerning costs, retrievals, additions, removals, charge-outs, returns, etc.
- Micrographic services
- Records construction capability
- Consulting services
- Onsite reference and conference rooms
- Communication systems

Cost

Costs are computed using different methods based on cubic feet used.

When the organization does not have or does not wish to allocate the resources necessary to establish and maintain its own records centre, the commercial centre offers a viable alternative. The organization, when making the decision regarding the commercial records centre most suitable for its particular needs, will want to evaluate the desired services in relation to the cost of providing those services. Five methods are commonly used for computing the costs of using a commercial facility. All of the methods are based on cost per cubic foot of storage space used.

In the first method, the costs of retrieval are included in the storage fee. The retrieval costs are difficult to evaluate because retrieval rates are not necessarily related to required storage space.

In the second method, an hourly fee for retrieval is added to the storage fee. This method, of course, relies on the commercial centre to provide quick and efficient retrieval and to charge accordingly for that service.

In the third method, fixed fees are charged for various types of services. The pricing is usually based on what the commercial centre considers to be the average time in which these services are performed.

In the fourth method, a service contract is used. This method is appropriate when companies can accurately predict retrieval requirements. However, if retrievals cannot be accurately predicted or if requests are sporadic, this method may be expensive.

In the fifth method, a combination plan is used. This plan includes a minimum guarantee for a given number of retrievals plus a flat rate for each search above that number. Most commercial centres allow customers the option of changing payment methods after the centre and the customer have an opportunity to evaluate the existing payment method. Certainly this item should be negotiated with the commercial records centre at the time of the original investigation.

Company-Owned Centres

Company-owned centres are an option.

One of the first options many organizations consider when storing inactive records is nonprime space within their own location—areas such as basement or attic spaces. The use of these areas is dependent on proper heating, lighting, humidity controls, and floor load capacity, as well as the amount of usable space. In addition to ceiling height, the amount of usable space is also dependent on the number of obstructions and odd-shaped spaces that may intrude on the available space. Conversion of these spaces may be an expensive, short-term solution. Planning for a records centre must include future needs as well as current space pressures.

Distance from storage 59.77 to 40-60%

In addition to conversion costs, the organization must be willing to commit resources to purchase appropriate storage tools, to create a system compatible with the existing active records system, and to hire the personnel necessary to operate and maintain the company-owned records centre. Resources must also be allocated for the rental costs of the converted space and the energy costs associated with its operation.

Organizations may, of course, go offsite for their records centre. A discussion of offsite storage is presented in the following section.

 Learning Check: Can you explain the advantages and disadvantages of the two types of records centre facilities?

SITE LOCATION

Although commercial records centres are offsite, company-owned centres may be either onsite or offsite. Often, the organization has little or no control over this decision. If only prime, high-cost space is available, the organization has little choice but to go offsite for records storage space.

Onsite

Onsite centres offer the advantage of onsite control.

If space capable of being converted to a records centre on a cost-effective basis is available, the organization may choose an **onsite records centre**. Onsite location offers many advantages to the organization. Some managers regard the information availability as necessary for effective performance. Also, a delivery system to get the information from one location to another is not needed. Other managers regard total control over the organization's records and information as important. The application of organizational policies and procedures to records availability and security provides a feeling of confidence to many managers.

Offsite

Offsite centres may be less costly.

Commercial **offsite records centres** offer low-cost storage at locations away from the organizational site. The locations of these records centres may be near to or hundreds of miles away from the organizational site. In either case, these facilities provide security for the records.

Company-owned records centres may also be located offsite. Constructing a new facility, renovating an existing building, or locating rental space appropriate for records storage are possible alternatives.

Facilities may be located above or below ground.

Offsite locations offer two options: aboveground or underground sites. Aboveground facilities are generally less expensive than underground facilities, but underground facilities offer greater security. Facilities located above ground may be constructed in a variety of geographic locations, while underground site availability is more limited. Underground vaults are located in salt mines, limestone mines, and under mountains and hills. A well-known example of a privately owned underground records facility is that of the Church of Jesus Christ of Latter-Day Saints, located in a granite mountain outside Salt Lake City, Utah. A lateral view of an underground storage facility is shown in Figure 17-1.

Figure 17-1
A Lateral View of an Underground Storage Facility

Source: Corporate Headquarters, Iron Mountain Group, Rosendale, New York

 Learning Check: Can you explain the advantages and disadvantages of onsite and offsite company-owned records centres?

Some experts estimate an annual cost of $200 to $300 to store one four-drawer file cabinet in a building in a prime location. This cost figure does not include expenses for clerical staff, equipment, and supplies. By comparison, offsite storage companies can store the contents of that same file cabinet for as little as $24 annually.

A provincial government records management specialist suggests that government departments can save a substantial amount of money by storing their inactive records in the provincial records centre. The example in Figure 17-2 bases amounts on square footage costs of a government office in a typical downtown location versus square footage costs in the offsite provincial records centre.

Figure 17-2

Onsite/Offsite Storage Cost Comparison

	Onsite	Provincial Government Records Centre
Storage Cost for 1 box	$30	$6
Storage Cost for 1,000 boxes	$30,000	$6,000

Government savings when 1,000 boxes are stored in the provincial records centre equals $24,000 ($30,000 less $6,000), a substantial cost reduction. Similar savings can be achieved for any organization with company-owned offsite storage due to lower space costs, lower equipment costs, and smaller staffing requirements.

Site Selection Criteria

Site selection involves many factors.

A number of factors must be considered when selecting an appropriate site. Major factors to be evaluated include cost, access to records, transportation, and safety and security of records.

Cost

The costs involved in setting up and maintaining the facility should be taken into consideration when selecting the site for the records centre. The cost of using a commercial records centre should be compared with that of operating a company-owned centre, and the long-term costs of each should be evaluated. The location of the site will also affect the costs incurred for pickup and delivery service. If the site is in a high-risk area, major expenditures will be required for security and insurance.

Access to Records

Efficient delivery services must be maintained.

Regardless of the type or location of the records centre, access to the records is of primary interest to the users. An onsite records centre obviously allows for ease of access. If the centre is located offsite, access is a greater problem. For company-owned centres located offsite, the organization has the responsibility for making the records easily accessible. Commercial centres located nearby may furnish document delivery or allow organizational representatives to come to the records centre to obtain necessary information and records. Often, the customer may exercise both of these options.

Commercial records centres located outside the organization's area have the entire responsibility for document delivery. Records may be delivered via facsimile, computer networks, courier services, Canada Post, or other express mail services. The type of delivery depends largely upon the required turnaround time and the size and nature of the records. In general, the original record is retained in storage and a copy of the record is sent to the user. Because 75 percent of all information requests can be answered verbally, telephone service is essential for prompt access to data.

Although most offsite storage centres guarantee 24-hour retrieval and delivery, many managers still fear that they will not have information when they need it. Several computer systems are available that will give managers a greater level of control. From a personal computer connected to the storage facility, clients can immediately learn the status of their records, place orders for retrieval, delivery, or pickup.

Transportation

Ease of commuting is a factor when selecting a site.

When evaluating sites for records centres, transportation of records and personnel must be considered. Even if the records centre is a company-owned onsite facility, procedures still have to be established for moving the records as they mature from active status to inactive status. Offsite centres present their own unique challenges for transporting records and personnel. The company-owned offsite location should have accessible roads that allow easy commuting to the centre. Commercial centres should be located in areas that allow prompt delivery by Canada Post, special messenger, or other express mail services.

Safety and Security

Security and safety are important considerations.

Records safety and security are of primary concern to management. If records can be accessed by unauthorized persons, lost, destroyed, or stolen, the site under consideration should be immediately discarded as a possible location for a records centre. Danger to records with regard to physical safety is discussed in Chapter 11, and with regard to records security, in Chapter 12. Safety and security are major factors to be evaluated when selecting a records centre site.

 Learning Check: Can you state the factors to be considered when selecting a records centre site?

SPACE UTILIZATION

Once the determination has been made regarding the type of records centre most appropriate for the company's needs, careful consideration is then given to maximizing the use of the available space.

Requirements

Maximizing space
utilization requires
careful
arrangement.

The volume of records and kinds of records (paper, fiche, film, disks, maps, and so forth) are determined by the records inventory report. This report identifies all of the organizational records classified as inactive. The space required to house this volume of records is determined by the storage method to be used.

Most records centres store the records in cartons, and the cartons are placed on steel shelving. The shelving is usually 30 inches deep by 42 inches wide and is placed back to back. This duplexing arrangement allows cartons to be placed back to back on the shelving. If cartons with lids are used, a depth of 32 inches is required for back-to-back placement. Organizations may single- or double-stack the cartons on the shelves, or very rarely, triple-stack them. A maximum of 50 feet of unbroken shelf length is recommended.

Not all records are
traditional size or
media.

Many records are not in $8\frac{1}{2}$-by-11-inch paper form and cannot be accommodated in traditional records housing. As organizations review their records and storage needs, many make the transition from paper records to other forms. This transition requires a different type of storage for both records centres and active records facilities.

The many forms of paper and other media records should be considered as plans are made for storage facilities. Some of these include audiovisual materials, cartographic materials, computer output, publications, microforms, and engineering drawings.

Plans must be made to accommodate storage of cassette tapes, transparencies, slides, video cassette tapes, phonographic records, and video disks. Cabinets are available to handle the special needs of these audiovisual materials. Maps classified as inactive may be stored in roll cabinets or in flat drawer cabinets. In records centres maps may be stored in specially designed containers.

Different media
types have different
storage
requirements.

Computer output may take the form of printouts, floppy disks, optical disks, magnetic tapes, or microforms. Each of these forms requires storage quite different from standard paper records. Computer printouts may be of varying sizes, and it may be impossible to stand them upright on storage shelves. Placing the printouts in hanging folders saves space and facilitates retrieval. Folders designed to house computer printouts upright on shelves are another storage option.

Floppy disks and magnetic tapes are placed in dustproof containers and stored upright in racks. When planning for storage, one must remember that magnetic media is very sensitive material and must be protected by climate controls. Because electrical and magnetic sources may cause tape erasure, the location of the storage racks is important.

Magazines and periodicals present some of the same storage problems as computer printouts; these publications are of varying sizes and lack the support needed to stand alone on shelves. As the periodicals accumulate, they should be bound and stored in the same manner as books.

Microfiche, roll or cartridge microfilm, microfilm jackets, and aperture cards require special types of storage cabinets. These cabinets are fully discussed in Chapter 5. As plans are made for a records centre, the special requirements for microforms must be considered.

Engineering drawings, like cartographic materials, may be stored in roll cabinets, in flat drawer cabinets, or in hanging files. The storage criteria used for engineering drawings are the same as those used for maps.

Special arrangements must be made for storing medical records and X rays.

Different types of cartons are available for micromedia than for other media.

Cartons for microrecords may be single-, double-, or even triple-compartmented, depending on the micromedia. Single-compartment boxes 6 by 4 by 24 inches will accommodate 3,000 fiche or 1,500 jackets. A single-compartment box 8 by 4 by 24 inches will accommodate 48 rolls of 16mm film or 24 rolls of 35mm film. Some records centres use pallets stacked on steel frames for rarely referenced records, records with short retention periods, or odd-sized material.

Mobile shelving may also be used in the records centre. This type of shelving allows for a greater density of records to be stored in the same area. Mobile shelving does, however, limit access to the records when more than one person is shelving or retrieving records.

The amount of space required for records can be determined by applying the general rule that three to four cubic feet of records will take one square foot of space. With multilevel storage, this ratio can be as high as nine cubic feet of records to one square foot of floor space. A documentation measurement guide is shown in Table 17-1.

Learning Check: Can you explain the necessity for special purpose storage in an inactive records facility and describe what these special purpose facilities might house?

Ceiling height affects storage cabinets.

Of course, ceiling height affects the amount of storage space available. Some organizations are realizing additional space by using "tall" storage, which makes use of catwalks for access (see Figure 17-3). Heights up to 14 feet may be accessed with safety or pulpit ladders; heights over 14 feet require catwalks or a system that uses automated storage and retrieval. Catwalks may be double-tiered (placed at levels between shelves 8 and 9 and shelves 15 and 16).

When estimating square footage required to house the volume of records to be stored, consider the type of storage container, type of shelving, height of ceiling, and any obstruction that reduces available storage space.

Table 17-1

Documentation Measurement Guide

Equipment Type	Conversion Table Equivalents	Cubic Feet*
Filing Cabinets	One letter-sized drawer One legal-sized drawer	1.50 2.00
Filing Cases	One 3" x 5" case One 4" x 6" case One 5" x 8" case	.10 .20 .25
Shelf Files	Letter-sized, 1 linear foot Legal-sized, 1 linear foot	.80 1.00
Tabulating Cards	10,000 cards	1.00
Magnetic Tape	7 reels	1.00
Microfilm	100 16mm reels (100 feet) 50 35mm reels (100 feet)	1.00 1.00
Still Pictures	2,300 35mm, 6-exposure strips 8,640 2" x 2" mounted slides 2,184 4" x 5" film sheets 5,960 2 1/4" x 3 1/4" film sheets	1.00 1.00 1.00 1.00
Machine Listings	1 linear foot	1.20
Still Pictures-Prints	2,350 8" x 10" glossies or contact sheets 9,400 4" x 5" glossies	1.00 1.00
Motion Pictures	6 35mm reels (1,000 feet) 11 16mm reels (1,200 feet) 15 16mm reels (800 feet) 32 16mm reels (400 feet)	1.00 1.00 1.00 1.00
Sound Recordings	76 16" disk recordings 144 12" disk recordings 48 7" audiotape reels 32 10" audiotape reels	1.00 1.00 1.00 1.00
Video Recordings	10 3/4" cassettes 3 2" reels 9 1" reels 43 1/2" reels	1.00 1.00 1.00 1.00
Transfer carton Transfile (long letter) Transfile (long legal)	1 15" x 12" x 10" 1 24" x 12" x 10" 1 24" x 15" x 10"	1.00 1.67 2.00

*May be rounded.

Source: Office Systems '85, Vol. 2, No. 6 (June, 1985).

Figure 17-3
Tall Storage with
Catwalks

Source: Reprinted from ARMA Records Management Quarterly, *January 1982 by permission of Records Managers and Administrators, Inc.*

Ceiling heights and stack heights have a major effect on the ratio of cubic feet of records to be housed to square feet of floor space required. As the ceiling and stack heights increase, the ratio of cubic feet of records to square feet of required floor space increases, and the space required to house the records decreases accordingly. This general guideline can be used to determine square foot requirements:

Ratio of Cubic Feet of Records to Square Feet of Required Floor Space*

8-Foot Stacks	10-Foot Stacks	12-Foot Stacks	14-Foot Stacks	22-Foot Stacks
2.7 to 1	3.3 to 1	3.9 to 1	4.5 to 1	7.1 to 1

*excluding aisle space

Applying the formula to a given situation in which the stacks are typical eight-foot stacks with 120,000 cartons to be stored (see Table 17-1—one standard transfer carton requires one cubic foot of space), the space required would be 44,444 (120,000 ÷ 2.7) square feet. In this case, if the stacks were 14 feet high, the space requirement would be reduced to 26,666 square feet (120,000 ÷ 4.5).

Another major consideration is the floor load capacity. **Floor load capacity**, as discussed in Chapter 5, is the weight of records and equipment that a floor can safely accommodate. A filled records carton weighs between 30 and 50 pounds. Care must be exercised in planning the records centre so that the weight of the current equipment and records does not exceed the floor load capacity and that future additions can be accommodated.

Floor load capacity is related to the structure of the building.

Physical Layout

The total system of records storage, retrieval, and disposition must be considered when the physical layout of the records centre is being planned. The records centre must accommodate not only the inactive records storage area but the administrative, receiving, preparation, and distribution areas also (see Figure 17-4). Plans should include:
- Records storage area
- Administrative areas
  - Reference area
  - Office area
- Receiving area
- Preparation area
- Distribution/disposition area

Figure 17-4
Records Centre
Layout

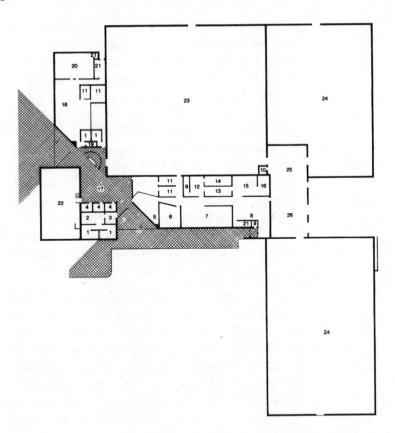

Source: Adapted from George Cunningham, Records Management Supervisor, Department of Library Archives and Public Records, Records Management Centre, State of Arizona, Phoenix

Records Storage Area

The layout of the facility should provide for user workspace.

The records storage area should provide feeder aisles of 30 inches to 36 inches with primary aisles 5 feet 8 inches to 6 feet 8 inches depending on the individual needs of the centre. Mobile storage equipment reduces the required aisle space. Humidity controls are critical in vault areas reserved for archival, vital, or security-type records. Fluorescent lighting is recommended for all work areas.

Administrative Areas

The administrative areas include reference and general office areas. These areas are labour-intensive and should provide for the comfort of the employees.

Reference areas should be comfortable.

The reference area should be an efficient, comfortable place for users. Tables and chairs, a copier, a microfilm/microfiche reader and, where appropriate, reader-printers are minimal requirements. Reference areas generally have limited space; therefore, efficient use must be made of the available area.

The general office areas provide the records centre supervisor and staff with their workspace. These office areas should be as suitably furnished as any other administrative area. While the amount of space per worker varies, each staff member (excluding the supervisor) should be provided with a minimum of 100 square feet. The office of the records centre supervisor should be larger and provide an attractive, comfortable area in which to work and to confer privately with others.

Since one function of the records centre is to serve as a reference area, indexes and controls necessary for prompt retrieval of records are required. The logical place to locate these retrieval tools is in the office area. Space, therefore, must be provided for housing indexes and retrieval equipment so that the records centre staff has easy access to them. If noncentre personnel have free access to the indexes and retrieval equipment, a more appropriate location might be the reference area.

Indexes and retrieval equipment should be accessible.

Receiving Area

The receiving area provides a place for records as they come into the centre. This area is usually adjacent to the loading dock to facilitate the process. Records (new files and refiles) cannot always be immediately shelved as they are received by the centre personnel. In these areas, shelving, if any, is usually minimal. Because records may be temporarily stored here, appropriate security precautions should be maintained. Forklifts and pallets are often used to deliver records to the receiving area. Doorways, therefore, must be wide enough to accommodate this equipment.

Preparation Area

The preparation area is where the records centre clerks prepare the incoming records for shelving and storage. The size of the preparation area is dependent upon the number and types of activities to be performed and the equipment necessary to accomplish the tasks. Equipment may run the gamut from manual sorters for refiles and interfiles to microfilming equipment for microfilm/microfiche production.

Disposition Area

The disposition area should be separated from the receiving area in order to minimize the risk of mistaking accessions for records scheduled for disposition. All records identified for disposal in the records retention and disposition schedule are transferred to the disposition area. If the quantity of records scheduled for disposal is small, the organization may wish to allow the records to accumulate until more are ready for destruction. If the organization is having a commercial company destroy its records, accumulating records is the most economical approach. (Destruction techniques are discussed below in this chapter.) Organizations with many records to be destroyed may have their own destruction equipment.

Preparation and disposition areas should be clearly separated.

The disposition area, as well as the receiving area, should be located near (preferably adjacent to) the loading dock. Also, as required in the receiving area, doorways must be wide enough to accommodate forklifts and pallets necessary to move the records.

 Learning Check: Can you describe the physical layout required for an inactive records centre?

Space Numbering Systems

A system is needed for finding the records once they have been shelved. In order to facilitate the location process, each carton is assigned an address (location) designation according to a **space numbering system**. Different organizations use different space numbering systems; however, one generally accepted method serves as a basis for many adaptations. This basic method is the row/space numbering method.

If the row/space numbering method is used, several steps are involved in assigning the numbers to the stack areas. First, each row is assigned a number. This number is posted at the front of each row. If rows are accessible from either front or rear, numbers are posted at each end of the row. Figure 17-5 shows four single rows of shelving, each shelf housing cartons stacked back to back, or two deep.

Figure 17-5
Back-to-Back
Shelves

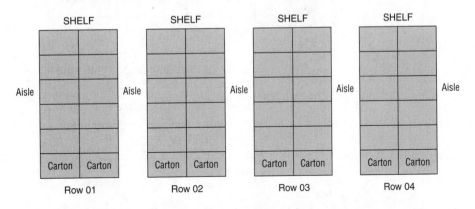

The row number provides the first part of the address. The second part of the address is the assigned space number. Each space accommodates one carton. Even numbers are usually assigned to the right side of the shelf; odd numbers are assigned to the left side. In Figure 17-6 each shelf in each row houses six boxes; only one shelf (the bottom shelf) in each row of shelves is shown. If each row has six shelves, the arrangement of row 01 would appear as illustrated in Figure 17-7.

Some records centre personnel find it easier to locate cartons of records if a shelf number is also assigned. In the previous illustration, the address for carton 030 in row 01 would be row number 01, shelf number 03, space number 030, or 01 03 030.

Figure 17-6
Row/Shelf Number
System

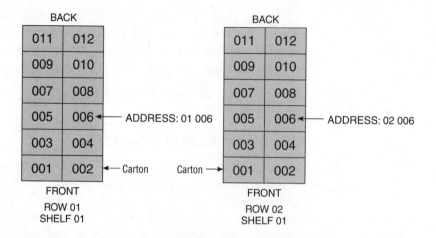

Learning Check: Can you illustrate and explain the row/space numbering system?

Figure 17-7
Row/Shelf/Space
Numbering System

RECORDS TRANSFER

Records are transferred from expensive office space and received at a records centre or other designated storage area. The transfer process is covered in Chapter 7.

Transfer Cartons

The records centre usually provides transfer cartons for the originating office.

The originating office prepares the records transmittal forms and packages the records in corrugated fibreboard cartons specially made for storing inactive records. Most records centres require that material in hanging folders or three-ring binders be transferred to manila folders and then placed in the boxes. The most frequently used carton size is 15 by 12 by 10 inches as this size is adaptable to both legal- and letter-sized records and fits all standard shelving equipment. The placement of records within these cartons is illustrated in Figure 17-8. When the time comes that legal-sized records no longer exist, companies will still be able to use these boxes; no waste occurs.

Figure 17-8
Transfer Box

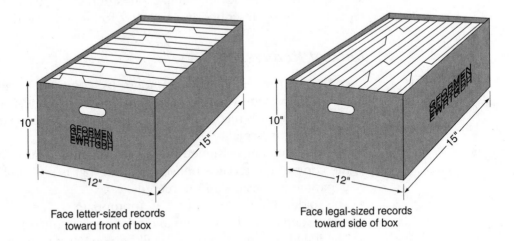

Face letter-sized records toward front of box

Face legal-sized records toward side of box

A 19-by-13-by-10-inch carton is also available for folders with side tabs for open-shelf files. These cartons require special shelving equipment. The storage carton for hanging folders, which is 15 by 12 by 11 inches, also requires special shelving in those instances in which removal of the records prior to storage is not required.

Special attention must be given to identifying and handling confidential records. These records must be protected from unauthorized access while in the storage area and properly disposed of when no longer needed.

Receiving Records

Receiving records is the responsibility of personnel in the records storage area. The number and contents of the cartons received must be checked against the records transfer list and any discrepancies noted. Discrepancies must be checked with the originating office immediately. Records may have been left in the office or misplaced between the office and the storage area. Any misplaced records must be located immediately.

Records storage location is noted on the transmittal form or locator file.

Once records have been checked in, they must be stored in the proper areas of the storage facility, and the locations noted on the records transmittal form shown in Chapter 5 (see Figure 5-20) or in a **locator file** (a special card file or automated index that lists records contents and their locations). This step is crucial to efficient retrieval of records while in storage.

Learning Check: Can you describe transfer containers and how records are received at the records centre?

RECORDS CHARGE-OUT AND FOLLOW-UP

A records centre is only as good as its record retrieval capability. Procedures to request records, retrieve, charge-out and follow-up are critical to efficient retrieval. Similar procedures are used for inactive records as those described in Chapter 7 for active records.

Record Request

Records may be requested in several ways.

Records may be requested by phone, by computer connection, by mail, or in person. Whatever the form used to request a record or information from a record, the requester should be prepared to give the following information to the records centre clerk:

- The box number (assigned by the records centre and noted on the copy of the records transmittal form that is returned to the department transferring the records).
- The folder title or description, if appropriate.
- Name, department, location, and telephone number of requester.
- The length of time the record will be needed, so a follow-up date can be listed on the form.

   If the request is made by phone or by mail, the records centre clerk will complete a form similar to the one shown in Figure 17-9. If the request is made in person, the requester will complete the form. Tracking software will provide the above information if the request is made by computer.

Charge-Out

Records may be retrieved and charged out manually, as described in Chapter 7, or electronically, as described in Chapter 10. Charge-out— by cards or electronically through a computerized system—should be consistently maintained. As each record is released to the requester, a charge-out is recorded. One type of reference control form is shown in Figure 17-10.

Follow-Up

Follow-up for manual systems is also described in Chapter 7, and follow-up electronically through a computerized system is described in Chapter 10. Some inactive records centres have manual retrieval, yet maintain their indexes, charge-outs, and follow-ups on computer.

Figure 17-9
Records Centre
Records Request

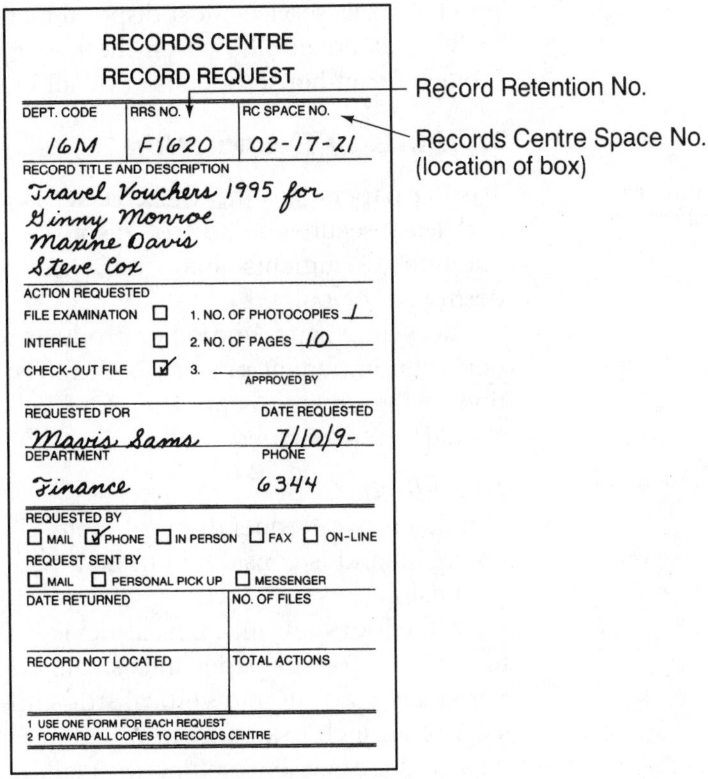

RECORDS CENTRE
RECORD REQUEST

——— Record Retention No.

——— Records Centre Space No.
(location of box)

DEPT. CODE	RRS NO.	RC SPACE NO.
16M	F1620	02-17-21

RECORD TITLE AND DESCRIPTION

Travel Vouchers 1995 for
Ginny Monroe
Maxine Davis
Steve Cox

ACTION REQUESTED

FILE EXAMINATION ☐   1. NO. OF PHOTOCOPIES _1_

INTERFILE ☐   2. NO. OF PAGES _10_

CHECK-OUT FILE ☑   3. _____
                          APPROVED BY

REQUESTED FOR	DATE REQUESTED
Mavis Sams	7/10/9-
DEPARTMENT	PHONE
Finance	6344

REQUESTED BY
☐ MAIL ☑ PHONE ☐ IN PERSON ☐ FAX ☐ ON-LINE

REQUEST SENT BY
☐ MAIL ☐ PERSONAL PICK UP ☐ MESSENGER

DATE RETURNED	NO. OF FILES
RECORD NOT LOCATED	TOTAL ACTIONS

1 USE ONE FORM FOR EACH REQUEST
2 FORWARD ALL COPIES TO RECORDS CENTRE

Figure 17-10
Control Form

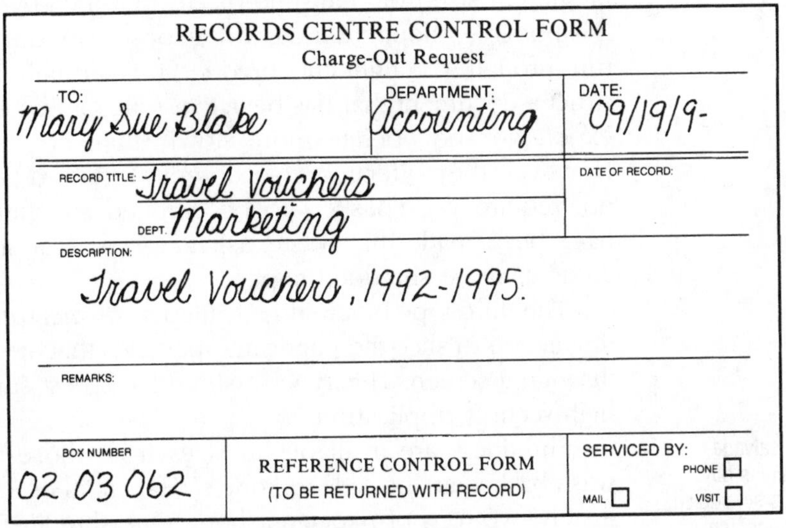

RECORDS CENTRE CONTROL FORM
Charge-Out Request

TO: *Mary Sue Blake*	DEPARTMENT: *Accounting*	DATE: 09/19/9-

RECORD TITLE: *Travel Vouchers*
DEPT. *Marketing*   DATE OF RECORD:

DESCRIPTION:
Travel Vouchers, 1992-1995.

REMARKS:

BOX NUMBER 02 03 062	REFERENCE CONTROL FORM (TO BE RETURNED WITH RECORD)	SERVICED BY: PHONE ☐ MAIL ☐ VISIT ☐

RECORDS DESTRUCTION

Records destruction is the disposal of records no longer needed by the organization. Disposal may be handled internally by the organization, by a commercial records centre, or contracted to a local company providing this service. Most disposal methods are available either internally or externally; however, the cost of some methods may be prohibitive for in-house operation by all but the largest organizations.

Methods of Destruction

Records are
destroyed by
several methods.

Tossing papers into the wastebasket is probably the most convenient and least secure method of disposing of unneeded documents. In addition documents may be shredded, incinerated, chemically destroyed, or pulped.

Recycling paper and other products resulting from records destruction is an important practice both for economy's sake and for protection of the environment. Therefore, whenever possible, this practice should be encouraged.

Shredding

Shredding is a frequently used method of destroying documents and microfilm and is considered to be a secure method of destroying confidential papers.

Shredders are mechanical devices that use a variety of methods to cut, pull, or rip paper into small, sometimes infinitesimal, pieces. Shredders may cut into vertical strips; the size of the strip varies from 1/32 of an inch to one inch in width. Shredders may also cut lengthwise and crosswise, resulting in small, rectangular confetti-like pieces, ranging in size from hair-fine pieces to 1-inch-by-1-inch pieces. While it is possible, though difficult, to reconstruct a document that has been run through a straight-cut shredder, it is virtually impossible to reconstruct a document that has been crosscut. Crosscut shredders are more expensive and operate more slowly than do straight-cut shredders. However, they offer more security and, due to the finer particles, do not require wastebaskets to be emptied so often. In fact, estimates have been made that wastebaskets of crosscut shredders hold up to 20 times more shredded paper.

The third type of shredder, called a *disintegrator,* uses a rotary-cutting action to slice the paper into particles that are fine enough to pass through a screen. This type of shredder is best suited to high-volume, high-security applications.

Paper salvage
companies buy
records scheduled
for disposition.

Shredders are available in sizes from those that fit on top of a wastebasket at the side of one's desk to those that shred approximately two tons of paper per hour. One shredder also accommodates both flat and crumpled paper (see Figure 17-11). Documents scheduled for destruction may be sold to a paper salvage company with or without having been shredded. Entrepreneurs, observing the need for small organizations to outsource paper disposal, have trucks containing shredding equipment that can shred volumes of paper onsite.

Figure 17-11
Paper Shredder

Source: Courtesy of Pitney Bowes

Incineration

There are
disadvantages to
destroying records
through
incineration.

Incineration was once the most accepted method of document destruction; however, incineration is now considered a problem-encumbered method. Although incineration was generally thought to be a secure method of destroying confidential documents, complete documents have occasionally blown out of the incinerator. This creates the possibility of confidential information becoming known to competitors or to the press. In addition, some bits of paper that are not completely burned remain legible, the labour to maintain an incinerator is costly, and in most areas environmental restrictions now prevent organizations from using this technique. Requiring that someone witness the destruction of records by incineration is time consuming and costly, adding a further disadvantage.

Chemical Destruction

Chemical destruction, or *maceration,* is the use of chemicals to soften the paper and obliterate the writing. This method also includes pulverization of records, including microfilm. Pulverizers, like shredders, are available in many sizes to accommodate the specific volume of documents to be destroyed. Chemical destruction is also used to recover the silver contained in X rays. Pulverizing may be more efficient than shredding or incineration.

Pulping

Pulping is an
economical way of
destroying
high-security
documents.

Pulping is an irreversible, safe, clean, convenient, and economical method of destroying confidential documents. Documents are mixed with water and forced through cutters and a screen. The size of the screen may vary according to the security requirements of the material to be pulped. The residue *(slurry)* that is created is pumped into a hydra-extractor, which squeezes out the water. The water is recirculated and the pulp is dumped into trailers for removal from the premises. Pulping is being used increasingly by banks and other organizations that generate a large amount of paper with high-security requirements. Depending on the size of the organization, pulping may be done internally or by a contractor. A further advantage is that the resulting material can be recycled.

 Learning Check: Can you compare methods of records destruction?

Method Selection

Many factors should be considered when reviewing destruction methods.

After examining the available destruction methods, the records manager should make a final decision, based on the answers to the following questions:

1. What is the volume of records to be destroyed?
2. Are these records of the same size and type of material? If not, which processes would destroy all types of records?
3. What percentage of the records are confidential?
4. What environmental standards affect the destruction of records in the community?
5. Are bonded contractors available in the area to provide the desired destruction method?
6. Can records be sold to a paper salvage company? Must they be shredded first?
7. What are the comparative costs of an in-house operation versus contracted destruction?

 Learning Check: Can you list criteria that affect an organization's selection of a destruction method?

Destruction Documentation

Records destruction authorization and confirmation should be documented.

Many organizations, especially large corporations and governmental units, are required to provide certification that records have been destroyed. Such certification forms include a description of the records destroyed and the date and method of destruction. Often, the records centre supervisor sends a notice to the originating office of impending destruction of records. The originating office then has a final opportunity to retain the records if a need to do so (such as ongoing litigation) exists. The authorization to destroy and the certificate of destruction may be contained on the same form.

Some organizations also maintain a records destruction register, which lists all destroyed records by date of destruction. This register is a permanent record of when and how records were destroyed. Tracking programs that follow records from their creation to their disposal offer real advantages in documenting records centre activities.

TERMINOLOGY REVIEW

Review the terms listed below in the Glossary on page 521.

chemical destruction
floor load capacity
landlord/tenant agreement
locator file
offsite records centre
onsite records centre

pulping
records centres
records destruction
shredders
space numbering system

REVIEW AND DISCUSSION

1. Describe the major uses of records centres.
2. Discuss the factors to be considered when deciding whether to use a commercial or a company-owned records centre.
3. Explain the advantages and disadvantages of onsite and offsite company-owned records centres.
4. State factors to be considered when selecting the site for a records centre.
5. Describe the physical layout required for an inactive records centre.
6. Explain the necessity for special storage needs for four media forms, excluding 8-by-11-inch paper records.
7. Illustrate and explain the row/space numbering system.
8. Describe the containers used to transfer and store inactive records.
9. Discuss records charge-out and follow-up.
10. Compare four methods of records destruction.
11. List three criteria that affect an organization's selection of a destruction method.

APPLICATIONS

1. Locate two advertisements for commercial records centres. Evaluate how well each records centre meets the site selection criteria outlined in this chapter.
2. From the information given in the advertisements evaluated in Application 1, determine whether the records centres are self-service or full-service records centres. Explain.
3. On the row/shelf/space numbering system illustration shown in Figure 17-7, locate the following addresses:
   Row 1, shelf 4, space 042
   Row 1, shelf 5, space 070
   Row 1, shelf 6, space 062
4. Draw and explain an illustration of a row/space numbering system.

CONCLUDING CASES

A. Victoria County Rehabilitation Centre

Victoria County Rehabilitation Centre is a residence rehab centre that serves Victoria County and its surrounding area. All of the records for its patients, both current and inactive, are housed in the individual departmental offices. There is some concern, however, about the lack of space to house the records, the security of the information, and the ability of the office clerks to locate records promptly.

Specifically, the cabinets are overstuffed, records are piled on desks as they are returned to the offices of two departments, and those records no longer in use are either stored in closets or, in some instances, thrown in the trash after several years.

As the new records manager, you realize that a number of problems exist. The rehab director has asked you what you think ought to be done about the records at Victoria County Rehabilitation Centre.

1. What will you tell him?
2. What kind of housing will you recommend for the inactive records?

B. Mattress Factory to You Wholesalers, Inc.

Mattress Factory to You Wholesalers, Inc., has allocated a recently vacated 40-by-50-foot space for use as a records centre. Inactive records are now housed in various locations throughout the building. The space allocated for the records centre is adjacent to the company offices in a 60-year-old building. The engineers have calculated the floor load capacity as 70 pounds per square foot. The ceiling height in the building will allow 14-foot stacks.

During the records inventory, the following records were classified as inactive:

- 50 four-drawer letter filing cabinets
- 45 transfer cartons (15" × 12" × 10"), letter size
- 500 linear feet of open-shelf files, letter size
- 75 100-foot 35mm rolls of microfilm

Given this information, calculate:

1. The ratio of cubic feet of records to square feet of space required
2. The cubic feet required for records
3. The floor load capacity

Prepare this information for T.C. Chong, vice president and chief information officer of Mattress Factory to You Wholesalers, Inc. Include any recommendations you might have regarding how these records should be stored (i.e., using filing cabinets, boxes, open shelves, etc.).

SUGGESTED READINGS AND RESOURCES

Allen, Michael. "Cleaning House: U.S. Companies Pay Increasing Attention to Destroying Files." *Wall Street Journal,* Vol. CCX, No. 46 (September 2, 1987), p. 1.

Brindza, Stephen. "Convenience Shredders Ease the Paper Problem." *Modern Office Technology,* Vol. 33, No. 4 (April, 1988), p. 82.

Brindza, Stephen. "Inactive Filing Proves Invaluable." *Modern Office Technology,* Vol. 33, No. 7 (July, 1988), p. 88.

Buyers Laboratory, Inc. "Control Security with Shredders." *Office Systems '87,* Vol. 4, No. 8 (August, 1987), p. 45.

Davis, James V. "Computerized Management of Inactive Record Centres." *IMC Journal,* Vol. 24, No. 1 (January/February, 1988), p. 16.

Diamond, Susan Z. "A Strategic Approach to Records Management." *Office Systems '87,* Vol. 4, No. 6 (June, 1987), p. 88.

Federal Records Centre Facility Standards. Rev. ed. Ottawa: Public Archives Canada, 1986.

Federal Records Centres Users' Guide. Ottawa: Public Archives Canada: Records Management Branch, 1987.

King, Susan L. "Moving the City of Charleston's Archives and Records Center." *Records Management Quarterly,* Vol. 27, No. 4 (October, 1993), p. 32.

Langemo, Mark. "Tips to Shape Up Your File System." *Office Systems '87,* Vol. 4, No. 4 (April, 1987), p. 48.

Romei, Lura K. "When Total Destruction Gives Peace of Mind." *Modern Office Technology,* Vol. 34, No. 6 (June, 1989), p. 79.

Sanders, Robert. "Escape from the 4-D* Monster (*Dirty Disgusting Document Disposition)." *Records Management Quarterly,* Vol. 22, No. 3 (July, 1988), p. 12.

Vollmart, Sara. "Shredders: A Powerful Office Security Tool." *The Office,* Vol. 117, No. 2 (February, 1993), p. 34.

Archives Management

Learning Goals

After completing this chapter, you should be able to:

1. Understand the history of archives.
2. Appreciate the roles and responsibilities required for interaction between archives and records management personnel.
3. Distinguish between private archives and public archives.
4. Explain the management of archives as a profession.
5. Describe the purposes of the archives.
6. Identify three approaches to archives management.
7. Describe records appraisal procedures for selection of archival records.
8. Define responsibility for archives management.
9. Describe procedures for archives storage.
10. Describe procedures for access to and security of archival records.

HISTORY OF ARCHIVES

Archives house
records selected
for long-term
retention and
preservation.

Archives are facilities where records are preserved because of their continuing value. These facilities house public or private records that have been selected for long-term retention and preservation. The term *archives* also refers to the records themselves, which have been preserved when the original reason for keeping them may no longer exist; their historical value becomes the reason for retaining the records. The term also refers to the part of an organization responsible for archival material.

For several centuries, governments have led the way in recognizing the importance of preserving historical information. From the time of the French Revolution in 1789 many European countries established national archival institutions. French, German, and Dutch archivists were responsible for developing archival theory and practice. In North America, the concern for selecting and caring for state papers of historical value can be traced to 1778 when Ebenezer Hazard received funds from Congress to collect state papers in order to document the history of the United States. A number of states as well as historical societies took action to safeguard the records of the government and American society.

The Public
Archives of Canada
was created in
1912.

Following the pattern established in other countries, the federal government of Canada not long after Confederation began to develop archival practices. In 1872 Canada created an Archives Branch as a part of the Department of Agriculture with journalist David Brymner as the first Dominion Archivist.[1] However, it wasn't until 1912 that the Public Archives of Canada was created with a mandate to collect and preserve Canada's official documents and historical materials under the leadership of the Dominion Archivist. Various orders in council and government directives from 1912 to 1987 strengthened the cultural role of the Public Archives in preserving the collective documentary memory of Canada and its functional role of managing records at the national level. In 1987, through the *National Archives of Canada Act,* the National Archives (formerly the Public Archives of Canada) was given a new and enhanced legislative mandate in managing federal government information having archival value; the Dominion Archivist became the National Archivist.

Canada's largest archival institution now acquires and conserves records of national significance; makes them available to researchers; acts as records management adviser to federal government agencies; requires producers or distributors of certain sound, film, and video

---

[1] W. Brian Speirs, "Canadian Public Archives," *Canadian Archives in 1992,* general ed. Marcel Caya, associate eds. Marion Beyea, Stan B. Hanson (Ottawa: Canadian Council of Archives, 1992), p. 17.

recordings to supply a copy of their productions; and supports the Canadian archival community in a variety of ways.[2] Technological advances, the need for automation services, new storage media, and conservation requirements will occupy the National Archives and other archival institutions well into the 21st century.

As mentioned in the introduction to *Canadian Archives in 1992*, several features identify the Canadian archival community:

- The development of a complex network among our national, regional, provincial, and local archival institutions, councils, and professional associations;
- The rapid growth in the number of public and private archival repositories;
- The "total archives" concept by which public archives acquire and care for both government records and related private records of organizations, societies, and individuals, no matter what the medium;
- The equal access to information by researchers of all types.[3]

TYPES OF ARCHIVES

In Texas Houston was called the meeting place but documents were moved to Austin.

Public archives are maintained by federal, provincial, and municipal governments.

Public archives are maintained by federal, provincial, and municipal governments to preserve the documents and other items that relate to the history of the area, its people, and all aspects of Canadian life. In addition to the federal government, Canada's 10 provinces and two territories maintain their own official archives. One of their primary responsibilities is for their own government's records. The provincial and territorial archives also characteristically consolidate archives and records management programs based on the life cycle of their records.

first Archives 1834

3od model established a new type of archive system

An example of material kept in a public archives is shown in Figure 18-1, which is a photograph by Joseph Rogers dated about 1861 of the Province Building in Halifax, the home of the Nova Scotia legislature. Under a permanent location was found for Nova Scotia's archives, maps and other valuable archival documents were kept in the basement and attic of Province Building (now called Province House) for many years.

Quebec's Archives nationale du Québec's has a mandate that is unique in Canada because of its broad responsibility for both archives and records management in 4,000 public areas—municipalities, universities, regional archives facilities, and court records and appeals.[4] Municipal archives outside the province of Quebec may be covered by

---

[2]Ibid., p. 19.

[3]Editorial Committee Marion Beyea, Françoise Bouvier, Marcel Caya, Stan B. Hanson, "Introduction," *Canadian Archives in 1992*, general ed. Marcel Caya (Ottawa: Canadian Council of Archives, 1992), pp. 12-13.

[4]W. Brian Speirs, "Canadian Public Archives," *Canadian Archives in 1992*, general ed. Marcel Caya (Ottawa: Canadian Council of Archives, 1992), p. 27.

provincial legislation but generally they concentrate on the social and economic history of their communities and often rely on assistance from local libraries, historical societies, or museums to preserve their heritage.

Figure 18-1
Province Building
Granville Street
Facade, Halifax

Source: The Joseph S. Rogers Collection, Public Archives of Nova Scotia, Halifax, Nova Scotia

manuscripts are archives

Private archives preserve the history of an institution, a corporation, or some entity other than government. Canadian university and college archives constitute the largest segment of private archives—every major university maintains an archival program. However, the archives of religious institutions, hospitals, health care facilities, and businesses such as banks also make up a significant segment of the Canadian archival community. An example from the archives of the Canadian Imperial Bank of Commerce (CIBC) is shown in Figure 18-2. The photograph depicts a nontraditional branch of the Canadian Bank of Commerce (as it was then known) in Cobalt, Ontario in 1905.

There are a number of active business archives in Canada; in addition, some Canadian companies have agreements with provincial archives to house their archival materials. For example, the T. Eaton Company records are housed with the Archives of Ontario and the Hudson's Bay Company with the Provincial Archives of Manitoba. A variety of thematic archives concentrate on specific subjects or research themes. Some examples are the Canadian Centre for Architecture, the Centre d'études acadiennes in New Brunswick, the Black Cultural Centre of Nova Scotia, and the Inuit Cultural Institute in the Northwest Territories.

Figure 18-2
Canadian Bank of
Commerce Branch
in Cobalt, Ontario,
1905

Source: CIBC Archives

 Learning Check: Can you distinguish between public archives and private archives?

THE ARCHIVES PROFESSION

The person
responsible for
archival activities is
the archivist.

The **archivist** is the person responsible for the following activities in an archive: acquisition, appraisal and disposition, accessioning, preservation, arrangement, description, reference service, exhibitions, publications, and outreach services. Archivists come into this profession with a variety of backgrounds, education, and experience.

As in other professions, archivists must understand and apply the principles of sound management to their work. They must know how to set goals and establish priorities, use resources wisely and efficiently, motivate and supervise staff, and develop resources to build support for an archives program. Archival facilities are extremely diverse, ranging from well-funded operations with a full range of archival services to limited archives that depend on part-time volunteer staff. They have been established by a great variety of public and private institutions from federal and provincial governments to labour unions and historical societies. Certificates, diplomas, undergraduate degrees, and master's-level graduate degrees are now offered in Canada; an archival technician program is also available. Individuals seeking a career in archives administration usually have an undergraduate and a graduate degree. Although undergraduate majors vary widely, many archivists come to their work with a master's degree in history or library and information management. Other areas of specialization include public administration and political science. Training and experience in conducting research in primary and secondary sources are helpful. With the growth of computers and electronic records, archivists must be familiar with new systems and storage media. There is a growing importance placed on continuing education through seminars and workshops as well as joint training sessions with other information management professionals.

The Canadian Council of Archives (CCA) is the main coordinating body of the Canadian archival system.

The **Canadian Council of Archives (CCA)** was founded in 1985 to coordinate the development of the Canadian archival system and foster partnerships within it. The CCA, an organization of archival institutions, is administered by a board made up of the National Archivist and representatives from the provincial and territorial councils, and from the Bureau of Canadian Archivists (the national association representing the **Association of Canadian Archivists** and the **Association des archivistes du Québec**). Many archivists in Canada are members of the Association of Canadian Archivists and the Association des archivistes du Québec, or professional archival organizations. These two associations encourage the development of the archival profession in Canada through their many professional activities and programs.

Many books, reports, technical leaflets, and journals are published in the archival field. In Canada, *The Archivist: Magazine of the National Archives of Canada* originates in Ottawa. The Association of Canadian Archivists has published *Archivaria,* a quarterly professional journal, since 1975. In the United States, the **Society of American Archivists (SAA)** publishes *The American Archivist* as well as a bimonthly newsletter. The British Records Association has published *Archives* semiannually since 1949.

✓ **Learning Check: Can you name three activities an archivist would perform?**

PURPOSES OF ARCHIVES

In a business sense, records are preserved and maintained in order to provide documentation that will help managers in their daily activities and also aid the organization to accomplish its established goals.

Archives are used to preserve corporate memory; provide production information, policy direction, personnel information, and financial information; maintain public relations activities; provide legal advantage and research service; and prepare commemorative histories.

Preserve Corporate Memory

Archives preserve corporate memory.

Historical records are used to document the activities of the organization and, in that way, preserve corporate memory. For example, it may be important to know issue dates of patents, initial distribution dates of products, and actions of the governing body, and to provide documentation of these facts.

Provide Product Information

Archives provide documentation of product development.

Documentation of product development, the success or failure of prior products, and marketing strategies used are all relevant to the creation, development, or introduction of a new product. For example, if a manufacturer is contemplating a change in product design, knowing the history of that product may be helpful.

Provide Policy Direction

Historical records provide policy direction.

Historical records may provide direction for reviewing the effectiveness of existing policies or in considering new ones. For example, access to records regarding the effectiveness of past policies and procedures would give direction for maintaining or changing policies.

Provide Personnel Information

Organizational history can help locate previous employees.

Personnel departments may find organizational history helpful when conducting employee orientations and building company identification. Personnel information may also be useful when it is necessary to contact previous employees. For example, in 1969 the archives staff of Eli Lilly and Company was asked to assist in locating surviving members of the families of deceased Lilly employees. When new benefits for survivors were added to the company's survivor benefits program, these benefits were made retroactive for eligible survivors of every qualified employee who had died at any time since the company began its retirement program. As a result of obtaining this personnel information, over 300 eligible survivors began receiving benefits.

Provide Financial Information

Financial records are valuable in long-term strategic planning.

The use of early financial records may prove valuable in forecasting activities. Planning departments frequently use financial records in long-term strategic planning.

Maintain Public Relations Activities

Public relations campaigns are enhanced by complete and accurate information.

Having complete and accurate information available for use in public relations campaigns is essential. A proven record of accomplishment, operational continuity, and length of service to the public provides a wealth of promotional material. For example, the Ford Motor Company once constructed an entire television commercial around a letter of approval the company received from the gangster Clyde Barrow (of Bonnie and Clyde fame). The Coca-Cola Company has offered trays and glasses that are facsimiles of those used many years ago to advertise Coca-Cola. In advertisements and promotions throughout 1995, the Hudson's Bay Company celebrated its 325-year history in North America from its beginnings under the royal charter of Charles II in 1670 as the Company of Adventurers of England Trading into Hudson's Bay.

Provide Legal Advantage

Historical records document legal positions.

Legal departments often need historical records to document their positions. For example, Eli Lilly and Company found archives information to be essential in establishing their right to a trademark registration. Other organizations have used their archives to justify tax positions, product rights, and so forth.

Provide Research Service

Original records provide essential tools for the historian.

Researchers need a source for their information. Original records are essential tools of the historian. Without original records, the researcher must rely on hearsay, tradition, recollections, and summary documentation. Archives provide the researcher with accurate information, which is accessible to users and preserved so that the information is still available. Often, knowing exactly when something happened allows for easier identification of the reason for or causes of the event.

Prepare Commemorative Histories

Businesses often wish to prepare a commemorative history for an anniversary. Historical records are essential to an accurate portrayal of the early years of a company. When there is no documentation, oral histories must be relied on to provide the necessary information. Although these personal recollections provide colour, they may be inaccurate or only partial recollections. Many companies prepare commemorative histories as they approach significant milestones in their lives; 25-, 50-, 75-, and 100-year anniversaries are typical commemorative years. Throughout 1995, for example, Hudson's Bay Company advertisements celebrated the company's 325 years of operation.

 Learning Check: Can you name four purposes of archives?

APPROACHES TO ARCHIVES MANAGEMENT

There are three approaches to archives management.

Archives management establishes control procedures to preserve history and provide the vehicle for using history in a beneficial way. Historically, there have been three successive approaches to archives management—an unstructured internal approach, a structured internal approach, and an external approach. Some organizations have progressed through all three approaches, with changes made as the needs of the organization changed.

Unstructured Internal Approach

In the unstructured internal approach to archives management, someone is assigned the task of sorting records to determine which records are valuable and should be preserved and which records have no lasting value and therefore should be destroyed. This is usually accomplished on an as-needed basis as a way of clearing out existing records in order to provide storage space for incoming records. Records tend to accumulate faster than they are destroyed, and the need for the process begins to occur more frequently as the need for storage accelerates. With the unstructured approach, the sorting is not usually a permanently assigned task. Several persons sorting and making decisions for retention or destruction may cause inconsistency and result in failure to preserve the most important records. This unstructured approach is often used by small businesses and organizations.

Structured Internal Approach

Beginning in 1943 with the establishment of a business archives by Firestone Tire & Rubber Co., other organizations began to see the value of establishing a formal system to collect and maintain their own historical records. This approach has been adopted by a number of large organizations, including Walt Disney Productions, the Ford Motor Co., the Coca-Cola Company, International Business Machines Corporation, the Bank of Nova Scotia, Bell Canada, Canadian Pacific, universities, and governmental agencies.

External Approach

Some organizations have elected to preserve and maintain their historical records in university archives, historical societies, and other archival repositories such as the provincial and National Archives. This approach provides a safe yet accessible place for historical records, although it does have disadvantages. The external approach separates important records by housing them in two places: active records within the organization, and selected inactive records outside the organization. Some of the records housed in the external depositories are bulky, little used, and expensive to maintain, presenting difficulties for the receiving repository. The external approach seems to be more appropriate for organizations that are no longer in business than for active organizations, although the Hudson's Bay Company and the T. Eaton Company both house their archives in provincial archives facilities. With proper records schedules and liaison between the organization and the archives, some of the disadvantages of separate housing can be overcome.

Learning Check: Can you name the three management approaches to archives management?

RECORDS APPRAISAL

Usually 2 to 5 percent of total records have lasting historical value.

Only a small percentage of all records, whether government or corporate, has any lasting archival value. This is generally in the range of 2 to 5 percent. The archivist is faced with the task of selecting the appropriate records to be kept in the archives. During the records survey and inventory, which was described in Chapter 3, archival records can be identified. Records are identified as having two basic types of values—primary (evidential or documentary) value and secondary (informational, research, or historical) value.[5]

In determining the records with archival value, the archivist must identify the records that document the programs, policies, or decision-making processes of an organization. These records help the archivist know when, where, why, and how a company flourished or did not flourish.[6] Financial records are important to give a complete historical picture of the organization, but records maintained in the archives must go beyond the financial records.

Archived records should include information about employee relations and civic involvement as well as biographical data about major personalities in the organization. Records may document why an organization was formed, what its priorities were, who wielded major influence, why the company succeeded or failed, how it expanded, how it adapted to new technology or changing markets, and how the company viewed itself. Documents that can be used to find this information include minutes of board of directors meetings, committee reports, annual reports, budget breakdowns, internal and external correspondence, policy and procedures manuals, special project reports, strategic planning statements, and organization charts.[7]

[5]Barbara Reed, "Appraisal and Disposal," *Keeping Archives,* 2nd ed., ed. Judith Ellis (Port Melbourne, Australia: Australian Society of Archivists, Inc., 1993), p. 158.

[6]Edie Hedlin, *Business Archives: An Introduction* (Chicago: Society of American Archivists, 1987), p. 15.

[7]Ibid., p. 16.

Records Selection

What records should be preserved and maintained in the archives? Records selection largely depends on the purpose for which each archives facility is established. In establishing a business archives, the following are some considerations that must be addressed:

- Will the archives function as a purely administrative tool of the business?
- Will its collections be available only to insiders?
- Will the archives serve scholars and other interested individuals?
- Will only company records be collected or will materials documenting the organization's role in community and civic affairs be included?
- Will the personal records of company officials be collected?

The answers to these questions, in addition to affecting the selection of the records being considered for preservation and archival storage, will determine the scope of the program.

Records Content

Records selection is a two-phase operation. The first phase is a determination of the administrative units most likely to produce records whose preservation may be important to the organization. The second phase is a determination of the record types to be preserved and maintained. The content of the records, rather than the age of the records, dominates the selection decision. Preserving records simply because they are old is difficult to justify when one considers the expense involved in preserving and maintaining the records in the archives program. Final selection is based on the organization's perceived value of the records for future reference and research.

Record Types

Most of the records selected for preservation and for archival storage are paper documents with different characteristics—bond paper, carbon paper, coated paper, copying paper, cover stock, decorated paper, facsimile paper, kraft paper, ledger paper, manila, newsprint, onionskin, parchment, book paper, and tracing paper. However, the records are not limited to paper and include magnetic media, video and audio cassettes, audio tapes, computer tapes, disks and diskettes, optical disks, animal skins such as vellum and parchment, microforms, textiles, and photographic materials.

Walt Disney Productions archivist David R. Smith identified for his unique archives three types of records—business, creative, and product. Included in the business category are all of the traditional records.

Creative records include the many types of materials generated in planning and producing films and in planning and constructing Disneyland, Walt Disney World, Epcot Center, and the Disney/MGM Studio Theme Park. The product records include films, books, comic books, phonograph records, press clippings, still photographs, insignia, character merchandise, employee publications, audioanimatronics, props, costumes, and Walt Disney memorabilia.

Another example of records other than paper that have been used to preserve corporate history are those items selected by Eli Lilly and Company for its archives. These include samples of Lilly products, anniversary souvenirs, advertising promotions, bottles, and packaging material.

Photographs are an important part of an archives collection. Pictures of people, equipment, products, and buildings add colour and dimension to the archival records maintained by an organization.

Oral histories—valuable assets of any company—are particularly valuable when based on the experiences of the organization's key personnel. These histories may be preserved in the form of tapes, transcripts, and videotapes. Original company catalogues are also a source of information.

All of these types of records are appropriate for archival preservation and storage. Final selection should be based on the needs of the individual organization.

✓ **Learning Check: Can you name and explain the two phases in the records selection operation?**

Determination of Information Value

Appraisal of records selected for archival storage continues through a determination of the value of the information contained in the records. The archival value may be primary reference value or secondary research value.

Primary Reference Value

Information from archival records used internally has reference value.

Differentiating between the reference value and the research value of records in archival storage is often difficult. In general, the distinction lies with the user and the intent rather than with the record and its content. Archives provide information regarding the organization's policies, philosophies, performances, products, and people. When this information is used internally, its value is primarily of **reference value**. Company personnel requiring information for the performance of their daily activities would benefit from the reference value of the archives. These records may provide validation or reinforcement for their decisions.

Secondary Research Value

Research value lies with external users.

The **research value** of archives most frequently lies with external users or with organizational personnel who are engaged in researching the development of the organization's policies, philosophy, performance, products, or people. The archives enable qualified historians to have the information required to write factual business histories.

 Learning Check: Can you explain the difference between reference value and research value?

RESPONSIBILITY FOR ARCHIVES MANAGEMENT

Efficient archives management requires defining responsibility for the preservation of the organization's history and an understanding of the need for coordination of shared responsibilities among those involved in the management of the archives.

Placement

Placement of responsibility for the archives program is not clearly defined.

The responsibility for an archives management program within an organization may be in one of a number of areas. There are three major schools of thought regarding who should have ultimate responsibility and authority for the establishment and maintenance of an archives program. One group believes that archives management is one element of a comprehensive records management system; therefore, the responsibility and authority should rest with the records manager. The second group believes that an archivist should have the responsibility and authority for administering the total system. The third group believes that a distinct delineation of functions exists between an archivist and a records manager; therefore, a delineation of responsibility and authority should exist. In this case, the records manager assumes the responsibility for efficient generation of records, arrangement and use of records for business purposes, and eventual records disposal when the records no longer serve a business need. The archivist assumes the responsibility for collecting, preserving, and making available for research the records selected for long-term preservation for historical value. As Figure 18-3 shows, there is some overlapping of interests in this arrangement. Overlapping functions and divided responsibility and authority can create problems, which may be resolved through coordination, cooperation, and communication.

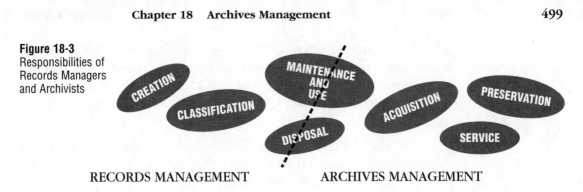

Figure 18-3
Responsibilities of
Records Managers
and Archivists

RECORDS MANAGEMENT   ARCHIVES MANAGEMENT

Source: Jay Atherton, "Archives and Records Management" (Presentation at Association of Records Managers and Administrators, Inc., Boston, 1980).

Coordination

Each of the three arrangements for sharing responsibility for records management and archives requires a high degree of coordination, cooperation, and communication among the participants. When the records manager is responsible for managing a total program that includes archives management, coordination of activities must be maintained between those who process active records and those who preserve inactive records. When the archivist is responsible for managing a total program that includes both functions, the same requirement for coordination exists. When the functions are divided and responsibility is shared, the degree to which coordination and cooperation exist determines the degree to which the program is effective.

✓ **Learning Check: Can you explain the three arrangements for sharing responsibility for archives management?**

ARCHIVES STORAGE

Storage of records in an archives involves ensuring that the records are maintained in the proper arrangement according to accepted archival principles. The records must be correctly prepared for storage and preserved so as to retain their value. Appropriate housing for the records must also be secured.

Arrangement

Archival rules of arrangement in Europe in the mid–nineteenth century stated that in order to provide the maximum information value, documents created by a body should be kept together and associated with that body.[8] Archivists refer to this original, inseparable group of records

---

[8]Terry Eastwood, "General Introduction," *The Archival Fonds from Theory to Practice*, ed. Terry Eastwood (Ottawa: Bureau of Canadian Archivists, 1992), p. 2.

as archival fonds—the whole of the documents produced by an administrative body or person in the course of practical activity.[9] **Respect des fonds** means honouring the concept of fonds in archival arrangement and the related principles of provenance and original order.

Provenance

The principle of **provenance** is that records of a given unit within the organization are retained as a separate group rather than being inter-filed with similar records of another unit. For example, under the provenance principle, the product division records regarding the manufacture of a specific product should not be merged with sales department records pertaining to that same product.

Original Order

The principle of **original order** preserves records in the same order in which they were filed in the office of origin. For example, if the specific product records were originally filed by subject classification, they should be filed by subject classification in the archives as well; they should be retained in the subject order in which they were received.

The principles of provenance and original order preserve file integrity by maintaining the original records in the arrangement in which they were created and used. Archivists recognize five levels of arrangement for archived records—the archival repository, archival fonds, records series, the filing unit, and the item.

 Learning Check: Can you explain respect des fonds and its relationship to the provenance arrangement of archival records and the original order arrangement of archival records?

Preparation

The selection of proper methods for preparing and storing records is important to their future accessibility and use.

Records Preparation

Records must be properly prepared for storage. All metal clips and staples should be removed unless they are rustproof. All rubber bands should be removed. Duplicate copies of records should be destroyed. Letters should be removed from their envelopes and unfolded. Records that are in poor condition should be noted for special treatment. Pressure-sensitive tape should never be used to repair valuable records.

---

[9]Ibid., p. 2.

Equipment

Open steel shelves are appropriate for storage of documents.

Storing archival records in filing cabinets is an unacceptable practice. Folders in file cabinets often become jammed, and searches create undue wear; documents have a tendency to curl. Additionally, file cabinets are expensive, inflexible, space-consuming, and conducive to slow retrieval. Open steel shelving is preferred for storage of documents. Other types of archives may require special storage equipment. Certain kinds of collectibles may require a glass-enclosed cabinet for protection from dust or handling. However, wooden shelves are not desirable for the storage of archival materials because of the possibility of pitch, resin, peroxide, and acidic products leaching out and damaging records. Oak, traditionally used for book cases and shelves, can damage records because of its particularly high formic acid content.[10] Tapes, disks, photographs, and maps require special housing, as discussed in Chapter 5, "Manual Systems of Active Records Management, Equipment and Supplies."

Description Systems and Finding Aids

Archival description must always follow archival arrangement. The Canadian archival community has adopted the *Rules for Archival Description* as its standard for the decryption of archival fonds regardless of the format of the records—text, photograph, film, video, map, plan, and so on. The detail to which a fonds or collection is described depends on the size of the archives, the way the archival materials are used, and the funds available for this time-consuming and expensive task. Descriptions contain standardized information about the arrangement and formats of the archival fonds so that researchers can find the information they need. Finding aids should be designed to serve the special needs of each collection and may be in the format of pamphlets, looseleaf binders, card indexes, magnetic or optical disks, microforms, or computer databases. In a card index, the record would be identified on the card by the records group, series, box, folder, and item number. Another type of finding aid is the accession log in which the type, amount, and date of arrival of new materials to be placed in the archives are recorded. If the processing of the records is delayed, the accession log can be used as a preliminary descriptive tool.

An inventory is a more detailed finding aid. The inventory describes a unit of records or a specific record collection. Included in the inventory is information concerning the source of the records, biographical information on major persons mentioned in the collection, background information on the office or unit, the general content of

---

[10]Mary Lynn Ritzenthaler, *Preserving Archives and Manuscripts* (Chicago: Society of American Archivists, 1993), p. 78.

the records, a box and folder listing of the letters or records included, a guide to where additional materials on the topic or unit might be found, and listings of different subjects mentioned in the collection and specifically where they might be found in the records. Computerized finding aids allow much more flexibility in describing records and provide a powerful search tool.

Preservation

Paper documents comprise a large portion of archival records. The length of time a paper document can be maintained without damage depends on the quality of the paper. See Figure 18-4 for recommendations for preserving books, papers, and photographs.

How to Preserve Books, Papers, and Photographs

1. Do not use tape or glue to repair documents. Most glues and all pressure-sensitive tapes are highly acidic and will cause brown stains on the documents.
2. Store documents flat, but do not flatten tightly curled documents with force. The force will break the fibres, weakening the paper.
3. Store documents away from sunlight or fluorescent light. All visible light will eventually damage documents; ultraviolet light destroys them.
4. Do not wrap documents with a rubber band. Rubber will harden and adhere to paper.
5. Do not use paper clips, straight pins, staples, or other metal objects to bind documents together. Metal objects will eventually rust and destroy the documents.
6. Do not use wooden or ordinary cardboard boxes to store valuable photographs and documents. These containers are highly acidic and will cause damage. Use metal containers or acid-free boxes.
7. Do not store photographs in scrapbooks that use plastic cover pages, adhesive-stripped backboards, or black construction paper. Archival-quality photograph storage supplies are available.
8. Do not store glass-based photographic materials flat, stacked, or in cardboard or wooden boxes. Use specially designed vertical storage systems.
9. Do not open a daguerreotype or ambrotype for cleaning. The balance of gases inside the seal will be upset, and the image will deteriorate rapidly.
10. Do not store negatives and slides in plastic storage sheets. These sheets will decompose and destroy the images.
11. Store all documents in archival containers. Place the containers in an environment where air circulates freely, the temperature is constant at 20 degrees Celsius, and the relative humidity is 50 percent.

Source: Adapted from "How to Take Care of Your Books, Papers, Photographs," a South Carolina Department of Archives and History Document Conservation Leaflet, South Carolina, 1989.

Sixteenth-century paper is stronger and more flexible than 20th century paper. Early manufacturers made paper from a pulp of linen or cotton rags that they bleached and then pounded either by hand or simple machinery into a slurry of long, strong fibres and water. They dried the slurry on frames and then sized it, often by hand, with alkaline materials to prevent inks from feathering. As the demand for paper increased, manufacturers replaced the rags with more plentiful, but acidic, ground wood pulp and looked for cheaper and faster ways to make their product.

Acids damage paper.

By the 19th century, cheaper, but potentially acidic, alum rosin had replaced the old sizing materials. After 1850 paper was plentiful and inexpensive. It was also weaker and highly acidic with its shorter fibres, high wood content, and alum rosin sizing. Acids damage paper and other organic substances by weakening their molecular bonds. Acidity causes paper to lose its strength, and the paper becomes weak, brittle, and stained. If deterioration continues, images and text may disappear entirely. Because many documents are prepared on "bad" paper (paper with a high acidic content), archivists must use special techniques to prepare the documents for storage.

Rather than attempting to treat records after damage has occurred, the archival community stresses preventive conservation throughout the whole life cycle. At the time documents are created, long-term preservation needs should be noted. This may prevent the necessity for costly treatment later. At the centre of the philosophy of conservation is the rule of reversibility: Do nothing which cannot later be undone without harm.[11] In many cases it may be best to do nothing at all. All archival records should be inspected regularly, and there are some methods of conserving these records that do not require expertise. Using acid-free papers, containers, and folders, carrying out basic repairs, encapsulating documents, and converting paper documents to microforms and electronic formats are some available techniques.

Deacidification of Paper

Alkali counteracts acid.

The acidity of paper is measured on the pH scale. The **pH scale** is an arbitrary numeric scale ranging from 0 to 14 that measures the acidity and alkalinity of paper. Figure 18-5 shows the pH scale.[12] The pH reading of 7.0 is the neutral point. All numbers above this point represent increasing alkalinity, and all numbers below 7.0 indicate increasing acidity. **Alkali** is a substance added to paper capable of neutralizing an acid. Because the scale is logarithmic, each number represents a 10-fold change in acidity or alkalinity. A pH of 4 is 10 times more acidic than a pH of 5 and a pH of 4 is 100 times more acidic than a pH of 6.[13] A number of methods are available to test the surface pH of paper

---

[11]*Rules for Archival Description* (Ottawa: Planning Committee on Descriptive Standards, Bureau of Canadian Archivists, 1990).

[12]Ibid., p. 25.

[13]Ibid., p. 144.

that do not require lab facilities or sophisticated training. If the pH is below 6, the deacidification of paper should be considered.[14] Acid-free and alkaline "permanent" papers with a pH of 8.5 to 10.0 are ideally suited for archival and preservation applications identified in the retention schedule.

Figure 18-5
pH Scale

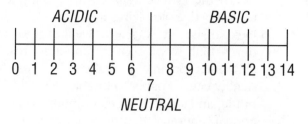

Source: Archives and Manuscripts: Conservation, A Manual on Physical Care Management, *Basic Manual Series (Chicago: Society of American Archivists, 1983).*

Containers

Acid-free containers should be used to store archival documents.

Acidity in storage containers destroys the records inside them. To combat possible destruction by acidity, records should be stored in acid-free boxes, folders, envelopes, and sleeves. All paper and board stock used in conjunction with archival materials should be acid-free and buffered to have an alkaline reserve with a minimum pH of 8.5.[15] Grey acid-free fibreboard boxes or cartons are available in various sizes to accommodate different types of records and are widely accepted as the most suitable containers for archival records. These acid-free boxes or cartons are more expensive than traditional records centre cartons, and when cost is a major factor, some organizations use the acid-free cartons for only the most valuable records. Corrugated, fitted-lid records centre cartons, together with acid-free folders, are used for all other records. Plastic containers are available in a variety of formats; however, polyvinyl chloride (PVC) should never be used to house archival records.

Folders

Acid-free folders are available in standard, legal and special sizes from most office supply firms. These acid-free folders protect their contents from acid damage. Blueprints, for example, require the special care of alkaline-buffered folders with sheets of polyester film on the top and bottom of a group of blueprints.

---

[14]Ibid., p. 144.
[15]Ibid., p. 82.

Basic Repairs

Repairs such as mending, reinforcement, and support of fragile documents can be very expensive procedures. Only simple procedures that do not require special equipment should be carried out by untrained staff. For example, surface dirt may be removed with a soft brush, a soft eraser, or a document cleaning pad.[16]

Encapsulation

Encapsulation is the process of placing a document between sheets of polyester film that have a neutral pH and sealing the edges. This process can be performed in-house by archives employees. Encapsulation requires no outside professional assistance, no expensive equipment, and no chemicals. The polyester film does not adhere to the document. The film simply encases the document to provide physical support for it. Once the records are enclosed within the polyester film, the documents can be handled, photocopied, and microfilmed. The process is easily reversed by simply unsealing the edges of the film around the document. Experts recommend that the documents be deacidified prior to encapsulation or that a sheet of acid-free buffered paper be included with the encapsulated material; otherwise, the paper will continue to deteriorate.

Microforms

Records may also be preserved by microfilming the originals. The original microfilm copies of long-term records should not be used for reference purposes. Negative or positive duplicates of the original camera film are made available for use; the original records and film are protected from damage caused by use. With proper care, microfilm can last for more than a hundred years.[17]

In 1947 the Dead Sea Scrolls were discovered. The original manuscripts are now showing increasing deterioration from exposure to light and humidity; predictions are that by the year 2010 the manuscripts will have deteriorated completely. To preserve their value for researchers, the Dead Sea Scrolls are being filmed and made available in both microfilm and microfiche.

Electronic Formats

Converting documents to electronic formats offers advantages similar to microfilming. However, the life of the storage media is much shorter than for microfilm, which means that electronic formats may not be suitable for long-term storage.

---

[16]Ibid., p. 82.
[17]Ross Harvey, "Preservation," *Keeping Archives,* 2nd ed., p. 95.

Housing

Proper storage conditions are important for archival records. Factors to consider when planning archival records storage include building construction, safety controls, temperature and humidity controls, light, and space allocations.

Building

The building housing the archives should comply with the requirements for three-hour fire-resistant construction. Fire walls, smoke-handling systems, and fire and smoke alarms are among the safety components that should be a part of the plan for the building or for its conversion. Clean air with good circulation must also be provided. A good ventilation system will provide the circulation of air needed. Appropriate filters that will eliminate specific pollutants from the environment must be installed.[18] Security systems must be in place to protect the archives.

Temperature and Humidity Controls

Temperature and humidity controls are necessary for the preservation and maintenance of the archives. As described in Figure 18-4, the recommended temperature for archival materials is 20 degrees Celsius and relative humidity of 50 percent.

50 - 70°
humidity

Light

Ultraviolet (UV) radiation and active visible light will cause deterioration of records and speed up chemical reactions. Ultraviolet radiation is emitted primarily from sunlight, and fluorescent lights pose great threats to archival materials if the materials are not boxed or wrapped. Incandescent lights pose no significant threats to archival materials from ultraviolet radiation and are the preferred light source in archives.[19]

Space

Space requirements for archival facilities are the same as those recommended in Chapter 17 for records centres—a stack area, processing area, office area, and reference area. The amount of space required depends on the volume of records in the facility, the projected accessions, and the reference activity within the facility.

---

[18]David Roberts, "Using Computers and Document Imaging," *Keeping Archives*, 2nd ed., p. 364.

[19]Mary Lynn Ritzenthaler, p. 56.

ACCESS TO AND SECURITY OF ARCHIVAL RECORDS

A system to secure the archival records must be established and implemented. The records must be secure when they are checked in and processed, used by researchers, or maintained in the archives. An evaluation should be made of the archives building including windows, doors, and skylights. The security system should deter unauthorized entrance by utilizing alarms, grilles or bars, monitoring panels, or motion detectors with remote alarms. Offsite storage must also be considered when establishing a security system.

Only archives personnel should have access to the stack areas. Visitors brought into any area of the archives should be supervised, and researchers using materials in the reading room should be monitored. Only archives staff should have keys to the archives area, and only staff members with a need-to-use should have access to stack or high-security areas. Maintenance and security staff should not have unsupervised access to the archives area.[20]

Archives management is a broad field of endeavour and cannot be completely addressed in one chapter. The purpose of this chapter is to provide an overview of archives management and to look at areas that differ from records management. For readers whose interests have been aroused by this discussion, further information may be obtained from the National Archives of Canada, the Association of Canadian Archivists, the Canadian Council of Archives, the Society of American Archivists, and the Australian Society of Archivists. The Society of American Archivists has published basic manuals dealing with surveys, appraisal and accessioning, arrangement and description, reference and access, security, and business archives. These manuals are available from the Society of American Archivists, 330 South Wells, Suite 810, Chicago, IL 60606. The Australian Society of Archivists has published a book called *Keeping Archives,* which contains chapters that discuss using computers, and document imaging and managing records in special formats. *A Manual for Small Archives,* published by the Association of British Columbia Archivists is also a very good source of information.

---

[20]Ibid., p. 59.

TERMINOLOGY REVIEW

Review each of the terms listed below in the Glossary on page 521.

alkali	pH scale
archival fonds	private archives
archives	provenance
archives management	public archives
archivist	reference value
Association of Canadian Archivists	research value
Association des archivistes du Québec	respect des fonds
Canadian Council of Archives	Society of American
encapsulation	Archivists (SAA)
original order	

REVIEW AND DISCUSSION

1. Briefly discuss the history of archives.
2. Explain the different roles and responsibilities of archivists and records managers.
3. Explain the difference between public archives and private archives.
4. What qualifications are needed to succeed in the management of archives as a profession?
5. Define archives management and explain its purpose.
6. List and describe three approaches to archives management.
7. Describe the records appraisal procedures used to select archival records.
8. Explain the three schools of thought regarding who should have ultimate responsibility and authority for the establishment and maintenance of an archives program.
9. Discuss archival fonds and its relationship with provenance and original order.
10. Describe three procedures for storage of archival records.
11. Discuss the factors that should be considered for housing archival records.
12. Discuss three procedures to secure archival records.

APPLICATIONS

1. Visit a museum, public archive, or private archive and prepare a report describing at least three methods the archivist uses to preserve documents.

2. Interview an archivist. Gather information concerning background, experience, and education. Ask about the career options of an archivist and the job titles of employees in the archives management field. Write a report on the information you compile.

CONCLUDING CASES

A. Casey Manufacturing Company

Casey Manufacturing Company was founded in 1920. You are the records manager and have been in that position for the last three years. For two years you have tried to establish an archives management program for the organization. Part of this procedure would be to hire an archivist to establish and manage the archives program. The CEO and other top managers in the organization do not see any benefit in an archives program and have refused to allow one to be established.

As records manager you were contacted when a forgotten warehouse full of records was discovered two months ago. Your staff was called to the location and asked to evaluate the records and decide the disposition of the records. Your staff members were amazed as they inventoried the records and found documents dating back to the beginning of the company. Many photographs, letters, drawings, and other documents were among the boxes located in the warehouse. The grandfather of the current CEO was the founder of the company, and many documents relate directly to him.

You see this as your opportunity to persuade current management of the importance of an archives management program and decide to draft a report detailing the advantages of an archives management program and the facilities needed to preserve these archival documents.

Write a report detailing the advantages of an archives management program, the management approach you would choose to manage the archives, and the facilities needed to house the archival documents.

B. Davi's Fashion House

Davi's Fashion House (DFH) is a fashion design business established in 1960. DFH just completed the buyout of a smaller fashion design business named Coast Fashion Design. Coast Fashion Design was a very well-known fashion design business that had been associated with numerous famous designers during the past 25 years.

As the two businesses merged into one, you, as the DFH records manager, did a complete records inventory of the Coast Fashion Design offices. During the inventory, you discovered several boxes of documents including letters, reports, and fashion sketches. The fashion sketches are preliminary and final sketches by three of the famous designers that had been associated with the Coast Fashion Design. The records are at least 20 years old and show some deterioration. You plan to add these documents, particularly the sketches by the famous designers, to the archives of Davi's Fashion House.

Explain the procedures you would use to preserve these documents and the preservation method you would choose to store the documents.

SUGGESTED READINGS AND RESOURCES

Acotia, Pino. "The National Archives of Ghana: New Responsibilities and Challenges." *Records Management Quarterly,* Vol. 28, No. 4 (October, 1994), p. 33.

A Manual for Small Archives. Vancouver: Association of British Columbia Archivists, 1988.

Barton, John P., and Johanna G. Wellheiser, eds. *An Ounce of Prevention: A Handbook on Disaster Contingency Planning for Archives, Libraries and Records Centres.* Toronto: Toronto Area Archivists Group, 1985.

Basic Conservation of Archival Materials: A Guide/Manuel de conservation des documents d'archives. Ottawa: Canadian Council of Archives, 1990.

Caya, Marcel, ed. *Canadian Archives in 1992.* Ottawa: Canadian Council of Archives, 1992.

Couture, Carol, and Jean-Yves Rousseau. Translated by David Homel. *The Life of A Document.* Montreal: Véhicule Press, 1987.

Cribbs, Margaret A. "Photographic Conservation—an Update." *Records Management Quarterly,* Vol. 22, No. 3 (July, 1988), p. 17.

Eastwood, Terry, ed. *The Archival Fonds: From Theory to Practice.* Ottawa: Bureau of Canadian Archivists, Planning Committee on Descriptive Standards, 1992.

Ellis, Judith, ed. *Keeping Archives, 2nd ed.* Port Melbourne, Australia: Australian Society of Archivists Inc., 1993.

Fortier, Normand. *Guide to Oral History Collections in Canada.* Ottawa: Canadian Oral History Association, 1993.

King, Susan L. "Moving the City of Charleston's Archives and Records Center." *Records Management Quarterly,* Vol. 27, No. 4 (October, 1993), p. 32.

Lowell, Howard P., "Elements of a State Archives and Records Management Program." *Records Management Quarterly,* Vol. 21, No. 4 (October, 1987), pp. 3–4.

Lowell, Howard P. "Preservation Microfilming: An Overview." *Records Management Quarterly,* Vol. 19, No. 1 (January, 1985), p. 22.

Neale, William E. "Archival Myths and Realities." *Inform,* Vol. 3, No. 10 (October, 1989), pp. 24-28.

Merz, Nancy M. "Archives and The One World of Records." *Inform,* Vol. 2, No. 4 (April, 1988), pp. 30-36.

Miller, Frederic M. *Arranging and Describing Archives and Manuscripts.* Chicago: Society of American Archivists, 1990.

Rhodes, Stephen B. "Archival and Records Management Automation." *Records Management Quarterly,* Vol. 25, No. 2 (April, 1991), p. 12.

Ritzenthaler, Mary Lynn. *Preserving Archives and Manuscripts.* Chicago: Society of American Archivists, 1993.

Sanders, Robert L. "Archivists and Records Managers: Another Marriage in Trouble?" *Records Management Quarterly,* Vol. 23, No. 2 (April, 1989), p. 12.

Shkolnik, Leon. "The Role of the Archive in the Corporate Structure." *Records Management Quarterly,* Vol. 24, No. 4 (October, 1990), p. 18.

Walch, Timothy, ed. *Guardian of Heritage, Essays on the History of the National Archives.* Washington, D.C.: National Archives and Records Administration, 1985.

Profile
Archivist

The university archivist for the archives and records management program of a major university has been in this position for five years. The university employs approximately 1,300 employees on five campuses; the archives and records management program, 10. The program position titles include university archivist, university records manager, graduate assistant, and student assistant.

Education and experience requirements for this position include a master's degree in history or library and information science and five years' experience in an archives setting. The position of archivist requires supervisory experience, oral and written communication skills, research skills, and extensive knowledge of archival theory and practice.

The major duties and responsibilities of the university archivist are to administer, coordinate, and direct a comprehensive records management program for all five campuses of the university system. The archivist is also responsible for all activities relating to accessioning, retrieving, appraising, conserving, arranging, and describing the holdings of the university archives. Additional duties include preparing and submitting grant proposals to provincial and national agencies to further develop the archives program. The archivist also formulates and coordinates production of exhibitions focusing on the university's history.

Changes that have occurred as a result of growth and technology include the application of computer technology to the arrangement and description of holdings of the archives. The archivist is also in the planning stage of establishing an offsite records centre for storage of semi-inactive records. The archivist plans to focus on the satellite campuses' recordkeeping activities through designation of staff at those campuses to be the liaison with the program at the main campus.

Currently the archivist holds the top position in the department so no further advancement is possible unless there is some administrative restructuring at the university that would affect the archives program.

The archivist is active in the Association of Canadian Archivists and the Council of Canadian Archives. The university records manager is the local ARMA chapter president. The archivist and records manager plan and participate in seminars and conventions sponsored by ARMA.

Conversions from Imperial to Metric Measures

(≐ means "is approximately equal to")

Length

1 inch = 25.4 mm (millimetres)

1 inch = 2.54 cm (centimetres)

1 foot = 30.48 cm (centimetres)

= 0.3048 m (metre)

1 yard = 0.9144 m (metre)

Area

1 square inch = 6.4516 cm² (square centimetres)

1 square foot ≐ 9.2903 dm² (square decimetres)

≐ 0.0929 m² (square metre)

1 square yard ≐ 0.8361 m² (square metre)

Volume

1 cubic inch ≐ 16.3871 cm³ (cubic centimetres)

1 cubic foot ≐ 28.3168 dm³ (cubic decimetres)

≐ 0.0283 m³ (cubic metre)

1 cubic yard ≐ 0.7645 m³ (cubic metre)

Standard Paper Sizes

(Canadian Government Specifications Board)

Size (designation)	Standard Sheet Size (centimetres)	Size Replaced (inches)
P1	56 × 86	22 × 34
P2	43 × 56	17 × 22
P3	28 × 43	11 × 17
P4	21.5 × 28	$8\frac{1}{2} \times 11$
P5	14 × 21.5	$5\frac{1}{2} \times 8\frac{1}{2}$
P6	10.7 × 14	$4\frac{1}{4} \times 5\frac{1}{2}$

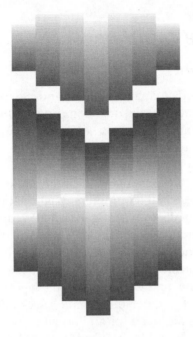

Appendix

Comprehensive Cases

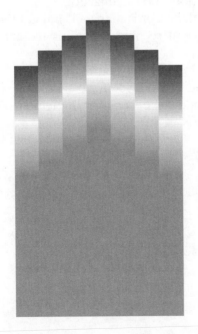

COMPREHENSIVE CASE I

Part 1: Background

Jim O'Brian is the records manager of Montand, Simpson, and Associates, a large-volume dealer of personal computers. MS&A sells and services personal computers from six different manufacturers; each manufacturer offers an extensive list of models from which to choose. MS&A has been very successful in its marketing, and, as a result, has gained a large share of the personal computer market.

The market for personal computers has quadrupled projected growth estimates. When MS&A was organized 10 years ago, only three major investors were active in the management of the organization: Cary Montand, president and officer in charge of administration; Joan Montand Kuriak, vice president in charge of sales and service (and the only salesperson for the first several months of operation); and Ty Simpson, vice president for personnel and jack-of-all-trades. As the organization expanded, the need for additional personnel became evident, and employees were added to all departments.

The records of MS&A are kept in individual departments within the organization. The fast growth of the company in volume of sales and in service calls and contracts has resulted in an even greater growth of required records. The sales and service growth has been enthusiastically received by management; the record growth has not. The primary reasons for the negative reaction to the record growth are that fast access to records is often difficult and there is a tremendous duplication of records throughout the organization.

All of this has led the records manager, Jim O'Brian, to decide that he should present several recommendations to management. If you were Jim,

- What recommendations would you make?
- What rationale would you provide for each of the recommendations?
- How would you outline the steps for implementation of each of the recommendations?

PART 2

The following information was obtained from the records inventory:

Records Inventory Data

Offices	Record Series	Records Media
Administrative	Reports Correspondence	Paper
Sales	Sales records	Paper
Service	Service manuals Customer records	Microfiche
Accounting	Financial records	Computer printouts Forms
Personnel	Personnel records	Microfiche

The records retention program has just been implemented. No records have been purged. You may assume that the general rule of one-third of records remaining in active files, one-third transferred to inactive files, and one-third remaining in each department will allow the organization to function effectively. If you believe other assumptions must be made, list them on a separate sheet.

From the information provided and the assumptions you make, recommend records to be transferred to inactive storage or discarded.

COMPREHENSIVE CASE II

Eric Faulkenbarry is the records manager of Citizens Trust Company (CTC), a provincewide trust company. The company directors recently approved Eric's request to begin in-house microfilming of several records applications. The trust company assigned part of one floor of a new building to Eric for office space, for timing activities, and for storage of microforms. The area is 40 feet by 40 feet. The space can be partitioned to Eric's specifications.

Eric has projected that the micrographics department will be filming some documents that are uniform in size; however, other documents will be in varying sizes and condition. He estimates that approximately 50 percent of the documents could be filmed using automatic feeding. Eric also projects that the department will be filming an average of 20,000 documents per day. Eric projects that each technician and each clerk will be able to film an average of 2,000 documents per hour. He anticipates that the micrographics department will receive an average of 65 requests daily for information or microforms. Since requests for information require more time than retrieving a microform, Eric projects that the average request will consume five minutes.

Based on the information above and any assumptions you want to make, help Eric with the following decisions:

1. What equipment and supplies would be needed to begin the micrographics department? Include the equipment for the micrographics department as well as any equipment needed throughout the trust company offices.
2. What would be the optimum number of employees for the micrographics department? Include the positions to which they should be assigned and give a rationale for your answer.
3. Based on the number of employees and positions in Number 2 above, draw a floor plan for the micrographics department. Indicate how the space should be apportioned and the location of each component of the micrographics department.
4. What additional responsibilities will Eric assume as a result of adding the micrographics department?

COMPREHENSIVE CASE III

Jean Alberts was hired as the records manager of Wright Insurance Company (WIC) three months ago. When she began work at WIC, she was aware that the company had several problems with the management of their records. Jean's job was to implement a formal records management program. She conducted a records inventory of all the active and inactive records.

The active records were crammed into the filing cabinets, and every department had its own procedures concerning the removal of records from the active files. Some departments simply waited until the cabinets were full and randomly removed records to the "inactive area." Many of the inactive records were stored in closets, basements, and other unsuitable storage areas. Many were not marked as to the content or date. Retention periods had not been established for the majority of the records being maintained. Jean identified the inactive records that were being maintained among the active records and purged them from the active files.

As a result of the inventory, Jean had the following active records:

Active Records

Dept.	Records Vol.	Housed In	Records Media
Adm. Offices	500 linear inches	5-drawer vertical cabinets	Paper
Sales	250 linear inches	Open shelves	Paper
Service	10 linear inches, fiche	Fiche cabinets	Microfiche
Accounting	230 linear inches, open shelves	Open shelves	Computer printouts
	310 linear inches, lateral cabinets	Lateral cabinets	Forms
Personnel	25 linear inches, fiche	Fiche cabinets	Microfiche

Jean must plan an active records facility. The active records facility will be a centralized records location for the organization. Only records that are confidential or needed in the departments will be housed outside the centralized area. The current records of the administrative offices will be housed in the administrative offices.

As part of the active records centre, Jean plans to use computer technology to track the active files as they are retrieved, and she also plans to establish the computer technology to maintain the retention schedules of all the records series in the organization.

1. Describe the type of facility that will be needed for the active records centre.
2. What types of hardware and software does Jean need to implement the electronic tracking system and the electronic retention schedule?

COMPREHENSIVE CASE IV

You have just been appointed records manager for Milady Shoe Manufacturers, Ltd. After several weeks of familiarizing yourself with Milady's records management system, you conclude that an important part of the system is not working. There seems to be, at best, minimal concern about the management of correspondence, copies, directives, reports, forms, microrecords, records security, or even any concern at all over computer-based records.

Before discussing this problem with management, you decide to investigate the management systems used by several other organizations. This investigation must take place while you are conducting your other duties as records manager; therefore, you decide to limit your investigation at this time to one of the programs. Select one of the following programs for evaluation:

- Correspondence management
- Copy management
- Directives management
- Reports management
- Microrecords management
- Computer-based records management
  For the program selected:
- Design a form to collect the information.
- Write letters to five organizations requesting that they supply the information needed.
- Analyze the information received.
- Write follow-up letters as required to obtain the information.

- Prepare a report that compiles and summarizes the collected information. The report may be in narrative, tabular, or a combination of narrative and tabular form.
- Add an evaluation section to the report that identifies the strengths and weaknesses of the programs analyzed. Recommendations may be made regarding the weaknesses. If assumptions are to be made, the assumptions should be stated.

Glossary

Access to Information Act A federal act giving Canadians the right to examine federal government records that are not of a personal nature.

Accession log A serial listing of numbers assigned to correspondents or subjects and numbers available for assignment.

Accuracy ratio A measure of the effectiveness of the records system and records personnel, which is determined by dividing the number of records located by the number of records requested.

Active record A record that is referenced (used) on a regular basis.

Active records staff Personnel responsible for controlling all records that are accessed at least once a month and for determining when records should be transferred to inactive status.

Administrative audit A review of the effectiveness of the system in terms of the functional quality and quantity of the records available.

Administrative procedures manual Contains standard operating procedures that facilitate the completion of tasks requiring the work of more than one unit of the organization.

Administrative value The value of a records series to the creating office in performing assigned operations within the organization.

Alkali A substance added to paper, which is capable of neutralizing an acid.

Alliance of Libraries, Archives and Records Management An alliance charged with developing a national human resource strategy in Canada's information resources sector.

Alphabetic classification system An arrangement of records alphabetically by letter, word, or unit.

Alphanumeric classification system An arrangement of records that uses a combination of words and numbers.

American Standard Code for Information Interchange (ASCII) A coding scheme for computer-processable information using bit patterns.

Aperture card A keypunch-sized card ($7\frac{3}{8}$ by $3\frac{1}{4}$ inches) into which an opening(s) has been cut to accommodate the insertion of a frame(s) of microfilm.

Archival fonds The whole of the documents produced by an administrative body or person in the course of practical activity.

Archives Facilities where records of an organization are preserved because of their continuing value.

Archives management Procedures to preserve history and provide the vehicle for using history in a beneficial way in the public and private environments.

Archivist The person responsible for or engaged in one or more of the following activities in an archive: acquisition; appraisal and disposition; accessioning; preservation; arrangement; description; reference service; exhibitions; publication; and outreach activities.

Ascending order The arrangement of numbers or letters from lowest to highest (*A* to *Z* or *1* to *100*).

Association des archivistes du Québec A professional archival organization in Quebec.

Association for Information and Image Management (AIIM) An international professional organization for records and information management professionals.

Association of Canadian Archivists A Canadian professional archival organization.

Association of Records Managers and Administrators, Inc. (ARMA) An international professional organization for records and information management professionals.

Audio teleconferencing Voice communication over telephone lines between two or more remote locations.

Audit A regular examination and verification of a specific activity.

Audit trail A procedure that provides documentation for regular examination and verification.

Automated storage and retrieval Storing, retrieving, and controlling information using a computer.

Bar coding A pattern of clear and opaque bars between images on roll microfilm.

Biometric devices Scanners that measure and record unique personal characteristics, such as fingerprints, voice, chromosomes in a strand of hair, or retinal eye patterns.

Bit mapping A process of image scanning using binary digital coded representations of information.

Bits Stands for *binary digits,* each 0 or 1 in the binary number system.

Blip coding A method of coding accomplished by placing a blip (an opaque or nonopaque optical rectangle in three sizes) below each image to identify it. Also called *image count marking.*

Block integrity An arrangement in which all records related to one subject are filed together.

Block numeric system A classification system ordering records by their function with blocks of numbers assigned to each major function.

Block sorting Rough sorting records into groups of alphabetic letters *(A, B, C, D, E, F)* or in groups of numbers (1–10, 11–20), and so forth.

Boolean logic The basis for most text retrieval query languages using the operators *AND, OR, NOT, EXCEPT, IF, THEN* to limit or expand a search.

Canadian Council of Archives (CCA) An organization of archival institutions with the goal of coordinating the development of and fostering partnerships within the Canadian archival system.

Canadian Information and Image Management Society (CIIMS) A professional organization concentrating on information technology.

Canadian Information Processing Society (CIPS) A professional organization concentrating on information technology.

Caption The name, letter, or number affixed to the tabs of guides and folders to identify the records to be stored in that section of the file or in that particular folder.

Card file A file that accommodates card stock in varying sizes.

Centralized records storage system A system providing housing for all active records in one location within the organization.

Centre hook file A method of storage that allows various media to be hung on hanger bars similar to hangers in a closet.

Certificate of authenticity/identification Frame on each roll of microfilm that identifies the date filmed and the operator and verifies the accuracy and completeness of the reproductions.

Certified Records Manager (CRM) The designation awarded to an individual who has met the experience and education requirements established by the Board of Regents of the ICRM and has satisfactorily passed a six-part examination.

Character Any symbol, digit, letter, or punctuation stored or processed by computers. Each character is represented by a group of eight binary digits called a byte.

Chemical destruction The use of chemicals to destroy paper records or microfilm; includes *maceration* and *pulverizing.*

Chip A piece of microfilm containing a microimage and optical or magnetic coding for automated retrieval.

Chronologic classification system An arrangement in which records are filed in sequence by date.

Cine mode The positioning of microimages on film that takes its name from cinema film and that is achieved by feeding documents into the camera with the heading or top of each sheet entering the camera first.

Classification system A logical, systematic ordering of records using numbers, letters, or a combination of numbers and letters for record identification.

Classified index An index in which the entries are not arranged in one straightforward alphabetic sequence, but where the subject of the work is divided into a number of main headings and these in turn are subdivided as necessary, each sequence of entries being arranged alphabetically (as in the Yellow Pages).

Coding Marking the filing segment on a record.

Colour coding The use of colours and colour patterns to improve efficiency in records storage and retrieval.

COM recorder A microfilm unit that converts computer data into human-readable language and records it on microfilm.

Combination manual Contains information on records policies, the structure and responsibilities of the records unit in relation to other units, administrative procedures, and operating procedures.

Combination records storage system A system for housing active records in individual departments under centralized control.

Comic mode The positioning of microimages on film that takes its name from the manner in which frames of a comic strip are presented and that is achieved by feeding the document into the camera with the side of each sheet entering the camera first and the heading or top toward the edge of the film.

Communication subsystem The means of getting information to users in a timely manner.

Compact disk read-only memory (CD-ROM) A read-only optical disk capable of storing audio, video, digital, and digitized data.

Compression A hardware- or software-based technique designed to reduce the amount of storage space required for a given quantity of information.

Computer-assisted retrieval (CAR) The use of various automation technologies to assist in timely location and retrieval of information.

Computer input microfilm (CIM) Microfilm containing images that are converted to electronic signals for storage on magnetic tape to be used as input to a computer.

Computer output microfilm (COM)
An integration of computer and microform technology that converts information on computer tapes or from computer memory to a microform.

Computer output to laser disk (COLD)
A technology that records computer-generated reports on optical disks as character-coded text.

Computer virus Unwanted instructions deliberately inserted into a computer system that can alter or destroy data.

Concurrent control A type of control that takes place as work is being performed.

Condition A specific criterion that a record must meet in order to be retrieved from the database.

Contact printing Method of duplication achieved by placing the emulsion side of the original developed camera film in contact with the emulsion side of the copy film and directing a light beam through the original image to the copy. The copy film is then developed.

Content security Provision for the protection against intentional destruction, disclosure, modification, or breach of confidentiality of information.

Control The function that compares achieved results with planned goals.

Convenience copiers Self-service, unattended copiers that are located throughout the facility to provide for convenient copies.

Conventional (vertical) cabinet A storage unit in which file access is vertical (from the top); records must be dropped into the unit for storage or lifted out for use.

Conveyor system A mechanical storage system that brings the desired folder to the user in response to dialing or keying in the folder number.

Copy A duplicate of the original record.

Copy control device Mechanism usually attached to copy machines to limit access to authorized users.

Copy management The management of copying practices, procedures, and devices to ensure the effective and economical creation of copies.

Copyright The sole right to produce or reproduce a work or any substantial part of it in any form.

Copyright collectives Licensing bodies in Canada designed to prevent copyright infringement while allowing users to copy materials for legitimate reasons.

Copyright infringement The production or reproduction without permission of a copyrighted work.

Correspondence manual Contains policies on the creation and distribution of correspondence, guidelines on efficient and effective document creation, form letters, formats for letters and other communications, guidelines for selecting the most effective type of communication, and guidelines on effective dictation techniques, if appropriate.

Cost benefit analysis A comparison of the benefits of a new procedure, system, or technology with its costs.

Cross-reference A notation that directs the user to another location where the record or information may be found.

Data Symbols that represent people, objects, events, or concepts.

Data character Any symbol, digit, letter, or punctuation stored or processed by computers.

Data field or *data element* A group of characters combined to create one unit of data.

Data file A collection of computer records consisting of numbers and text with each record containing the same fields of information.

Data integrity The accuracy of data contained in database files.

Data processing The use of a computer to manipulate data to achieve a desired result.

Data redundancy The duplication of data fields in more than one data file.

Data set Groups of data or information stored on magnetic tape.

Database A collection of interrelated data files.

Database management A method of managing data in database files using special software.

Database management system software (DBMS) An integrated set of software programs that allows the user to create databases, maintain databases, and retrieve information from those databases in a predetermined report format.

Decentralized records storage system A system for housing records in individual departments or offices that create or receive the records.

Density A numeric measurement of the amount of light that passes through a black background of negative microfilm.

Descending order The arrangement of letters or numbers from highest to lowest (*Z* to *A* or *100* to *1*).

Dictionary order A subject files arrangement in which records are in alphabetic order by subject with no real attempt made to file related subjects together.

Direct access A storage system that permits access to records without reference to an index.

Directive An instruction from management, usually addressing policy and/or procedure.

Directive on directives A document describing the framework and philosophy of the directives management program.

Directives manual Handbook containing all of the organizational directives and the directive on directives.

Diskettes Removable magnetic storage media also known as *floppies* or *flexible disks*.

Dispersal A method of providing a copy of an original document for records reconstruction by having access to a copy distributed externally or internally.

Document imaging system A system employing computer hardware and software components to store, retrieve, transmit, process, and manage pictorial copies (images) of documents.

Duo mode A method of microfilming in which images are placed in consecutive order down one half of a strip of film and then back up the other half.

Duplex mode A method of microfilming both sides of a document simultaneously with the images presented side by side.

Duplex/duo mode A combination of duo and duplex modes.

Duplex order An arrangement of records using numbers with two or more parts separated by a dash, space, or comma.

Duplication A method of providing a copy of an original document by reproducing the original in paper, microfilm, microfiche, magnetic, or other media used by the organization.

Edit check Feature of certain forms software packages that prevents certain errors from occurring when the data are being keyed into a form.

Electronic Data Interchange (EDI) The technology that enables organizations to process business transactions electronically without the need to generate paper documents.

Electronic information system　The use of computer technology to process information.

Electronic record　A record that contains machine-readable information consisting of text, data, and image files.

Encapsulation　The process of placing an archival document between sheets of polyester film and sealing the edges.

Encyclopedic order　Records arranged alphabetically by major subjects and sub-groupings, as in an encyclopedia.

Ergonomics　The applied science that fits the working environment and equipment to the needs of people.

Essential records　The term used in Canada to refer to *vital records;* those records essential to the operation of the organization, continuation and/or resumption of operations following a disaster, re-creation of legal or financial status, or fulfilment of the organization's obligations to shareholders and employees after a disaster.

Extended Binary Coded Decimal Interchange Code (EBCDIC)　A coding scheme developed by IBM that specifies bit patterns for computer-processable information; similar to ASCII.

Facilitative area　The section of a form, usually at the top, that provides printed information such as organization name, form number, and instructions. Although necessary, this information is peripheral to the main purpose of the form.

Facsimile transmission　The electronic transmission of hard-copy data over telephone lines.

Feasibility study　An examination of the practicality of implementing new or modified procedures, methods, or technologies.

Feedback control　A type of control that concentrates on comparison of historical data with current performance data.

Fibre optics　Transparent glass fibres that may transmit both analogue (tonal) and digital signals by lasers.

Field　(data element) A group of characters combined to create one unit of data.

File　A collection of related records treated as a unit and arranged according to a predetermined system. In database applications these records contain the same fields.

File backer　A document-sized cardboard sheet to which paper documents are attached; only the backer and attached documents are transferred to the records centre.

File folder　Container used to hold correspondence or other documents in files.

File group　A collection of records with similar characteristics that should be separated from other record groups.

File integrity　Accuracy and completeness of the file.

Filing　The action of storing a record.

Filing manual　Contains rules and regulations for filing that standardize procedures, assist in training personnel, and make storage and retrieval more efficient.

Filing segment　The entire name, subject, or number that is used for filing purposes.

Filing time　A measure of the time per item spent in filing, which is obtained by dividing the total time used to file by the number of items filed.

Filing unit　Each element of a name that will be considered when employing alphabetic-by-name filing rules.

Fiscal value　The value attributed to a record series that provides documentation of use of governmental funds necessary for audit or operational purposes, data necessary to compile the annual report or to complete the organization's tax return, or documentation of other financial transactions such as purchases and sales.

Flash targets   Method used to divide a roll of film into batches of information.

[...] eight of [...] or can

[...] uments [...] rmation [...] ns and

[...] f deter- [...] and, if [...] assure

[...] m   A [...] gned to [...] d distri- [...] e use of

[...] Soft- [...] ns man-

[...] oftware [...] business

[...] ible for [...] cedures, [...] d spec- [...] trolling [...]

[...] depart- [...] se or in

[...] s man- [...] cording

Functional reports file   A reports management file that maintains information about reports having a similar function.

General folder   A folder used to contain records for which there is not a special or individual folder.

Geographic order   An arrangement in which related records are grouped by place or location.

Goals   General statements of the philosophy and aspirations of management for the organization.

Guides   Items used for separating records into sections to facilitate storage and retrieval and for supporting folders by keeping them upright in a cabinet or on a shelf.

Hierarchical database   A database that organizes data into related groups much like a family tree. This organization is sometimes called the *tree structure*.

Historical reports file   A reports control file that maintains a history of each report.

Historical value   A value based on the quality or content that causes a record of an event related to a particular project to be retained for purposes of history and not necessarily for business purposes.

Hypertext markup language (HTML) An electronic publishing standard that preserves text features separately from the content of a document.

Image files   Electronic records consisting of digitally coded "pictures" of documents, drawings, or graphics.

Image orientation   The positioning of images on microfilm.

Image technology   The capture, storage, and retrieval of information that includes text, graphics, tables, and pictures using micrographics and/or optical disks.

Important records   Those records necessary to the continued life of a business; also called *Class 2 records*.

Inactive record A record that is referenced fewer than 10 times annually.

Inactive records centre staff Personnel responsible for controlling all inactive records of the organization.

Index A dictionary-type listing used as a search tool to show the location of information.

Indexing The mental process of deciding by which filing segment a record is to be stored.

Indirect access A storage system that requires reference to an index before a record can be accessed.

Individual folder A folder used to contain records concerning one correspondent or subject.

Information Data placed into a meaningful context for users.

Information highway The term given to integrated computer, communication, and cable TV networks.

Information Technology Association of Canada (ITAC) A professional organization that concentrates on information technology.

In-house copy facilities Copying facilities located within an organization as either centralized or decentralized operations.

Institute of Certified Records Managers (ICRM) A group of CRMs who administer and evaluate the Certified Records Manager examination.

Integrated information system A group of automated subsystems working together and communicating with each other to process information, distribute it to the appropriate persons in a timely manner, store information (records) for efficient retrieval, and dispose of stored information (records) when it is no longer needed.

Jacket A transparent plastic carrier for strips of microfilm.

Job analysis The systematic study of a job to determine its characteristics—its function, specific duties, and qualifications.

Job description A written summary of the job that states (or lists) duties to be performed by the employee; the description will include areas of responsibility and specific duties.

Jukebox (or *autochanger*) Robotic equipment that stores optical disks, magnetic tape, or microfilm cartridges and automatically selects the correct one on demand.

Key (or *common field*) Data that are unique to each record in a database.

Label Item used to identify the contents of folders, drawers, shelves, binders, trays, and boxes.

Landlord/Tenant Agreement A self-service type of commercial records centre operating under agreement between the owner of the records and the renter of the space.

Lateral file A storage unit in which files are accessed from the side (horizontally).

Legal sufficiency The requirement for a records retention program to adhere to government regulations and provide litigation protection and support.

Legal value A value attributed to a records series that documents business ownership, agreements, and transactions.

Life cycle The evolution of a record through creation and receipt, distribution, use, maintenance, and disposition.

Local area network (LAN) A network of nodes and their links serving a small area such as a building or an organization.

Locator file A special card file or automated index that lists records contents and their locations.

Logic statement Uses operators such as *AND, OR, NOT, EXCEPT, IF, THEN* to limit or expand a search of information stored electronically.

Long-term cross-reference An additional notation that is used to provide a trail or forwarding address for a record.

Long-term record A record that documents organizational history, policies or procedures, or individual papers having historical significance—records, in other words, having continuing value to the organization. Vital records are also considered long-term records.

Magnetic media Storage media in the form of magnetic tapes, disks, diskettes, or optical disks.

Manual storage and retrieval The process of storing and retrieving records without the aid of mechanical or automated devices.

Mapping A part of the design process for electronic forms in which each fill-in space or data field is programmed to restrict information that can be entered in that field.

Maximum-minimum periodic transfer A variation of periodic transfer to inactive storage in which records are kept in the active files for a specified minimum and maximum period of time, for example, a minimum of 6 months and a maximum of 18 months.

Microfiche A sheet of film containing multiple miniature images in a grid pattern.

Microform Any medium that contains miniature images.

Micrographics The procedures for creating, using, and storing microforms.

Micrographics staff Personnel responsible for converting certain records or types of records to microforms.

Microimage storage and retrieval The process of storing and retrieving records that have been reduced in size and stored on roll film, fiche, aperture cards, jackets, or opaques.

Microrecord file A vertical storage container with shallow drawers to accommodate the size of the microforms.

Microrecords Records stored on microfilm.

Middle-digit order A duplex-numeric arrangement in which the middle two or three digits of each number are the primary digits under which the record is filed.

Mobile aisle system A space-conserving cabinet of shelves or trays that move on track (either manually or electrically) to create aisles for accessing records.

Multifunctional media A combination of several types of optical disks for specialized applications such as instructional materials.

Name order An arrangement in which records are classified by name of organization, person, agency or business.

Network A communication network consisting of nodes such as workstations and printers and the links between them.

Network database A database similar to the hierarchical database organization; however, in the network database organization each child record can have more than one parent.

Nonessential records Those records having no present value to the organization; also called *Class 4 records*.

Nonrecord copy A copy of a record maintained in addition to the record copy and in another location, such as materials not identified in the retention schedule; documents not required to be retained; materials available from public sources.

Numeric classification system An arrangement of records by number rather than by name.

Numeric forms file A forms control file that documents the history of each form and contains such information as the original request for the form, a sample of the original form and each subsequent revision, a reorder record, and any correspondence related to that form.

Object A small, reusable chunk of code in a computer program.

Object relational database Uses objects to build a complex database.

Objective A statement of how one step in reaching a goal is to be achieved and measured.

Odometer indexing Method of indexing that indicates the distance of each image from the beginning of the roll of microfilm.

Offsite records centre A storage facility located away from the organization site.

On-line computer storage The depositing of information in a computer database or in the memory of a computer.

Onsite records centre A storage facility located on the same site as the organization.

Open-shelf file A lateral file container consisting of horizontal open shelves similar to open bookshelves. Records are accessed from the side; guide and folder identifiers are on the side.

Operating system The set of programs that allows the computer system to direct its own resources and operations.

Operational audit A review of the effectiveness of the system as a process to ensure

that specific tasks are performed effectively and efficiently.

Operational manual Contains detailed information on the structure, policies, and procedures of one department or division of the organization.

Optical character reader (OCR) Reads printed information and digitizes it so that the computer can transform it to printed words on a screen.

Optical media Disks, tapes, and cards on which information is recorded by means of a highly focused laser beam; information can be retrieved and read by optical reader equipment.

Organization chart A formal representation of the firm's organizational structure— a diagram of who reports to whom within an organization.

Organizational manual Describes the structure, duties, and responsibilities of each department or division and explains the relationships between other departments and divisions and the records unit.

Original order The principle of storage that preserves records in the same order in which they were filed in the office of origin.

Originating subsystem The means of putting information into the integrated information system.

Originating unit Department responsible for the creation of the directive or for the function or subject described in the directive.

Out indicators Plastic or cardboard guides, folders, or sheets showing where materials have been taken from a file.

Periodic transfer The transfer of inactive records at regularly scheduled intervals.

Perpetual transfer The transfer of records to storage as they become inactive.

Personnel ratio A measure of the adequacy of the records staff to perform specific functions, which is determined by analyzing the staff requirements for specific tasks.

pH scale An arbitrary numeric scale ranging from 0 to 14 that measures the acidity and alkalinity of paper.

Pixels (picture elements) The millions of black and white dots in an imaginary grid that represents a document page.

Planetary camera A flatbed camera used to film standard and large documents.

Planning Determining where the organization wants to go (goals) and how it will get there (strategy).

Polarity The light to dark relationship of a film image. In *positive polarity* black characters are produced on a clear background; in *negative polarity* clear characters are produced on a black background.

Policy Guideline for decision making.

Policy manual Contains written general guidelines used for consistent decision making.

Power carousel file A storage unit arranged in a circular format that rotates. Files are accessed horizontally on one or more levels.

Power elevator lateral file A multiple-tier storage unit that utilizes a Ferris wheel approach to electrically bring the desired shelf to the user when needed.

Precontrol A type of control that takes place before work is performed and concentrates on preventing problems before they occur.

Primary guide The guide used to begin a major division or subdivision in a file drawer or on a file shelf.

Privacy Act A federal act giving Canadians the right to have access to information held about them by the federal government.

Private archives Archives that preserve the history of an institution, a corporation, or some entity other than a government entity.

Procedure Statement of how to implement a policy.

Processing subsystem The means of manipulating data within the information system to achieve desired results.

Provenance The arrangement principle that records of a given unit within the organization be retained as a separate group rather than being interfiled with similar records of another unit.

Public archives Archives maintained by federal, provincial, and municipal governments to preserve the documents and other items that relate to the history of the area and the people.

Pulping A method of destroying confidential paper documents in which the documents are mixed with water and forced through cutters and a screen.

Quick copy Centralized copying facility representing one of the forms of in-house copying.

Record Recorded information, regardless of medium or characteristics, made or received by an organization that is useful in the operation of the organization. In database applications, a group of related fields describing one occurrence in the file.

Record copy The official copy of a record that is retained for legal, operational, or historical purposes, usually the original.

Records analyst A specialist in systems and procedures used in creating, processing, and disposing of records.

Records analyst staff Personnel responsible for providing assistance in reviewing existing records systems and preparing revisions for improvement.

Records appraisal   An examination of the data gathered through the records inventory to determine the value of each records series to the organization.

Records centres   Storage facilities to house inactive records.

Records destruction   The disposal of records no longer needed by the organization.

Records disaster prevention and recovery manual   A document that details the course of action required to prevent or minimize the effects of a disaster and to recover, to the extent possible, those records that sustain damage.

Records inventory   A detailed review of the quantity, type, function, and organization of records.

Records management   The systematic control of records from their creation, or receipt, through their processing, distribution, organization, storage and retrieval to their ultimate disposition.

Records management manual   Contains information about how the records management system works.

Records retention and disposition manual   Contains the records retention schedule, procedures for establishing retention periods, procedures for transferring inactive records to the records centre, and procedures for the destruction of records.

Records retention program   Provides a timetable and consistent procedures for maintaining the organization's records, moving the records to inactive storage when appropriate, and destroying records when they are no longer valuable to the organization.

Records series   A group of records that is filed together as a unit, used as a unit,

and usually transferred to inactive storage or destroyed as a unit.

Records time/activity chart   A chart that provides information regarding the volume of records, types of records activities within each department or file station, and time spent in records activities.

Records transfer   The physical movement of records from expensive office space to a records centre or other designated storage area.

Reduction ratio   The size of a microimage as compared to the size of the original document, usually expressed as 24x, 30x, or 24:1, 30:1, and so forth.

Reference ratio   A measure of file activity that is determined by dividing the number of retrieval requests by the number of pieces stored.

Reference value   The value of archival material based on its use internally by personnel of the organization.

Relational database   A database that organizes data in tables, called relations.

Relative index   Shows all possible words or word combinations by which the material may be requested.

Release mark   A notation that the immediate need for the record has passed and that the record may now be stored.

Report   A written presentation of information useful in the decision-making process.

Reports staff   Personnel responsible for the development, implementation, and control of reports throughout the organization.

Research value   The value of archival material based on its use by external users or by organizational personnel who are engaged in researching the development of the organization's policies, philosophy, performance, product, or people.

Resolution The sharpness of a microimage. In electronic records management, the quality of an image displayed on a screen or printed by a laser printer.

Respect des fonds Honouring the concept of archival fonds and the related principles of provenance and original order.

Retention schedule A timetable that identifies the length of time a record must be kept in active and inactive storage before its final disposition.

Retrieval Finding and removing a requested file or information contained within the file.

Retrieval time The time required to locate a record, which is determined by dividing the total time in minutes used to retrieve items by total number of requests received.

Reversal processing A procedure that changes the polarity of film.

Rewritable optical disk A type of optical disk that allows erasure and overwriting of previously recorded information.

Risk assessment An evaluation of the probabilities of a disaster occurring and the possible extent of the damage.

Roll film 100- or 200-foot lengths of microfilm stored on an open reel or encased in a cartridge or cassette.

Root directory The main directory of a hard disk.

Rotary camera A type of microfilm camera that photographs documents while the documents and film are being moved by transport mechanisms at the same speed.

Rotary file A circular single- or multiple-tier storage unit in which each tier turns individually.

Scanner (or *document/image digitizer*) A device that captures information from

paper or microfilmed documents using laser technology and stores the electronic signals in a computer.

Scroll A roll of extra-wide microfilm (105mm) used in some automated retrieval systems.

Searching The process of finding a particular record or piece of data.

Semiactive record A record that is referenced once a month.

Serial order An arrangement of records using consecutive numbers.

Shredders Mechanical devices that use a variety of methods to cut, pull, or rip paper into small pieces.

Smart card A credit-card-sized device incorporating a tiny computer chip holding more memory than a magnetic strip.

Society of American Archivists (SAA) The professional organization for archivists in the United States.

Sorting Arranging records in filing order according to the classification system used.

Space numbering system A method of designating the storage location of records.

Special film targets Special indicators used during microfilming to indicate unique filming procedures or to identify sequences on the film; for example, cross-reference targets, missing document targets, substandard document targets, correction targets, camera operator targets or organization of information targets.

Special folder A folder used to contain records concerning a special topic or a special section in the file.

Special guide (or *secondary guide*) A special guide targets a special section within the file drawer or on a file shelf.

Specifications forms file A forms control file that groups forms according to the manner in which they are printed.

Standard general markup language (SGML)   A widely used electronic publishing language that preserves text features separately from the content of a document.

Statute   An act or a regulation passed by Parliament or by a provincial legislature.

Statute of limitations   A law that specifies the period of time during which a person or organization can bring action in a lawsuit or be sued.

Step and repeat camera   A flatbed camera designed to expose images in uniform rows and columns for the preparation of microfiche.

Storage subsystem   The means of storing, retrieving, and disposing of information according to the organization's needs.

Strips   Short lengths of film containing microimages that are containerized and coded for use in automated retrieval systems.

Structured query language (SQL)   The industry standard for languages by which a user can formulate requests for information and update, add, or delete information from a database.

Structured full-text query language (SFQL)   A proposed standard for a query language to be used with full-text databases.

Subject order   An arrangement of records by their subjects.

System   A group of interrelated parts acting together to accomplish a goal.

Tab   A projection from the top or side of a guide or folder used to identify the contents.

Telecommunications   Communication sent over telephone lines.

Templates   Blank forms stored electronically in a computerized information processing system.

Temporary record   A record that does not have continuing or lasting value to the organization; sometimes called a *transitory record*.

Terminal-digit order   A duplex-numeric arrangement in which the last two or three digits of each number are the primary digits under which the record is filed.

Text files   Electronic records consisting of character-coded letters, digits, punctuation marks, and other symbols.

Tree structure   See **Hierarchical database**.

Ultrafiche   A microfiche produced at a reduction ratio of 90× or greater and containing microimages of 4,000 or more pages.

Uniform Classification System (UCS)   A standard classification system used throughout an organization.

Unit box lateral file   A shelf filing system that uses specially designed boxes that hang from rails to hold file folders.

Useful records   Those records needed for the uninterrupted operation of the business; also called *Class 3 records*.

Utility program   A computer program that automatically searches for specific information, converts files from one form to another, and performs sort/merge operations.

Vacuum drying   A process by which wet paper materials are placed into a chamber that pulls out the moisture by means of a vacuum.

Vacuum freeze drying   A process by which paper materials are frozen and then dried in a high-heat chamber.

Vertical refresh rate The number of times per second the image on a computer screen is redrawn. Higher refresh rates avoid an image flicker causing eye strain.

Videoconferencing Live, full-motion video transmission to multiple locations.

Vital records Those records that are essential to the operation of the organization, the continuation and/or resumption of operations following a disaster, the re-creation of legal or financial status of the organization, or to the fulfilment of its obligations to shareholders and employees in the event of a disaster; also called *Class 1 records*.

Vital records manual Contains policies on how to determine whether a record is vital, what to do to protect a vital record, and how to access and retrieve a vital record.

Vital records protection manual A manual listing all vital records of an organization according to department; contains both the vital record code number and the retention date.

Wild card A symbol representing one or more unknown characters and used to search a database.

Workflow An automated management system in which documents are routed in the correct sequence to the employees who process transactions, perform designated operations, or complete specific activities.

Working area The section of a form that requests information necessary to achieve the purpose for which the form was designed.

WORM (Write once read many) disk A form of optical disk on which data are written once and may be read many times.

Index

To the owner of this book

We hope that you have enjoyed *Information and Image Management: A Records Systems Approach,* Canadian Third Edition, and we would like to know as much about your experiences with this text as you would care to offer. Only through your comments and those of others can we learn how to make this a better text for future readers.

School _____ Your instructor's name _____

Course _____ Was the text required? _____ Recommended? _____

1. What did you like the most about *Information and Image Management: A Records Systems Approach?*

_____

_____

_____

2. How useful was this text for your course?

_____

_____

_____

3. Do you have any recommendations for ways to improve the next edition of this text?

_____

_____

_____

4. In the space below or in a separate letter, please write any other comments you have about the book. (For example, please feel free to comment on reading level, writing style, terminology, design features, and learning aids.)

_____

_____

_____

_____

Optional

Your name _____ Date _____

May ITP Nelson quote you, either in promotion for *Information and Image Management: A Records Systems Approach* or in future publishing ventures?

Yes _____ No _____

Thanks!

Nelson

MAIL▶POSTE

Canada Post Corporation
Société canadienne des postes

Postage paid	Port payé
if mailed in Canada	si posté au Canada
Business Reply	**Réponse d'affaires**

0066102399   01

0066102399-M1K5G4-BR01

ITP NELSON
MARKET AND PRODUCT DEVELOPMENT
PO BOX 60225 STN BRM B
TORONTO ON M7Y 2H1